Felsensprengerin, Brückenbauerin, Wegbereiterin. Die Komponistin Ethel Smyth
Rock Blaster, Bridge Builder, Road Paver: The Composer Ethel Smyth

AF001693

Beiträge zur Kulturgeschichte der Musik
Herausgegeben von Rebecca Grotjahn
Band 2

Felsensprengerin, Brückenbauerin, Wegbereiterin. Die Komponistin Ethel Smyth

Rock Blaster, Bridge Builder, Road Paver: The Composer Ethel Smyth

Herausgegeben von Cornelia Bartsch, Rebecca Grotjahn und Melanie Unseld

Weitere Informationen über den Verlag und sein Programm unter:
www.allitera.de

Bibliografische Information der Deutschen Nationalbibliothek:
Die Deutsche Nationalbibliothek verzeichnet diese Publikation in der
Deutschen Nationalbibliografie; detaillierte bibliografische Daten sind im
Internet über <http://dnb.d-nb.de> abrufbar.

Januar 2010
Allitera Verlag
Ein Verlag der Buch&media GmbH, München
© 2010 Buch&media GmbH, München
Umschlaggestaltung: Kay Fretwurst, Freienbrink
Herstellung: Books on Demand GmbH, Norderstedt
Printed in Germany · ISBN 978-3-86906-068-2

Inhalt

Einleitung 7
Introduction 14

Gunilla Budde
„In pre-Suffragette days". Mädchenerziehung und Frauenleben im
19. Jahrhundert im deutsch-englischen Vergleich 21
    Abstract: "… in pre-Suffragette days": Women's Life and Education in the
    19th Century in Germany and England 37

Rebecca Grotjahn
Das Komponistinnenparadox. Ethel Smyth und der musikalische
Geschlechterdiskurs um 1900 39
    Abstract: The Women Composers' Paradox: Ethel Smyth and the
    Discourse on Music and Gender around 1900 53

Elicia Clements
"As Springy as a Racehorse": *Female Pipings in Eden* as Rejoinder to
Virginia Woolf's *A Room of One's Own* 55
    Abstract: „Lebhaft wie ein Rennpferd". *Female Pipings in Eden* als Antwort
    auf Virginia Woolfs *A Room of One's Own* 69

Amanda Harris
"Comrade" Ethel Smyth in the "great liberative war of women":
An English Musical Feminism 70
    Abstract: „Comrade" Ethel Smyth im „großen Befreiungskampf der Frauen".
    Zum musikalischen Feminismus in England 83

Susan Wollenberg
Ethel Smyth as Honorary Doctor of the University of Oxford 85
    Abstract: Ethel Smyth als Ehrendoktor der Universität Oxford 97

Elizabeth Kertesz
Creating Ethel Smyth: Three Variations on the Theme of Struggle 98
    Abstract: Ethel Smyth kreieren. Variationen über das Thema des Kampfes 107

Melanie Unseld
Identität durch Schreiben. Ethel Smyth und ihre autobiographischen Texte 108
    Abstract: Creating Identity by Writing: The Autobiographical Oeuvre of
    Ethel Smyth 120

Cornelia Bartsch
Schön Rohtraut und das Sattelpferd. Lyrisches und biographisches
Ich in Ethel Smyths Liedkompositionen der 1870er Jahre 121
    Abstract: Schön Rohtraut und das Sattelpferd: The 'Lyrical and Biographical
    I' in Ethel Smyth's Early Lied Compositions 151

Pavel B. Jiracek
Empire zwischen den Zeilen. Eine postkoloniale Perspektive 153
    Abstract: Empire between the Lines: A Postcolonial Perspective 160

Margaret R. Hunt
Same-sex Love before *Psychopathia Sexualis*: Or, What Young Ethel Knew 161
    Abstract: Gleichgeschlechtliche Liebe vor *Psychopathia Sexualis* oder
    Was die junge Ethel wusste 174

Kordula Knaus
Mere Mates or Mainly Monsters: Homoeroticism and Homosexuality
in Operas Around 1900 175
    Abstract: Harmlose Freundschaft oder pathologische Monstrosität.
    Homoerotik und Homosexualität in Opern um 1900 187

Christa Brüstle
Hell, dunkel, männlich, weiblich: „So shall I at last be whole".
Musik und Homosexualität bei Michael Tippett 189
    Abstract: Light, Dark, Male, Female: "So shall I at last be whole" –
    Music and Homosexuality in the Works of Michael Tippett 199

Erik Dremel
„All there was in my heart". Ethel Smyth, ihre *Mass in D* und ihre Freundschaft zu Pauline Trevelyan 201
    Abstract: "All there was in my heart": Ethel Smyth, her *Mass in D*,
    and her Friendship with Pauline Trevelyan 217

Aidan J. Thomson
Decadence in the Forest: Smyth's *Der Wald* in its Critical Context 218
    Abstract: Dekadenz im Wald. Smyths *Der Wald* im Kontext der Kritik . . . 248

Jürgen Schaarwächter
A British Choral Symphony? Ethel Smyth's *The Prison* in Context 250
    Abstract: Eine britische Chorsinfonie? Ethel Smyths *The Prison* im Kontext . 259

Die Autorinnen und Autoren 260

> „Sie ist vom Stamm der Pioniere, der Bahnbrecher.
> Sie ist vorausgegangen und hat Bäume gefällt und
> Felsen gesprengt und Brücken gebaut und so
> den Weg bereitet für die, die nach ihr kommen.
> So ehren wir sie nicht nur als Musikerin und Schriftstellerin [...],
> sondern auch als Felsensprengerin und Brückenbauerin."[1]

Einleitung

Ethel Smyth (1858–1944) zählt zu den interessantesten Persönlichkeiten ihrer Epoche. Ihre Musik, ihr politisches Engagement und ihre autobiographischen Texte dokumentieren eine erstaunliche Freiheit im Umgang mit Grenzen und Konventionen. In einer Zeit, als die Geschlechterfrage zu den meistdiskutierten gesellschaftlichen Themen gehörte und Frauen künstlerische Kreativität oft grundsätzlich abgesprochen wurde, verstand sie sich als professionelle Komponistin und trat mit großer Vehemenz für ihre eigenen Werke ein. Zwei Jahre ihres Lebens widmete sie der englischen Frauenwahlrechtsbewegung – eine für die Angehörige der englischen *upper class* keineswegs selbstverständliche politische Betätigung, für die sie sogar ins Gefängnis ging. Auch als Komponistin zeichnet sich Ethel Smyth als Grenzgängerin aus: Aufgrund ihrer Ausbildung in Leipzig zeitlebens der deutschen Musikkultur verbunden, stellt zugleich das ‚Britische' ein unüberhörbares Element in ihrer Musik dar. Vor dem Hintergrund der politischen Spannungen zwischen Deutschland und England insbesondere seit dem zweiten Burenkrieg war diese Mischung durchaus von einiger Brisanz. Von Bedeutung für das Selbstverständnis wie für das Schaffen Ethel Smyths sind nicht zuletzt die von ihr gelebten Liebesbeziehungen, die vor dem Hintergrund der zeitgenössischen Vorstellungen von Geschlecht, Sexualität und Moral als Grenzüberschreitungen wahrgenommen wurden.

Aus Anlass von Ethel Smyths 150. Geburtstag wurden im Jahre 2008 zwei wissenschaftliche Konferenzen ausgerichtet. Anfang November fand im Rahmen des *Ethel Smyth Festivals 2008* in Detmold das internationale Symposion *Felsensprengerin, Brückenbauerin, Wegbereiterin: Die englische Komponistin Ethel Smyth (1858–1944)* unter der Leitung von Cornelia Bartsch, Rebecca Grotjahn, Pavel Jiracek und Melanie Unseld statt, veranstaltet vom Musik-

---

[1] Virginia Woolf über Ethel Smyth, in: [Speech before the London/National Society for Women's Service, January 21 1931], in: Virginia Woolf, *The Pargiters. The Novel-Essay Portion of* The Years, hrsg. von Mitchell A. Leaska, New York 1977, S. xxviif.

wissenschaftlichen Seminar der Universität Paderborn und der Hochschule für Musik Detmold sowie der Fachgruppe Frauen- und Genderstudien der Gesellschaft für Musikforschung. Es folgte drei Wochen später die von Sophie Fuller und Susan Wollenberg konzipierte Tagung *Ethel Smyth (1858–1944) and Her Generation* an der Faculty of Music der University of Oxford. In diesem Band wird ein großer Teil der bei beiden Veranstaltungen vorgetragenen Referate dokumentiert. Die Beiträge vermitteln nicht nur Einsichten in das Werk einer der bedeutendsten Komponistinnen der Musikgeschichte, sondern auch neue Erkenntnisse über eine Zeit umwälzender geschlechtergeschichtlicher Wandlungen sowie über die Rolle, die die Musik hierbei spielte.

Wer war Dame Ethel Mary Smyth? Wie ist ihre Musik in der europäischen Musikgeschichte des späten 19. und des frühen 20. Jahrhunderts zu verorten? Wie war ihr künstlerisches und politisches Selbstverständnis? Wie wandelte sich die Rezeption ihrer Musik im Laufe ihres Lebens und nach ihrem Tod? Keine dieser Fragen lässt sich unabhängig vom zeitgenössischen kulturgeschichtlichen Kontext beantworten. Als Komponistin, als Frauen liebende Frau, als Engländerin in Deutschland, als Suffragette und nicht zuletzt als passionierte Orient-Reisende steht Ethel Smyth so sehr inmitten der zentralen Diskursfelder der Zeit, dass sich von ihrem Leben und Schaffen ausgehend zahlreiche Einsichten in die Zeit um 1900 gewinnen lassen, und zwar vor allem im Hinblick auf die Kultur- und Geschlechtergeschichte.

Zentral ist dabei der Diskurs um Geschlechterrollen und Geschlechteridentitäten, der die Gesellschaft seit dem ausgehenden 18. Jahrhundert maßgeblich prägte und der in den letzten Jahrzehnten des 19. Jahrhunderts in eine neue, überaus konfliktreiche Phase eintrat: Aus den ‚bürgerlichen', auf gegenseitige Ergänzung angelegten Geschlechterpolaritäten, die als Modell stabiler gesellschaftlicher Strukturen konstruiert waren, wurde eine aggressiv getönte Polarisierung. Während sich dabei die Diskussion in England auf politische Fragen konzentrierte,[2] arbeiteten deutschsprachige Autoren intensiv an der Beantwortung der ‚Frauenfrage' auf der Basis von naturwissenschaftlichen und philosophischen Überlegungen. Die Frauenrechtsbewegung des ausgehenden 19. Jahrhunderts wurde durch misogyne Schriften beantwortet, die die Minderwertigkeit der Frau zu belegen suchten. So definierte Otto Weininger auf der Basis von Grundannahmen über die männliche und weibliche Sexualität das Weibliche als nicht-seiend und wesenlos: „Die Frau-

---

[2] Vgl. dazu etwa die Forschungen von Krista Cowman, etwa *Mrs. Brown is a Man and a Brother. Women in Merseyside's Political Organisations, 1890–1920*, Liverpool 2004, oder dies., *The Militant Suffragette Movement in York*, York 2007.

en haben keine Existenz und keine Essenz, sie *sind* nicht, sie sind *nichts*."³
Und so wie in solchen Argumentationen immer wieder auch künstlerische
und insbesondere musikalische Aspekte eine wichtige Rolle spielen, so finden die neu definierten Geschlechterrollen ihren Ausdruck in der Literatur,
der Bildenden Kunst und der Musik.⁴ Als Opfer von Vorurteilen und als
Gegenstand zahlreicher Publikationen, die sich mit der ‚Frauenfrage' allgemein oder speziell mit Komponistinnen (manchmal sogar mit ihr persönlich
als Beispiel) befassten, war Ethel Smyth auf der einen Seite Objekt dieses
Diskurses; andererseits war sie aktiv an ihm beteiligt – als Schriftstellerin
und als Suffragette ebenso wie als Komponistin, die in zahlreichen ihrer
Werke Geschlechterverhältnisse und -rollen künstlerisch gestaltete. Die wissenschaftliche Auseinandersetzung mit ihrer Person und ihrem Schaffen
füllt somit nicht nur eine Leerstelle in der Musikgeschichtsschreibung, sondern zeigt darüber hinaus die Bedeutung musikkultureller Aspekte für die
Geschlechtergeschichte insgesamt auf.

Der Reigen der hier dokumentierten Beiträge wird mit einem Text eröffnet, der grundlegende Bedingungen für die historische Kontextualisierung von
Leben und Werk Ethel Smyth skizziert. Gunilla Budde zeichnet die geschlechtergeschichtliche Entwicklung in der Epoche Smyths nach und akzentuiert
dabei den Vergleich der Verhältnisse in England und Deutschland. Anschließend widmet sich Rebecca Grotjahn dem Geschlechter- und Sexualitätsdiskurs, in dem sowohl misogyne und differenzfeministische Theorien als auch
der entstehende feministische Künstlerinnendiskurs auf Fakten aus Musikgeschichte und Musikleben zurückgreifen. Mit dem Verhältnis zwischen Ethel
Smyth und Virginia Woolf vor dem Hintergrund dieses Künstlerinnendiskurses befasst sich Elicia Clements. Sie entdeckt in den Schriften beider Autorinnen nicht nur starke gegenseitige Einflussnahmen, sondern erkennt darüber
hinaus das Anliegen, den Dialog zwischen weiblichen Intellektuellen öffentlich
zu führen. Amanda Harris stellt Smyths musikalische und schriftstellerische
Tätigkeit in den Kontext der europäischen Frauenbewegungen und zeigt, dass
gerade Smyths Aktivitäten mit dafür verantwortlich waren, dass in England
die Musik von Frauen einen besonderen Stellenwert in der feministischen Politik bekam. Dem gegenüber akzentuiert Susan Wollenberg die Verbesserung der
Ausbildungssituation und der Frauenrechte an der University of Oxford seit

---

3   Otto Weininger, *Geschlecht und Charakter. Eine prinzipielle Untersuchung.*
    Wien 1903 (Reprint München 1997), S. 383.
4   Vgl. z. B. *Der Kampf der Geschlechter. Der neue Mythos in der Kunst 1850–
    1930*, hrsg. von Barbara Eschenburg (Katalog zur Ausstellung in der Städtischen
    Galerie im Lenbachhaus München, 8.3.–7.5.1995), München/Köln 1995.

1900, die dazu beitrug, dass Ethel Smyth im Jahre 1926 zum ersten weiblichen Doctor of Music dieser renommierten Institution ernannt werden konnte.

Zentrale Motive der Ethel-Smyth-Rezeption der vergangenen zwei Jahrzehnte sind das politische Engagement der Komponistin als Suffragette sowie ihr vehementer Einsatz für die eigene Musik und gegen ihre Benachteiligung als Komponistin. In ihrer Studie über die Rezeption der Hauptwerke Smyths in englischen und deutschen Rezensionen hat Elizabeth Kertesz darauf aufmerksam gemacht, dass das (Selbst-)Bild der Komponistin als ‚Kämpferin' zu einem Bruch in der Rezeptionsgeschichte ihrer Musik geführt hat, die in den 1920er Jahren bis zu ihrem Tod im Jahr 1944 mehr von der Frage nach dem nationalen Einfluss und des spezifisch ‚Britischen' ihrer Musik geprägt war als von Genderaspekten.[5] Kertesz' Untersuchungen sind ein wichtiger Anknüpfungspunkt für die Frage nach den geschlechterhistorisch bedingten Konstruktionen von Selbst- und Fremdbildern, die Ethel Smyths Schaffen wie dessen Rezeption beeinflussten.[6] In ihrem Beitrag für den vorliegenden Band thematisiert sie die Wechselwirkungen zwischen Smyths eigener Selbstdarstellung als kämpfende englische Komponistin und der Berichterstattung in der zeitgenössischen Presse, wobei sich herausstellt, dass die Komponistin ihr öffentliches Image durchaus aktiv mit zu gestalten wusste. Melanie Unseld arbeitet die Funktion von Smyths autobiographischen Schriften innerhalb eines bewusst gestalteten Selbstbildes heraus und geht der Frage nach, mit welchen Schreibstrategien Smyth ihren Anspruch verfolgte, sich einerseits in den Kanon der Musikgeschichte einzuschreiben und andererseits ihrer qua Geschlecht von der typischen Künstlerbiographie abweichenden Lebensgeschichte gerecht zu werden. Das Verhältnis von biographischem und lyrischem Ich reflektiert Cornelia Bartsch anhand einer Parallellektüre der Memoiren und der frühen Lieder Ethel Smyths, aus der sich Schlüsse auf Subjektkonstruktionen ziehen lassen. Zugleich ergeben sich neue

---

[5] Elizabeth Kertesz, *Issues on the Critical Reception of Ethel Smyth's Mass and First Four Operas in England and Germany*, Diss. University of Melbourne 2000. Siehe auch dies., „Gender and beyond: Talking About the Critical Reception of Ethel Smyth", in: *Gender Studies & Musik. Geschlechterrollen und ihre Bedeutung für die Musikwissenschaft*, hrsg. von Stefan Fragner, Jan Hemming und Beate Kutschke, Regensburg 1998, S. 65–74.

[6] Auch Michaela Brohm geht in ihrer im Jahre 2000 eingereichten Dissertation von dem ‚kämpferischen' Charakter der Komponistin aus, thematisiert jedoch die Konstruiertheit dieses Images nicht und kommt daher zu einer überaus einseitigen Wertung der Kompositionen Smyths. Vgl. Michaela Brohm, *Die Komponistin Ethel Smyth (1858–1944). Ursachen von Anerkennung und Misserfolg. Eine Untersuchung zum Spannungsfeld zwischen biographisch-psychosozialen, werkimmanenten und historischen Faktoren*, Berlin 2007.

Erkenntnisse über die Zyklizität der Liedopera 3 und 4. Aus der Perspektive der *postcolonial studies* befasst sich Pavel Jiracek mit Smyths problematischem Verhältnis zu ‚fremden' Kulturen, für das er Anzeichen in ihren Reiseberichten, aber auch in ihren exotistisch anmutenden Werken wie den *Four Songs for Mezzo-Soprano* findet.

In der noch jungen wissenschaftlichen Auseinandersetzung mit Ethel Smyth spielt der Aspekt der Homosexualität eine zentrale Rolle. Hier hat vor allem die Diskussion um die kulturelle Konstruiertheit von Gender und Begehren neue Impulse gesetzt. Insbesondere Elizabeth Wood hat sich als Vertreterin der *New Musicology* mit Konstruktionen des Begehrens in der Produktion, Reproduktion und Rezeption von Musik befasst.[7] In ihren Arbeiten geht sie der Frage nach, wie Ethel Smyth sich als lesbische Komponistin in den musikalischen Kodierungen ihrer Zeit bewegt und in wiefern der versteckte oder offene Bruch mit herkömmlichen Mustern die Rezeption ihrer Musik beeinflusst. Den Veranstalterinnen und Veranstaltern der hier dokumentierten Tagung war es in diesem Zusammenhang ein Anliegen, die Geschichte homosexueller Lebensformen und den historischen Sexualitätsdiskurs stärker zu berücksichtigen. Wie Sabine Mehlmann gezeigt hat, ist nicht nur Geschlecht kulturell konstruiert. Vielmehr darf bereits die Vorstellung einer sexuellen ‚Identität', die – sei sie nun der heterosexuellen ‚Norm' entsprechend oder als abweichend definiert – einem Körper bzw. einer Person gewissermaßen anhaftet, keineswegs als ahistorische Größe betrachtet werden; sie ist ihrerseits kulturelles Konstrukt, das mit Diskursen um Individualität und Person in Beziehung steht.[8] Vor die-

---

[7] Elizabeth Wood, „Gender and Genre in Ethel Smyth's Operas", in: *The Musical Woman: an International Perspective*, Bd. 2, hrsg. von Judith Lang Zaimont u. a., Westport 1987, S. 491–507; dies., „Lesbian Fugue: Ethel Smyth's Contrapunctal Arts", in: *Musicology and Difference. Gender and Sexuality in Music Scholarship,* hrsg. von Ruth A. Solie, Berkeley/Los Angeles/London 1993, S. 164–183; dies., „Performing Rights: a Sonography of Women's Suffrage", in: *The Musical Quarterly* (1995), S. 606–643; dies., „Sapphonics", in: *Queering the Pitch: the New Gay and Lesbian Musicology*, hrsg. von Philip Brett, Elizabeth Wood and Gary C. Thomas, London 1994, S. 27–66; dies., „The Lesbian in the Opera: Desire Unmasked in Smyth's Fantasio and Fête galante", in: *En travesti: Women, Gender Subversion, Opera*, hrsg. von Corinne E. Blackmer und Patricia J. Smith, New York 1995, S. 285–305; dies., „Women, Music, and Ethel Smyth: A Pathway in the Politics of Music", in: *The Massachusetts Review* (1983), S. 125–139.

[8] Vgl. Sabine Mehlmann, *Unzuverlässige Körper. Zur Diskursgeschichte des Konzepts geschlechtlicher Identität,* Königstein 2006. Siehe zu diesem Themenfeld auch Heike Schader, „Konstruktionen weiblicher Homosexualität in Zeitschriften homosexueller Frauen in den 1920er Jahren", in: *Homosexualitäten in der Weimarer Republik 1919–1933*, hrsg. vom Fachverband Homosexualität und

sem Hintergrund ließe sich provokant die Frage stellen, ob Ethel Smyth im Sinne der zeitgenössischen Diskussionen überhaupt ‚lesbisch' war, zumal es um die Wende zum 19. Jahrhundert zum misogynen Argumentationsmuster gehörte, Frauen, die aus den ihnen zugewiesenen Rollenmustern ausbrachen, als ‚Mannweiber' oder ‚konträrsexuelle Frauen' zu titulieren, ihnen zumindest latente Homosexualität zu unterstellen und ihr ‚Frausein' abzusprechen. In ihrem Beitrag räumt Margaret Hunt mit zahlreichen Klischees insbesondere zu weiblicher Homosexualität auf und stellt Identitäts- und Handlungsmöglichkeiten der Zeit um 1900 differenziert dar. Zwei weitere Texte beschäftigen sich mit Homosexualität in Musik von Zeitgenossen Smyths. Kordula Knaus' Thema sind die abwesenden männlichen sowie die entweder als bloße Freundinnen oder aber als pathologische Monster dargestellten weiblichen Homosexuellen in Opern zu Beginn des 20. Jahrhunderts. Mit einem jüngeren Zeitgenossen Smyths, Michael Tippett, beschäftigt sich Christa Brüstle, die aufzeigt, dass sich die musikalischen Denkweisen des Komponisten nicht von seinen Erfahrungen als Teil der (britischen) Gesellschaft und auch als Teil der ‚homosexual community' trennen lassen. Erik Dremel schließlich widmet sich Smyths *Mass in D*, die als Reflex ihrer Liebe zu Pauline Trevelyan gilt, und arbeitet heraus, wie sehr hier Liebe und Religiosität zu einem religiösen Gefühl verschmelzen, das sich auch in der Zuneigung und Liebe zu einem Menschen kristallisiert.

Im Vergleich zu Aspekten von Biographie und Rezeption sind kompositions- und gattungsgeschichtliche Aspekte in der Smyth-Forschung bisher weniger berücksichtigt worden. Zwei abschließende Beiträge nutzen analytische Zugänge, aus denen auch die musikgeschichtliche Bedeutung Smyths erkennbar wird. Aidan Thomson stellt die Entstehungsgeschichte und frühe Rezeption von *Der Wald* dar, um dann strukturelle Aspekte des Werks im Lichte sowohl der Wagner-Rezeption der Komponistin als auch der spezifisch britischen Wagner-Rezeption ihrer Kritiker herauszuarbeiten. Mit dem 1931 uraufgeführten Werk *The Prison* befasst sich der abschließende Beitrag von Jürgen Schaarwächter, der der Frage nach der Gattungszugehörigkeit des Werks vor dem Hintergrund der britischen Sinfonik nachgeht.

Die an den beiden Tagungen beteiligten Wissenschaftlerinnen und Wissenschaftler einte das gemeinsame Anliegen, die Forschung zu Ethel Smyth als einer interessanten Persönlichkeit der Kultur ihrer Zeit, einer politischen Akti-

Geschichte e. V. in Zusammenarbeit mit Bernd-Ulrich Hergemöller, Rüdiger Lautmann und Manfred Herzer (Invertitio, Jahrbuch für die Geschichte der Homosexualitäten, 2/2000), S. 8–33, sowie Sabine Hark, *Grenzen lesbischer Identitäten*, Berlin 1996

vistin und vor allem einer großartigen Komponistin zu intensivieren. Zugleich wurde jedoch auch deutlich, wie schmal das Fundament dafür noch immer ist. Zahlreiche Dokumente warten noch immer auf ihre Aufarbeitung, ja erst einmal auf ihre Entdeckung in Archiven und Bibliotheken. Dies gilt für musikalische Quellen – von denen heute vor allem diejenigen bekannt sind, die zu Lebzeiten der Komponistin gedruckt wurden, nicht jedoch Autographen und Skizzen – als auch für die weitläufige, in verschiedenen Bibliotheken Deutschlands, Österreichs, Englands und den USA verstreute Korrespondenz, die von großem kulturgeschichtlichen Wert zu sein verspricht. Die im Anschluss an die hier dokumentierten Symposien ins Leben gerufene Ethel Smyth Forschungsstelle in Detmold wird dieses Desideratum systematisch angehen.[9]

Wie die Symposien in Detmold und Oxford ist der vorliegende Band bilingual konzipiert – ausgehend von der Überzeugung, dass die Muttersprache bessere Bedingungen für eine adäquate sprachliche Umsetzung komplexer Gedankengänge bietet als eine nur mangelhaft beherrschte *lingua franca*. Jedem Text ist daher ein abstract in der jeweils anderen Sprache beigegeben. Beim Übersetzen und beim Lektorat der englischen Texte waren dankenswerterweise Victoria Viebahn und Alan Schelten behilflich. Für die Mitarbeit bei der Redaktion und der technischen Herstellung von Abbildungen und Notenbeispielen danken wir Luisa Brünger und Stefanie Rauch. Marleen Hoffmann und Heidi Schafmeister sowie allen weiteren Helferinnen und Helfern im Vorfeld der Symposien, die diesem Band vorausgingen, sei ebenfalls gedankt. Die Symposien sowie die Drucklegung dieses Bandes wurden durch die Deutsche Forschungsgemeinschaft, die Mariann Steegmann Foundation Zürich, das Musikwissenschaftliche Seminar Detmold/Paderborn sowie die University of Oxford finanziell und ideell unterstützt.

Detmold/Paderborn und Oldenburg, im Oktober 2009

Cornelia Bartsch, Rebecca Grotjahn und Melanie Unseld

---

[9] Siehe http://muwi-detmold-paderborn.de/internationale-ethel-smyth-gesellschaft.html. Vorbereitet werden hier u. a. Editionen der musikalischen Werke sowie der Briefe Smyths sowie ein Verzeichnis ihrer Werke.

> "She is of the race of pioneers, of path-makers.
> She has gone before and felled trees and blasted rocks and built bridges
> and thus made a way for those who come after her.
> Thus we honour her not only as a musician and as a writer [...],
> but also as a blaster of rocks and the maker of bridges."[1]

Introduction

Ethel Smyth (1858–1944) numbers among the most intriguing figures of her time. Her music, her political commitment and her autobiographical writings document her astonishingly free approach to dealing with borders and conventions. At a time when the gender issue was one of the most discussed social topics, and artistic creativity among women was frequently denied in principle, she held herself to be a professional composer, advocating her own works with considerable vehemence. Two years of her life she devoted to the English suffragette movement – a political activity that was by no means a matter of course for those belonging to the English upper classes, and one for which she even went to prison. As a composer, too, Ethel Smyth stood out as a *Grenzgängerin*, a crosser of borders: due to her training in Leipzig, she maintained a life-long connection with German musical culture, yet at the same time 'Britishness' constitutes an unmistakable element in her music. Against the background of the political tensions between Germany and England particularly apparent since the second Boer War, this was something of an explosive mixture. Significant factors contributing to Ethel Smyth's perception of herself and her creative activities include not least her love relationships which, against the background of contemporary concepts of gender, sexuality and morality, were regarded as overstepping borders.

Two academic conferences were held to mark the 150th anniversary of Ethel Smyth's birth, which fell in 2008. Early in November, the international symposium 'Rock blaster, bridge maker, road paver: The English Composer Ethel Smyth (1858–1944)' took place in Detmold, within the framework of the 2008 Ethel Smyth Festival, under the direction of Cornelia Bartsch, Rebecca Grotjahn, Pavel Jiracek and Melanie Unseld. This symposium was held by the Department of Musicology of the University of Paderborn and the Hoch-

---

[1] Virginia Woolf on Ethel Smyth, in: [Speech before the London/National Society for Women's Service, January 21 1931], in: Virginia Woolf, *The Pargiters. The Novel-Essay Portion of* The Years, ed. by Mitchell A. Leaska, New York 1977, p. xxviif.

schule für Musik Detmold, together with the Section for Women's and Gender Studies of the Gesellschaft für Musikforschung. It was followed three weeks later by the meeting inspired by Sophie Fuller and Susan Wollenberg, 'Ethel Smyth (1858-1944) and Her Generation' at the Faculty of Music, University of Oxford. The present volume documents a large proportion of the papers delivered at the two events. The contributions provide not only insights into the oeuvre of one of the most significant female composers in music history, but also new findings on a period of dramatic upheavals in the development of gender issues and the role played by music therein.

Who was Dame Ethel Mary Smyth? Where should her music be placed within European music history of the late 19th and early 20th centuries? How did she see herself as an artist and as a political figure? In what way did the reception of her music evolve in the course of her lifetime and after her death? None of these questions can be answered without reference to the contemporary context of cultural history. As a composer, as a woman who loved women, as an Englishwoman in Germany, as a Suffragette, and not least as a passionate traveller in the Orient, Ethel Smyth occupies such a central position amid the key fields of discourse of her time that, taking her life and work as a starting point, numerous insights into the period around 1900 may be won above all with respect to the history of culture and gender.

At the core of such considerations is the discourse on gender roles and gender identities that had been predominant in society since the late 18th century and was entering a new, highly conflict-ridden phase in the last decades of the 19th century: from the bourgeois, mutually-endorsing gender polarities, which were construed as a model of stable social structures, grew polarisation displaying an aggressive tinge. While in England the discussion was focussed on political issues,[2] German-speaking authors were working intensively to answer the '*Frauenfrage*' (women's question) on the basis of considerations from the natural sciences and philosophy. The women's rights movement of the late 19th century was answered by misogynistic writings seeking to prove the inferiority of women. Based on fundamental assumptions on male and female sexuality, Otto Weininger, for example, described the feminine state as non-existent and being-less: "Women have no existence and no essence, the *are* not, they are *nothing*."[3] And hence, just as artistic and especially musical

---

[2] Cf. research conducted by Krista Cowman, for example, including *Mrs Brown is a Man and a Brother. Women in Merseyside's Political Organisations, 1890–1920*, Liverpool 2004, or idem: *The Militant Suffragette Movement in York*, York 2007.
[3] Otto Weininger, *Geschlecht und Charakter. Eine prinzipielle Untersuchung.* Vienna 1903 (Reprint Munich 1997), p. 383.

aspects consistently play a major role in argumentation of this kind, the newly-defined gender roles likewise find their expression in literature, the visual arts, and music.[4] As a victim of prejudice and the subject of numerous publications dealing with the *Frauenfrage* in general or with female composers in particular (some of them even going so far as to cite her personally as an example), Ethel Smyth was, on the one hand, herself an object these discourses; on the other, she participated in them actively – as a writer and a Suffragette, and equally as a composer who modelled gender relations and gender roles artistically into many of her works. The scholarly analysis of her person and her oeuvre thus not only serves to fill a gap in music history as it has been written but, beyond this, also demonstrates the significance of aspects of musical culture in the study of gender history as a whole.

The conference proceedings as reproduced here begin with a text outlining the fundamental conditions for the historical contextualisation of Ethel Smyth's life and work. Gunilla Budde traces the development of gender history in Smyth's era, highlighting the comparison of circumstances in England and Germany. Rebecca Grotjahn then considers the gender and sexuality discourse in which both misogynistic theories and those of difference feminism, as well as the emerging feminist discourse among female artists, draw on facts from music history and musical life. The relationship between Ethel Smyth and Virginia Woolf against the backdrop of this discourse among female artists is examined by Elicia Clements, who not only discovers strong mutual influence in the writings of the two authors, but also detects the perceived need for the dialogue between female intellectuals to be conducted in public. Amanda Harris places Smyth's musical and literary activities in the context of the European women's movement and shows that it was through Smyth's activities in particular that music composed by women assumed a special position within the sphere of feminist politics in England. Susan Wollenberg, on the other hand, highlights the considerable extent to which the education and rights of women at the University of Oxford had improved since 1900, developments which helped to pave the way for Ethel Smyth to become the first woman to be awarded a D. Mus. by this renowned institution, in 1926.

Central motifs running through the reception of Ethel Smyth over the past two decades have been the composer's political engagement as a Suffragette, and her vehement activities towards promotion of her own music and against

---

[4] Cf. for example *Der Kampf der Geschlechter. Der neue Mythos in der Kunst 1850–1930*, ed. by Barbara Eschenburg (Catalogue to the exhibition at the Städtische Galerie im Lenbachhaus München, 8.3.–7.5.1995), Munich/Cologne 1995.

Introduction

her discrimination as a composer. In her study of the reception of Smyth's central works in English and German reviews, Elizabeth Kertesz draws attention to the fact that the (self-)image of the composer as a 'fighter' led to a turning point in the history of her music's reception, which from the 1920s until her death in 1944 was concerned more with national influence and the specific 'Britishness' of her music than with gender aspects.[5] Kertesz' investigations establish an important link with the question as to the shaping of image by self and others in the historical gender context, an issue with impact on Ethel Smyth's output and its reception.[6] In her contribution to the present volume, she addresses the interplay between Smyth's self-representation as an English composer of fighting spirit and contemporary reporting, from which it becomes clear that the composer indeed knew how to contribute to the shaping of her own public image. Melanie Unseld elaborates on the function of Smyth's autobiographical writings within a consciously crafted image of herself. She looks into the question of the writing strategies Smyth applied with a view to featuring in the canon of music history while at the same time doing justice to the history of her life, which deviated qua gender from the typical biography of an artist. On the basis of a parallel reading of Ethel Smyth's memoirs and her early songs, from which conclusions can be drawn with regard to subject structures, Cornelia Bartsch reflects on the relationship between the 'biographical and the lyrical I'. At the same time, new perceptions emerge on the cyclical nature of the Liedopera 3 and 4. From the perspective of postcolonial studies, Pavel Jiracek considers Smyth's problematic relationship to 'strange' cultures, indications of which he finds in her travel accounts as well as in her 'exotic' works such as the *Four Songs for Mezzo-Soprano*.

In the scholarly debate surrounding Ethel Smyth, which is still in its early days, the aspect of homosexuality plays a central role. New impulses have been given

---

[5] Elizabeth Kertesz, *Issues on the Critical Reception of Ethel Smyth's Mass and First Four Operas in England and Germany*, Diss. University of Melbourne 2000. See also id. "Gender and beyond: Talking About the Critical Reception of Ethel Smyth", in: *Gender Studies & Musik. Geschlechterrollen und ihre Bedeutung für die Musikwissenschaft*, ed. by Stefan Fragner, Jan Hemming and Beate Kutschke, Regensburg 1998, pp. 65–74.

[6] In her dissertation submitted in 2000, Michaela Brohm likewise assumes that the composer was '*kämpferisch*' (of fighting spirit) in character, but does not deal with the construed nature of this image and hence arrives at a distinctly one-sided view of Smyth as a composer. Cf. Michaela Brohm, *Die Komponistin Ethel Smyth (1858–1944). Ursachen von Anerkennung und Misserfolg. Eine Untersuchung zum Spannungsfeld zwischen biographisch-psychosozialen, werkimmanenten und historischen Faktoren*, Berlin 2007.

17

here, above all by the discussion concerning the culturally construed nature of gender and desire. In particular Elizabeth Wood, a representative of *New Musicology*, has dealt with constructions of desire in the production, reproduction and reception of music.[7] Her studies examine the question of how Ethel Smyth functions as a lesbian composer in the musical encodings of her day, and to what extent the covert or overt rejection of conventional patterns influences her music. The organizers of the meeting documented here sought to take the history of homosexual lifestyles and the historical discourse on sexuality more strongly into account in this connection. As Sabine Mehlmann has shown, not only gender is construed through culture. Rather, even the idea of a sexual 'identity', which – be it defined in accordance with the heterosexual 'norm' or in deviation from it – is to a certain degree attached to a body or a person, may by no means be considered to be an a-historical factor; it is in turn a construction and one that stands in relation to discourses concerning individuality and person.[8] Against this background, the provocative question may be posed as to whether Ethel Smyth was, in the sense of contemporary discussion, indeed 'lesbian'. This question is all the more justified since at the turn of the 19th century it was part of the misogynistic line of argumentation to call women who broke out of their appointed role-models 'Mannweiber' (viragoes) or 'konträrsexuelle Frauen' (contrary sexual women), or at least to insinuate their latent homosexuality and deny their 'womanhood'. In her paper, Margaret Hunt deals with

[7] Elizabeth Wood, "Gender and Genre in Ethel Smyth's Operas", in: *The Musical Woman: an International Perspective*, vol. 2, ed. by Judith Lang Zaimont et al, Westport 1987, pp. 491–507; id., "Lesbian Fugue: Ethel Smyth's Contrapunctal Arts", in: *Musicology and Difference. Gender and Sexuality in Music Scholarship*, ed. by Ruth A. Solie, Berkeley/Los Angeles/London 1993, pp. 164–183; id., "Performing Rights: a Sonography of Women's Suffrage", in: *The Musical Quarterly* (1995), pp. 606–643; id., "Sapphonics", in: *Queering the Pitch: the New Gay and Lesbian Musicology*, ed. by Philip Brett, Elizabeth Wood and Gary C. Thomas, London 1994, pp. 27–66; id., "The Lesbian in the Opera: Desire Unmasked in Smyth's Fantasio and Fête galante", in: *En travesti: Women, Gender Subversion, Opera*, ed. by Corinne E. Blackmer and Patricia J. Smith, New York 1995, pp. 285–305; id., "Women, Music, and Ethel Smyth: A Pathway in the Politics of Music", in: *The Massachusetts Review* (1983), pp. 125–139.

[8] Cf. Sabine Mehlmann, *Unzuverlässige Körper. Zur Diskursgeschichte des Konzepts geschlechtlicher Identität*, Königstein 2006. See also on this topic group Heike Schader, "Konstruktionen weiblicher Homosexualität in Zeitschriften homosexueller Frauen in den 1920er Jahren", in: *Homosexualitäten in der Weimarer Republik 1919–1933*, publ. by the Fachverband Homosexualität und Geschichte e. V. in cooperation with Bernd-Ulrich Hergemöller, Rüdiger Lautmann and Manfred Herzer (Invertitio, Jahrbuch für die Geschichte der Homosexualitäten, 2/2000), pp. 8–33, and Sabine Hark, *Grenzen lesbischer Identitäten*, Berlin 1996

numerous clichés concerning female homosexuality, providing a differentiated account of the various possibilities regarding identity and activity that existed in the period around 1900. Two further texts deal with homosexuality in music by Smyth's contemporaries. Kordula Knaus takes as her theme the fact that in opera in the early 20th century, female homosexuals were either absent or were represented as mere female friends, or, even, as pathological monsters. Christa Brüstle deals with Michael Tippett, a younger contemporary of Smyth's, showing that his musical mindset cannot be separated from his experience as a member of (British) society and as a member of the 'homosexual community'. Lastly, Erik Dremel contemplates Smyth's *Mass in D*, a work thought to constitute a reaction to her love of Pauline Trevelyan, and demonstrates the great extent to which love and religiosity fuse here to produce a religious feeling, as also crystallises in the attraction to, and love for, a person.

In comparison with the biographical and reception-related aspects, areas of Smyth research concerned with compositional issues and generic history have received little attention up to now. Two last contributions take analytical approaches that allow Smyth's significance to become apparent also in terms of music history. Aidan Thomson describes how *Der Wald* came into being and was first received, before elaborating on structural aspects of the work, in the light of both the composer's attitude towards Wagner and of her critics' specifically British Wagner reception. The final paper by Jürgen Schaarwächter deals with the work *The Prison*, which received its premiere in 1931, examining where the work stands with respect to genre against the background of British symphonic compositions.

The scholars who participated in the two symposia were united in their pursuit of a common objective, that of intensifying the research into Ethel Smyth as a fascinating personality within the culture of her day, a political activist and, above all, a brilliant composer. At the same time, it became clear just how narrow the foundation remains upon which this work rests. Numerous documents are still awaiting scrutiny, or indeed discovery, in archives and libraries. The same applies with regard to musical sources – those known today being primarily the items printed during the composer's lifetime, but not the manuscripts and sketches – as well as to the copious correspondence. The latter, scattered far and wide in various libraries in Germany, Austria, England and the USA, promises to be of great historico-cultural value. The Ethel Smyth Research Centre in Detmold that came into being following the symposia documented here will take a systematic approach to tackling this desideratum.[9]

[9] See http://muwi-detmold-paderborn.de/internationale-ethel-smyth-gesellschaft.html,

Cornelia Bartsch, Rebecca Grotjahn and Melanie Unseld

Like the symposia in Detmold and Oxford, the present volume is bilingual in its conception – based on the conviction that the native tongue is better suited to realising complex trains of thought in an adequate linguistic form than is a *lingua franca* of which one has only a poor grasp. Each text is therefore provided with an abstract in the other of the two languages. Assistance in the work of translating and editing the English texts was kindly given by Victoria Viebahn and Alan Schelten. We are grateful to Luisa Brünger and Stefanie Rauch for their contributions to the editing and production of illustrations and musical examples. We further thank Marleen Hoffmann, Heidi Schafmeister and all those who helped to prepare the symposia that preceded the publication of this volume. Both the symposia and the publishing of the volume were supported financially and conceptually by the Deutsche Forschungsgemeinschaft (German Research Foundation), the Mariann Steegmann Foundation Zürich, the Detmold/Paderborn Department of Musicology and the University of Oxford.

Detmold/Paderborn and Oldenburg, October 2009

Cornelia Bartsch, Rebecca Grotjahn and Melanie Unseld

where editions of Smyth's musical works and correspondence, as well as a catalogue of her works, are in preparation.

Gunilla Budde
„In pre-Suffragette days". Mädchenerziehung und Frauenleben im 19. Jahrhundert im deutsch-englischen Vergleich

"My father left England on 30 June 1857, and I was born on the 23rd day of the following April – a ten month' child. In pre-Suffragette days I was proud of this fact, having heard that such children are generally boys and always remarkable!"[1] Ein bemerkenswerter Junge zu sein, war, dies ahnte Ethel Smyth schon als kleines Mädchen, deutlich attraktiver als als „Tochter aus gutem Hause" aufzuwachsen. Namentlich im Vergleich mit den Brüdern erfuhren Bürgertöchter bereits in frühester Kindheit eine oft schmerzlich empfundene Begrenzung ihres Bewegungsspielraums. Früh wurden die Töchter in eine familienfixierte Frauenrolle eingepasst, die die Mütter ihnen vorlebten.

Im Folgenden geht es zunächst darum, Entstehung und Eigenarten des bürgerlichen Geschlechtermodells zu erläutern. Zum Zweiten werden die daraus resultierenden Erziehungswerte, Erziehungserfahrungen und Lebensentwürfe für Bürgertöchter und -frauen beleuchtet. Drittens und abschließend wird im deutsch–englischen Vergleich nach Ähnlichkeiten und Unterschieden in Mädchenerziehung und Frauenleben gefragt.

1. Geschlechterbeziehungen auf dem Reißbrett

Die europäische Aufklärung war als Befreiungsschlag gedacht. Mit seinem Diktum „Habe Mut, dich deines eigenen Verstandes zu bedienen",[2] forderte der Königsberger Philosoph Immanuel Kant seine Zeitgenossen energisch zur Emanzipation auf. In den Studierstuben aufklärerisch gesinnter Meisterdenker wurde mit der bürgerlichen Gesellschaft ein Gesellschaftsmodell entworfen, in dem eigenständiges Denken gefragt und zur Überwindung ständischer Ungleichheit und absolutistischer Staatsgewalt eingesetzt werden konnte. Empha-

---

[1] Ethel Smyth, *The Memoirs of Ethel Smyth*, hrsg. von Ronald Crichton, Harmondsworth 1987, S. 23.
[2] Immanuel Kant, „Beantwortung der Frage: Was ist Aufklärung", in: *Berlinische Monatsschrift* 1783, S. 481–494, hier S. 484.

tisch verkündete man den Abschied von geburtsständischen Privilegien, obrigkeitsstaatlicher Gängelung und klerikaler Deutungsmacht. Entworfen wurde die Vision einer von Vernunft, Individualität und Humanität bestimmten Gesellschaft, in der die staatliche Macht im Sinne des liberalen Rechts- und Verfassungsstaats einerseits begrenzt und andererseits über Öffentlichkeit, Wahlen und Repräsentationsorgane den Einflüssen des mündigen Bürgers unterstand.

Es war ein im Prinzip universalistisch gedachtes Programm. Alle sollten daran partizipieren und davon profitieren. Doch die Realität des 19. Jahrhunderts strafte die Gleichheitsrhetorik, die in ihm mitschwang, Lügen. Denn die Aufklärung war ein Befreiungsschlag, der zunächst ausschließlich die männlichen Mitglieder der Bürgergesellschaft betraf. Die gleichen Aufklärer, die Emanzipation großschrieben, konzipierten eine Geschlechterordnung als Säule der Bürgergesellschaft, die der Entfaltungsfreiheit ihrer weiblichen Mitglieder enge Grenzen setzte. Die vermeintlich ‚natürlichen Geschlechtscharaktere' von Männern und Frauen gaben gemäß der seit dem 18. Jahrhundert gängigen Argumentation vor, in welchen Handlungs- und Wirkungssphären sie sich zu bewegen hatten. Dass Bürgermänner die familienferne Berufswelt beherrschen, die Bürgerfrauen dagegen die öffentlichkeitsferne Familiensphäre, wurde als biologisch vorgegeben und damit unveränderbar deklariert.[3] Zeitgenössische Lexikonartikel halfen eifrig mit, dieses Modell zu untermauern. Frauen werden darin als passiv, bewahrend, emotional, irrational, anpassungsbereit, wankelmütig, emsig und bescheiden charakterisiert, Männer als aktiv, selbständig, tapfer, vernünftig, energisch, zukunftsorientiert und weitblickend. Mit der polar entworfenen Geschlechterordnung wurden nicht nur Ungleichheiten festgezurrt, sondern gleichzeitig auch in einem System der Über- und Unterordnung verankert.

Wie aber vertrug sich die Idee weiblicher Unterordnung mit der bürgerlichen Utopie allgemeiner Chancengleichheit ohne Rücksicht auf Geburt und damit auch Geschlecht? Dass hier im egalitären Grundton der zivilgesellschaftlichen Utopie Missklänge zu hören waren, entging auch den Vor- und Meisterdenkern des emphatischen Programms nicht. Eine Vielzahl von Publikationen theologischer, philosophischer, pädagogischer und naturwissenschaftlicher Provenienz bezeugt den Wunsch, eine offensichtliche Unstimmigkeit zu legitimieren und zu harmonisieren. Selbst kluge und liberale Männer kamen dabei

---

[3] Vgl. hierzu den mittlerweile klassischen Aufsatz von Karin Hausen, „Die Polarisierung der ‚Geschlechtscharaktere'. – Eine Spiegelung der Dissoziation von Erwerbs- und Familienleben", in: *Der Strukturwandel der Familie im industriellen Modernisierungsprozess – Historische Begründung einer aktuellen Frage*, hrsg. von Werner Conze, Stuttgart 1985, S. 363–393.

offensichtlich in Erklärungsnotstand. Fraglos reagierten sie mit ihren hilflosen Bemühungen nicht nur auf selbst erkannte Spannungen des Gedankengebäudes, sondern auch auf die allerorts sich wandelnde Geschlechterordnung, deren reale Beweglichkeit im Alltag es zu domestizieren galt. Ungeachtet der geschlechtsspezifischen Einfärbung der Privatheit und der Öffentlichkeit erwiesen sich ihre Ränder in der sozialen Praxis als historisch höchst variabel, durchlässig und fließend.[4] Die Ausrichtung eines repräsentativen Diners für die Kollegenfamilien ihres Mannes, bei dem eine Bürgerfrau Regie führte, ebenso wie das ehemännliche, durch das Allgemeine Landrecht von 1792 zugestandene Entscheidungsrecht über die Länge der Stilldauer, der Ankauf von Gemälden für die Familienwohnung, den ein Bürger tätigte, sind nur einige Beispiele solcher ständigen Grenzüberschreitungen. Fraglos waren auch im 19. Jahrhundert Geschlecht und Geschlechterdifferenz Produkte diskursiver Konstruktion und situativer Interaktion und damit keineswegs irreversibel. Sie wurden in verschiedenen Kontexten auf verschiedene Art mit unterschiedlichen Konsequenzen immer wieder neu ausgehandelt und hervorgebracht. Die Geschlechterordnung entstand im Zusammenspiel von normativen Entwürfen und subjektiven Erfahrungen.

2. Mädchenerziehung und Frauenleben

Diese Geschlechterordnung, so beweglich sie auch war, stellte die wesentlichen Weichen für eine geschlechtsspezifische Erziehung. Nicht nur von den Spielen der Brüder wurden die Töchter früh ausgeschlossen, auch ihre Erziehung und Bildung verlief in gänzlich anderen Bahnen.[5] Eigene Bedürfnisse sollten dabei tunlichst hintangestellt werden. „Boys are to be happy in themselves, the girls are to make others happy", brachte eine englische Zeitgenossin dieses Erziehungscredo auf den Punkt.[6] Spiel und Spielzeug sollten diese selbstlosen und opferbereiten Tugenden der Töchter befördern helfen. Mit Puppen und Puppenhäusern bekamen die Mädchen ihre künftige, eng begrenzte Frauenwelt en miniature vor Augen geführt.

Erfüllten die Mädchen und jungen Frauen die an sie gestellten Weiblichkeitserwartungen nicht, wurde dies streng geahndet. Sich „wie ein Junge zu

---

[4] Gunilla Budde, „The Family – A Core Institution of Civil Society: A Perspective on the Middle Classes in Imperial Germany", in: *Civil Society and Gender Justice. Historical and Comparative Perspectives*, hrsg. von ders. u. a., New York/Oxford 2008, S. 119–134.

[5] Gunilla Budde, *Auf dem Weg ins Bürgerleben. Kindheit und Erziehung in deutschen und englischen Bürgerfamilien 1840–1914*, Göttingen 1994.

[6] Cicely Hamilton, *Marriage as a Trade*, London 1909, S. 53.

verhalten" galt als verpönt. Marianne Weber etwa, die sich in Worten und Taten für die Frauenemanzipation stark machte, vertrat in ihren Lebenserinnerungen eine eher traditionelle Vorstellung, was Mädchen zieme und was nicht. 1870 besuchte sie ein ‚Töchterinstitut' in Hannover, wo sie bald wenig mädchenhafte Neigungen an den Tag legte. „Gewalten gewannen Herrschaft über mich, von denen sich bisher gar nichts gezeigt hatte: brennender Ehrgeiz, der Drang nach Anerkennung. Ich wollte mich hervortun und auf diese Weise nicht nur Beachtung, sondern auch Zuneigung erringen". Dass dieses „Strebertum", wie sie es selbst verächtlich abwertete, einem Mädchen nicht zustand, wurde ihr bald sehr drastisch vor Augen geführt: Die beiden von ihr verehrten Schulleiterinnen straften sie mit Nichtachtung und hielten auch die Mitschülerinnen dazu an. Erst nach Wochen kam es zur klärenden Aussprache: „Es war", so schreibt Weber, „eine große Überraschung; meine Pflichttreue, mein Eifer – tadelnswerter Ehrgeiz, Geltungsbedürfnis, Selbstsucht?" Zumindest wenn Mädchen sie zeigten, so erfuhren es viele Bürgertöchter schmerzlich, waren es unerwünschte Eigenschaften; bei Jungen hingegen wurden sie erwartet und mit Lob bedacht. Webers resümierende Selbstkritik zeigt, wie sehr sie selbst diese Anschauung verinnerlicht hatte: „Wahrscheinlich war ich unausstehlich, in meinem tugendhaften Eifer, meinem Strebertum".[7]

Zumindest die Ausbildung der Töchter war wenig dazu angetan, Ambitionen zu nähren. Oberflächlichkeit, Zufälligkeit, Wissenschaftsferne und weitgehend fehlende Planmäßigkeit und Normierung zeichneten das Curriculum in viktorianischer und wilhelminischer Zeit aus. Neben dem Elementarunterricht im Lesen und Schreiben gehörten dazu anstelle von Latein und Griechisch, je nach Nationalität, rudimentäre Englisch-, Deutsch- sowie auch Grundkenntnisse des Französischen. Besonderes Gewicht erhielt in beiden Ländern die Lektüre von Dramen, Gedichten und Romanen der Klassiker.

Auch die Ausbildung in musikalischen Fertigkeiten stand für Bürgertöchter auf dem Stundenplan. Die Feminisierung der Hausmusik, die sich im 19. Jahrhundert abzeichnete, erwuchs nicht zuletzt aus Vorstellungen des weiblichen „Geschlechtscharakters", der vor allem mit Emotionalität und Häuslichkeit assoziiert wurde. In der Hausmusik gingen diese beiden Eigenschaften eine ideale Verbindung ein. Als Medium der Gefühlsexpression, die jedoch durch ihren Austragungsort unter Kontrolle blieb, erfüllte das im privaten Kreis gepflegte Musizieren in idealer Form die Reproduktions- und Rekreationsaufgabe, die Bürgertöchtern und -frauen gegenüber den männlichen Familienangehörigen auferlegt wurde. Die Zeitgenossen wurden nicht müde, ein solches Bild golden einzufärben. So hieß es in einer Publikation aus dem Jahre 1879:

---

[7] Marianne Weber, *Lebenserinnerungen*, Bremen 1948, S. 44f.

„Es kommt der Vater verstimmt nach Hause, weil sie ihm draußen im feindlichen Leben gar hart zugesetzt haben; da öffnet das Töchterlein das Clavier, greift in die Tasten und singt dem Vater sein Lieblingslied – ist's nicht, als gienge auf dem Antlitz des Vaters die Sonne auf und schlichen von dannen die bösen Schatten?"[8]

Seit der Jahrhundertmitte häuften sich europaweit Gemälde vor allem aus der impressionistischen Schule, denen solche Phantasien als Modelle dienten. Nicht zufällig ist es darauf vor allem das Klavier, auf dem die jungen Bürgerinnen ihrer Musizierlust frönen.[9] Das bürgerliche 19. Jahrhundert war, diesen Eindruck vermittelt zumindest ein Großteil der schriftlichen und bildlichen Quellen, voll von Klavieren, Eduard Hanslick war nicht der Einzige, der gar von der „Clavierseuche" schrieb.[10] Ein Klavier, besser noch ein Flügel, gehörte unabdingbar zur angemessenen Einrichtung eines guten Hauses dazu. Unübersehbar führte das Instrument als repräsentatives Möbelstück die Kunstbeflissenheit seiner Besitzer vor Augen.

Und es waren vor allem die Töchter, die auf den Klavierhockern Platz nahmen. Eine 1897 veröffentlichte Umfrage, die der Direktor einer Berliner „höheren Töchterschule" unter seinen Schülerinnen gemacht hatte, kam zu dem Ergebnis, dass 25 % der neunjährigen und über 75 % der vierzehnjährigen Mädchen privat im Klavierspiel unterwiesen wurden.[11] Anders als sonst bei den Ausbildungskosten üblich, mussten hier nicht selten die Brüder den kürzeren ziehen, vor allem dann, wenn in der Geschwisterschar Schwestern als Konkurrentinnen um musische Investitionen vertreten waren. Die in der Relation zu einem durchschnittlichen bürgerlichen Familienbudget hohen Aufwendungen für Musikstunden galten als sinnvolle Investition in die töchterliche Zukunft. Nicht nur der Vater sollte, wie oben skizziert, unterhalten

---

[8] H. A. Köstlin, *Die Tonkunst. Einführung in die Aesthetik der Musik*, Stuttgart 1879, zit. in: Gunilla Budde, „Musik in Bürgerhäusern", in: *Le concert et son public. Mutations de la vie musicale en Europe de 1780 à 1914*, hrsg. von Hans Erich Bödeker u. a., Paris 2002, S. 427–457.

[9] Zu der im Folgenden dargestellten Rolle des Klaviers und des Klavierspiels in der Gesellschaft vgl. Andreas Ballstaedt und Tobias Widmaier, *Salonmusik. Zur Geschichte und Funktion einer bürgerlichen Musikpraxis*, Wiesbaden 1989 (= *Beihefte zum Archiv für Musikwissenschaft*, Bd. 28), sowie Freia Hoffmann, *Instrument und Körper. Die musizierende Frau in der bürgerlichen Kultur*, Frankfurt am Main und Leipzig 1991.

[10] Unter anderem in: Eduard Hanslick, „Ein Brief über die ‚Clavierseuche'", in: *Die Gartenlaube* 35 (1884), S. 572–575.

[11] Budde, *Musik*, S. 443f.

und erbaut werden, sondern vor allem auch der künftige Ehemann. Für die Töchter des Bürgertums und der middle class zählte musikalische Meisterschaft zur angemessenen Ausbildung und Aussteuer der zukünftigen Ehefrau und Mutter. Schon Mitte des Jahrhunderts hatte Johanna Kinkel diese Funktion erkannt, indem sie schrieb: „Ich meine, dass wir so vorherrschend im musikalischen Zeitalter leben, dass singende und klavierspielende Mädchen sich vor ihren nicht musizierenden Schwestern eines ungerechten Vorzugs erfreuen. Sie werden schon in frühester Jugend in größere Kreise gezogen, mehr beachtet, und verheiraten sich eher als andere."[12] Für junge Bürgerinnen und Bürger, deren Verkehrsformen vor der Verheiratung einem strikten Reglement unterlagen, bot das gemeinsame Musizieren überdies die seltene Chance, miteinander zu kommunizieren. Das starre Korsett der Konventionen, über das die Gesellschaft mit Argusaugen wachte, schien hier leicht gelockert. Das Vierhändigspiel erlaubte im tête-à-tête der Hände, zudem noch im Schutze der Kunst, eine unter Brautleuten unübliche und unerlaubte körperliche Nähe und war ein willkommener und unangreifbarer Vorwand häufiger Rendezvous'. Dass dabei häufig gleichsam „durch die Note" gesagt werden konnte, was sonst als unaussprechlich galt, belegen Musiktitel wie „Liebesblicke", „Liebesgeflüster", „Offenes Geständnis", „Süßes Kosen" und „Sprechen Sie mit Mama". Entsprechend seiner Kupplerfunktion gewann das Klavier dann vor allem für die „Haustöchter im Wartestand" an Bedeutung. Jetzt spielten die Töchter im wörtlichen Sinne um ihre Zukunft. Bereits von klein auf mit der Forderung „play your piece" vertraut, hieß es für die heranwachsende Tochter dann, bei größeren Gesellschaften ihre Herkunft aus „gutem Hause" zu dokumentieren und die Aufmerksamkeit vor allem der Männerwelt auf sich zu ziehen.

Auch die Machart der Musik fügte sich diesem Schema. Offensichtliche Virtuosität, eingängige Melodik und wohltemperierte Gefühle waren dabei die gewünschten Merkmale, die den Musikvortrag auszeichnen sollten. Diesen Anforderungen kamen eine Vielzahl von Komponistinnen und Komponisten beflissen entgegen, indem sie ein „Salonstück" nach dem anderen aus der Taufe hoben. Diese waren primär einer jungen weiblichen Klientel zugedacht, was aus der Vielzahl von Stücken erkennbar ist, deren Titel die Mädchentypen der damaligen Backfischliteratur wieder aufgriffen. Auch auf den Flügeldeckeln tummelten sich Herzblättchen, Trotzköpfchen, Lachtäubchen, Plappermäulchen, Zankteufelchen und Nesthäkchen. Sie waren alle leicht spielbar, täuschten jedoch durch die Aneinanderreihung von Arpeggien Virtuosität vor und hatten selten einen Umfang, der über zwei Seiten hinausging. Unbestrittene

[12] Johanna Kinkel, „Musik als Mode", in: *Frau und Musik. Die Frau in der Gesellschaft. Frühe Texte*, hrsg. von Eva Rieger, Frankfurt am Main 1980, S. 50.

Heldin dieses Genres war Thekla Badarzewska-Baranowska, die im Jahr 1856 in Warschau das *Gebet einer Jungfrau* schrieb, das bald nach seinem Erscheinen die europäischen Notenständer eroberte. Der Grund für den Siegeszug dieser pianistischen Trivialität lag nicht zuletzt darin, dass sie die Charakteristika der sich im Aufwind befindlichen Salonmusik par excellence erfüllte. Nach vier Takten mit beidhändigen Oktavsprüngen folgt eine sich über sechs Takte erstreckende Melodie, die ihre Interpretinnen bis in die höchsten Sphären der Tastatur führt, um sich dann auf zwei Seiten zu wiederholen, lediglich variiert durch Ornamentierungen und Verzierungen, während die linke Begleithand Kadenzen repetiert.

Nur in Notfällen schlugen Bürgertöchter aus ihren häufig durchaus großen musikalischen Fertigkeiten Kapital, indem sie als Klavierlehrerin oder Gouvernante, für die das Klavierspiel zur notwendigen Zusatzqualifikation gehörte, ihren Unterhalt oder zumindest einen Teil davon verdienten.[13] Vor einem „massenhaften Andrang des weiblichen Geschlechts zum Virtuosenthum" meinte ein zeitgenössischer Musikprofessor als einer „bösen Krankheitserscheinung der Zeit"[14] warnen zu müssen. Die meisten Eltern, Ethel Smyth wusste ein Lied davon zu singen, stimmten ihm zu. Verhaftet dem Ideal der vom Erwerb freigestellten Frau, musste jede Abweichung davon als unweiblich abgekanzelt werden. Strebten Töchter gar eine Künstlerkarriere an, die mit öffentlichen Auftritten verbunden war, widersprach dies umso mehr dem herrschenden Weiblichkeitsideal zurückhaltender Bescheidenheit.

Den Drahtseilakt zwischen Kunstbeflissenheit und Künstlerskepsis galt es von daher vor allem in der Mädchenerziehung durchzuhalten. Wo diese vonstatten ging und wer sie vollzog, differierte sowohl national als auch temporal. Da gab es zum einen den reinen Unterricht zu Hause, wobei die ersten Unterweisungen nicht selten von den Eltern, älteren Geschwistern oder anderen Verwandten kamen. Danach zogen Privatlehrer und Gouvernanten in die vermögenden städtischen, vor allem aber die ländlichen Bürgerhäuser ein. Gern wurden auch Ausländerinnen eingestellt. Schließlich war auf diese Weise die fremdsprachige Konversation am besten zu erlernen. In England war eine Ausbildung ausschließlich durch Gouvernanten weitaus üblicher als in Deutschland. Zum einen lag dies daran, dass öffentliche Grundschulen erst nach dem 1870 erlassenen „Education Act" aufkamen und sich eher zögerlich

---

[13] Zur professionellen Musikausbildung der Frauen vgl. Rebecca Grotjahn, „Das Konservatorium und die weibliche Bildung", in: *Zwischen bürgerlicher Kultur und Akademie. Zur Professionalisierung der Musikausbildung in Stuttgart seit 1857*, hrsg. von Dörte Schmidt und Joachim Kremer, Schliengen 2007, S. 147–165.

[14] Otto Gumbrecht, zit. in: Hanslick, „Ein Brief über die ‚Clavierseuche'".

durchsetzten. Auch private Mädchenschulen gab es in England noch bis Ende des 19. Jahrhunderts nur in bedeutend geringerer Zahl als in Deutschland. Zum anderen verbrachte ein Großteil zumindest der englischen upper middle class einen Teil des Jahres auf dem Land und bezog nur für einige Wochen während der „season" eine Stadtwohnung, so dass dieses Pendeln keinen stetigen Schulbesuch erlaubte.

Die stark individualisierte Methode des häuslichen Privatunterrichts hatte durchaus zwei Seiten. Einerseits gaben diese jungen Pädagoginnen, die in der Regel „in quick succession" diverse Bürgerhäuser durchliefen, einer großen Willkür Raum. Je nach Eignung und Neigung bestimmte die jeweilige *governess* die Unterrichtsschwerpunkte. Im Hause eines vermögenden englischen Geschäftsmannes und Vaters von fünf Töchtern und zwei Söhnen gaben sich beispielsweise in den 70er und 80er Jahren des 19. Jahrhunderts fast alljährlich wechselnde Gouvernanten unterschiedlicher Nationalität die Klinke in die Hand, so dass die Schwestern sowohl „deutsche Kinderreime und deutsche Disziplin", irische Gebete und französische Chansons lernten, als auch englische Königsdramen aufführten.[15] Andererseits barg diese Konstellation, die keinem strikten Curriculum unterstand, in nicht seltenen Einzelfällen die Chance in sich, dass in einem harmonischen Lehrerinnen-Schülerinnen-Verhältnis die Bürgertöchter eine besondere, auf ihre Interessen und Talente zugeschnittene Förderung erhielten. Ethel Smyth selbst ist ein treffliches Beispiel dafür:

> "The whole course of my life", so schreibt sie in ihren Memoiren, "was determined [...] by one of these governesses. When I was twelve a new victim arrived who had studied music at the Leipzig Conservatorium, then in the heyday of its reputation in England; for the first time I heard classical music and a new world opened up before me. Shortly after, a friend having given me Beethoven's Sonatas, I began studying the easier of these and walked into the new world on my own feet. Thus was my true bent suddenly revealed to me, and I then and there conceived the plan, carried out seven years later, of studying at Leipzig and giving up my life to music. This intention was announced to everyone and of course no one took it seriously, but that troubled me not at all. It seemed to me a dream that I knew would come true in the fullness of time, but I was in no hurry as to the when."[16]

---

[15] Mary Carbery, *Happy World. The Story of a Victorian Childhood*, London 1941, S. 13, 88 u. 220–223.
[16] Smyth, *Memoirs*, S. 45.

Die zweite Variante lag in einer Kombination von privatem Elementarunterricht und daran anschließenden wenigen Jahren auf einer „Höheren Töchterschule". Diese waren in Deutschland wie in England primär privat geführt. Noch gegen Ende des 19. Jahrhunderts dominierte die Meinung – so ein bekannter Schulmann im Jahr 1865, dessen Vorträge und Schriften nicht nur die konservative *Kreuzzeitung* feierte – dass „weibliche Staatsschulen" als Widerspruch in sich „unnatürlich und unausführbar" seien.[17] Begründet wurde dies damit, dass Frauen ihrer „Natur" nach für den privaten Bereich zuständig wären und entsprechend auch ihre Ausbildung vonstatten gehen sollte. 1900/1901 etwa gab es in Preußen noch dreimal so viele Privatschulen für Mädchen wie öffentliche,[18] und in England, wo sich eine normierte Schulausbildung allgemein langsamer durchsetzte, lag die Relation noch eindeutiger zugunsten der privaten. Generell galt auch hier der Leitsatz, dass Mädchen und Frauen stärker an den familiären Haushalt gebunden sein sollten als ihre Väter und Brüder.

Dass Töchter nach dem Schulabschluss einen anderen Beruf als die ihr angeborene Berufung wählten, galt in den Augen ihrer Eltern als nicht tolerable Extravaganz. Allerdings konnte man, nicht zuletzt auf Anstoß der Feministinnen, die immer wieder den vermeintlichen „Frauenüberschuss" als Waffe nutzten, um ihre Forderungen nach Frauenbildung zu unterfüttern, sowohl in Deutschland als auch in England seit der zweiten Hälfte des 19. Jahrhunderts nicht umhin, die wachsende Zahl von unverheirateten Frauen zu registrieren und zu diskutieren. Doch auch wenn Lehr- und Pflegeberufe langsam als Alternative zum Hausfrauendasein toleriert wurden, geschah dies keineswegs ohne Stirnrunzeln. Es herrschte in beiden Ländern Konsens, dass es sich dabei nur um Notlösungen handeln könne und eine Heirat noch immer vorzuziehen sei.

Doch dass wir in beiden Ländern in der Publizistik des ausgehenden 19. Jahrhunderts immer mehr inbrünstige Appelle an die weibliche Häuslichkeit finden, deutet auf eine Defensivstrategie hin, die gegenläufigen Trends entgegen wirken sollte. Unhinterfragte Selbstverständlichkeiten hätten einer solchen gebetsmühlenartigen Betonung nicht bedurft. Die „Frauenfrage" war in aller Munde und wurde Ende des Jahrhunderts immer lauter gestellt. Doch bei aller Öffnung der Diskurse: Noch zu Beginn des 20. Jahrhunderts ernteten töchterliche Ambitionen, die der weiblichen Bestimmung zuwider-

---

17   Rezension zu Ludwig von Wiese, „Deutsche Briefe über Englische Erziehung, nebst einem Anhang über belgische Schulen", in: *Neue Preußische Kreuzzeitung* 129, 4.6.1865.
18   James C. Albisetti, *Mädchen- und Frauenbildung im 19. Jahrhundert*, Bad Heilbrunn 2007, S. 53f.

liefen, in der Regel elterlichen Groll und gesellschaftliches Grummeln. Die Reederstochter Charlotte Behrend-Corinth erinnert sich an folgende Szene mit ihrem Vater:

> „,Papa, ich möchte nach dem Schulabgang studieren.' ,Drücke dich nicht so überaus wichtig aus. Was meinst du damit? Ein Blaustrumpf werden? Nicht heiraten?' Seine Stimme war drohend. Ich blieb tapfer: ,Man ist kein Blaustrumpf, weil man nicht einfach dasitzen will, bis ein Freiersmann kommt. Ich will nicht Klavier klimpern, Deckchen sticken, Französisch parlieren!' ,Dann willst du eine Emanzipierte werden?!' ,Ich will Malerin werden, Papa.' ,Eine Künstlerin? So eine von diesen verwahrlosten?' ,Es ist ein Lehrgang, strenger als auf der Schule' [...]. ,Wie lange dauert der Lehrgang?' ,Viele Jahr.' ,Viele Jahre? Viele Jahre, Jahre? Darüber vergeht deine Jugend! Also doch ein Blaustrumpf? Eine alte Jungfer!'"[19]

Auch Ethel Smyths Vater sah, wie er ihr in einer harten Aussprache zu Verstehen gab, seine Tochter „knocking to late at doors in the marriage market,"[20] falls sie mit ihren Plänen eines Musikstudiums in Deutschland ernst mache.

Die väterliche Empörung und das töchterliche Aufbegehren verdeutlichen einerseits, wie wenig selbst noch zu Beginn des 20. Jahrhunderts von einer gesamtgesellschaftlichen Toleranz, geschweige denn Akzeptanz die Rede sein konnte, wenn Bürgertöchter andere Wege außerhalb der Ehefrauen- und Mutterrolle suchten. Besonders schweres Geschütz wurde aufgefahren, wenn Frauen Bestrebungen zeigten, sich öffentlich als Künstlerin feiern zu lassen oder auch in die Männerdomäne Universität einzubrechen. Galt künstlerisches Tun als Widerspruch zur weiblichen Zurückhaltung und Bescheidenheit, wurde akademische Bildung gar als Gefährdung der Weiblichkeit verdammt. Wie viel Bildung verträgt eine Frau? Diese Schlüsselfrage wurde in der zweiten Hälfte des 19. Jahrhunderts europaweit gestellt und äußerst kontrovers diskutiert. Doch weite Teile der Männerwelt zeigten sich hier einig. Geistliche, aber vor allem auch Mediziner in Deutschland wie England, kamen mit zum Teil abenteuerlichen Argumentationen daher. Manche von ihnen griffen gar zu Zollstock und Waage. 130 Gramm, so der Befund von Theodor von Bischoff, machten dabei den berühmten „kleinen Unterschied" aus. So viel weniger, das hatte der durchaus anerkannte Anatom in den 1870er Jahren errechnet, brächte das weibliche Gehirn auf die Waage. Ein kleiner Unterschied mit großen Folgen. Gewogen und zu leicht befunden, stritt man dem weiblichem Gehirn

---

[19] Charlotte Berend-Corinth, *Als ich ein Kind war*, Hamburg-Bergedorf 1950, S. 162f.
[20] Smyth, *Memoirs*, S. 49f.

die Studierfähigkeit ab.[21] In seinem Essay „Sex in mind and education", der 1874 in der Zeitschrift *Fortnightly Review* publiziert wurde, vertrat der Arzt Henry Maudsley die Ansicht, dass intellektuelle Schulung von heranwachsenden Mädchen die Gefahr einer bleibenden Schädigung des Fortpflanzungssystems und ihres Gehirns in sich berge.[22]

Die Frauen, die – nachdem die Zulassungsschranken zu Beginn des 20. Jahrhunderts gefallen waren – den Sprung an die Alma Mater wagten, mussten strengen Blicken standhalten. Mit dem weiblichen Eindringen in ihre Domäne glaubten viele eine unweibliche Anpassung an männliches Gehabe erkennen zu können. So auch der Beamtensohn und spätere Soziologe Max Weber im Dezember 1885 in einem Brief an seine Cousine über die weiblichen Gasthörer an seiner Universität: Eine „gewisse Energie in den Bewegungen [...,] welche nicht immer ästhetisch wohltuend" seien, sowie „eine gewisse wissenschaftliche Art der Ausdrucksweise auch bei sehr unwissenschaftlichen Unterhaltungsgegenständen" glaubte er beobachten zu können.[23] Doch diese Skepsis war keinesfalls nur auf die Männerwelt beschränkt. Als sich Franziska Tiburtius als „Fräulein Doktor" zusammen mit einer Freundin als erste approbierte deutsche Ärztin im vornehmen Berliner Stadtteil Charlottenburg niederließ, reagierte auch die weibliche Patientenschaft zunächst sehr zögerlich. „Es war", so schreibt sie in ihren Erinnerungen, „absolut nicht so, wie einige begeisterte Frauenrechtlerinnen uns anfangs glauben machen wollten, als ob die Frauenwelt nur auf uns warte. [...] Es geschah wohl, daß aus den reichen und vornehmen Häusern erst die Hausangestellten gesandt wurden, die Hausmädchen, Köchinnen um Umschau zu halten, fiel der Bescheid günstig aus, so erschien dann wohl die gnädige Frau selbst."[24]

Die gesellschaftliche Stimmungslage war kaum dazu angetan, Mädchen zum Aufbegehren, zum Schwimmen gegen den Strom zu ermutigen. Frauen mit Hochschulabschluss vor dem Ersten Weltkrieg, die als große Vorbilder hätten dienen können, waren und blieben noch lange Zeit vereinzelte, wenig anerkannte und wenig Mut machende Pionierinnen. Die Regel blieb die Frauenexistenz als Hausfrau, Ehefrau und Mutter. Dass diese mit einer Fülle von Arbeiten einherging, sollte zumindest vor den Augen der Öffentlichkeit verborgen bleiben. Öffnete ein Dienstmädchen Besuchern die Tür, galt dies als Indiz für den Wohlstand einer Familie, in der die Frau einzig ihre Mutterrolle

---

[21] Theodor L. W. Bischoff, *Das Studium und die Ausübung der Medizin durch Frauen*, München 1872.
[22] Henry Maudsley, „Sex in Mind and Education", in: *Fortnightly Review* 1874.
[23] Max Weber, Brief an seine Cousine Emmy Baumgarten vom 3.12.1885, in: Max Weber, *Jugendbriefe*, Tübingen 1936, S. 186.
[24] Franziska Tiburtius, *Erinnerungen einer Achtzigjährigen*, Berlin 1925, S. 196.

zu erfüllen hatte, körperliche Arbeiten hingegen an Untergebene delegieren konnte. Dies entsprach zwar keineswegs der Realität, doch nach außen hin wurde alles getan, diese Illusion aufrecht zu erhalten. Die müßige Bürgerfrau, die lediglich den erreichten Status ihres Ehemannes durch elegante Kleidung, wohlerzogene Kinder und distinguierte Umgangsformen zur Schau stellen sollte, wurde zum Idealbild der Frau des 19. Jahrhunderts.

In den ersten Ehejahren standen für deutsche wie auch für englische Bürgerfrauen eine Reihe von Schwangerschaften und Wochenbetten auf dem Programm. Diese besonderen und „anderen Umstände" schotteten die Bürgerfrauen noch stärker als ohnehin schon vom öffentlichen Leben ab. Paradoxerweise sah es dieselbe bürgerliche Öffentlichkeit, die so wortreich das Ideal der Mutterschaft verfocht, nicht gern, wenn sich sichtlich schwangere Frauen außerhalb ihrer eigenen vier Wände zeigten. Da Bürgerväter die Erziehungsverantwortung für die ersten Lebensjahre ihrer Kinder weitestgehend an ihre Frauen abtraten, lag die Verantwortung primär bei den Müttern. Die Briefflut, die bei der in den 1850er Jahren ins Leben gerufenen Frauenzeitschrift *The Englishwoman's Domestic Magazine* einging, kurz nachdem diese auf ihren letzten Seiten unter dem Titel „The Englishwoman's Conversazione" eine Art „Kummerkasten" eingerichtet hatte, zeugte von der großen Verunsicherung vieler Frauen, ihrer ideologisch so überfrachteten Mutterrolle gerecht zu werden. Die Vielzahl von Erziehungsratgebern, die nun vor allem an die Mütter adressiert waren, unterstreicht die Tendenz einer zunehmenden Verwissenschaftlichung der Mutterrolle. Diese Fachliteratur trug einerseits dazu bei, ihre Erziehungsfunktion zu festigen und aufzuwerten, andererseits verlieh sie ihr eine vordem unbekannte Komplexität, die zur Legitimation des Ausschlusses der Frauen aus anderen Funktionen beitrug.

So wie die Pflege und Erziehung der Kinder eine Verwissenschaftlichung erfuhr, wirkten sich allgemein-gesellschaftliche Professionalisierungs- und Rationalisierungstendenzen auch auf die Führung des bürgerlichen Haushalts aus. Schlüsselwörter der weitverbreiteten und vielgelesenen Hausfrauenratgeber waren „Organisation", „Zeiteinteilung", „Sparsamkeit", „Selbständigkeit", „Verantwortung" sowie ihre englischen Pendants „management", „regularity", „economy", „autonomy" und „responsibility", also Qualitäten, die auch in der männlichen Berufswelt gefragt waren. So wünschte um die Mitte des 19. Jahrhunderts die deutsche Haushaltsexpertin Henriette Davidis, nachdem sie die obige Liste von Hausfrauentugenden entwickelt hatte: „[...] möge in diesem Sinne und in dieser Auffassung ihres Berufes die junge Frau [...] den vollen Erfolg und damit auch die wahre Befriedigung in ihrer waltenden Thätigkeit finden." Ihre englische Zeitgenossin Isabella Beeton, deren

Book of household management gemäß seiner ebenso starken Auflagenhöhe wohl in jedem Haushalt der middle class zu finden war, verglich die „mistress of a house" mit einem „leader of any enterprise".²⁵

Darüber hinaus wurde von ihnen erwartet, ihren Teil zu Statuserhalt und -erhöhung der Familie beizutragen. Zum einen als Heiratspartnerinnen, die entweder zum ökonomischen Erfolg des Mannes eine kapitalkräftige Mitgift beisteuerten und ihm Verwandtschaftsbeziehungen erschlossen, die sein Unternehmen festigen oder seine Amtskarriere fördern konnten. Zum anderen indem sie durch Herkunftsmilieu und Erziehung „kulturelles Kapital" und Kapazitäten einbrachten, die den Mann auf seinem Karriereweg weiterbrachten. In einer Zeit, in der Banken und andere Finanzinstitutionen erst im Entstehen waren, entschieden nicht nur das Auftreten des Mannes, sondern auch das äußere Erscheinungsbild seiner Frau und seiner Familie über seine Kreditwürdigkeit. Viele Bürgerfrauen, wie etwa Pfarrfrauen oder Arztgattinnen erfüllten zudem Funktionen, die über ihre „natürliche Berufung" hinausgingen und eng verknüpft waren mit dem Beruf des Mannes. Viele Bürgerfrauen genossen aber auch die beruflichen Erfolge des Mannes, wie wiederum Frau Marx, die in einem Brief an Ernestine Liebknecht vom 28. April 1866 aufatmend den Abschluss des 1. Bandes des *Kapital* verkündete: „Es ging ihm famos von der Hand u. ich kann Ihnen nicht beschreiben, mit welcher stillen Genugtuung ich, nach so viel langen, bangen, fast hoffnungsvollen Sehnen, das Manuscript stolz zu großem Umfange heranwachsen sah."²⁶

Bürgerfrauen mussten nach außen Schwäche mimen, nach innen hingegen ständig Stärke beweisen. Weder die müßige, kränkelnde, sich pflegende und sich langweilende „Gnädige" noch die tagaus, tagein schuftende „Familiensklavin" trafen die Wirklichkeit der Mehrheit deutscher und englischer Bürgerfrauen. Gerade die kontrastierende Doppelrolle, in der nach Vermögen und Verlangen die eine oder andere Facette mehr oder minder stärker akzentuiert wurde, war es, die die Frauenbürgerlichkeit in Deutschland und England ausmachte. Aufs Stichwort, und das hieß, wenn das Dienstmädchen Besucher anmeldete, das Kränzchen oder der „At Home Day" auf dem Kalender stand oder zu einer größeren Abendgesellschaft geladen wurde, war die Rolle der schönen, gebildeten, gewandten und elegant gewandeten Gastgeberin gefragt. Über diese Metamorphose ihrer Mütter verwunderten sich viele Autorinnen

---

[25] Henriette Davidis, *Praktisches Kochbuch für die gewöhnliche und feinere Küche*, Bielefeld 1898, S. 2 u. 721f., Isabella Beeton, *The Book of Household Management*, London 1861, S. 1f. u. 6.

[26] Brief an Ernestine Liebknecht vom 28.1.1866, in: Jenny Marx, *„Sie können sich denken, wie mir oft zu Muthe war ..."*. *Jenny Marx in Briefen an eine vertraute Freundin*, hrsg. von Wolfgang Schröder, Leipzig 1989, S. 82.

und Autoren in ihren Kindheitserinnerungen. Auch die Art der Kleidung der Bürgerfrau wurde, unterstützt von weitverbreiteten Modejournalen, mehr und mehr zum Statussymbol.

3. Deutsch-englische Unterschiede

Doch der Grad der Akzeptanz der gesellschaftlich oktroyierten Rolle wies in beiden Ländern erkennbare Abstufungen auf, die zwischen Identifikation und Rebellion eine Vielzahl von Nischen bereithielten. Neben kleinen Fluchten ihrer Mütter, die in Romanlektüre und Klavierspiel ihren Ausdruck fanden, fällt auf, dass über die Hälfte der hier zu Rate gezogenen Quellen eine von Zeit zu Zeit kranke Mutter zeigen. In der Regel handelte es sich dabei nicht um schwerwiegende Erkrankungen, sondern um „zeitweise Migräneanfälle", „headaches", „schwache Nerven" oder generelle „Kränklichkeit" und „angegriffene Gesundheit". Wie krank deutsche und englische Bürgerfrauen wirklich waren, lässt sich keiner Statistik entnehmen. Sicherlich kann davon ausgegangen werden, dass bedingt durch zahlreiche Schwangerschaften und Geburten und durch noch mangelhafte medizinische Betreuung im 19. Jahrhundert der Gesundheitszustand auch von Frauen des Bürgertums starken Belastungen ausgesetzt war. Dennoch legen die in den Kindheitserinnerungen, Tagebüchern und Briefen geschilderten Symptome die Vermutung nahe und stützen damit die häufig geäußerte Forschungsthese, dass viele Frauen des englischen und stärker noch des deutschen Bürgertums das Stereotyp des „schwachen Geschlechts" in ein Instrument der Verweigerung verwandelten. Mit der Krankheit, die sie im Gegensatz zu ihren Männern öffentlich machen durften, kämpften sie mit den vermeintlich ureigensten Waffen der Frau. Sie erlaubte ihnen mehr oder weniger kurze Rückzugsmöglichkeiten aus dem Familienalltag mit seinen Anforderungen und Verpflichtungen, denn die Tür zum Krankenzimmer der Mutter stellte ein ebensolches Tabu dar wie die Tür zum väterlichen Arbeitszimmer.

Die leise Rebellion, die in zeitweiligen und kaum gravierenden Krankheiten zum Ausdruck kam, wurde nur in Ausnahmefällen zu öffentlichen Protest. Die bürgerliche Frauenbewegung beider Länder war, auch wenn sie in Deutschland für „mütterliche Politik" votierte, nicht von Müttern, sondern primär von unverheirateten Frauen getragen. Dass Ethel Smyth als „Tochter aus gutem Hause", ungeachtet ihres unorthodoxen Lebensstils sich mit der englischen Suffragettenbewegung erst so spät und nur auf Drängen von außen anfreundete,[27] war durchaus typisch. Skepsis überwog. Diese schien in Deutschland

---

[27] Smyth, *Memoirs*, S. 293f.

ausgeprägter als in England, obwohl die deutsche Frauenbewegung, zumindest ihr bürgerlicher Teil, schon deutlich moderatere Töne anschlug als die mit spektakulären Aktionen kämpfenden Schwestern in England. Es verwundert kaum, dass die englischen Suffragetten, die in den Hungerstreik traten, sich am Zaun des Buckingham Palace anketteten oder vor die Pferde in Ascot warfen, es eher auf die Titelseiten der Zeitungen brachten und zum allgemeinen Gesprächsthema wurden.

Auch weniger frauenbewegte Bürgerinnen in Deutschland arrangierten sich offenbar mit ihren eingeschränkten Spielräumen eher als englische Zeitgenossinnen, die in wachsendem Maße Wege außerhalb der Familie suchten und gingen und generell bei der Durchsetzung eigener Interessen weniger konzessionsbereit waren. Zu Hilfe kam ihnen dabei das offenbar nicht so apodiktisch propagierte Ideal der Mutterschaft. Eine Nanny zur Entlastung von mütterlichen Pflichten zu engagieren, um sich zivilgesellschaftlich philanthropisch engagieren zu können, war eine in England allgemein akzeptierte Regel. Die Kindererziehung auch nur zeitweilig an Familienfremde zu delegieren, galt dagegen in Deutschland als äußerst verpönt.

Ein Aufbegehren gegen dieses Leitbild war nicht selten gepaart mit einem schlechten Gewissen. Wenn Jenny Marx, im zweiten Ehejahr und bereits Mutter von zwei Kindern, im „Scherz und Ernst" in einem Brief an ihren Mann klagte, dass die „verwaschnen, vernähten, verkindeten Tage" schon sehr mit dem inneren Drang kollidierten, „sich betätigen und the happiness of mankind an sich selbst empfinden" zu können, so war dieser Tenor in den Briefen, die sie zwei Jahrzehnte später mit Ernestine Liebknecht wechselte, einem resignierten, sich selbst zurücknehmenden Sich-Abfinden gewichen: „[...] doch ich will nicht weiter von mir reden – Sie können sich denken, wie mir oft zu Muthe war u. ist".[28]

Am Jahrhundertende findet man in England dann neben solch privaten Klagen durchaus öffentliche Diskurse, in denen die Frauenoptionen kritisch diskutiert wurden. Im Jahr 1894 startete die Januar-Ausgabe der Zeitschrift *The Nineteenth Century* mit dem Aufsatz „The revolt of the daughters" einen regen Gedankenaustausch zwischen Frauen verschiedenster Generationen und Ansichten über die Rechte, Pflichten, Chancen und Grenzen der Frau. Dabei stießen traditionelle und emanzipatorische Ideen aufeinander. Eine eher vermittelnde Stimme plädierte dafür, auch den Töchtern, denen man doch durch eine verbesserte Mädchenbildung andere Wege auch außerhalb der Familie gewiesen habe, sie diese wenigstens ein Stück weit gehen zu lassen: "Why not

---

[28] Jenny Marx an Karl Marx, 24.8.1845, in: *MEGA*, III. Abt., 1. Bd., Berlin 1979, S. 479f., u. dies., *„Sie können sich denken"*, S. 61.

allow the possibility that nice girls, well-disposed girls, may also desire a mild sort of wanderjahre period, during which they, too, want not to break fences, but to get occasional glimpses of the landscape beyond the family domain." Eine Tochter, die sich zu Wort meldete, klagte über den „long course of trivialities and mental starvation", den Bürgertöchter zu überstehen hätten: "A great deal is said about the duty and the beauty of 'self-sacrifice'", um zum Schluss ihre „Schwestern" aufzurufen: "She must sacrifice herself, not to people, but for principles."[29]

Was sich hier vor den Augen der englischen Öffentlichkeit abspielte, fand so auch mehr oder minder ausgeprägt hinter den verschlossenen Türen vieler deutscher und englischer Bürgerfamilien statt. Traditionell verfestigte und feministisch inspirierte Ideen über die Rolle der Frau lieferten besonders gegen Ende des Jahrhunderts die Basis für einen weiblichen Generationenkonflikt. Je weiter eine verbesserte Bildung im Ansatz auch den Töchtern das Tor zur außerfamiliären Welt öffnete, desto härter musste es in ihren Ohren klingen, wenn es nach Schulabschluss und Rückkehr in die Familie wieder hinter ihnen ins Schloss fiel.

Die meisten Bürgerfrauen in Deutschland und England zogen offenbar noch bis ins frühe 20. Jahrhundert hinein, ungeachtet der seit der Mitte des 19. Jahrhunderts immer lautstärker verkündeten emanzipatorischen Ideen, den traditionellen Weg des geringsten Widerstands einem Kampf um Gleichberechtigung vor. Da die bürgerliche Gesellschaft noch weit entfernt davon war, alternative Lebensentwürfe mit der gleichen Emphase zu begrüßen wie die hochgejubelte Mutterrolle, ermutigten die meisten Bürgermütter ihre Töchter keinesfalls zum Ausscheren, sondern wiesen ihnen den eingefahrenen Weg. Damit halfen sie aber mehr oder minder freiwillig mit, das alte Schema zu verfestigen. Diese Doppelzüngigkeit der Frauen, die sich einerseits selbst als Opfer stilisierten, andererseits ihre Töchter wieder in diese Rolle zwangen, stellte das Hauptmotiv der 1852 erschienen Schrift von Florence Nightingale dar, die sie mit dem flammenden Aufruf schloss: "Oh! Mothers, who talk about this hearth, how much do you know of your Sons' real life, how much of your daughters' imaginary one? Awake, ye women, all ye that sleep, awake! If this domestic life were so very good, would your young men wander away from it, your maidens think of something else?"[30]

---

[29] „The Revolt of the Daughters", in: *The Nineteenth Century*, Januar 1894, S. 27 u. März 1894, S. 425; „A Reply from the Daughters", in: *The Nineteenth Century*, März 1894, S. 447–449.

[30] Zit. nach: Carol Dyhouse, *Feminism and the Family in England, 1880–1939*, Oxford 1989, S. 9f.

Doch es würde zu kurz greifen, deutsche und englische Bürgerfrauen allein in eine Opferrolle zu drängen. Dass die Familie auch ein Terrain darstellte, auf dem gerade Frauen Einfluss und Macht ausüben und dadurch Selbstbewusstsein und -befriedigung erlangen konnten, betonte die Gründerin des „Allgemeinen Deutschen Frauenvereins", Louise Otto, im Jahr 1869:

> „Die Familie ist vor der Hand auf der Culturstufe, welche wir gegenwärtig einnehmen, fast die einzige Institution, in welcher nicht nur die Männer, sondern auch die Frauen, ja diese vorzugsweise ihre Eigenthümlichkeiten entwickeln, und die Kräfte bethätigen können, welche in ihnen ruhen. Nur in Familien-Angelegenheiten hat die Frau eine Stimme, und zwar nicht allein eine berathende, sondern oft eine entscheidende, ihr Einfluß ist hier meist der mächtigere, ist derjenige, der bewußt oder unbewußt gewissermaßen den Ton angibt, den Grundton, der durch das ganze Haus erklingt, und alle Glieder desselben in gleichgestimmten Accorden zu einer schönen Harmonie zusammentönen läßt."[31]

Der Stolz auf diese wenn auch begrenzte Macht mag es mit erklären, warum deutsche wie auch englische Bürgerinnen sich so lange mit ihren eingeschränkten Rechten und Optionen abfanden. Es brauchte erst eine Reihe von wagemutigen Pionierinnen, zu denen auch Ethel Smyth gehörte, damit neue Frauenwege akzeptiert und auch beschritten wurden.

Abstract

"... In pre-Suffragette days": Women's Life and Education in the 19th Century in Germany and England

"My father left England on 30 June 1857, and I was born on the 23rd day of the following April – a 'ten month child'. In pre-Suffragette days I was proud of this fact, having heard that such children are generally boys and always remarkable!" In the Victorian middle class into which she was born, being a remarkable boy was, as Ethel Smyth already suspected as a little girl, considerably more attractive than growing up as a daughter "coming from a good family". This was the experience of middle-class women all across Europe. The social concept of a middle-class society, based on the ideas of the enlightenment, gave the male members of society more and more options of freedom, independence and self-realization, while at the same time a gender model was constructed in which women drew the short straw: lengthy con-

---

[31] Louise Otto, *Der Genius des Hauses. Eine Gabe für Mädchen und Frauen*, Wien 1869, S. 165.

cepts were developed, telling women how to be and where they should find their "true place". In the first part of my article I outline these concepts; in the main part I illustrate the education and experiences of German and English middle-class women in "pre-Suffragette days", and in conclusion I search for German-English similarities and differences.

Rebecca Grotjahn
Das Komponistinnenparadox. Ethel Smyth und der musikalische Geschlechterdiskurs um 1900

„Es ist gewiß eine auffallende, aber doch bestehende Tatsache, daß dem weiblichen Geschlechte im allgemeinen die Gabe des Komponierens versagt ist, wohingegen wir eine ganze Reihe bedeutender Malerinnen, Dichterinnen und Schriftstellerinnen zählen. Komponistinnen sind jedoch eine seltene Erscheinung. Und wenn man auch hin und wieder einmal einer Dame begegnet, die komponiert, so sind doch weibliche kompositorische Geistesprodukte immer nur recht harmloser Natur und haben eben immer nur die Tatsache bestätigt, daß dem schönen Geschlechte die Gabe geistigen Schaffens auf kompositorischem Gebiete verschlossen ist. Diese Bemerkung haben wir auch am Samstag wieder gemacht, wo ein Einakter, betitelt ‚Der Wald‘, von einer englischen Komponistin mit Namen Ethel M. Smyth, an unserem Stadttheater zur Aufführung gelangte. Wir geben zu, – zumal nach unserem oben Ausgeführten – daß es immerhin von Interesse ist, das Geistesprodukt einer komponierenden Dame überhaupt kennen zu lernen. Galanterie verbietet uns, näher auf den musikalischen Wert des Werkes einzugehen und an die kompositorische Befähigung der englischen Miß eine kritische Sonde zu legen."[1]

Auf frauenfeindliche Kritiken wie diese – anlässlich der Aufführung von Ethel Smyths *Der Wald* am 13. Februar 1904 in Straßburg – musste eine Komponistin im ausgehenden 19. und beginnenden 20. Jahrhunderts stets gefasst sein. Anders als viele ihrer Geschlechtsgenossinnen zog Smyth daraus jedoch bekanntlich nicht die Konsequenz, ihre künstlerischen Ambitionen herunterzuschrauben. Vielmehr führte die sich wiederholende Erfahrung, aufgrund ihres Geschlechts in ihrer kompositorischen Laufbahn benachteiligt und behindert zu werden, zum aktiven Engagement in der militanten Suffragettenbewegung.

Ethel Smyths Epoche war ein Zeitalter des aggressiv geführten „Kampfes

---

[1] *Neueste Nachrichten* [Straßburg], Nr. 38, 15.2.1904. Für den Hinweis auf diese Quelle danke ich Jeroen van Gessel.

der Geschlechter"[2], ausgetragen nicht zuletzt in Schriften wie Möbius' *Über den physiologischen Schwachsinn des Weibes* auf der einen und Helene von Druskowitz' *Pessimistischen Cardinalsätzen* – mit dem vierten Kapitel „Der Mann als logische und sittliche Unmöglichkeit und als Fluch der Welt" – auf der anderen Seite.[3] Rund ein Jahrhundert nach der biologistischen Wende war der Geschlechterdiskurs erneut in Bewegung gekommen, nun mit der Sexualität als Dreh- und Angelpunkt, und er spielte sich keineswegs in Randbereichen der Wissenschaft ab. Vielmehr dominierte das Thema in der Publizistik ebenso wie in der Literatur, der Kunst und der Musik.[4] Auch im Diskurs über das Komponieren war die Diskussion um Geschlecht und Sexualität allgegenwärtig, und die Auffassung, Frauen könnten nicht komponieren, verfestigte sich zu einem festen, bis heute einflussreichen Denkmodell. Dieses wurde nicht nur in explizit musikbezogenen Schriften konstruiert. Auffällig oft streifen die zahlreichen Texte zum Themenbereich Sexualität und Geschlecht dieser Zeit das Gebiet Musik. Zwar nimmt sie hier keine zentrale Stellung ein – etwa, indem die Autorinnen oder Autoren spezielle Kapitel hierzu verfasst hätten –, sondern sie dient dazu, Aussagen allgemeiner Bedeutung zu stützen oder zu verdeutlichen. Gerade daran ist jedoch erkennbar, wie verbreitet und selbstverständlich bestimmte Vorstellungen über das weibliche Komponieren waren.

---

[2] So der Titel der aufschlussreichen Ausstellung im Lenbachhaus München 1995. Siehe den Katalog von Barbara Eschenburg, *Der Kampf der Geschlechter. Der neue Mythos in der Kunst 1850–1930*, hrsg. von Helmut Friedel, München 1995.

[3] Zu Möbius siehe unten S. 45ff./Fußnote 27. Helene von Druskowitz, *Pessimistische Cardinalsätze. Ein Vademekum für die freiesten Geister*, Wittenberg o.J. [1905]. Nachdruck in elektronischer Form auf ngiyaw eBooks (http://ngiyaw-ebooks.org/index.htm, Abruf: 6. Juni 2009; dort auch biographische Daten). Helene von Druskowitz (1856–1918) war übrigens am Wiener Konservatorium ausgebildete Pianistin.

[4] Zum Niederschlag des Geschlechterdiskurses in Werken und Texten zur Musik vgl. vor allem: Melanie Unseld, *„Man töte dieses Weib!" Weiblichkeit und Tod in der Musik der Jahrhundertwende*, Stuttgart/Weimar 2001; Susanne Rode[-Breymann], *Alban Berg und Karl Kraus. Zur geistigen Biographie des Komponisten der „Lulu"*, Frankfurt am Main u.a. 1988 (= Europäische Hochschulschriften, Reihe 36 Musikwissenschaft Bd. 36); *Kordula Knaus: Gezähmte Lulu. Alban Bergs Wedekind-Vertonung im Spannungsfeld von literarischer Ambition, Opernkonvention und „absoluter Musik"*, Freiburg 2004.

Eine Art höherer Männlichkeit:
Otto Weininger und die Frau in der Musik

Zu den meistgelesenen Schriften der Epoche zählt Otto Weiningers *Geschlecht und Charakter: Eine prinzipielle Untersuchung*.[5] Seine Verbreitung bezeugt die Volksausgabe des Buches aus dem Jahr 1926,[6] die eine Liste der zwischen 1903 und 1925 erschienenen 26 [!] Auflagen beinhaltet und darüber hinaus Übersetzungen ins Englische, Dänische, Norwegische und Schwedische, Italienische, Polnische, Ungarische und Russische nennt. Weiningers Text konnte sicherlich nur in der Wiener Atmosphäre um 1900 entstehen, aber die Rezeption seiner misogynen Theorie ist ein weltweites Phänomen.[7]

In dem Buch des Musikliebhabers Weininger, der zentrale Thesen von *Geschlecht und Charakter* in Wagners *Parsifal* wiederzufinden glaubte[8] und der sich wenige Monate nach dem Erscheinen seines Hauptwerks für seinen Suizid ein Zimmer in Beethovens Sterbehaus mietete, kommt die Musik im Zusammenhang mit dem Aspekt Genialität zur Sprache. Dieser spielt eine zentrale Rolle bei der Definition der „sexuellen Typen", dem Gegenstand des Hauptteils von *Geschlecht und Charakter*: In der provokanten Formulierung, Genialität offenbare sich als „eine Art höherer Männlichkeit",[9] fokussiert sich der Kerngedanke des Werks. Weininger zielt in seiner Argumentation nicht auf empirische Männer und Frauen, sondern versteht das Männliche und das Weibliche – abgekürzt durch die Buchstaben M und W – im Sinne von Idealtypen (ohne diesen 1904 von Max Weber in die wissenschaftstheoretische Diskussion eingeführten Begriff explizit zu verwenden): „[S]o können wir einen idealen Mann M und ein ideales Weib W, die es in der Wirklichkeit nicht gibt, aufstellen als ideale Typen. Diese Typen können nicht nur, sie müs-

---

5   Otto Weininger, *Geschlecht und Charakter. Eine prinzipielle Untersuchung*, Wien 1903. Im Folgenden zit. nach dem Nachdruck München 1997. Auf eine Wiedergabe der zahlreichen Hervorhebungen im Sperrdruck wird in der Regel verzichtet.
6   Otto Weininger, *Geschlecht und Charakter. Eine prinzipielle Untersuchung. Im ersten und zweiten Teil vollständige, lediglich im Anhange gekürzte Volksausgabe*, Wien und Leipzig 1926.
7   Vgl. Chandak Sengoopta, *Otto Weininger. Sex, Science, and Self in Imperial Vienna*, Chicago and London 2000, bes. S. 137–156. Zu Weiningers Antifeminismus siehe auch Jacques Le Rider, *Der Fall Otto Weininger: Wurzeln des Antifeminismus und Antisemitismus*. Aus dem Französischen von Dieter Hornig, Wien 1985.
8   „Über den Gedankengehalt der Werke Richard Wagners, insbesondere seines ‚Parsifal'", in: Otto Weininger, *Über die letzten Dinge*. Mit einem biographischen Vorwort von Moritz Rappaport, 5. Auflage, Wien und Leipzig 1918, S. 85–92.
9   Weininger, *Geschlecht und Charakter*, S. 141.

sen konstruiert werden."¹⁰ In der empirischen Wirklichkeit finde man weder einen vollkommenen Mann noch ein vollkommenes Weib, sondern nur die verschiedensten, mehr oder weniger zur einen oder anderen Seite tendierenden „sexuellen Zwischenformen".¹¹ „Es gibt in der Erfahrung nicht Mann noch Weib könnte man sagen, sondern nur männlich und weiblich"¹² – diese Aussage wird mit dem Hinweis auf die zahlreichen Abweichungen von den idealtypischen körperlichen Merkmalen belegt: Männer mit breiten Becken und spärlichem Bartwuchs, Frauen mit tiefen Stimmen und flachen Brüsten usw.¹³

Anders als die heutige Leserin mit ihren Leseerfahrungen von Judith Butler bis Jeffrey Eugenides vermuten könnte, wird von diesem Punkt aus jedoch nicht etwa der Geschlechtergegensatz in Frage gestellt, im Gegenteil. Wie Sabine Mehlmann gezeigt hat, wird gerade dadurch, dass Weininger die „Unzuverlässigkeit" der körperlichen Unterschiede anerkennt, der Dualismus der Geschlechter nachhaltig gefestigt.¹⁴ Mehlmann interpretiert Weiningers Position als Antwort auf die Problemgeschichte des Sexualitätsdiskurses, der zu dieser Zeit an einem Punkt angelangt war, der den Abschied von der traditionellen hierarchischen Geschlechterordnung nahe gelegt hätte. Erstens war es nicht mehr zu leugnen, dass viele Menschen den traditionellen Vorstellungen körperlicher Weiblichkeit und Männlichkeit nicht entsprechen, und zweitens wurde Homosexualität – eines der zentralen Themen des Diskurses – nicht mehr unbedingt als krankhafte Abweichung von der heterosexuellen Norm verstanden, sondern als eigenständige, angeborene Form der Sexualität. Wenn auf diese Einsichten nicht mit dem Abschied von Geschlechterdualismus und ‚Zwangsheterosexualität' reagiert werden sollte – was vielleicht erst in der zweiten Hälfte des 20. Jahrhunderts möglich wurde –, galt es eine Argumentation zu finden, die der unabweisbaren Flexibilität der Geschlechtergrenzen Rechnung trug, ohne den Gegensatz und die Hierarchie der Geschlechter aufzugeben. Dies gelingt Weininger durch zwei miteinander verbundene Strategien. Die eine ist die erwähnte Zurückführung der empirischen Männer und Frauen auf zwei Grundtypen M und W, die in den tatsächlichen Menschen in unterschiedlichen Mischungsverhältnissen vorkommen. Unter dieser Voraussetzung stellen Abweichungen das binäre Konzept nicht in Frage: Wenn

10   Ebd., S. 9.
11   Ebd. Wie „ideal" ist auch der Begriff „vollkommen" hier nicht als Wertung zu verstehen, sondern im Sinne der vollständigen Verbindung sämtlicher als typisch und der Abwesenheit aller als untypisch postulierten Eigenschaften.
12   Ebd., S. 10.
13   Ebd., S. 4–6 sowie 11.
14   Sabine Mehlmann, *Unzuverlässige Körper. Zur Diskursgeschichte des Konzepts geschlechtlicher Identität,* Königstein/Ts. 2006, bes. S. 270–299.

beispielsweise eine Frau eine gute Mathematikerin ist, dann sind dafür ihre in besonders hohem Maße vorhandenen männlichen Anteile verantwortlich; W – das Weibliche an sich – jedoch bleibt dessen unbeschadet durch die Unfähigkeit zu abstraktem Denken definiert. Die zweite Strategie besteht darin, das Konzept des Geschlechts nicht mehr an den Körper, sondern an die Psyche zu binden. Weininger definiert M und W vor allem durch ihre mentalen Potenzen. Dabei wird W an die Sexualität geknüpft: Das Weib ist idealtypischerweise ein vollständig sexuelles Wesen, dessen ganzes Denken, Trachten und Begehren sich nur auf den Geschlechtsakt richtet. Es kann nicht abstrakt und klar, sondern nur „mehr oder minder in Heniden" denken,[15] und sein Gedächtnis beschränkt sich auf eine einzige „Klasse von Erinnerungen: es sind die mit dem Geschlechtstrieb und der Fortpflanzung zusammenhängenden".[16] Der Idealtypus M hingegen ist verbunden mit der Fähigkeit zu bewusstem Denken, zur Abstraktion, zur exakten Erinnerung und zum Bewusstsein für das Ich. All dies verleiht dem Männlichen die Möglichkeit zur Existenz, während es über die Frauen heißt: „Sie sind nicht, sie sind nichts. Man *ist* Mann oder man *ist* Weib, je nachdem, ob man wer *ist* oder nicht."[17] Abstraktionsfähigkeit wie exakte Erinnerung jedoch sind Weininger zufolge die Voraussetzungen für Genialität,[18] die mithin nicht einfach eine von vielen maskulinen Fähigkeiten ist, sondern Inbegriff der Männlichkeit:

> „So ist das geniale Bewusstsein am weitesten entfernt vom Henidenstadium; es hat vielmehr die größte, grellste Klarheit und Helle. Genialität offenbart sich bereits als eine Art höherer Männlichkeit; und darum kann W nicht genial sein."[19]

Obwohl Weiningers Argumentation auf der Abstraktion von der Realität und der Harmonisierung der in der Wirklichkeit aufzufindenden Widersprüche basiert, scheut sich der Autor nicht, die Erfahrungswelt heranzuziehen, um seinem System Überzeugungskraft zu verleihen, und die von ihm oft in polemischem Ton geschilderten Alltagsbeobachtungen und Klischees dürften mit für den überwältigenden Erfolg seines Werks verantwortlich sein. Zu seinen

---

[15] Weininger, *Geschlecht und Charakter*, S. 127. „Henide" ist eine Weiningersche Begriffsschöpfung, die eine vage, unstrukturierte Gesamtheit von Gedanken (das „einfachste psychische Datum", ein „dumpfes Eines") meint. Vgl. ebd., S. 117–130; die beiden Zitate: S. XV und S. 126.
[16] Ebd., S. 158.
[17] Ebd., S. 383, Hervorhebung im Original.
[18] Weininger unterscheidet nicht grundsätzlich zwischen künstlerischer und intellektueller Genialität, sondern postuliert eine „Universalität des Genies", siehe ebd., S. 142.
[19] Ebd., S. 141.

besonders evidenzstarken ‚Beweismitteln' gehört nun die Musik, konkret: die „absolute Bedeutungslosigkeit der Frauen in der Musikgeschichte".[20] Hier holt der Autor seine Leserinnen und Leser an ihren kulturellen Erfahrungen ab. Wo ist der weibliche Beethoven? Beweist das Fehlen von Komponistinnen, die einem Bach, Mozart oder Wagner das Wasser reichen könnten, nicht schlagend, dass Frauen unfähig zu musikalischem Schöpfertum sind? Darüber hinaus bietet der Themenbereich Musik dem Autor Gelegenheit, auf den schon zu seiner Zeit von feministischer Seite vorgebrachten Hinweis auf die Benachteiligung von Frauen in der Ausbildung und im realen gesellschaftlichen Leben zu antworten. Gerade die Situation in der Musik beweise die Richtigkeit seiner Auffassungen – „weil in der Musik nicht wie anderswo die Ausrede der Frauenrechtler und -Rechtlerinnen gilt: der Zugang zu ihr sei den Frauen zu kurze Zeit erst freigegeben, als daß man schon reife Früchte von ihnen fordern dürfe."[21] Geradezu triumphierend wird der Hinweis vorgebracht: „Sängerinnen und Virtuosinnen hat es immer, bereits im klassischen Altertum, gegeben. Und doch ..."[22] – und doch, so ist zu ergänzen, sei ausgerechnet in der Musik die Bedeutung der Frauen besonders gering, geringer noch als in der Malerei oder in den Wissenschaften.

Daraus zieht der Autor den Schluss, dass die Gründe für das Fehlen genialer Komponistinnen anderswo liegen müssen als in den angeblichen Hindernissen: in der Psyche, der intellektuellen Ausstattung. An dieser Stelle schließt sich der argumentative Kreis. Weininger setzt voraus, dass für die musikalische Schöpferkraft die Fähigkeit zur Abstraktion eine noch wichtigere Voraussetzung darstellt als in den andere Künsten und in den Wissenschaften. Denn diese haben alle „deutlichere Beziehungen zur empirischen Realität":[23] Bildende Kunst, Literatur, Wissenschaften gehen von der Wirklichkeit aus, die sie nach- oder abbilden bzw. erklären. Aber die Musik sei nicht mimetisch:

> „zur musikalischen Produktivität gehört unendlich viel mehr Phantasie als selbst das männlichste Weib besitzt: viel mehr als zu sonstiger künstlerischer und wissenschaftlicher Tätigkeit. Nichts Wirkliches in der Natur, nichts Gegebenes in der sinnlichen Empirie entspricht einem Tonbilde. Die Musik ist wie ohne Beziehungen zur Erfahrungswelt: es gibt keine Klänge, keine Accorde, keine Melodien in der Natur, sondern hier hat erst der Mensch auch die letzten Elemente noch selbständig zu erzeugen."[24]

[20] Ebd., S. 151.
[21] Ebd., S. 152.
[22] Ebd., S. 152.
[23] Ebd., S. 151.
[24] Ebd.

Die Unfähigkeit zu abstraktem Denken ist es, was das Weibliche kennzeichnet – und dies scheint bewiesen durch das Fehlen genialer Komponistinnen.[25]

Das Argument der musikgeschichtlichen „Thatsachen" im misogynen und feministischen Musikdiskurs

Mit seiner Behauptung, es gäbe keine genialen Komponistinnen, greift Weininger auf einen Topos zurück, der sich im misogynen Diskurs bereits bewährt hatte. Vielleicht ist er für den Plagiatsvorwurf mitverantwortlich, den Paul Julius Möbius, der Autor von *Über den physiologischen Schwachsinn des Weibes*, gegen Weininger erhob.[26] Dieser ist zwar im Hinblick auf die generelle Aussage untriftig, denn Möbius hält an dem durch Weininger überwundenen Ansatz fest, aus der Anatomie eine reale Zweigeschlechtlichkeit abzuleiten. Das Musik-Argument allerdings begegnet bei Möbius ebenfalls, und zwar in derselben Struktur. Es wird eine Spannung zwischen zwei vermeintlichen Fakten aufgebaut: dem Fehlen von genialen Komponistinnen in der Musikgeschichte und der Feststellung, dass es niemals eine Benachteiligung der Frauen in der Musikausbildung gegeben habe. Auch die vermeintlich zwingende Schlussfolgerung ist dieselbe: Der Grund dafür, dass es keine großen Komponistinnen gebe, könne nur die mangelhafte mentale Ausstattung der Frauen sein:

„Dreister, als es die ‚Feministen' thun, kann man der Wahrheit gar nicht ins Gesicht schlagen. Am einfachsten ist es, auf die Gebiete hinzuweisen, die den Weibern jederzeit offen gestanden und auf denen sie sich nach Belieben bewegt haben. Die Musik z. B. ist doch nie männliche Domäne gewesen, im Gegentheile werden mehr Mädchen als Knaben in der Musik unterrichtet. Was ist nun dabei herausgekommen? Die Weiber singen und spielen zum Theile ganz gut, aber damit ist die Sache zu Ende. Wo ist der weibliche Componist, der einen Fortschritt bedeutete? [...] Der Mangel am Vermögen, zu combiniren, d.h. in der Kunst der Mangel an Phantasie, macht die weibliche Kunstübung im Grossen und Ganzen werthlos."[27]

[25] An dieser Stelle ließe sich Weiningers Musikbegriff diskutieren, der der Idee der absoluten Musik verpflichtet ist. Vgl. hierzu von der Autorin: „Deutsche Frauen, deutscher Sang – Nation, Gender und die *idea of serious music*", in: *Deutsche Frauen, deutscher Sang – Musik in der deutschen Kulturnation,* hrsg. von ders. (Beiträge zur Kulturgeschichte der Musik, Bd. 1), München: Allitera 2009, S. 173–193.

[26] Vgl. Romana Weiershausen, *Wissenschaft und Weiblichkeit. Die Studentin in der Literatur der Jahrhundertwende* (Ergebnisse der Frauen- und Geschlechterforschung, N. F., Bd, 5), Göttingen 2004, S. 43.

[27] P[aul] J[ulius] Möbius, *Ueber den physiologischen Schwachsinn des Weibes.* 5. veränderte Auflage, Halle a.d.S. 1903, S. 24.

Wie bei Weininger hat bei Möbius der Hinweis auf die musikgeschichtlichen "Thatsachen" die Funktion, die geringeren mentalen Kapazitäten von Frauen im Allgemeinen – nicht nur in der Musik – zu belegen und zugleich auf die Gegenargumente der "Feministen" zu antworten:

> "Sie meinen, wenn man die Mädchen nur genug unterrichtete und die Schranken der Sitte und des Gesetzes niederrisse, dann würden die Geistesfähigkeiten des weiblichen Geschlechts nicht von denen des männlichen verschieden sein. Mit diesen wunderlichen Heiligen ist schwer zu reden. Wenn man sie auf Thatsachen hinweist, z. B. auf die Musikgeschichte u. A., so gehen sie nicht darauf ein."[28]

Das Buch von Möbius erschien erstmals 1900. In späteren Auflagen enthält es Auszüge aus Rezeptionszeugnissen – Besprechungen und Privatbriefen –, in denen das Musik-Argument immer wieder Resonanz findet:

> "Das Erfinden, das Schaffen neuer Methoden ist dem Weib versagt; in der *Musik* selbst gibt es keine bedeutenden Komponistinnen [...]."[29]

> "Man kennt weder einen weiblichen Beethoven noch einen weiblichen Goethe oder Rubens."[30]

> "Wo sind die Komponistinnen, die Malerinnen und Plastikerinnen, die durch ihre ‚Arbeiten' etwas zur Berechtigung des ungeheuren Apparates, den die Frauenrechtlerinnen in Szene gesetzt haben, beitragen können."[31]

Belegen diese Zitate, wie verbreitet der Topos vom fehlenden weiblichen Kompositionsgenie in dieser Epoche war, so zeigt die ablehnende Rezension von Hedwig Dohm – einer der wichtigsten feministischen Politikerinnen ihrer Zeit –, dass auch Gegenargumente, die bis heute in Gebrauch sind, bereits Verwendung fanden. Sie empfiehlt dem Autor;

> "Er lese in den Mendelssohn'schen Briefen, wie Abraham Mendelssohn, ein für seine Zeit ungemein intelligenter und vorurteilsloser Mann, sich energisch gegen den Musikberuf seiner Tochter, als durchaus unweiblich wehrte. Ihre Lieder [...] mußte sie unter dem Namen ihres Bruders drucken lassen."[32]

---

[28] Ebd., S. 65.
[29] Rezension in *Psychiatrische Wochenschrift* II (1900), zit. nach P[aul] J[ulius] Möbius, *Ueber den physiologischen Schwachsinn des Weibes*. 9. vermehrte Auflage, Halle a. D. S. 1908, S. 104.
[30] Rezension in *Die Heilkunde* II (1901), zit. ebd., S. 91.
[31] Rezension in *Der Litterat*, ohne Jahresangabe, zit. ebd., S. 99.
[32] Rezension in *Die Frauenbewegung* II (1901), zit. ebd., S. 128.

Allerdings sind die Seiten im Musikdiskurs nicht so klar aufgeteilt, wie es den Anschein haben mag. Vielmehr findet sich auch in zahlreichen Texten der Frauenbewegung dieser Zeit eine Position, die die angebliche Unfähigkeit der Frauen zu kompositorischer Genialität als Tatsache behauptet. Die Basis hierfür ist eine differenzfeministische Position, die von einer grundsätzlichen Unterschiedlichkeit der Geschlechter ausgeht und das Streben nach konsequenter Gleichbehandlung ablehnt, aber soziale oder rechtliche Ungleichheiten bekämpft. Ein Beispiel ist die weltweit gelesene schwedische Frauenrechtlerin und Reformpädagogin Ellen Key, die im „Neuschaffen auf dem Gebiete der geistigen und materiellen Kultur [...] die höchste Kraftäußerung des Mannes" sieht.[33] Key stimmt mit Möbius und Weininger darin überein, dass man bei der Frau das „Kombinationsvermögen" und den „höchsten Flug der Phantasie" nur in geringem Maße antreffe,[34] was auch bei ihr das angebliche Faktum erklärt, dass Frauen keine großen Werke schaffen können. Anstatt allerdings weibliche Genialität generell auszuschließen, definiert sie eine spezifisch weibliche Genialität, die sich aus der Liebesfähigkeit speise:

> „Auch die großen epischen und dramatischen Dichtungen, die Hauptwerke der Musik und der bildenden Kunst fordern jene Stärke, welche die Frau nicht besitzt. Der Mann holt seine Inspiration aus den großen Gefühlen. Er aber beherrscht sie, wenn er aus ihnen gestaltet; er dichtet sich aus in seinen Werken und befreit sich so von der alles absorbierenden Macht der Gefühle. Das männliche Genie verdoppelt sich so zu sagen beim Schaffensakt: ist zugleich Mann und Weib. Auch das weibliche Genie verdoppelt sich, aber dadurch, daß es *zwei Male Weib* wird. Die Genialität des Genies verstärkt ihre weibliche Genialität, welche die ist: lieben zu können."[35]

Dadurch ist die Frau zur reproduzierenden Künstlerin prädestiniert:

> „Diese geniale Kraft ist auch die Ursache, weshalb die Frau der Assimilation so fähig ist, weshalb sie den Stoff, den die männlichen Genies ihr gegeben, in sich so gut aufnehmen und verarbeiten kann, indem sie die Werke zum zweiten Male auf der Bühne gestaltet oder sie als reproduzierende Künstlerin wiedergiebt."[36]

---

[33] Ellen Key, *Mißbrauchte Frauenkraft*, 2. Auflage, Berlin 1904, S. 14. (Die schwedische Originalausgabe *Missbrukad kvinnokraft och Naturenliga arbetsområden för kvinnan* erschien 1896 in Stockholm, die erste deutsche Übersetzung in Paris 1898.)
[34] Ebd., S. 61.
[35] Ebd.
[36] Ebd.

Stärker auf die Musik fokussiert wird dieser Gedanke von Johannes Müller, einem Differenzfeministen, der in seinen Schriften dafür eintritt, dass jede Frau einen Beruf erlernen solle. Dieser müsse allerdings ihrer weiblichen „Natur" entsprechen, welche im Gegensatz zur produktiven Männlichkeit reproduktiv sei – woraus sich ergibt, dass Frauen als „Komponisten" nicht Großes leisten können:

> „Ein [...] Unterschied zwischen männlicher und weiblicher Natur ist der, daß der Mann vorwiegend produktiv, die Frau rezeptiv und reproduktiv ist. Es werden also die Berufszweige mit Männern versorgt werden müssen, wo das schöpferische Moment in der Tätigkeit vorhanden sein muß, wenigstens in den Stellungen des Arbeitsgebietes, wo es nicht entbehrt werden kann. Das gilt tatsächlich für alle Erwerbszweige, ob es sich um künstlerisches Schaffen und Nachschaffen oder wissenschaftliche Forschung oder um das technische und kaufmännische Gebiet handelt. [...] In der Musik z. B. werden sie als Virtuosen zweifellos Hervorragendes leisten können, aber nicht als Komponisten. Sie verstehen sich ja auf das Nachempfinden besser als die Männer. Aber schon die Kapellmeisterkarriere wird ihnen verschlossen bleiben, weil sich hier zur Notwendigkeit, das Kunstwerk einheitlich neu zu schaffen, die Aufgabe gesellt, eine große Zahl Individualitäten einheitlich zu beherrschen."[37]

Von einer differenzfeministischen Basis aus argumentiert auch die sozialdemokratische Frauenrechtlerin Lily Braun in ihrem Kapitel „Das geistige Leben des Weibes" für das ambitionierte dreibändige Werk *Mann und Weib*. Für sie ist es selbstverständlich, dass „die Geschlechtsunterschiede sich nicht nur auf das rein Körperliche beschränken, sondern das seelische Leben und die geistige Entwicklung auf das nachhaltigste beeinflussen."[38] Dabei sieht sie die besonderen Fähigkeiten der Frau in der Mütterlichkeit begründet, durch die sich eine besondere Tiefe des Gefühlslebens ergäbe. Ähnlich wie Ellen Key leitet sie daraus eine spezifisch weibliche Genialität ab: Ihre „weltumfassende Mütterlichkeit [ist] die Triebkraft ihres Handelns, die Muse ihres künstlerischen Genius".[39] Wie um Weininger zu bestätigen, ist es allerdings tatsächlich die Musikgeschichte, die die Feministin Braun in Erklärungsnotstand bringt:

---

[37] Johannes Müller, *Der Beruf und die Stellung der Frau*, 2. Auflage Leipzig 1903, S. 92. (1. Aufl. 1902).

[38] Lily Braun, „Das geistige Leben des Weibes", in: Robby Koßmann und Julius Weiß, *Mann und Weib. Ihre Beziehungen zueinander und zum Kulturleben der Gegenwart*. Unter Mitwirkung von Th. Achelis et al., 3 Bände, Stuttgart o.J. [1908], 1. Band: *Der Mann. Das Weib. [2.] Das Weib*, S. 231–287, hier S. 231.

[39] Ebd., S. 276.

„Wenn es die Tiefe der Empfindung, wenn es der Subjektivismus der Frauen ist, der sie beherrscht und leitet, wie kommt es dann, daß die subjektivste aller Künste, die *Musik*, ihrer Schöpferkraft verschlossen blieb? Zu keiner Zeit hat man sie an der Ausübung der Musik verhindert; sie ist von jeher ein wichtiger Teil weiblicher Erziehung gewesen; als reproduzierende Künstlerinnen haben es Frauen auf allen Gebieten zu vollendeter Meisterschaft gebracht. Und doch kennt die Musikgeschichte keine einzige Komponistin von nennenswerter Bedeutung! Wirft das nicht unsere Beweisführung, daß das Gefühl das stärkste Element weiblicher Produktionskraft ist, sofort über den Haufen?"[40]

Zur Auflösung der Spannung zieht Braun eine Theorie heran, mit der sie bereits zuvor die Entwicklung in anderen Künsten und in der Wissenschaft beschreibt: Die Frau folge dem Mann in ihrer Entwicklung stets nach, individuell und kulturell. Erst nach einer Phase der Nachahmung des Mannes, der Reproduktion, finde sie zum Ausdruck der weiblichen Individualität. Da jedoch die Musik sich ohnehin langsamer als die anderen Künste entwickelt habe und historisch erst spät zu dem geworden sei, was sie heute ist – nämlich zu einer subjektiven Ausdruckskunst –, müsse die Frau hier noch auf einer niedrigeren Stufe stehen als etwa in der Literatur oder der bildenden Kunst:

„Die Entwicklung der Musik zu dem, was sie heute ist, hat selbst für die Männer verhältnismäßig spät ihren Anfang genommen. Um in Tönen zu empfinden, aus Tönen eine Welt aufzubauen, dazu gehört Vertiefung des Innenlebens, eine Verfeinerung der Empfindung, eine Stärke und Abgeschlossenheit der Persönlichkeit, die die Frau erst nach einer langen Zeit allmählicher Menschwerdung erreichen kann. Sie steht in der Musik erst auf jener Stufe, die sie auf anderen Gebieten des Geisteslebens schon überschritten hat: sie reproduziert, sie schmiegt sich dem Denken und Fühlen des Mannes an, sie ist die Saite, auf der er spielt."[41]

„Nothing to prevent?" Otto Weininger, Ethel Smyth und die weibliche Genialität

Zweifellos hätte Lily Braun andere, vielleicht tragfähigere Erklärungen für die Spannung zwischen den „Thatsachen" über die Frau in der Musik finden können – etwa indem sie auf die kompositorischen Leistungen einer Ethel

---

[40] Ebd., S. 276f. Hervorhebung im Original.
[41] Ebd., S. 277.

Smyth[42] oder auf das Problem der Professionalität als Voraussetzung für kompositorischen Erfolg hingewiesen hätte. Aber diese Art von Gegenargumentation, die sich ebenfalls auf musikgeschichtliche Tatsachen bezogen hätte, findet man in der Diskussion kaum – was angesichts des Forschungs- und Kenntnisstandes dieser Zeit vielleicht nicht überrascht. Zu den seltenen Gegenbeispielen zählt eine Quelle aus dem Jahr 1920, die gleichzeitig belegt, welche Relevanz der misogyne Diskurs – und die Weininger-Lektüre – für die Welt Ethel Smyths besaß.

Im Herbst 1920 erschien im Magazin *New Statesman* eine Rezension des Buches *Our Women* von Arnold Bennett[43] von dem unter dem Pseudonym „Affable Hawk" (freundlicher Falke) schreibenden Journalisten Desmond MacCarthy.[44] Dieser beschreibt das Buch ein wenig gelangweilt als eines von vielen zur Geschlechterthematik, das wieder einmal die intellektuelle Unterlegenheit der Frauen nachweise. Zustimmend referiert er Bennetts Aussagen über fehlende herausragende Frauen in Literatur, Wissenschaft, Philosophie etc. – und natürlich in Kunst und Musik. "No woman at all has achieved either painting or sculpture that is better than second-rate, or music that is better than second-rate", so zitiert der Kritiker aus dem rezensierten Buch, um selbst in Klammern hinzuzufügen: "True; remember the standard is the masterpieces of the world."[45] Ausnahmen werden zugestanden, aber relativiert: "Some women undoubtedly have genius, but genius in a lesser degree than Shakespeare, Newton, Michel Angelo, Beethoven, Tolstoy."[46] All diesen Aussagen stimmt der Kritiker zu, findet sie aber weder neu noch spektakulär – da sei doch *Sex and Character* von Otto Weininger[47] viel aufregender gewesen mit seinen radikalen Positionen, die „Affable Hawk" knapp und zugespitzt zusammenfasst, ohne dass ganz klar wird, was er davon hält.

Eine Woche später wird in derselben Zeitschrift eine Antwort von Virginia Woolf abgedruckt, die mit spitzer Feder verschiedene Behauptungen der Rezension aufgreift – und damit ein paar Tage später wiederum „Affable

---

[42] Hedwig Dohms Hinweis auf Fanny Hensel wurde bereits oben zitiert, s. S. 46/Fußnote 32.
[43] Arnold Bennett: *Our Women. Chapters on the Sex-Discord*, London 1920.
[44] Die Rezension und die im Folgenden dargestellten Reaktionen sind vollständig abgedruckt in: „The Intellectual Status of Women", in: Virginia Woolf, *Killing the Angel in the House. Seven Essays*, hrsg. von Rachel Bowlby, London 1993, S. 19–33.
[45] „The Intellectual Status of Women", S. 21.
[46] Ebd.
[47] Gemeint ist die 1906 im Londoner Verlag Heinemann erschienene englische Übersetzung von *Geschlecht und Charakter*.

Hawk" zu einer Replik herausfordert. Dieser beharrt auf seiner Meinung, Frauen seien intellektuell unterlegen, und verwendet nun zur Untermauerung das bekannte ‚Musikgeschichtliche-Thatsachen-Argument', das ihm aus seiner Weininger-Lektüre bekannt gewesen sein mag: Es habe doch in der Musik niemals Hindernisse für Frauen gegeben – warum also gäbe es dann nicht mehr Komponistinnen? An diesem neuralgischen Punkt hakt Virginia Woolf in ihrer neuerlichen Erwiderung ein und begegnet der Behauptung des Kritikers mit dem Hinweis auf musikgeschichtliche Tatsachen. Ihr Fallbeispiel ist Ethel Smyth:

> "'There was nothing else [but intellectual inferiority] to prevent down the ages, so far as I can see, women who always played and sang and studied music producing as many musicians from among their number as men have done,'[48] says Affable Hawk. Was there nothing to prevent Ethel Smyth from going to Munich? Was there no opposition from her father? Did she find that the playing, singing and study of music which well-to-do families provided for their daughters were such as to fit them to become musicians? Yet Ethel Smyth was born in the nineteenth century."[49]

Es würde zu weit führen, die anderen – noch heute lesenswerten – Argumente Woolfs (die den mit der Schriftstellerin befreundeten Kritiker[50] übrigens offenbar zur Einsicht brachten) wiederzugeben; worauf es ankommt, ist, dass dem gängigen ‚Thatsachen-Argument' mit dem Hinweis auf Fakten widersprochen wird. Woolfs Hinweise auf Ethels Smyths Erfahrungen dürften auf dem erst ein Jahr zuvor erschienenen Memoirenband der Komponistin, *Impressions That Remained*, basieren, denn erst zehn Jahre später lernten sich Smyth und Woolf persönlich kennen. Wie Woolfs zwei Jahre später verfasste Rezensionen zu den *Impressions* and *Streaks of Life* (1922) müssen die Repliken auf „Affable Hawk" wohl mit zur vorbereitenden Arbeit an dem berühmten Essay *A Room of One's Own* (1929) gezählt werden, in dem

---

[48] Hier zitiert Woolf wörtlich den Text von Affable Hawk („The Intellectual Status of Women", S. 29); Interpolation im Text von Virginia Woolf.
[49] „The Intellectual Status of Women", S. 30. (Virginia Woolf bringt hier die Orte durcheinander, an denen sich Ethel Smyth aufhielt – statt „Munich" müsste es natürlich „Leipzig" heißen.)
[50] Die Auseinandersetzung im *New Statesman* endet mit dem Satz des Kritikers: "If the freedom and education of women is impeded by the expression of my views, I shall argue no more." (Ebd., S. 33.) Zu Woolfs Verhältnis zu Desmond MacCarthy vgl. Quentin Bell, *Virginia Woolf. Eine Biographie*. Aus dem Englischen von Arnold Fernberg, Frankfurt am Main 1982 (passim).

es heißt: "The woman composer stands where the actress stood in the time of Shakespeare".[51]

Zu Recht wird heute oft davor gewarnt, Frauengeschichte in erster Linie als Opfergeschichte, als Geschichte von Verhinderungen und Unmöglichkeiten zu schreiben. Dabei darf jedoch nicht in Vergessenheit geraten, dass von der Benennung der realen Hindernisse eine befreiende Wirkung ausging, die vor dem Hintergrund der misogynen Theorien der Jahrhundertwende besonders deutlich zutage tritt. Dass die Ausbildung von Mädchen nicht auf die volle Entfaltung ihrer Potenziale zielte, sondern oft geradezu auf deren Verkümmerung, dass Frauen berufliche Möglichkeiten vorenthalten wurden, dass Musikerinnen nicht die notwendige Bewegungsfreiheit genossen, dass Komponistinnen sich mit Vorurteilen und Missachtung auseinandersetzen mussten – all diese in jeder Komponistinnenbiographie nachweisbaren massiven Schwierigkeiten bedeuten, dass der scheinbar zwingende Schluss der misogynen Autoren auf die weiblichen mentalen Strukturen in sich zusammenfällt. Gerade durch das um 1900 moderne Konzept einer psychischen Unfähigkeit der Frau jedoch wurden Komponistinnen tiefgreifender eingeschränkt als je zuvor. Gegen Verdikte, die lediglich auf die Einhaltung von sozialen Normen zielten, lässt sich leichter verstoßen als gegen Konzepte, die mentale Bedingungen postulieren. Eine junge Frau, die eine gewisse Portion Mut und Unangepasstheit mitbrachte, konnte sich über das Verbot, Musik zu studieren oder unbegleitet ins Konzert zu gehen, einfach hinwegsetzen. Steht jedoch generell das Potenzial zur künstlerischen Kreativität in Frage, so nährt jeder – auf dem Weg zur Karriere unausweichliche – Misserfolg, jede schlechte Kritik grundsätzliche Selbstzweifel. Dies gilt umso mehr, wenn Kreativität und Genialität aneinander gekoppelt werden. In diesem Fall genügt es nicht, dass eine Komponistin komponieren kann. Sie hat genial zu sein; denn jede mittelmäßige Komponistin bestätigt, dass Frauen keine Genies sein können.

Daraus ergibt sich ein Dilemma, das ich als ‚Komponistinnenparadox' bezeichnen möchte. Wenn sich – dem *state of the art* der Epoche Ethel Smyths entsprechend – Geschlecht in psychischen Strukturen realisiert, so sind Abweichungen zwar möglich, aber nur unter Strafe der Unweiblichkeit. Möbius zufolge drohen als Folge von allzu intensiver intellektueller Tätigkeit Schädigungen des weiblichen Fortpflanzungsapparates. Für Weininger belegt eine geniale Frau nicht etwa, dass Genialität eine Möglichkeit der Weiblichkeit ist, sondern lediglich, dass die betreffende Frau starke männliche Anteile besitzt. Sie

---

[51] Virginia Woolf, *A Room of One's Own*, London 1929, Reprint 1946, S. 82. Zum dialogischen Verhältnis zwischen Woolf und Smyth siehe den Beitrag von Elicia Clements in diesem Band.

widerlegt also nicht die Männlichkeit des Genies, sondern ihre eigene Weiblichkeit.

Eben dieses Paradox spiegelt sich in Kritiken, wie wir sie aus Ethels Smyths Biographie kennen: Entweder sind die Werke einer Komponistin schlecht oder allenfalls mittelmäßig; dann sind sie ‚weiblich', d. h. sie belegen, dass Frauen nicht komponieren können.[52] Oder sie sind gut – aber dann sind sie ‚männlich':

> "This work [die *Mass in D*] definitely places the composer among the most eminent composers of her time, and easily at the head of all those of her own sex. The most striking thing about it is the entire absence of the qualities that are usually associated with feminine productions; throughout it is virile, masterly in construction and workmanship, and particularly remarkable for the excellence and rich colour of the orchestration."[53]

Abstract

The Women Composers' Paradox: Ethel Smyth and the Discourse on Music and Gender around 1900

Gender discourse around 1900 repeatedly contains the following observation concerning music: although women had never encountered obstacles when they wanted to study music, music history had evidently produced no great women composers. The only possible explanation for this 'fact' was the assumption that their mental potential differed clearly from that of men. Not only antifeminist authors like Otto Weininger or Paul J. Möbius use this argument of 'facts' to underline their misogynistic concepts. Followers of the difference feminism – e. g. Ellen Key, Johannes Müller or Lily Braun – used it as well, to argue that men and women were different, but equal.

The idea that mental incapacity made women unfit to compose put women composers in a paradoxical situation. If gender is based on psychic structures, deviation would indicate lack of femaleness. A woman composer of genius would not be considered proof of the female potential for genius but would raise question marks about her femininity. In a discussion in the *New Statesman* Virginia Woolf showed a way out of this female composers' paradox

---

[52] Vgl. das zu Beginn dieses Aufsatzes zitierte Beispiel aus den Straßburger *Neuesten Nachrichten*.

[53] J. A. Fuller-Maitland, [Kritik der Erstaufführung der *Mass in D*], in: *The Times* [London, Januar 1893], zit. nach: Christopher St John, *Ethel Smyth. A Biography*, London, New York und Toronto 1959, S. 86.

by pointing out that women had indeed suffered discrimination, and referred to the numerous problems which Ethel Smyth relates in her autobiography *Impressions that Remained*. Therefore, the *Impressions* should be regarded as a work that helped engender one of the most important feminist books of the 20th century: Woolf's *A Room of One's Own*.

Elicia Clements
"As Springy as a Racehorse": *Female Pipings in Eden* as Rejoinder to Virginia Woolf's *A Room of One's Own*

Perhaps it was the following phrase from Virginia Woolf's *A Room of One's Own* (1929) that compelled Dame Ethel Smyth to introduce herself to the famed writer in 1930: "The woman composer stands where the actress stood in the time of Shakespeare".[1] Their meeting would affect both their lives in significant ways for the next 11 years, until the time of Woolf's death in 1941. With this relationship, Smyth gained a colleague and a friend, but also a valuable reader of her prose. While some critics have assessed Smyth's effect on Woolf's texts,[2] much less scholarship exists that explores the reverse: Woolf's impact on Smyth's feminist ideas and her writings. Thus, the focus of this paper will be on the latter exchange. Woolf had been enjoying Smyth's texts since *Impressions that Remained* (1919) and *Streaks of Life* (1922), which she reviewed favourably in 1922. Woolf also read *Female Pipings in Eden*, Smyth's collection of essays, at least twice before publication in 1933, and gave Smyth constructive suggestions about both the content and the methods of her arguments.

Female Pipings in Eden has its genesis in Smyth's earlier journalistic writings, but also in her contribution to the platform she shared with Woolf on 21 January, 1931 for the London/National Society for Women's Service. I would suggest further that it also thoroughly engages with Woolf's statement about the restricted status of female composers in *A Room of One's Own*. Indeed, it is Smyth's central claim: "as things are to-day it is absolutely impossible in this country for a woman composer to get and to keep her head above water; to go on from strength to strength, and develop such powers as she may possess."[3]

---

[1] Virginia Woolf, *A Room of One's Own and Three Guineas*, Oxford 1992, p. 70.
[2] In my paper "Virginia Woolf, Ethel Smyth, and Music: Listening as a Productive Mode of Social Interaction", in: *College Literature* 32.3 (2005), pp. 51–71, I review the literature. See also the contribution of Rebecca Grotjahn in this volume.
[3] Ethel Smyth, *Female Pipings in Eden*, London 1933, p. 4.

I contend, therefore, that Smyth attempts to open up an expressly public dialogue among female intellectuals with her book of 1933. Smyth's text instigates a conversation among professionals to resist the silencing of women's voices in the public sphere.

First, a clarification: I am not suggesting that Smyth simply takes Woolf's argument from *A Room of One's Own* and repeats it. On the contrary, by examining the textual strategies Smyth employs in the first, quite lengthy, and eponymous essay of *Female Pipings in Eden*, I find a variety of devices are used to stimulate dialogue and create a female-centered community within what was, for women, a new and fearfully provisional professional sphere. Smyth deploys two approaches to this end. One is overt: she applies Woolf's thesis to her own discipline to make a similar materialist feminist argument – that a woman must have money and a room of her own to create and be productive. The other tactic is covert: to build and support new communal relationships – and put into practice a feminist materialism, Smyth makes intertextual and interdisciplinary gestures that resonate with *A Room of One's Own,* as well as with other female professionals. Ultimately, I argue, Smyth's text is informed by Woolf's earlier feminist tract, but also responds to, extends, and reassesses it. In turn, not only does Smyth engage with her colleague's ideas dialogically, she also crafts methods that enable her to perform her feminist ideas in her own work.[4]

Part I: Dialogic Exchange

Whether Smyth's approach is explicit or implicit it is, in both cases, dialogic. I am using Mikhail Bakhtin's term to suggest two things: that language is a social phenomenon (it does not exist in isolation, is never neutral nor free from

---

[4] In his comparison of Woolf and Smyth, Christopher Wiley maintains that "Smyth's published writings quite literally told an altogether different story from that of her music", a narrative that adhered to "the normative masculine model" ("'When a Woman Speaks the Truth about her Body': Ethel Smyth, Virginia Woolf, and the Challenges of Lesbian Auto/biography", in: *Music & Letters* 85.3 (2004), pp. 388–414, at p. 412). Wiley interprets Smyth's writing as largely conservative; referring to the construction of a resistant lesbian auto/biographical subject, he contends that Woolf "wrote the silences *into* her works where Smyth merely left them out" (Wiley, "When a Woman", p. 406). I am arguing, on the contrary, that by reading Woolf and Smyth together dialogically, Smyth's intertextual play with Woolf reveals a female-centered exchange that works toward building alternative communities in the public sphere. Her books, therefore, often deploy indirection to resist masculinist discourse.

the effects of other discourses); and, by extension, that texts do not merely answer each other, they are always in a state of dialogic relation. Any construction of language – including rhetorical prose –"permits a multiplicity of social voices and a wide variety of links and interrelationships".[5] Thus, the personal interchange between Smyth and Woolf plays out in productive ways in their texts. Conceptual, textual, and disciplinary boundary crossings enable both authors to forge, restructure, and exercise new possibilities in the public sphere.

As is well-known, Woolf declares in *A Room of One's Own* that there were fewer recognizable female writers because of a systemic lack of financial support and a dearth of autonomous space. As the critic Laura Marcus summarizes, Woolf's materialist stance is revealed in her "emphases on education and experience as the necessary conditions for women's cultural and intellectual life".[6] Such a focus on the everyday and communal aspects of life demonstrate, as Marcus continues, that "the environment and the social sphere become far more significant determinants of literary capacity and production than any concept of creativity as a purely personal property".[7] Smyth clearly agreed with Woolf on this point. Her essay in *Female Pipings in Eden* illuminates the particular economic disadvantages faced by female musicians. But she also explicates how such constraints play out in the material world. For a composer, this means the arena of performance (an experience with which Woolf would have been understandably less familiar). This disciplinary shift in focus assists Smyth in gleaning new insights concerning the status and capabilities of female professionals.

The educational focus of Chapter II, "Women's Training Hitherto", is a good example of Smyth's concern to articulate the material conditions for women attempting to enter the professional sphere. Interestingly, Woolf admired this section in particular. In a June 1933 letter Woolf lauds the segment, telling Smyth

> "its [sic] well worth saying – well worth printing. I think much of it very convincing, interesting, forcible. I mean by 'much of it' all the impersonal objective part. I mean the facts about education. I think they could not be

---

[5] Mikhail Bakhtin, *The Dialogic Imagination: Four Essays by M. M. Bakhtin*, ed. Michael Holquist, Texas, U.S.A., 1981, p. 263.
[6] Laura Marcus, "Woolf's Feminism and Feminism's Woolf", in: *The Cambridge Companion to Virginia Woolf*, eds. Sue Roe and Susan Sellers, Cambridge 2000, pp. 209–44, at p. 213.
[7] Ibid., p. 213.

better, more musically, more persuasively, put. And no one I expect has any notion of them. I am sure they are valuable in the extreme."[8]

Undoubtedly, Woolf understood the double significance of documenting and publicizing the indisputable imbalance of power in the field of music.

Smyth discloses, for example, that despite new gains for the "professional female orchestral player"[9], they are still belittled and ghettoized in many instances. Making the link between the economy and the body even more explicit – a connection Woolf would enumerate throughout the 1930s partly because she witnessed her friend's courage to do so in print – Smyth discloses that simply being female affects the choice of instrument a woman plays and, more importantly, any consequent financial remuneration. Thus, when it comes to orchestras "women cellists are banned! Why, [she] cannot conceive!";[10] yet, the "solitary white-armed presence" of a woman playing the "cumbrous and rather unlucrative instrument," the harp, is endearingly prized.[11] She brings this point home, so to speak, in her tell-tale, humorously effective way, by suggesting that the men in the orchestra treasure this singular woman as soldiers "cherish the regimental goat".[12] As Woolf recalled in reference to Smyth's speaking abilities, she certainly was adept at "liquidat[ing] [her] whole personality in speaking and thr[o]w[ing] in something never yet written by being [her]self there in the flesh".[13] Smyth also notes that choirs, which typically have the same amount of women as they do men, are "generally voluntary, and in no case demand the large fees of orchestral players".[14]

These examples divulge that Smyth's material world was somewhat different from Woolf's. Indeed, throughout the essay, Smyth details the highly communal nature of the musical performance network – a term I take from Carolyn Abbate to signify an arrangement comprised from a set of connections that include the composer, the performer, various interpretative forces such as the stage and musical directors, the moment of realization in the theatre, as well as the mechanisms involved in reproduction.[15] Smyth is keenly aware of the

[8] Virginia Woolf, *The Letters of Virginia Woolf*, eds. Nigel Nicolson and Joanne Trautmann. Vol. 5, New York 1977, p. 191.
[9] Smyth, *Female Pipings*, p. 11.
[10] Ibid., p. 11.
[11] Ibid., p. 11.
[12] Ibid., p. 12.
[13] Virginia Woolf, *The Letters of Virginia Woolf*, eds. Nigel Nicolson and Joanne Trautmann. Vol. 4, New York 1977, p. 280.
[14] Smyth, *Female Pipings*, p. 9.
[15] Carolyn Abbate, *In Search of Opera,* Princeton 2001, xiii.

multiple bodies – both personal and institutional – that enable or delimit women's opportunities in the public sphere. As she explains, "in order to master music *as a trade* ... you have to be right down in the rough and tumble of music life, and no sooner did a woman leave college than she became aware of men's firm intention to keep her out of that arena".[16] Moreover,

> "All the best music, ancient and modern, passes in procession across your desk; here as nowhere else can you learn instrumentation, phrasing, conducting, rhythm; here the beautiful workaday part of your vocation gets into your blood automatically and gratis."[17]

Elaborating Woolf's argument in an adjacent discipline, therefore, leads Smyth to the important conclusion that strictures are especially confining for female musicians precisely because performance is so dependent on publics – conductors, audiences, critics, venue owners, publishers. Unlike writing, initially an isolated adventure, music needs the medial step of performance to be realized. Smyth is acutely conscious that this component necessitates entrance into the very sphere from which women had been both openly and surreptitiously excluded. This point is convincingly made in the last paragraph of "Women's Training Hitherto":

> "So much for the training of musical maidens who fondly believe they have something worth saying to say, and ask but one thing: a chance of hearing their work in public and finding out whether or no they are harbouring illusions. For until a work is publically performed, it is impossible even for the composer to form a true judgment on its merit."[18]

In the chapter that follows, Smyth casts her net even wider. "Literary and Musical Careers Contrasted," which indirectly refers to Woolf's comparison in *A Room of One's Own* (not to mention Woolf herself), reveals that publication is integral to the musical performance network. In reality, Smyth contends, publication in music is fundamental to its practice.[19] For the composer, in the 1930s at least, a work needed to be published even before a reliable rendition could be heard. And a choral work, in particular, needed to be reproduced to be performed. Hence, the difficulty for a "tyro to bring his work and public

---

[16] Smyth, *Female Pipings*, p. 8.
[17] Ibid., p. 8–9.
[18] Ibid., p. 13.
[19] In literature, Woolf herself attests in the 1925 Introduction to the American edition of *Mrs Dalloway*, once a novel is printed, it is not longer the property of the author.

together",[20] a dilemma that again depends precisely on conditions in the public domain. Thus, Smyth too reveals that such exclusionary procedures are systemic, a result of social, legal, and political limitations in the "real world" that are just as criminal, she suggests, as "taxing the voteless more than sixty years after John Stuart Mill had pointed out that thereby one of the most fundamental principles of our constitution was being violated".[21] As Smyth reiterates later in the essay, "at the bottom of everything lies the question of bread and butter"[22]. Practical implications are always at issue.

Crossing disciplinary borders afforded other realizations as well. Indeed, Smyth understood the value of public relations, as her memoir writing bears out. Discussing her life in a public venue did other work for her: it enticed readers to listen to her music. In Chapter VI, "The Writer's Good Fortune," Smyth chronicles her own experiences to further her argument. As she frames it, "[i]n default of courage to resume the Sisiphus-task of wearing down cold-shouldering by the Powers, the writing of memoirs was taken up as pastime. Result: a certain curiosity as to the author's music".[23] Although Woolf thoroughly enjoyed Smyth's biographical and autobiographical facility, she believed that memoir material was out of place in a feminist polemic. Indeed, Woolf tended to shy away from such personal exposés in her earlier essays. She makes her case as follows to Smyth, who, truth be told, basically ignored her except for one proviso, which I will discuss below: "I hesitate to go on to criticism [Woolf writes]; because as you will guess what I criticize is what you say to be necessary – that is the autobiography. I hate it. I don't think it adds any thing to what you have said. I think the personal details immensely diminish the power of the rest".[24] In a follow-up letter Woolf clarifies,

> "But my dear Ethel your case is that there are a thousand others. Leave your own case out of it; theirs will be far far stronger.... I didnt [sic] write 'A room' without considerable feeling even you will admit; I'm not cool on the subject. And I forced myself to keep my own figure fictitious; legendary. If I had said, Look here am I uneducated, because my brothers used all the family funds which is the fact – Well theyd [sic] have said; she has an axe to grind; and no one would have taken me seriously...."[25]

[20] Smyth, *Female Pipings*, p. 16.
[21] Ibid., p. 5.
[22] Ibid., p. 31.
[23] Ibid., p. 37.
[24] Woolf, *The Letters*, v.5, p. 191.
[25] Ibid., p. 195.

Woolf is cautioning Smyth as she cautioned readers of *A Room of One's Own*: however warranted, anger is unproductive. It can overwhelm the person and the text, and provide new fodder for misogynist backlash.

Nevertheless, the autobiographical domain is vexed for Woolf; sometimes, inevitably, even *A Room of One's Own* trespasses there in indicative ways. Woolf acknowledges, for example, that having her own independent income was absolutely essential to any success she enjoyed as a writer. Smyth makes the same significant admission in *Female Pipings in Eden*: "[T]he cards put by kind Fate into the hands of the present writer were, good health, a fair dose of persistence and fighting instinct, and, most important of all, a small independent income which rendered possible a continuous struggle for musical existence such as no woman obliged to earn her livelihood in music could have carried on".[26] Both authors, therefore, incorporate candid, personal facts from their own lives to persuade listeners.

Moreover, Woolf's stance changes in the 1930s particularly because of her relationship with Smyth. The very issue Woolf mentions in the letter from June 8th 1933 about *Female Pipings in Eden* – that she is "uneducated, because [her] brothers used all the family funds" – is one of her central concerns in *Three Guineas*, a text that courageously includes an incensed tone, in striking contrast to her earlier feminist essay. Indeed, several critics suggest this shift in Woolf's rhetorical strategy is largely due to her relationship with Smyth.[27] Yet, in typical Woolf fashion, instead of overtly and specifically alluding to her own situation in *Three Guineas*, she cites Mary Kingsley, the nineteenth-century English traveler, as the central example to demonstrate her point about the self-educated daughters of learned men. Smyth can be heard in such a dialogic method, I would suggest, just as Woolf echoes in *Female Pipings in Eden*.

---

[26] Smyth, *Female Pipings*, p. 37.
[27] In "Virginia Woolf and her violin" (collected in *Mothering the Mind,* edited by Ruth Perry and Marine Watson Brownley. New York: Holmes and Meier Publishers, Inc., 1984), Jane Marcus asserts Smyth was a mothering figure for Woolf, while Suzanne Raitt ("'The tide of Ethel': Femininity as Narrative in the Friendship of Ethel Smyth and Virginia Woolf". *Critical quarterly* 30.4 (Winter 1988): 3–21) contends the friendship elicited personal narratives of the self from Woolf. Additionally, Hermoine Lee documents the significance of the relationship for Woolf's imagination in her comprehensive biography (*Virginia Woolf.* London: Chatto & Windus, 1996).

Part II: Intertexts

Although Smyth does not change her autobiographical method, as I have just discussed, she does take another tack that is indebted to Woolf's comments about limiting anger concerning gendered injustices: she utilizes indirect intertextual gestures. According to Julia Kristeva, intertextuality occurs when two texts speak to each other; it is "a mosaic of quotations; any text is the absorption and transformation of another".[28] Significantly, Smyth never explicitly cites Woolf or her earlier text – to which, as I have shown, she owes a substantial debt. Instead, Smyth uses intertextuality not only to speak to *A Room of One's Own* but to put into practice dialogic transformations.

As Woolf had done in the 1929 text, Smyth also attempts to think back through many of the same historical mothers, referring directly to the Brontës and Jane Austen. These citations, however, only serve to illuminate the lack of a similar tradition to draw upon in music. (She is, of course, incorrect about this, as feminist musicologists have subsequently done the excavation work needed to assemble a history of female composers that was largely unwritten.[29]) Smyth's argument indirectly alludes to Woolf's when she suggests, "Few deny that the Brontës and Jane Austen brought a new note into our literature," and then asks, "Why then should not our musical contribution be equally individual and pregnant?".[30] Reading Woolf's essay, therefore, elucidated blind spots (or deaf moments) for Smyth in her own discipline; she attempted to gather similar histories but was unable to. Her strategies in *Female Pipings in Eden* speak specifically to this dilemma: she is intent on making connections to Woolf, and a female-centered community more generally, precisely to counter-balance such neglect.

But there are also other covert allusions to Woolf and her text. Smyth's reference to Dr Johnson, for example, recalls a similar quotation in *A Room of One's Own*, one that foregrounds the issues of gender and music. In Woolf's essay, Dr Johnson's misogyny is made obvious when she applies his dictum concerning female preachers and dancing dogs to Cecil Gray's *A Survey of Contemporary Music* (1924), suggesting the same about female composers:

---

[28] Mary Orr, *Intertextuality: Debates and Contexts*, Cambridge 2003, p. 21.
[29] See especially Sophie Fuller, *The Pandora Guide to Women Composers: Britain and the United States 1629–Present*, London 1994. For a discussion of the gendered processes of canonization in music history see Marcia J. Citron, *Gender and the Musical Canon*, Cambridge 2000.
[30] Smyth, *Female Pipings*, p. 9–10.

"and here, I said, opening a book about music, we have the very words used again in this year of grace, 1928, of women who try to write music. Of Mlle Germaine Tailleferre one can only repeat Dr Johnson's dictum concerning a woman preacher, transposed into terms of music. "Sir, a woman's composing is like a dog's walking on his hind legs. It is not done well, but you are surprised to find it done at all." So accurately does history repeat itself [Woolf concludes]."[31]

Smyth's Dr Johnson is similarly prejudiced. In James Boswell's *The Life of Samuel Johnson*, the wit's slights are chronicled in a conversation constructed between Mrs Knowles and Mr Boswell: "'I hope,' said Dr Johnson's Quaker friend Mrs Knowles, 'that in heaven men and women will be equal.' 'That, Madam,' cried Boswell, 'is to be too ambitious! We might as well aspire to be equal to the angels!'".[32] Woolf's point resonates in Smyth's excerpt. As she uncompromisingly testifies, "The idea can only be to keep women in their place".[33] Whether the comparison features a dog on hind legs or men audaciously aspiring to angelic status, Dr Johnson's sexism is exposed by both writers, as are the systemic constrictions for women in the field of music.

Smyth also mentions Woolf's uncle, James Fitzjames Stephen, several times, most notably in the final chapter, "Last Thoughts," a section that Woolf appreciatively affirmed was "imaginative and tranquil".[34] J.F. Stephen, the older brother of Woolf's father, was an anti-libertarian, lawyer, and judge. Despite his anti-democratic leanings, Smyth refers to his definition of "originality" in her text,[35] an issue she mentions is her "King Charles's Head," a phrase that became popular in the 1890s to describe an obsession that keeps intruding irrelevantly into other matters.[36] And indeed, she does return to the issue of "originality," as she notes, in another essay in the volume, "[w]here Musical Criticism Goes Astray."[37] If Woolf suggests in *A Room of One's Own* that women have "served all these centuries as looking-glasses possessing the magic and delicious power of reflecting the figure of man at twice its natural

---

[31] Woolf, *A Room*, p. 71.
[32] Smyth, *Female*, p. 11.
[33] Ibid., p. 11.
[34] Ibid., p. 192.
[35] Ibid., p. 54.
[36] "king, *n.15*", *The Oxford English Dictionary*, 2nd ed. 1989. *OED Online*. Oxford University Press, 31 Aug. 2009, <http://dictionary.oed.com.ezproxy.library.yorku.ca/cgi/entry/50126785>
[37] Smyth, *Female*, pp. 71–86.

size",[38] Smyth asserts, via Stephen, that "the great business [for women] is to find out what we ourselves think and feel (supposing we think and feel anything), and try to say exactly that".[39] The interplay among the texts and their authors is palpable. Smyth's rejoinders to Woolf's suppositions respectfully recall her argument, but they also extend and resituate them at the same time.

Another quite remarkable yet elusive reference occurs when Smyth falsely credits the novel *Orlando* to Vita Sackville-West, also a covert allusion to same-sex love.[40] Woolf explicitly told her that she was incorrect about this in a letter dated 21 November, 1933: "I'm amused and delighted to find (in Pipings – odious name [she reiterates]) that you attribute Orlando to V. Sackville West".[41] Although she flags the mistake here, she does not ask Smyth to change it and almost encourages the inaccuracy by alluding to her amusement; elsewhere she requests specifically that Smyth not refer to her in the book. Thus the slippage, which is actually quite apposite given the dislodgement of identity performed in *Orlando*, is maintained – even in the second edition.

The moment to which Smyth refers in Woolf's innovative fictional biography is also important: it is the intrepid scene in which Orlando, the male protagonist, turns into a woman. Fittingly, then, while critiquing the exclusion of women from orchestras, Smyth suggests that the status of their inclusion has actually diminished in recent years: "But as the season went on (I am speaking of only two or three years ago) a metamorphosis such as we read in V. Sackville-West's *Orlando* took place, only the other way round. By degrees these female backbenchers turned into men; and as in the 'Orlando' business it seemed impossible to learn how and when and why the change had come

[38] Woolf, *A Room*, p. 45.
[39] Smyth, *Female Pipings*, p. 54.
[40] Clearly, the *Orlando* reference is also a Sapphicistic allusion, given that Woolf wrote the text in honour of her lover at the time, Vita Sackville-West. Indeed, in contrast to Christopher Wiley, who suggests Smyth only "obfuscated her sexuality in her writings" through "silence rather than subtextual encodification" (Wiley, "When a Woman", p. 403, n.116), I would contend that a codified and ambiguous slippage is at play here precisely to "voice" the unsayable. Smyth's (stubborn?) inclusion of Woolf's lover's name as the text's author functions not only as a beacon that illumines same-sex love, but also as another gesture toward an alternative community (one that obliquely includes the author of *Female Pipings in Eden*). For more on Woolf and Smyth's mutual concern with and pleasure in female same-sex desire see Patricia Moran, "The flaw in the center." *Tulsa studies in women's literature* 17.1 (Spring 1998): 101–121.
[41] Woolf, *The Letters*, v.5, p. 250.

about".⁴² The scene in Woolf's text is, as noted, particularly radical in terms of crossing the borders of gender, sexuality, and knowledge. An impossible event in so-called "reality," Woolf's ploy extricates the typical truth-claims that demarcate women by ascribing their abilities and actions to biology. This is precisely what Smyth is also illuminating in her passage: the limitations placed on female musicians simply by virtue of having women's bodies.

But there is more to this ambiguous allusion. Woolf's scene is also particularly musical. In fact, instrumentalists – trumpeters – actually announce Orlando's sex change:

> "Would that we might spare the reader what is to come and say to him in so many words, Orlando died and was buried. But here, alas, Truth, Candour, and Honesty, the austere Gods who keep watch and ward by the inkpot of the biographer cry No! Putting their silver trumpets to their lips they demand in one blast, Truth! And again they cry Truth! And sounding yet a third time in concert they peal forth, The Truth and nothing but the Truth!"⁴³

After the three goddesses of Purity, Chastity, and Modesty are dispelled for attempting to dissuade "truth" from coming out of its "horrid den",⁴⁴ we are

> "left entirely alone in the room with the sleeping Orlando and the trumpeters. The trumpeters, ranging themselves side by side in order, blow one terrific blast: –
>
> 'THE TRUTH!'
>
> at which Orlando woke.
>
> He stretched himself. He rose. He stood upright in complete nakedness before us, and while the trumpets pealed Truth! Truth! Truth! We have no choice left but confess – he was a woman."⁴⁵

Woolf's text, which foregrounds and indeed makes absurd the presupposed binaries of male/female (and all of the attendant imbalances of power), employs sound because the moment, through parody and hyperbole, upends the certainties of "truth".⁴⁶ As Smyth states in the chapter titled "Hopes and Du-

---

42 Smyth, *Female Pipings*, p. 10.
43 Virginia Woolf, *Orlando*, Oxford 1992, p. 129.
44 Ibid., p. 131.
45 Ibid., p. 132.
46 In my paper "Transforming Musical Sounds into Words: Narrative Method in Virginia Woolf's *The Waves*" I argue that Woolf often deploys the concept of music to unsettle the assumption that meaning in language is transparent.

ties," "Art is bi-sexual, the female element implicit with the male".[47] Thus, correlating *Orlando* and *Female Pipings in Eden* reveals a salient intertextual play between them, one that demonstrates how both authors disrupt assumptions about gender, sexuality, and social codes. Smyth's deployment of this doubly indirect allusion is acutely effective because it exposes fissures in the possibility of meaning. Springing, one could aptly say, from Woolf's musical tropes and enactments, Smyth listens to, converses with, and responds to her friend and colleague in the public sphere.

Part III: Interdisciplinary Gestures

Smyth's intertextual rejoinders are extremely informative; their covert nature, I would propose, suggests a respect for Woolf and her methods. But in addition to applying Woolf's argument in *A Room* to her own discipline, Smyth also enacts a strategy that branches out to include other fields of knowledge. This tactic both enumerates for the reader the many professional women active in a variety of disciplines and reaches across such borders to perform acts of inclusion. Most obviously, the dedication to Emmeline Pankhurst in the final section of the essay collection both validates and elucidates Smyth's feminist mentor. Woolf thought the other sections of the book "profound, and harmonious. But then they dont [sic] preach; they expound. There you gallop over turf as springy as a race horse – I'm thinking of Pankhurst and HB, which I've just re-read; and kept thinking how fresh, how full, how wise they are".[48]

But even in the first essay, Smyth chronicles a community of professional women. The examples are various and purposeful, in effect building an albeit loosely aligned social network in the public sphere. Such a strategy was crucial in 1933 as such possible connections were just beginning to emerge. As Christine Froula confirms, when Woolf and Smyth shared the platform in 1931, "a society of professional Englishwomen had materialized".[49] Thus, Smyth is sure to mention other female musicians, such as Dame Clara Butt (the English contralto) and Wilma Norman-Neruda (the stage name of the violinist, Lady Halle). She also refers to other performers, including Ellen Ter-

---

[47] Smyth, *Female Pipings*, p. 47.
[48] Woolf, *The Letters*, v.5, p. 249. When Woolf refers to HB she is alluding to Smyth's close friend Henry Brewster. In *Female Pipings in Eden* Smyth includes a chapter on her companion: "Henry Brewster: A Memoir; and Letters" (pp. 87–121). Smyth sent Woolf his letters, which arrived at Monks House on 7 August 1933 (v.5, p. 211).
[49] Christine Froula, *Virginia Woolf and the Bloomsbury Avant-Garde: War, Civilization, Modernity*, New York 2005, p. 213.

ry (the well-known English actress), Lillian Baylis (the theatrical producer), and Edith Craig (a theatre director and women's suffrage activist, in addition to being Ellen Terry's daughter). Smyth also includes visual artists, such as Annie Swynnerton, the Pre-Raphaelite painter and first woman to be elected an Associate to the Royal Academy – Smyth points out, of course, that she had to wait until she was over seventy for this esteemed honour. Reaching further afield to embrace other accomplished professional women Smyth cites Amy Johnson, the pioneering English aviatrix; the Nobel prize-winning physicist and chemist Madame Curie; and Lady Margaret Rhondda, who founded the feminist journal *Time and Tide*.

These testimonials signify more than just name dropping; they are an attempt to enact – to put into practice – the subject matter of her text. A camouflaged but appreciably anti-territorial strategy, Smyth's inclusion of several different fields of inquiry speaks to her overt complaints in the fourth chapter concerning the exclusionary politics of musical groups and institutions. Lines are drawn similarly to war strategies, she argues, an exposé that such procedures always concern the seizure of terrain, whether literal of figurative. And so she asks, "surely there are enough rocks, papyri, flowers, insects, stars and corpses to go round?".[50] (Interestingly, given the mapping metaphors, this is the chapter in which she discusses Amy Johnson's literal record flights across national borders.) It is no accident then that Smyth branches out to include a variety of different disciplines in her feminist text, for, as Julie Thompson Klein has argued, when fields of knowledge are under inquiry, the rhetoric of territories often situates and defines the terms: "All knowledge is located, whether ... the space of inquiry is a routine, practiced place or a negotiated, contested space. The question of knowledge space is not unlike the question of cartography, an analogy reinforced by the metaphor of mapping knowledge".[51] By thoroughly incorporating women as examples she is not only informing her audience but also reiterating her peers' accomplishments in print – the very sphere from which they have been explicitly excluded. In the process, she questions how such boundaries are constructed in the first place. Indeed, in the final section, Smyth makes this argument for the inclusion of difference in eloquent terms, and once again alludes to Woolf to do so (although she remains unnamed):

> "A great woman writer of to-day has said of her books that they are all experiments. That is what I mean, only put in another form; I have always felt it must be, for women, a question of something yet unvoiced, unless

[50] Smyth, *Female Pipings*, p. 24.
[51] Julie Thompson Klein, *Crossing Boundaries: Knowledge, Disciplinarities, and Interdisciplinarities*, Virginia, U.S.A. 1996, p. 3.

in flashes by men like Shakespeare and Donne [two of Woolf's favourites]. And as time goes on, even the Faculty, an all-male body ... may come to perceive that something not quite negligible is being uttered though in a language different to their own; while non-creative women, listening to the song of their sisters, be it literature, painting, or music, will say: 'O what is this that knows the way I came?'".[52]

Smyth unsettles territorial procedures conventionally deployed in the professional sphere by creating her own alternative networks.

Smyth's dialogic exchanges with Woolf, her texts, and professional women more generally, both inform and comprise *Female Pipings in Eden*. Concomitantly, Woolf, too, was creatively motivated by Smyth and her work; she gleaned much inspiration for her writing in the 1930s, her most overtly political phase. As I have noted, Woolf was most likely emboldened by Smyth's spirited acts of resistance in the public sphere to compose the daringly assertive follow-up to *A Room of One's Own*, *Three Guineas*. Additionally, her 1937 novel, *The Years*, depicts the suffragette character Rose Pargiter, often linked to the composer (Rose's quirky cousin, Sara, a pianist and singer, also echoes many of Smyth's attributes, as Woolf conceived of them). And, finally, Miss La Trobe, from her last novel *Between the Acts* (1941), is substantially indebted to her musical friend. Their relationship, therefore, represents a sometimes contested but largely collegial exchange between two women who made momentous strides within and without predominantly restrictive circumstances. A serendipitous note I found in a copy of *Female Pipings in Eden* owned by the Music Library at the University of Toronto speaks poignantly to their mutually inclusive methods, methods that crisscross the borders of music and literature, essays and novels, private and public lives. Imagine my surprise when I opened the book and discovered, on the inside cover, Smyth's handwriting and a personal message to another female composer. The inscription reads, "Muriel Talbot-Hodge a memento of June 1st 1933.... 'She maketh a path to shine after her.' Dame Ethel Smyth." Indeed Smyth did, and so she continues to do so.

[52] Smyth, *Female Pipings*, p. 55.

Abstract

„Lebhaft wie ein Rennpferd". Female Pipings in Eden *als Antwort auf Virginia Woolfs* A Room of One's Own

Die Begegnung von Virginia Woolf und Ethel Smyth im Jahre 1930 sollte das Leben beider in den nächsten elf Jahren bis zu Woolfs Tod im Jahre 1941 nachhaltig beeinflussen. Woolf gewann nicht nur eine Freundin und Kollegin, sondern wurde in den 1930er Jahren, ihrer nach außen hin politischsten Phase, auch von Smyth inspiriert. Während Smyths Einfluss auf Woolfs Texte schon oft Thema der Forschung war, gibt es wesentlich weniger Studien, die sich mit dem Umgekehrten beschäftigen: dem Einfluss Woolfs auf die feministischen Ideen und den Schriften Smyths. Woolf las *Female Pipings in Eden* (1933) zwei Mal vor der Drucklegung und machte Smyth konstruktive Vorschläge sowohl zum Inhalt als auch zur Systematik ihrer Argumente. Smyths Buch greift die Behauptung aus Virginia Woolfs *A Room of One's Own* auf, die Komponistin stehe gegenwärtig auf dem Stand der Schauspielerin zu Shakespeares Zeiten, und entwickelt daraus ihre Hauptthese: „So wie die Dinge heute stehen, ist es für eine Komponistin in diesem Land vollkommen unmöglich, Fuß zu fassen, ihre Stärken zu fördern und alle Fähigkeiten zu entwickeln die sie haben könnte."

Female Pipings in Eden ist als Versuch anzusehen, einen öffentlichen Dialog zwischen weiblichen Intellektuellen zu eröffnen. Mit ihrem Text, den Woolf an einigen Stellen „lebhaft wie ein Rennpferd" fand, zielt Smyth darauf ab, die Unterdrückung weiblicher Stimmen im öffentlichen Leben zu bekämpfen. So schreibt sie mit Blick auf die Romane Woolfs: „Eine große Schriftstellerin dieser Zeit sagte über ihre Bücher, sie seien alle nur Experimente. Das ist es, was ich meine, nur anders ausgedrückt; ich habe immer gefühlt, es müsse für Frauen um etwas noch Unausgesprochenes gehen." Smyths Dialog mit Woolf war ein Mittel, solche Vorstellungen in die öffentliche Diskussion einzubringen.

Amanda Harris
"Comrade" Ethel Smyth in the "great liberative war of women": An English Musical Feminism

Ethel Smyth is as well known as a suffragette as she is as a composer, even though it was her composition that she strove to promote throughout her life. The militancy of her two-year commitment to the Suffragettes from 1911 to 1913 was but two years of her eighty-six, but the image of Smyth as militant Suffragette persisted well beyond her death in 1944. The sensationalism of the Suffragettes' militant tactics is perhaps the principal reason for this persistent representation, however it is also important to understand the militancy of Smyth's gender politics in the context of her broader approach to life and career. Smyth's feminist stint was not as sudden a change of heart as has been suggested in some accounts of her life. Rather, it was consistent with her overall approach to life and particularly to the promotion of her music. Once Smyth withdrew from the feminist movement, she continued her militant approach to fighting for women's rights in music and managed to retain the respect of her fellow suffragists into her old age. This mutually beneficial relationship between Smyth as a committed musician and her political colleagues was not echoed in the experiences of composing women and feminists throughout Europe. The feminist press at the time in France and Germany reveals the otherwise ambivalent relationship that existed between those who publicly claimed their political affiliation with women and those who did not.

Smyth's view of the world prior to 1910 was increasingly a feminist one, even while, as she suggested later in life, she had known "little and cared less about the Suffrage".[1] She quoted many instances of her feminist awakening in her first volume of memoirs, *Impressions that Remained*. In the years Smyth had lived in Leipzig, she had already begun to formulate unconventional ideas about women's place in society and decided that it would not be in her best interest to marry, although she was aware of the financial burden this placed on her father.[2] During this time, she wrote to a friend asserting that she would not marry, "having other views"[3], and in 1877 wrote two letters to her sisters

---

[1] Ethel Smyth, *What Happened Next*, London 1940, p. 210.
[2] Ethel Smyth, *Impressions that Remained*, London 1919, p. 96.
[3] Smyth, *Impressions*, pp. 101–102.

Nina and Alice, one asserting the importance of her independence in her current life situation:

> "I don't think I ever appreciated the necessity of temporary spinsterhood (at any rate, if not total) to certain kinds of lives, till I came here!! You may rely upon that and fear no brother-in-law…"[4]

and the second linked marriage with the failure of women to succeed in music:

> "Every day I become more and more convinced of the truth of my old axiom, that why no women have become composers is because they have married, and then, very properly, made their husbands and children the first consideration. So even if I were to fall desperately in love with BRAHMS and he were to propose to me, I should say no!"[5]

In excusing her first autobiographical volume for its lack of "orthodox love-affairs to relate, neither soulful sentiment for musician of genius, nor perilous passion", Smyth clarified her reasons for not wanting to marry, which had been affirmed over the years:

> "Where should be found the man whose existence could blend with mine without loss of quality on either side? My work must, and would always, be the first consideration."[6]

It is perhaps the reference to "orthodox" love affairs that indicated that this memoir would not delve into the "soulful sentiments" and "perilous passions" of her romances with Lisl von Herzogenberg, Emmeline Pankhurst, Lady Ponsonby or the other important female figures of her love life. Indeed the one man with whom she shared a twenty-four year romantic relationship, Henry

---

[4] Ethel Smyth to Nina Smyth, 9 October 1877, printed in Smyth, *Impressions that Remained*, p. 197.

[5] Ethel Smyth to Alice Smyth, 19 August 1877, printed in Smyth, *Impressions that Remained*, pp. 190–191.

[6] Smyth, *Impressions*, p. 258. It was not only publicly that Smyth declared these views on marriage. She noted in her diary in 1920 that she had no regrets about not having married. Ethel Smyth, *Diary*. VI. 12 December 1920. Special Collections, Harlan Hatcher Graduate Library, University of Michigan, 195. She later wrote of a nightmare she had had before the First World War in Egypt in which she "woke dripping", having dreamt that she was "engaged to be married on the morrow to some unknown person, and couldn't get out of it." Smyth acknowledged that in early Victorian days such a nightmare may have expressed the opposite fear – of never marrying. Ethel Smyth, *Beecham and Pharaoh*, London 1935, p. 110.

Brewster, seems to have encouraged both Smyth's commitment to her work and her budding feminism. When they discussed marriage in their unpublished letters of 1895, Brewster accepted Smyth's assertion that she could not give up her independence and concluded that it was not possible to broker a form of marriage on her terms, which included living in different countries.[7] Smyth had puzzled in 1892 over her strong attraction to women over men:

> "I wonder often why it is so much easier for me (as I believe for a great many English women) to love my own sex passionately than to love yours. I can't make it out – for I think I am a very 'healthy' minded person… it is an everlasting puzzle to me – What say you?"[8]

Brewster's reply indicates the extent to which he supported her inclination towards women as well as her emerging feminist politics. His reassurance of Smyth's anxiety was characteristically rational:

> "You wonder why so many women prefer friends of their own sex… Probably there are several reasons; among others this one that these affections entail no duties, no sacrifice of liberty or of tastes, no partial loss of individuality; whereas friendships of equal warmth with men have that danger (and others) in the background."[9]

Several events during Smyth's years in Germany radicalised her and ultimately led to her militant suffragist views. In 1877 she went to see a friend at Breitkopf and Härtel in an attempt to have some of her works published. Following a long lecture by this friend about the inability of female composers to succeed and the failure of any of women's published works to sell, Smyth found herself meekly agreeing to his terms and neglecting to ask a fee for the publication of her compositions. Writing in retrospect in 1918, she admonished herself for her stupidity, having clearly struggled under the weight of the history of her sex at the time of the incident.[10]

A number of other minor events give an indication of Smyth's growing awareness of discrimination and her reactions to it. In the late 1870s Smyth had made the acquaintance of Brahms, of whose music she was an avid admir-

---

[7] See their negotiations about marriage in letters between Ethel Smyth and Harry Brewster September and October 1895 held in Private Brewster Collection of letters owned by the great-grandson of Harry Brewster.
[8] Ethel Smyth to Harry Brewster 6 October 1892. Private Brewster Collection. This was also quoted in part in Christopher St. John, *Ethel Smyth: A Biography*, London 1959, p. 9.
[9] Harry Brewster to Ethel Smyth 14 October 1892. Private Brewster Collection.
[10] Smyth, *Impressions*, pp. 211–212.

er. She later complained that she was angered at the time by Brahms' views on women, which she had not realised were actually the prevalent views in Germany. She criticised Brahms to her friend Lisl von Herzogenberg, who was also his close friend and was disappointed with Herzogenberg's response. Herzogenberg had resembled many of the "anti-suffragist women" that Smyth had known since, who "for some reason or other on the pinnacle of man's favour themselves, had no objection to the rest of womenkind being held in contempt".[11] In the decade that followed, Smyth would come to receive negative reviews of her music which explicitly tied what the reviewers saw as the inadequacy of her composition with her sex. When her Violin Sonata was performed in 1887, "the critics unanimously said it was devoid of feminine charm and therefore unworthy of a woman – the good old remark I was so often to hear again".[12]

By 1890 Smyth was already discussing her views on women in music and had raised the issue of women's exclusion from orchestras with the violinist Joseph Joachim. When Joachim admitted that it was not muscle strength that made a good violinist, Smyth immediately confronted him with the question of why women should be barred from playing along with men.[13] The issue of Smyth's sex in relation to her attempts at being taken seriously as a musician had become an increasingly insistent preoccupation in her years as a student, and later practising musician, in Germany. By 1899, she had already lived through several decades of struggle against the limitations placed on her sex and in a letter to Harry Brewster, she wrote of her experience of the "awful difficulty of sex and nationality".[14]

Smyth's years in Germany marked a shift from the relative naivety of her twenties to the actions of her mature life. Her views on sexual morality were certainly changing and so was her political perspective on women. In a letter to conductor Hermann Levi in 1902, Smyth wrote: "I feel I must fight for *Der Wald* [her opera]… I want women to turn their minds to big and difficult jobs; not just to go on hugging the shore, afraid to put out to sea."[15] Even at this early stage, a decade before she is recognised as having actively become a part of the women's movement, Smyth had already formed the notion that she wished to devote her efforts to fighting for the cause of women musicians. Rather than seeing herself as one of many women who might form a front for

[11] Ibid., pp. 235–236.
[12] Ibid., p. 396.
[13] Ethel Smyth, *Female Pipings in Eden*, Edinburgh 1934, p. 11.
[14] Ethel Smyth to Harry Brewster, 14 December 1899, printed in Smyth, *What Happened Next*, p. 151.
[15] Smyth, *What Happened*, p. 210.

the suffrage fight, Smyth seems to have developed the view of herself as a lone crusader from early on, deeming it her duty:

> "to encourage other women on the path of high adventure, since, not being compelled to work for my living, I was better equipped than many of my sex for carrying on what I had already learned would be a long and painful fight against prejudice." [16]

Smyth had long experienced the capriciousness of public opinion so easily swayed by an inherent disbelief in the merit of anything composed by a woman. Several times in her writing, she recounted a conversation with Hermann Levi in the years of her residence in Germany, who admitted to having been almost unable to believe that a woman wrote Smyth's *Mass in D*. Smyth responded "'No and what's more, in a week's time you *won't* believe it!'" suggesting that once the tide of "reason" had overcome his initial impression, popular opinion would triumph.[17] It was perhaps this conversation which influenced her, years later, to write about the perception of women's compositions by the general public and other musicians:

> "My present aim is to point out that until woman after woman has emerged in the front rank of music, as they have already done in literature, no woman-composer can expect objective treatment. Between the perceiver and the thing perceived rises like a mist the thought: 'There never have been great women composers – *and there never will be*'."[18]

Smyth's early experiences as a budding composer led her to the position she took in 1910 when the question of women's suffrage was brought to her attention. Although her induction into the Suffragette movement has often been portrayed as the result of her infatuation with Emmeline Pankhurst,[19] Smyth

---

[16] Smyth, *What Happened*, p. 210.
[17] This quote is drawn from Ethel Smyth, *A Final Burning of Boats*, London 1928, p. 10, although the anecdote was also told in Ethel Smyth, "Reflections on Prejudice", in: *Music Bulletin* 5 (3) (1923), p. 81; Ethel Smyth, "A Burning of Boats", in: *London Mercury* 9 (52) (1924), p. 382, and Smyth, *Female Pipings*, p. 26.
[18] Smyth, "A Burning of Boats", p. 383.
[19] Emmeline's daughter, Sylvia Pankhurst may have been one of the first to suggest this in 1931 where she wrote that Smyth had joined the movement in 1910 "subjugated by the charm of Mrs. Pankhurst", then a few years later and with somewhat of an axe to grind against the composer (see the letters between Ethel Smyth and Sylvia Pankhurst in 1934 for examples of the vitriol exchanged between the two women in Add. 56813 BL), she wrote of Smyth: "Recently she had been an anti-Suffragist; now she was a red-hot militant, entirely subjugated by Mrs. Pankhurst, panting with joy and excitement when she could manage to inveigle her idol to her

came to the movement on her own terms and was introduced to Pankhurst at the first suffrage meeting she attended. Indeed in her reflections following the news of Pankhurst's death, by which time her affection had cooled, she implied that the friendship had originally "perhaps after all depended a lot on the Suffrage fight."[20] After being awarded an honorary doctorate by Durham University in 1910, she had received a letter from the WSPU asking her views on the suffrage movement and had revised her initial dismissal of the letter after a conversation with her Austrian friend, Hermann Bahr. Bahr had suggested that the militant suffrage movement was the most vibrant movement in England at that time and that he "could not imagine how a woman like myself had not joined them long ago".[21]

In the book she was writing when she died, Smyth wrote of how Mary Dodge and her "inseparable companion" Munie Delawarr who were "ardent militants" agreed to take her along with them to one of Mrs Pankhurst's meetings.[22] In Smyth's account of this time, she was indeed swept off her feet by Emmeline Pankhurst, but was also convinced by the values of the movement and their resonance with her own politics. In aligning herself with them, she was forced to consider the viability of maintaining her career in music alongside a commitment to political militancy:

> "If I thought I should be a welcome recruit, I was to be disappointed. Mrs. Pankhurst, to whom Munie introduced me, received me with marked coolness, as one who ought long ago to have joined them; and Christabel was still more aloof. But the personality and style of her mother swept me off my feet at once – in fact in less time than it would take to relate the

---

cottage near Woking, delighted to be the one member of the Union who addressed the leader familiarly as 'Em". E. Sylvia Pankhurst, *The Suffragette Movement: an Intimate Account of Persons and Ideals*, London 1977, p. 377 (first published in 1931); E. Sylvia Pankhurst, *The Life of Emmeline Pankhurst: the Suffragette Struggle for Women's Citizenship*, London 1935, p. 106. See also Sophie Fuller, *The Pandora Guide to Women Composers: Britain and the United States 1629 – Present*, London 1995, p. 293 and Sylvia Kahan, *Music's Modern Muse: A Life of Winnaretta Singer, Princesse de Polignac*, Rochester 2003, p. 172.

[20] Smyth, *Diary*. V3. 8 July 1928. Special Collections, Harlan Hatcher Graduate Library, University of Michigan, p. 26.
[21] Smyth, *Female Pipings*, p. 191.
[22] Smyth's account of this time was recorded in Smyth, *Female Pipings*, p. 190–192, and in the initial chapters of a book she was working on in 1941 and neither finished nor published before her death: Ethel Smyth, *A Fresh Start*, unpublished 1941, pp. 16–17, 23 (of manuscript). Special Collections Harlan Hatcher Graduate Library, University of Michigan.

story I had become her slave. The difficulty about music was brushed aside by Christabel with a touch of scorn, but her mother, all in seemingly taking amused pride in the uncompromising attitude of her one-idead daughter ... at once understood how the land lay. Eventually I decided to give up two years to what I knew was wholly incompatible with artistic creation, the Suffrage fight, and then go back firmly to my own job."[23]

Shortly after pursuing her interest in the Suffragettes and meeting Pankhurst for the first time, Smyth intended to introduce her to some of her Paris friends and wrote to the writer Augustine Bulteau about her new acquaintance:

"She's the best thing I have ever met in England & I am so thankful I became a Suffragist before I ever saw or heard her... So that I am quite certain it was not personal magnetism!... I don't know her very well – But this I can say, – but for my own duty to my own inside, I would do any mortal thing she told me... Even go to America! (my equivalent for going to Hell)."[24]

The period beginning in 1910 marked a new phase of Smyth's political life: she not only joined the WSPU but also became an Honorary Board Member of the Society of Women Musicians (SWM).[25] Smyth saw the progression to her involvement in the women's movement as the natural conclusion of her life-long attachment to women in general. Speaking of the time she spent in Holloway prison, serving a short sentence for throwing a rock through a government minister's window, Smyth wrote: "I had always... thought all the world of women – but now I saw (and have never forgotten it) that they are bigger, more wonderful, than I had even dreamed".[26] Shortly after her spell in gaol, having achieved this ultimate goal of her personal militancy, one that she saw as badge of honour,[27] Smyth left England for Vienna to escape the

[23] Smyth, *A Fresh Start*, p. 24.
[24] Ethel Smyth to Augustine Bulteau 25 December 1910. N.A.Fr 17527, Département des Manuscrits, Bibliothèque Nationale de France.
[25] However there is some evidence that Smyth resisted becoming too involved in the SWM in favour of spending time on the suffrage cause. In a letter probably dating from 1912 Smyth wrote to Gertrude Eaton "I think you know I am a very close friend of Mrs Pankhurst's & my preoccupations just now are ... specialised. I hope "The Times" will print a letter on the subject in a day or two which will further explain." Ethel Smyth to Gertrude Eaton 18 April [1912]. Box 2 of the papers of the Society of Women Musicians. Royal College of Music Library, London.
[26] Ethel Smyth, *A Fresh Start*, pp. 32–33.
[27] Smyth wrote to Constance Lytton on 30 November 1911: "I can't settle down till

pull of the movement away from the career to which she wished to return. But having left, she found herself still torn away from the musical life she was trying to pursue by demands to speak at meetings and do many of the things she had left England to escape.[28] On the suggestion of her friend Ronald Storrs she then left for Egypt where she began work on her opera *The Boatswain's Mate*.[29] She continued to correspond avidly with the suffrage leader, and their correspondence reflects Smyth's preoccupation with Pankhurst and women's suffrage as much as it does her commitment to work on her new opera.[30]

Perhaps it was the timing of Smyth's move away from her active involvement in the suffrage movement which saved her from the criticism of fellow activists. Aside from the tacit disapproval from Emmeline's daughter and fellow movement leader, Christabel Pankhurst, Smyth was not openly criticised by feminists.[31] The First World War, which followed quickly on the heels of Smyth's departure, brought an end to the WSPU's militancy for four years, after which, the battle for the vote having been won in 1918, the suffragettes turned their attention to other tasks.[32] The fact that she had committed herself so wholeheartedly to the cause during those two years may have silenced much

---

I've earned what I'd rather have than any distinction in the world – the little prison brooch – After that it is over for me." Quoted in Sophie Fuller, *Women Composers During the British Musical Renaissance, 1880–1918*, PhD London, King's College 1998, p. 40.

[28] See the article about Smyth's suffrage lectures in Anon., "Composer and Suffragist: Dr Ethel Smyth in Vienna", *The Suffragette*, 15 November 1912, p. 66.

[29] Smyth, *A Fresh Start*, p. 41–42.

[30] In fact Smyth's involvement continued even here, the letters are peppered with her account of the discussions she had with fellow hotel guests and acquaintances about women's suffrage and give the impression that she talked about little else at the time. See the correspondence between Ethel Smyth and Emmeline Pankhurst in the collection of Jackson Library, University of North Carolina. She also wrote an article from Egypt which was published in *The Suffragette* although she had hoped it might be published in the *English Review*. Referred to in Ethel Smyth to Emmeline Pankhurst 9 May 1914. Jackson Library, University of North Carolina. Ethel Smyth, "Venus, The Bishops, and a Moral", in: *The Suffragette*, 1 May 1914.

[31] Smyth commented that although Emmeline was happy that Smyth was pursuing her music career, Christabel "very rightly from her point of view, looked upon all women primarily as cannon-fodder". Ethel Smyth, *Female Pipings in Eden*, Edinburgh 1934, p. 215.

[32] For a discussion of Smyth's activities in Word War I see Rebecca Grotjahn, "Eine Suffragette im Ersten Weltkrieg: Ethel Smyths *March of the Women* und das *King Albert's Book*", in: *Blickwechsel Ost | West. Gender-Topographien*, ed. by Nina Noeske and Melanie Unseld (Jahrbuch Musik und Gender 2 [2009]), p. 163–166.

of the potential criticism from those within the movement. Whatever the reason, Smyth was able to continue pursuing her compositional ambitions after the war largely without the disapproval of her former sisters in arms.

In the English feminist press, Ethel Smyth's musical aspirations were in fact seen as consistent with the overall goals of the feminist movement, even though at least for the WSPU those goals otherwise chiefly focused on obtaining the vote for women. Smyth wrote several articles for *The Suffragette*, a paper founded by Christabel Pankhurst in 1912, which combined radical militant politics and articles of general interest to women. Interestingly, her articles on music and on politics, approximately equally represented in her early writing in this paper, were distinct and separate, and her writing only crossed into the politicisation of women in music late in 1913.[33]

In 1911 the first published indication of Smyth's new political stance on women in music had appeared in an interview with *The Vote* (a non-militant suffragist paper) when she told an interviewer that she had introduced a female flautist to the orchestra for one of her performances and encouraged the public to let go of its prejudices against women playing orchestral instruments.[34] In October 1913, Smyth published the first article of her own on this topic, one she would later dub "musical feminis[m]".[35] In this article, Smyth praised Henry Wood's initiative in including women in his Queen's Hall orchestra. The question of women musicians' inclusion in orchestras was later to become a key focus of Smyth's politics. She went on to publish further press articles on the topic in 1916 and 1918 and intermittent items in the 1920s including a section of her memoir *Streaks of Life* in 1921. Eventually this topic formed a central part of her book *Female Pipings in Eden* in 1934, a memoir which functioned as a kind of feminist manifesto.[36]

---

[33] Smyth's early articles on music in 1912 and early 1913 included musical reviews of Richard Strauss and Schoenberg's new works and political writing on the hypocrisy of male Members of Parliament and the "cat and mouse" act in relation to the arrest of Emmeline Pankhurst. See her articles in editions of *The Suffragette* on the 8 November 1912, 14 February, 14 March, and 30 May 1913.

[34] M. O. Kennedy, "Dr. Ethel Smyth on Women in Orchestras", in: *The Vote*, 28 January 1911, p. 165.

[35] Ethel Smyth, "Dame Ethel Smyth" in *More Points of View: A Second Series of Broadcast Addresses*, London 1930, p. 88.

[36] See Ethel Smyth, "England, Music and – Women", in: *The English Review* 22 (1916), p. 195; Ethel Smyth, "Women as Orchestral Players", in: *The Englishwoman*, March 1918, p. 170–171; Ethel Smyth, *Streaks of Life*, London 1921, p. 231–246; Smyth, *Female Pipings*. For more on *Female Pipings in Eden* see also the contribution of Elicia Clements in this volume.

Other feminist writers took up the cause of Smyth's struggle in music, well before she had publicly done so, as one which would be of interest to militant feminists in general. An article in 1912 celebrated the positive reception of several of Smyth's orchestral works by Viennese audiences. The author went on to describe Smyth's address to an organisation for women's suffrage in Vienna at which not only feminists, but also numerous representatives of the music world were present. Smyth's musical success was lauded as a triumph for women:

> "Who did not feel the significance of the spectacle of a woman receiving as a creator, not, as so often before, as an interpreter in the realm of music, the homage of the public?"[37]

Her political speech was then described as an opportunity for her respectable appearance to dispel some of the misconceptions about militancy. The fact that Smyth announced her return to focus on her career in music during this trip was also reported with a distinct lack of criticism.

One of Christopher St John's earliest articles concerning Smyth appeared in *The Suffragette* as well. In her review of a performance of Smyth's works by the London Symphony Orchestra, St John directly linked Smyth's musical efforts with the struggle for women's rights, donning her: the "composer whom every fighter in the great liberative war of women calls by the name of 'Comrade'."[38] The composer would later become something of a preoccupation for St John when she became music reviewer for *Time and Tide*; in many of her reviews, Smyth was held up as the (often sole) example of women's abilities in music, and other women's attempts at composition were compared unfavourably to Smyth's.[39]

The collaboration between Smyth and English suffragists is especially notable when viewed in the context of female musicians' relationship to feminists in other parts of Europe at this time. Smyth was unique amongst composers

---

[37] Anon., "Composer and Suffragist", p. 66. *The Vote* also celebrated Smyth as "the greatest British composer of the day" on 8 April 1911.

[38] Christopher St John, "Review", in: *The Suffragette*, 27 June 1913, p. 612. St John was born Christabel Marshall.

[39] See for example St John's review of a work by Katherine Eggar in: *Time and Tide*, 29 May 1920, p. 66; her article on *The Wreckers*, in: *Time and Tide*, 13 May 1921; Christopher St John, "A Forgotten Masterpiece", in: *Time and Tide*, 22 February 1924, p. 178; Christopher St John, "Too Much Noise", *Time and Tide*, 10 December 1926; Christopher St John, "A Triumph for Ethel Smyth", in: *Time and Tide*, 18 March 1927; Christopher St John, "Behold Ethel Smyth", in: *Time and Tide*, 16 March 1928 and Christopher St John, "The March of the Women", in: *Time and Tide*, 7 December 1928, p. 1205.

in her unequivocal alignment with the feminist movement. In other European nations, composing women may have asserted their right to work and yet they distanced themselves from feminism itself. In 1902, in reaction to Juliette Toutain's attempts to be admitted to the *Prix de Rome*, Max Rivière, writing for *Femina*, interviewed various women musicians currently active in the music world, including Augusta Holmès, Cécile Chaminade, Juliette Toutain, Jane Vieu, Cécile Dufresne and Wanda Landowska to gain their opinion on the *Prix de Rome* and on women in music in general. For composer Jane Vieu, it was important to emphasise that while being an artist, her first priority was still her role as mother and wife. The author's portrayal of Vieu distanced her from "feminism" while emphasising her belief in a woman's right to work (alongside women's natural inclination towards family):

> « Mlle Jane Vieu n'est d'ailleurs pas une ‹féministe'› au sens précis du mot. Elle a sur le féminisme des opinions très raisonnables: elle se borne à réclamer pour les femmes le droit au travail. Elle ajoute que c'est leur devoir de travailler, et que jamais le travail ne les empêchera d'être de bonnes épouses, de bonnes mères et des femmes d'intérieur.‹ Ne cherchons pas à concourir pour de vagues prix de Rome, conclut-elle; il y a dans la vie des besognes plus intéressantes. L'important pour une femme, c'est de travailler. Donc travaillons.› »⁴⁰

This excerpt is interesting in the way that it differentiated Vieu's belief in women's right to work from feminism, "in the true sense of the word". Such an ambivalent relationship with feminism as an ideology and a movement appeared throughout the feminist press in relation to artists' and musicians' association with feminism.

Another example of this ambivalence is an article by A. de Sivry in *Le Monde Musical* of 1904 which took up an issue, contentious at the Paris *Conservatoire* at the time, that the numbers of women students in string instrument classes were due to be restricted to no more than ten percent of the class numbers. This article was one of several on this topic which appeared in feminist and musical periodicals, among others from the Groupe Français d'Études

---

40   "Moreover, Mlle Jane Vieu is not a 'feminist' in the true sense of the word. She holds very intelligent views on feminism: she is content to reclaim for women the right to work. She adds that it is their duty to work, and that working should never prevent them from being good wives, good mothers and homemakers. 'Do not seek to compete for distant composition prizes [Prix de Rome]' she concludes 'there are more interesting occupations in life. What is important for women is to work. So let's work'. " Max Rivière, "Nos Musiciennes et le Prix de Rome", in: *Femina*, 15 April 1902, p. 116. (This and all following translations: A. H.)

Féministes (French Group for Feminist Studies), disputing the justification for these new rules and asserting that selections should be made on the basis of skill and not on gender.[41] Following de Sivry's articulation of the arguments against the new restrictions, the author saw fit to distance herself from feminism, apparently distinguishing the fairness and equality she was calling for from other demands of the feminist movement:

> « Nous ne sommes pas féministes à outrance; nous ne souhaitons pas voir des électeurs en jupons; mais nous nous efforçons d'être justes et il nous semble que la femme étant fort bien douée pour jouer du violon, il n'est pas équitable d'opposer à son talent une barrière, si éloignée soit-elle et sous quelque faux prétexte que ce soit. »[42]

Outside of England, in spite of articles in the music press which constantly associated women's successes in music with feminism, the feminist press itself took very little interest in the activities of women musicians. To glean a sense of what feminists did think of women musicians, we can look to articles which levelled explicit criticism at women whose actions may have furthered the cause of women generally, but who did not acknowledge the debt they owed to the greater movement. The successful painter Louise Abbéma, was exemplified by the paper *Le Droit des Femmes* in 1912 as the kind of semi-emancipated decadent whom feminists begrudged. The paper's criticism was chiefly based on the fact that Abbéma declined to show her works in an exhibition of women artists (*l'Exposition des Femmes peintres et sculpteurs*) on which the paper reported later that year. Abbéma believed that exhibiting in women-only exhibitions sent the message to men that women were not worthy of competing in mixed-sex contexts. Feminists retaliated: Mlle Abbéma *"n'a pas de notions bien claires du droit, de la justice et de l'avenir des races humaines. Elle n'a appris que le dessin"*.[43] The scientist Marie Curie was similarly criticised in the

---

[41] A letter from this group was published in an article by Arthur Pougin, "Le Violon, Les Femmes et le Conservatoire", in: *Le Ménestrel*, 3 April 1904 and reproduced in *La Fronde*, 1 May 1904.

[42] "We are not excessively feminist; we have no wish to see voters in skirts; but we try hard to be fair, and it appears to us that, should a woman be a talented violin player, it is not equitable to place obstacles in the way of her talent, as unconnected as they are, and under whatever false pretences." (Transl.: A. H.) A. de Sivry, "La Question Féministe au Conservatoire", in: *Le Monde Musicale*, 15 April 1904, pp. 105–106.

[43] Mlle Abbéma "does not have very clear notions of the law, of justice and of the future of the human race. She studies nothing but drawing." (Transl.: A. H.) Eugenie Potonié-Pierre, "Exposition Feminin", in: *Le Droit des Femmes*, 3 May 1891.

paper *La Suffragiste* by those who thought her "problablement [sic] une demi-émancipée".[44] The feminist journalist who wrote this article was incensed that Curie should not acknowledge the battle which underlay her success: « Les membres des groupes féministes ne sont pas toutes docteurs ès-sciences ; mais c'est quand même leur agitation qui a créé l'état d'esprit dont Mme Curie a profité. »[45]

Likewise in Germany, 1907 saw a debate between two feminist newspapers, *Die Frau* and *Die Frauenbewegung*. In a discussion on "Die 'undankbaren' Studentinnen", Helene Lange and Minna Cauer argued about female students' responsibilities to the feminist movement. Cauer wrote that students indulged in high-minded idealism and argued that they possessed no social conscience, in other words they were not engaged in the women's movement. Lange's view was that the actions of women students not actively involved in the movement brought different things to women in general.[46]

> „Es ist ein ganz richtiger Instinkt, der den Studentinnen sagt, daß es nicht ihre Aufgabe sei, an der Agitation für die Frauenbewegung tätigen Anteil zu nehmen. Die Frauenbewegung kann in zwei Stadien zerlegt werden: ein Stadium der Vorbereitung und eines der Erfüllung, eine Epoche der Agitation und eine Epoche der Tat. In der ersten galt es, das Gerüst aufzuschlagen, in der zweiten, den Bau aufzuführen, um dessentwillen das Gerüst da ist."[47]

These two papers, very similar in orientation and general politics, took vehemently different stances on this issue which reflected the concerns of many feminists. An author for the moderate French feminist paper, *La Française* explored some of the grounds for this kind of debate and attempted to explain why women in certain professional positions distanced themselves from femi-

[44] "probably semi-emancipated". Madeleine Pelletier, "A Propos de Mme Curie. Les demi-émancipées", in: *La Suffragiste*, January 1912.
[45] "The members of feminist organisations are not all Doctors of Science, but it is nevertheless their agitation which has created the frame of mind from which Mme Curie has benefited." Madeleine Pelletier, "A Propos de Mme Curie. Les demi-émancipées", in: *La Suffragiste*, January 1912.
[46] Helene Lange, "Die 'undankbaren' Studentinnen", in: *Die Frau*, October 1907, p. 41.
[47] "It is a very correct instinct that tells the [female] students, that it is not their responsibility to take an active part in the agitation of the women's movement. The women's movement can be divided into two stages: a stage of preparation and one of realisation, an era of agitation and an era of action. In the first, the structure must be erected, in the second it must be enacted for the sake of those for whom the structure exists." Lange, "Die 'undankbaren' Studentinnen", p. 41.

nism. In questioning why academic women were not feminists, the anonymous author suggested that because many female academics were still single, they would not empathise with their married sisters who had now lost many of their rights, and would believe that feminists' desire for equality would mean an equality of vices; women living out the faults of men, including taking multiple lovers. She suggested that female academics saw the feminists as ridiculous because they understood them little, seeing only that: "feminists are all viragos with short hair, masculine clothing, running through the streets and organising public meetings."[48]

In summary, not all women who focused their energies on their careers or on furthering the cause of women in their particular field were accorded the status of 'Comrade' which Smyth's direct action earned her. Women's ambivalence towards the mutual relevance of their pursuits indicates an uncertainty about the compatibility of professional women's goals with those of feminist activism. When Vera Brittain looked back on her life of feminist engagement however, commenting that "neither music nor painting seems to be an appropriate medium for conveying the essence of a democratic revolution", Smyth and Marion Scott (of the Society of Women Musicians) were cited as the exceptions which proved the rule.[49] Smyth's direct engagement with feminism spared her the contempt of political activists towards creative practitioners. She was one of the few to bridge the gulf between politics and the arts, and to convince feminists through her actions of the centrality of feminist values to women's pursuits in music. In doing so, she became a willing example of the march of women into new territories of creativity and political agency.

Abstract

„Comrade" Ethel Smyth im „großen Befreiungskampf der Frauen". Zum musikalischen Feminismus in England

Der Beitrag untersucht die feministische Politik, mit der sich Ethel Smyth lebenslang beschäftigte. Ihre Motivation für ihr Engagement in der Suffragettenbewegung wird oft in ihrer Leidenschaft für Emmeline Pankhurst gesehen, die sie 1910 kennen lernte. Ihre Wurzeln sind jedoch in einer früheren Lebensphase zu suchen: in der Zeit, die sie als junge Frau in Deutschland verbrachte.

---

[48] "*les féministes sont toutes des viragos aux cheveux courts, aux vêtements masculins, parcourant les rues, organisant des réunions publiques*" Anon., "L'Université et le Féminisme", in : *La Française*, 18 October 1908.

[49] Vera Brittain, *Lady Into Woman: a History of Women From Victoria to Elizabeth II*, London 1953, p. 212.

Hier stieß sie erstens auf ausgeprägte Vorurteile gegenüber Komponistinnen, zweitens festigte sich in dieser Zeit auch ihre Haltung gegen Heirat und Ehe. Wenn auch für Smyth feministische Politik und Musik zwei gleichermaßen wichtige Teile ihres Lebens und ihrer Persönlichkeit blieben, ist es auffällig, dass die Beziehung zwischen aufstrebenden Musikerinnen und in der feministischen Presse schreibenden Frauen oft ambivalent war. In Frankreich und Deutschland schwankten feministische Journalistinnen zwischen der Befürwortung des Kampfes der Musikerinnen und der Kritik an deren unpolitischer Einstellung. Im Gegensatz dazu war die Beziehung zwischen Feministinnen und Komponistinnen in England symbiotisch, ja sogar intim. Ein Grund dafür dürfte in Smyths Teilnahme an den militanten Aktivitäten der Suffragetten liegen. Obwohl sie sich 1913/14 plötzlich von der Bewegung löste, blieben ihr ihre Mitstreiterinnen ihr ganzes Leben lang treu und unterstützten ihre Versuche, ihre Karriere voranzutreiben und sich für die Sache von Musikerinnen einzusetzen. Die Darstellung Smyths durch die Feministinnen wird mit der Darstellung ihrer Politik durch ihre musikalischen KollegInnen verglichen. Während Ethel Smyth den Übergang von Musikerin zur Feministin und zurück reibungslos bewältigte, sind in Frankreich und Deutschland immer wieder Konflikte zwischen kreativen Frauen und Feministinnen zu beobachten.

Susan Wollenberg
Ethel Smyth as Honorary Doctor of the University of Oxford

On 23 June 1926 a remarkable event took place at the University of Oxford, that ancient monastic establishment.[1] As the local newspaper reported on the following Friday, under the heading of "The Commemoration: University Honours Distinguished Visitors":

> "Some of the glories of an old-time Encaenia were revived on Wednesday, when the Chancellor, Viscount Cave, conferred degrees on some of the country's most distinguished men (sic)."[2]

Tucked away among the long list of men receiving Honorary degrees in Law and other "mainstream" subjects in the Sheldonian Theatre on that occasion, one of the only two exceptions to the norm is noted as follows: "Honorary Degree of D. Mus. – Dame Ethel Mary Smyth, D.B.E."[3] The customary encomium that featured in the Public Orator's presentation of the honorands

---

[1] For the history of the University see Trevor Aston, ed., *The History of the University of Oxford*, 8 vols., Oxford 1984 ff.
[2] *Oxford Times* [*OT*], 25 June 1926, p. 11. However, in the Creweian Oration (given in memory of Nathaniel, Lord Crewe, benefactor to the University, printed in the same issue of *OT*) the Public Orator, Mr A. B. Poynton, referred specifically to the fact that the Lord High Chancellor, Chancellor of the University, had added "great pleasure and distinction" to the occasion "by his presence and by bringing with him so many eminent men *and women* to receive academic honours" [my emphasis]. The Encaenia ceremony, normally held during June in the Sheldonian Theatre, the University's great assembly room (designed by Christopher Wren and opened in 1669), involved the giving of honorary degrees and the recitation of prize literary compositions. The ceremony was presided over by the Chancellor of the University. Honorands are traditionally presented for their degrees by the Public Orator, whose speeches are given in Latin.
[3] *OT*, 25 June 1926, p. 11. Other honorands in the Arts included the playwright Sir J. M. Barrie (Bart.), who received the Hon. D. Litt. See also the leading article in the *Oxford Magazine*, June 1926, where Smyth and the only other female candidate are remarked on (quoted on p. 94 below). Smyth had been made a Dame of the British Empire in 1922. See Sophie Fuller, "Smyth, Dame Ethel", *Grove Music Online* accessed 16 December 2008.

85

was quoted in the newspaper report quite extensively in respect of Ethel Smyth:

> "A leader of the militant suffragettes, who wrote their song, comes to receive our welcome today, draped as a very different 'leader'. We all admire her grand and impressive Mass, the power and variety of her musical works and 'operas' – the 'Wreckers' and the 'Boatswain's Mate'. In her music and librettos there is humour. Her force of character has advanced her to a prominent place among musicians. She has given us a vivid record of her life in 'Impressions that Remain' and 'Streaks of Life'. I leave it to you to honour our Pallas."[4]

Smyth herself wrote in a letter to her great-niece, Elizabeth Mary Williamson: "We had a great reception at the Encoenia (sic) which really was a lovely sight, the sun blazing through the S[outh] windows of the Sheldonian ..."[5] We read later in the *Oxford Times* report that "A large company luncheoned at All Souls College at the conclusion of the ceremony". Ethel Smyth is listed among the lunch guests; besides the honorands these included a large throng of visiting dignitaries, members of the aristocracy, eminent parliamentarians, and leading University figures including the Principals of Lady Margaret Hall and Somerville College.[6]

The celebrations continued through the day:

> "All those who had honorary degrees conferred upon them at the Encaenia were the guests of the President and Fellows of St. John's College at a garden party given in the College groves during the afternoon. The picturesque groves made an admirable setting and, favoured with ideal weather, the party proved a successful function, [with] about 900 attending. The band of the Irish Guards played selections throughout the afternoon."[7]

---

[4] *OT*, 25 June 1926, p. 11.

[5] Letter from Ethel Smyth to Elizabeth Mary Williamson [EMW], 25 June 1926 (private collection); I am grateful for the kind permission to quote from this source, which became known to me only in the final stages of preparing the edited version of this paper.

[6] Both of these were women's colleges, founded in 1878–9. The other women's colleges were St Hugh's (1886), St Hilda's (1893), and St Anne's (originally the "Society of Oxford Home Students", formally thus titled from 1898). See Janet Howarth, "'In Oxford but ... not of Oxford': The Women's Colleges", in: *Nineteenth-Century Oxford, Part 2* [NCO], History of the University of Oxford, vol. 7, ed. Michael Brock and Mark Curthoys, Oxford 2000, pp. 237–307; and J. Howarth, "Women", in: *The Twentieth Century* [TCO], History of the University of Oxford, vol. 8, ed. Brian Harrison, Oxford 1995, pp. 345–375.

[7] *OT*, 25 June 1926, p. 11.

The letter from Smyth to her great-niece documents in some detail and with considerable enthusiasm her continuing presence during the celebrations at Oxford.[8] Besides enjoying the lunch party, she visited two of the women's colleges. At Somerville College (where she was 'very happy') Smyth was a guest of the principal, Miss Penrose ('the last person to be my hostess, you'd think; tho' I believe she is an excellent Principal ... and won my heart in spite of very conventional manners by her adoration of Greece and her lovely paintings ...'). And at Lady Margaret Hall, as she reported:

> "I made greatest pals at the dinner for me and the D[uchess] of Atholl at Lady Marg[are]t Hall with the Greek Tutor, such a goodlooking woman about 30, who went and fetched various translations of Theocritus to compare the passage I love so in the 'Two Fishermen' Idyll ... At that place I felt most deeply that a chief aim of your life should be to master ancient Greek. The forehand drive is important but O, Eliz! With your gift of tongues, gather, gather that rosebud while you are young! Later on languages become much more difficult. Miss Penrose talks it fluently and was urging even me to begin! But Mr Sidgwick who mysteriously turned up for that dinner (not for the Encoenia!) explained that my life was very full ..."[9]

Behind this event lie a number of vital threads connected with it, and belonging to the history of the University. Chiefly these are: first, the role of music in the University; secondly, the development of the system of awarding honorary degrees; and finally, the introduction of women into the University environment at Oxford, which had been for so many centuries an all-male institution. As for the background to the University's award of the honorary degree to Smyth, this is essentially "shrouded in secrecy", since "the proceedings of the University's Hebdomadal council, in accordance with the protocol of the time, maintain[ed] a high level of confidentiality over the decision-mak-

---

[8] Letter from Smyth to EMW, 25 June 1926 (all quotations in the remainder of this paragraph are derived from this source).
[9] The 'forehand drive' refers to the game of golf. The 'Greek tutor' may have been Catherine Mary Chilcott (1898–1983), who was tutor in Classics at LMH between 1922 and 1929. The college's annual record, the 'Brown Book', December 1926, mentions that when the honorary degrees were conferred on the Duchess of Atholl and Ethel Smyth 'our Principal had the honour of giving hospitality [i.e. as her house guest] to the former, and of entertaining both'. (The Principal at the time was the distinguished economist Lynda Grier). I am extremely grateful to the college archivist at LMH, Oliver Mahony, for his help in locating the relevant information.

ing process".[10] What is known is that this particular Encaenia was termed a 'Chancellor's Encaenia', being the first to take place after the installation of a new chancellor of the University, in this case Viscount Cave.[11] On these extra-special occasions the honorands were nominated personally by the newly installed Chancellor. No records of the specific details concerning Viscount Cave's decisions have been found in the University archives, although Smyth herself recorded that "He told me I was his own choice 'tho' of course I consulted musicians."'[12]

There is, however, some other information available to set alongside the Chancellor's choice of Smyth. The year 1926 was a special year for music in the University in a number of respects. That year marked the tercentenary of the Heather Professorship of Music at Oxford (endowed by William Heather in 1626–7), a post which survives to this day. For the Heather Festival of 1926, celebrating the tercentenary, the Music Board was invited to put forward names for honorary degrees, and at a meeting of the Board on 6 February 1926, it was resolved

> "to recommend to Council the names of the following to receive the degree of Doctor of Music <u>honoris causa</u> at the Heather Tercentenary Festival:
>
> Sir Henry Wood
>
> Frederick Delius (even if in absence)
>
> Charles Wood
>
> John Blackwood McEwan
>
> ([with] in reserve, Gustav Holst)".[13]

This list serves to highlight the fact that in 1926 Smyth was distinctly in a minority in this context with regard to gender.[14]

[10] Information kindly supplied by Alice Millea, Assistant Keeper, University Archives (Bodleian Library, Oxford) in an email communication.
[11] Viscount (George) Cave (1856–1928), lawyer and politician (Home Secretary and Lord Chancellor) was a graduate and later Honorary Fellow of St John's College; he was elected Chancellor of the University in 1925, remaining in office until 1928. By this time the Chancellor's role was of a formal and ceremonial nature, involving presiding over such University occasions as the Encaenia.
[12] Letter from Smyth to EMW, 25 June 1926.
[13] Board of Studies for Music, meeting papers 1911–55, University Archives, Bodleian Library, Oxford, FA4/12/1/1 (6 February 1926).
[14] Although the Board put forward all four names (and presumably the fifth as reserve) it seems that only three were promoted by the University's Council to receive the Hon. D. Mus.: Dr J.B. McEwen (Principal of the Royal Academy of Music), Prof. Charles Wood (Professor of Music at Cambridge), and Sir Henry

As it happens, the ratio of 4 to 1, male to female, reflects approximately the ratio of men to women within the University at the time. Numbers of resident female undergraduate students had risen from 400 in 1918 to 751 by 1925, thus "not far short of one woman to four men, a trend that created alarm".[15] The many centuries of the men's colleges at Oxford stood in stark contrast to the not quite half-century of the women's colleges' existence by the mid-1920s.[16] Yet, writing in 1923, Elizabeth Wordsworth (first Principal of LMH), remarked that:

> "Already these women's colleges, though they have not yet existed half a century, have begun to feel that they have traditions to maintain, examples to admire and, if possible imitate, an *esprit de corps* to live up to – a Sparta to adorn."[17]

The period was certainly one of great significance for women's education. By 1918, in her memoir *A Writer's Recollections*, Mrs Humphry Ward (the novelist Mary Ward) referred to the improvement in girls' schooling in England as "worthily representative of that astonishing rise in the intellectual standards of women, which has taken place in the last half century".[18]

The introduction of women students into the collegiate university was a complex process that generated a variety of comment and debate, often reflecting attitudes to women held in wider society.[19] When Emily Davies, the founder of Girton College, Cambridge, visited Oxford in 1867 to test the possibility of situating her college there, she found that "Oxford people brought home to her the difficulty of introducing women students into a University with monas-

---

Wood (conductor and concert innovator, famous for his London Promenade Concerts). Perhaps Delius was excluded since it was feared he would not be able to be present. For a full description of the Heather Tercentenary festival and its central feature, the Heather Commemoration held on 6 May 1926, see Cyril Bailey, *Hugh Percy Allen*, London 1948, pp. 47–9.

[15] Janet Howarth, in: *TCO*, p. 350.
[16] For most of that time, women students at Oxford had been barred from actually taking the degrees they had earned through their studies and by undergoing University examinations: until 1920 they were not able to be awarded degrees from Oxford. In May of that year the University voted to admit its women students to full membership.
[17] Elizabeth Wordsworth, "A Retrospect", in: *Lady Margaret Hall: A Short History*, ed. Gemma Bailey, London 1923, p. 18.
[18] Mrs H. Ward (Mary Ward), *A Writer's Recollections, 1856–1900*, London 1918, p. 97.
[19] This process is documented in detail by Janet Howarth in *NCO* and *TCO*: her important work has formed the main starting-point for the discussion here.

89

tic traditions, rowdy undergraduates, a lively interest in gossip, and a large population of prostitutes".[20] Some forty years later, D.G. Hogarth, writing in the *Anti-Suffrage Review* on the subject of "Oxford Degrees for Women", summarized the objections raised against the proposal to allow these. If women gained the MA, they might enter university politics "and become eligible to University offices" (the author comments that some fear this, and some do not, but "there is no reason to suppose that their vote and interest would be used less intelligently than those of men").

Furthermore, Hogarth reported, "many doubt how far women can stand the pressure of the courses and terms prescribed for men", though in fact women in charge of women students themselves "express no fear on this count". And many feared also that the increased presence of women which would inevitably follow if degrees were granted, might disturb the stability of the student community: "At present the Oxford boys can be boys without coming into much relation with girls".[21] Hogarth concluded that since women had already been admitted to Oxford's class-rooms and examination halls the University could "hardly in reason withhold for ever that which constitutes the chief value of its favours to the poorer student".[22]

Even before women students were admitted to Oxford's "class-rooms and examination halls", women scholars were to be seen in the Bodleian Library. The novelist Mary Ward, herself a scholar, in her pamphlet "A Morning in the Bodleian" referred to the variety of "readers for whose present benefit these priceless stores are opened; readers of both sexes and of every age"; and she characterized the woman reader as convincing the observer by "her liveliness and warmth ... that it is possible for a woman to be a student without being a pedant – without in fact ceasing to be a woman".[23]

The subsequent founding of the women's colleges gave the female scholar a place of her own in Oxford. My own college, Lady Margaret Hall [LMH], was, as indicated above, among the earliest of the women's colleges; it was

[20] Howarth, *NCO*, p. 237. Howarth has documented the beliefs of those who thought that "examinations were bad for women's health and character" (*TCO*, p. 347).

[21] D.G. H[ogarth], "Oxford Degrees for Women", in: *Anti-Suffrage Review*, May 1909, p. 5. David George Hogarth (1862–1927), archaeologist and traveller, was educated at Magdalen College, Oxford where he became a Fellow and Tutor in 1886. For a caricaturist's fantasy of young women students alluringly attired in academic dress (cap and gown) see Howarth, *NCO*, p. 254, Figures 10.4a and 10.4b.

[22] Hogarth, "Oxford Degrees for Women", p. 5.

[23] Mary Ward, "A Morning in the Bodleian", Fox How 1871, p. 2 and p. 6.

launched in 1878 as a Church of England foundation.[24] Ethel Smyth's teenage years coincided with the movement for women's higher education in Oxford; as an early chronicler of LMH phrased it, "The 'sixties and 'seventies were years of stirring life and reform in Oxford".[25] If Ethel Smyth at the age of 19 or 20 had contemplated going to University to study (that is, had she not set her sights on the Leipzig Conservatorium) and had she waited for LMH to open its doors to its first students, she might well have relished the escape from home that Oxford could provide:

> "An Oxford education gave women freedoms that were, for many students, undreamt of in their family homes. The study with a door that could be shut against interruptions was the prerogative of the father, while control of hospitality rested with the mother. Winifred Knox (LMH 1901–5) recalled 'the glorious freedom of one's own kettle' and the novel experience of 'privacy ensured by the simple expedient of putting up the notice "Engaged" on one's door'."[26]

The women's colleges rapidly acquired the plethora of clubs and societies (including sports and music-making) that characterized the male university. Their doings are reported in *The Fritillary*, the magazine of the women's colleges, founded at the same date as the male equivalent, *Isis*. Here we read of the discussion by the Women's Debating Society on the motion: "That Fashions in dress are morally and socially injurious". One woman student claimed that "The large sleeves of the present day [were] a sign of the desire for space in which to develop mentally and physically".[27] It was in that year, 1896, that a proposal to grant degrees to women was brought before Congregation, the University's Parliament, where it was defeated by a large majority. A recent commentator, Kristin Ewins, notes that in the same year *Isis* ran "a futuristic

---

[24] The Revd E. S. Talbot, who with his wife conceived the original plan of starting "a small residentiary enterprise", recalled that their scheme was modified so as to avoid "confining the Hall to members of the Church of England". While "their reception was its main object, we gave the Principal liberty to admit members of other religious bodies". E. S. Talbot, "The Foundation", in: Bailey, *Lady Margaret Hall*, p. 22. See also, on the early history of LMH, Frances Lannon, *Lady Margaret Hall, Oxford: The First 125 Years, 1879–2004*, Oxford 2004. As Dr Lannon puts it in her Introduction (p. 4), "Lady Margaret Hall was founded to change Oxford University forever".

[25] Bailey, *Lady Margaret Hall*, p. [3]. Among the ladies of the 1870s movement were, besides Mrs Talbot, Mrs Max Müller, wife of the Professor of Comparative Philology; Mrs Humphry Ward (Mary Ward), a granddaughter of Dr Arnold; and Clara Pater, sister of the writer Walter Pater (Fellow of Brasenose College).

[26] Howarth, *NCO*, p. 278.

[27] *Fritillary*, 8 (June 1896), p. 152.

satire around the time of the vote [on degrees for women]: the 'Diary of a Lady Undergrad. A.D. 1920'". In this imaginary Oxford of the future, women were elected to the presidency of the Oxford Union Society, and smoked pipes, among other unfeminine activities; at the same time they are mocked for missing chapel because they could not finish styling their hair in time.[28]

But if Smyth had come to Oxford as a student in the late 1870s she would in fact have been unable to study Music in the modern sense at the University. Just as women were on the fringes of the University, not in the mainstream, so Music as an academic subject had a Cinderella-like status in comparison with more "mainstream" academic disciplines such as Philosophy and Theology. The modern Faculty of Music did not exist until 1944, and it was only in 1950 that the Honour School of Music, offering a residential degree course in the subject comparable to other arts subjects, was finally established.

The "Cinderella-like" situation of music at Oxford in the past is exactly the image used by a mid nineteenth-century commentator on the state of Music in the University. As the Reverend Peter Maurice (Chaplain of New and All Souls Colleges) put it in his reflections of 1856: "Of all the progeny of Alma Mater, she [music] alone is allowed to grow up without training and education".[29] As with the sweeping changes made by the introduction of women students (and women tutors) at Oxford, so with the radical changes to the musical degrees in the second half of the nineteenth century (involving the gradual increase in content and extent of the degree examinations), the process of reform was surrounded by debate and controversy.

When, in 1870, an attempt to "compel candidates for musical degrees to reside three years in Oxford and to pass all examinations required for a degree in Arts" was defeated in Congregation, the *Musical Times* commented:

"It is hardly necessary to point out that [this rule] [...] would have virtually closed Oxford degrees against professional musicians, few of whom can spare the time to pass three years in Oxford [...]."[30]

[28] *Isis*, 7 March 1896, pp. 198–9, quoted in Kristin Ewins, "The Women's Degree in Oxford Magazines of the 1890s", in: *Oxford Magazine*, Second Week, Michaelmas Term 2008, p. 8. As Ewins points out, it is curious that the date chosen for this fantasy is the very year in which women were admitted to degrees.

[29] Peter Maurice, *What shall we do with Music? A Letter*, Oxford 1856, p. 5. Essentially the B. Mus. and D. Mus. were external degrees granted, on successful submission of a compositional exercise, to candidates who were not required to be in residence at the University.

[30] Quoted in Percy Scholes, *The Mirror of Music 1844–1944: A Century of Musical Life in Britain as reflected in the pages of the Musical Times*, vol. 2, London 1947, p. 654.

Later in the century the great educator and musical writer William Henry Hadow waxed eloquent on the subject of the music degree's still anomalous status:

> "Under the present system the connexion between musical graduates and the University is restricted to matriculation, the work of the examination-room, and the ceremony of the degree. Successful candidates bear an Oxford distinction without having [...] contributed anything to Oxford life or gained anything from its experience [...] it leaves the successful candidate in a position always anomalous and often misunderstood."[31]

At this point we can bring together women and music in the University: for, following the introduction of the statute in 1885 permitting the "admission of women to the first examination for the degree of Mus. Bac. at Oxford University",[32] in 1892 the "first two ladies" to supplicate for the B. Mus. degree, having passed their final B. Mus. examination, were congratulated on this distinction in a report in the local press.[33] These pioneering candidates were Emilie B. Grant and Adelaide Thomas. They were, however, "not allowed to take the degree".[34] By the 1890s the examinations for the B. Mus. degree had been developed (largely by Frederick Gore Ouseley and John Stainer, successive Heather Professors of Music) to lengths undreamt of by earlier Professors, who simply had to judge candidates' compositions sent in as their degree "exercises". The 1892 examinations required a panel of examiners and encompassed, besides the candidate's submitted composition, a series of papers in harmony and counterpoint, instrumentation, history of music, and set works to be studied in score. Books recommended for study included Berlioz's treatise on instrumentation, Burney's and Hawkins's great histories of music, and Hubert Parry's article on form in *Grove's Dictionary*.[35]

Another new dimension to the musical degrees had developed from the late eighteenth century onwards: this was the University's awarding of the D. Mus. as an honorary degree to distinguished exponents of the art, the first famous example being Joseph Haydn on his visit to England in 1791 (hence his 'Oxford'

---

[31] Minutes of Hebdomadal Council, 3/16 (1898), p. 38 (University Archives, Bodleian Library, Oxford). Further on the development of the musical degrees see Susan Wollenberg, *Music at Oxford in the Eighteenth and Nineteenth Centuries*, Oxford 2001.

[32] The event was of sufficient general interest to be reported in the *Musical Times*, xxvi (1885).

[33] *Jackson's Oxford Journal*, 5 November 1892.

[34] See Scholes, *Mirror of Music*, pp. 681–2.

[35] Summarised in Ibid, pp. 654–6.

symphony). With the stiffening of the academic requirements for the examined degree in the later nineteenth century, there came the establishment of the honorary D. Mus. as a regular and distinctive award. From 1879 a series of composers, including many of acknowledged international standing, received the honorary D. Mus. from Oxford. (Some of these were similarly honoured by Cambridge also.) One of the earliest was Sir Arthur Sullivan (1879). The tradition of awarding the honorary degree primarily to composers continued into the early twentieth century: among the names of honorands besides Smyth were Elgar (1905), Grieg (1906), Glazounov and Saint-Saëns (1907).[36]

From 1920, when women were permitted to take their degrees, "the University was now free to confer special honours on distinguished women".[37] In May 1921 Queen Mary was offered and accepted the degree of Hon. D.C.L. (Doctor of Civil Law). On her visit the Queen met students from the five women's "Societies" and inspected and criticized the domestic arrangements at LMH.[38] In June 1925 "the Hon. D. Sc. was conferred [...] on Miss Annie Cannon, a distinguished American astronomer, on the suggestion of Professor H.H. Turner who had once been so strong an opponent of the admission of women to the University that he at one time refused to admit them to his lectures".[39]

Returning now to the exceptional Chancellor's Encaenia of 23 June 1926 when Smyth received the honorary D. Mus., I conclude with two further extracts from documents pertaining to that event. "H.W." in "The Oxford Point of View", a leading article in the *Oxford Magazine*, Special Commemoration Number (17 June 1926), commenting on the "candidates for the degree of Doctor, *honoris causa*, upon whom [...] he [Lord Chancellor Cave] will confer himself that signal honour at his enthronement at the Encaenia on Wednesday next", observed that Lord Cave's list was "distinctly select", and further that:

> "Viewed more closely, it contains a number of interesting and novel elements. If there is no crowned head or prince of the blood, there is the President of the French Republic, who is to be treated as a reigning sovereign [...]. But the newest and most interesting figures perhaps of all will be those of the two ladies, her Grace the Duchess of Atholl, M.P. [member of parliament], and Dame Ethel Mary Smyth."[40]

---

[36] Others honoured during these years included leading conductors (Richter in 1885, Manns in 1903) and university musicians (Oakeley, Professor at Edinburgh, in 1879) as well as occasionally performers (Joseph Joachim, 1888).
[37] Annie Rogers, *Degrees by Degrees*, London 1938, p. 146.
[38] Ibid, p. 147.
[39] Ibid, p. 148.
[40] *Oxford Magazine*, Special Commemoration Number, 17 June 1926, p. [567].

The pictures in the local press are unhelpful with regard to providing a photographic record of Smyth's participation in the event, although they are worth reproducing if only for their unintentionally amusing caption (see Fig. 1, p. 96). Smyth noted in her letter to her great-niece:

> "The Mus. Docs come last and I was the only one, at the tail of the procession, so doubt if I shall be much to the fore in the photographs. They probably took one for the housekeeper or a female Bedel."

She did, however, mention that she saw herself in the *Times*, "sitting next to Sir A. Chamberlain".[41]

In characteristically wry and eccentric fashion, Smyth later gave her view of the basis on which her award of the Oxford degree, *honoris causa*, had come about:

> "As regards the final honour conferred upon me by the University of Oxford at the Encaenia, 23 June 1926, I believe the present Chancellor is more literary than musical. And since I learned that my inclusion in the list was his own, unprompted idea, I cannot help hoping, just to complete the tale, that if it is now my privilege to wear the handsomest of all the Oxford doctors' gowns, my books may have been a contributory cause."[42]

---

[41] Letter of Smyth to EMW, 25 June 1926. The Bedels were University officials who assisted on ceremonial occasions.
[42] Ethel Smyth, *A Final Burning of Boats*, London 1928, pp. 40–1. (In the same section, Smyth claimed to attribute her DBE to her contribution to women's golfing rights, as asserted by her in a scene at the Woking Golf Club in 1922: Ibid, pp. 39–40).

Figure 1: Famous men receive degrees June 1926 [43]

[43] *Oxford Illustrated Journal*, 30 June 1926, front page. Smyth is not obviously visible in these photographs, although the Duchess of Atholl, Katharine Marjory Stewart, née Ramsay (1874–1960), distinguished public servant and politician and Scotland's first woman Member of Parliament, is included.

Abstract

Ethel Smyth als Ehrendoktor der Universität Oxford

Frauen und Musik wurden in der Geschichte der Universität Oxford vor Beginn des 20. Jahrhunderts ähnlich stiefmütterlich behandelt. Aber sowohl für den Status der Frauen als auch für die Rolle Musik an der Universität bedeutete die Periode vom späten 19. bis zum frühen 20. Jahrhundert einen radikalen Umbruch. So eröffnete die Gründung der *women's colleges* ab 1878 ebenso neue Möglichkeiten wie die Reform der Abschlüsse im Fach Musik ab den späten 1850er Jahren. In dieser Zeit wurde auch der Ehrendoktor in Musik, der „D.Mus", wiederbelebt, der kaum noch vergeben worden war, nachdem ihn Joseph Haydn im Jahre 1791 erhalten hatte.

Ab 1879 wurde der Oxforder Ehrendoktor in Musik an eine Reihe international anerkannter Komponisten verliehen, darunter Edward Elgar (1905), Edvard Grieg (1906), Alexander Glazounov und Camille Saint-Saëns (1907). Die Reihe der Würdenträger bekam eine neue Qualität, als bei der traditionellen Feierlichkeit zur Verleihung der akademischen Grade im Sheldonian Theater (dem Versammlungsraum der Universität) im Jahre 1926 Ethel Smyth den D. Mus. erhielt und der Ehrentitel damit erstmals einer Komponistin verliehen wurde.

Der Aufsatz erläutert die Umstände dieses Ereignisses und bezieht sowohl die musikalische Ausbildung als auch die Ausbildung der Frauen mit ein, um es zu kontextualisieren.

Elizabeth Kertesz
Creating Ethel Smyth: Three Variations on the Theme of Struggle

The notion of struggle lies at the heart of Ethel Smyth's creative endeavour. Her constantly evolving musical style reflects her internal struggle to keep responding to the development of her creative voice, while Smyth's external struggles to hear her music played publicly are crucial to our understanding of her. This paper presents three reflections spanning Smyth's life and career. Three variations, if you like, on the theme of struggle, teasing out how Smyth's creative identity was intertwined with her constant sense of being up against the odds.

Variation 1 takes us to Berlin, to reconsider the troubles that beset *Der Wald*'s first production in 1902. Variation 2 finds Smyth in Egypt, struggling with convention and her musical past as she created a new genre in *The Boatswain's Mate*. In Variation 3 we see Smyth in later life, exploring a new outlet for her creative voice, while contending with the powerful sense that she must continue to fight alone.

Variation 1

Growing up in England's home counties, in an upper middle class home, Smyth's first struggle was to discover her own creative identity and find a way to express it. Once she had recognised her own gifts, she fought to escape from the role that had been allotted her as a gentleman's daughter, expected either to marry or to care for her aging parents.

Smyth focused her desires on the goal of study in Germany, and once she had achieved this and was living in Leipzig, we see her continuing her creative struggle on several fronts: she sought to become part of this new world where her feelings about music were understood and recognised as valid, and which provided a context for developing her passion and talent. In the private / public sphere of Leipzig's elevated domestic musical culture she found a nurturing and listening environment, a milieu which allowed her to start searching for her compositional voice and constructing a creative identity that reached even beyond the academicising confines of her circle.

Smyth's abiding passion was for opera, and her first opera, *Fantasio*, achieved two German productions, in court theatres in Weimar (May 1898) and Karlsruhe (February 1901). Her second opera, *Der Wald*, was accepted for production at Covent Garden, an uncommon feat for an English composer in this period. Smyth never found it easy to secure performances of her music in England, and she learnt early that as a double outsider (a foreign-trained woman) she would often be excluded by what she termed the 'Machine'. This group, she said, was "made up [...] of units from every section of our music life; heads of Musical Colleges, leading publishers, dominant members of music committees throughout the country, the Press, and so on."[1] And so she deployed her own networks of female sociability when faced with difficulties she could not overcome with her own charm and persistence, calling on royal and aristocratic friends or congenial members of the musical elite.

According to Smyth, the Covent Garden Syndicate, in the person of Harry Higgins, expressed interest in staging *Der Wald* in late 1900, but she continued to pursue the dream of German performance. After unsuccessful negotiations with Dresden, Smyth turned her sights on Berlin, having met the Hofoper's conductor Carl Muck in London. She travelled to the German capital to launch her campaign in Autumn 1901, armed with an introduction from her sister Mary to the English ambassador Sir Frank Lascelles and secure in her well-established friendship with Maria von Bülow, whose husband was now *Reichskanzler* [German Chancellor].[2]

Smyth gained a hearing from Henry Pierson,[3] director of the *Intendanz*, who offered to schedule a production of *Der Wald* early in 1902. Pierson reminded Smyth that she might face difficulties both due to the anti-English sentiment aroused by the Boer War and the prejudice of the Berlin press. She was equally aware that neither Pierson nor his *Intendant* Count Bolko von Hochberg were untainted by intrigue and corruption.[4] Undeterred, Smyth called on Muck to discuss the score, and described him overcoming the fanatical hatred of all things English inspired in him by the war – he liked her opera and would conduct it well, for "'Art is Art'".[5] But she failed to obtain an interview with Hochberg,

[1] Ethel Smyth, *As Time Went On ...*, London 1936, pp. 292–293.
[2] Smyth dated her arrival quite precisely as September 22. [Ethel Smyth, *What Happened Next*, London 1940, p. 192] Sir Frank Lascelles (1841–1920) was ambassador in Berlin 1895–1907. Bernhard von Bülow (1849–1929) was German Foreign Secretary from 1897 and Chancellor 1900–09.
[3] Georg Henry Pierson (1852–1902), son of the German-English composer Henry Hugh Pierson, was a Dresden bookseller before moving to work in the Berlin Court Theatre. He was married to the singer Bertha Bréthol.
[4] Smyth, *What Happened Next*, p. 190; Ethel Smyth, "A Winter of Storm", in: *Streaks of Life*, London 1921, pp. 143–144; Graf Bolko von Hochberg (1843–1926) was a Silesian nobleman known as an amateur composer and musician, who was a diplomat before devoting himself to music. He was *Generalintendant* of the *Königliche Schauspiele* [Royal Theatres] in Berlin 1886–1902.
[5] Smyth, *What Happened Next*, p. 191; Smyth, "A Winter of Storm", pp. 144–145.

whose approval was the final requirement. And so Smyth wielded the weapon that had removed such obstacles before and would continue to help her out of impossible situations: patronage and influence. She asked the ladies of the Bülow household to intercede for her, was instantly granted an interview with the *Intendant*, and a contract was signed before the end of October. Smyth had approved a possible cast and been promised that *Der Wald* would receive its premiere early in 1902 when she left Berlin in late October.[6]

But signing a contract is only the first stage, and Smyth's real travails had yet to begin. Poor management was endemic at the Hofoper, and the production was postponed in the new year. The chaotic situation only worsened when Pierson died in mid-February amid scandal and rumour, and general criticism of his choice of new repertoire. Hochberg found it difficult to keep things going, and *Der Wald*'s rehearsals suffered from absenteeism and general lack of discipline, some of which Smyth attributed to the cast's unwillingness to risk damaging their reputations by association with an English work. Smyth seriously considered asking Ambassador Lascelles to give a letter to Kaiser Wilhelm, asking him to intervene, but in the end decided against it. Finally Muck took over the rehearsal process, and having narrowly avoided further postponements, a slightly unpolished premiere took place on 9 April 1902 before a largely attentive audience. Some hissing and booing greeted the end of the work, but after some delays three further performances were presented, to positive audience response. It was too close to the end of the season for *Der Wald* to achieve a run that might have attracted the interest of other theatres, and the contracted fifth night was cancelled.

Smyth declared the press "atrocious",[7] and indeed the opera was criticised in the strongest possible terms. The local critics did not engage with it musically, simply declaring it the worst opera ever staged in that theatre and revelling in the opportunity for snide mockery. Smyth claimed that they treated *Der Wald* as "an excuse for an anti-Boer-War demonstration",[8] but examination of the reviews themselves reveals no comments on her English nationality, whereas many critics reflected on the administration's poor choice of works that season. Their extreme response to *Der Wald* must be seen in the context of the whole season, quite apart from the internal disarray of the company.[9]

---

[6] Smyth, *What Happened Next*, p. 192; Smyth, "A Winter of Storm", p. 157.
[7] Smyth, "A Winter of Storm", p. 203; Smyth, *What Happened Next*, p. 199–200.
[8] Smyth, "A Winter of Storm", p. 193.
[9] For a more detailed discussion of the situation of the Berliner Hofoper in that season, see Elizabeth Kertesz, *Issues in the Critical Reception of Ethel Smyth's Mass and First Four Operas in England and Germany,* PhD, University of Melbourne, 2001 (Chapter 2), http://repository.unimelb.edu.au/10187/621.

Smyth constructed several narratives based on her experiences in Berlin with *Der Wald*, both in her volume *What happened next...* and her essay "A winter of storm". The very title of the latter is indicative of the difficulties she had encountered. Her vivid account makes much of the anti-English sentiment she witnessed in Berlin and the poor treatment meted out to her opera as a result. Despite this frank acknowledgement of *Der Wald*'s troubled career in Berlin, Smyth re-framed her tale into one of success, and deployed this narrative both in subsequent campaigns for performance in England, and in the volumes of memoir and commentary she published in later life.

It must be admitted that *Der Wald* achieved remarkable success after its shaky start in Berlin. Not only was it mounted at Covent Garden on 18 July 1902, shortly after its Hofoper premiere, in what Smyth described as "one of [her] few almost wholly delightful operatic experiences,"[10] but it was taken to New York's Met by Maurice Grau in March 1903 and revived at Covent Garden that summer, a truly extraordinary achievement for an English opera at this time. None of these productions took place without some drama, and Smyth had to call in the aid of her Society friends and royal connections several times to avert postponements.

But it was Smyth's *German* experience which she exploited when trying to build her career. When Covent Garden staunchly refused to show interest in her next opera, *The Wreckers*, she declared in a letter to Percy Pitt "I think that I who have fought the good fight for English art abroad, as no one else has [...] should have first chance here".[11] Smyth's personal battle for performance and recognition was thus transformed into a battle for English music, which should be rewarded at home. And recalling her English career in the 1928 essay "A Final Burning of Boats", Smyth wrote of her "successes [in Germany] on the strength of which it was difficult to refuse to perform [her] second opera, *Der Wald*, at Covent Garden, conductor and performers being of course Germans".[12]

Even during Smyth's most musically productive decades, between 1890 and 1920, her incessant struggle to obtain a hearing for her music occupied a significant amount of time and energy, at times more than she could devote to composing. Although she faced considerable obstacles achieving performance in both Germany and England, she felt keenly the contrast between musical life in the two countries, always extolling the German tradition that honoured

---

[10] Smyth, *What Happened Next*, p. 204.
[11] Ethel Smyth, Letter to Percy Pitt, 19 March 1908, Letters to Percy Pitt 1908–29. Eg. 3306, British Library, fo.75.
[12] Ethel Smyth, "A Final Burning of Boats", *A Final Burning of Boats Etc.*, London 1928, pp. 18–19. This essay was first published in a shorter version in 1924 as "A Burning of Boats", in: *London Mercury* (February 1924), pp. 381–393.

her beloved art, an attitude she found so lacking at home.

As Smyth began to identify herself as a fighter in the battle for the recognition of English music abroad, she also engaged in debates about the state of English opera and later took up the cause of women musicians. Her growing public profile led the suffrage movement to seek her involvement, and her eventual decision to join them for two years from 1910 provided her with fresh creative stimulus at a time when she was grieving the loss of her long-time creative partner Henry Brewster, who died in 1908.

Variation 2

This brings us to the 2nd variation, in which a reflection on Smyth's fourth opera, *The Boatswain's Mate* reveals her struggle to achieve a working synthesis between her own creative voice and the evolving musical structures that defined the genres she was working in.

Smyth's musical style developed steadily after her student days, and with each new work she tried something new in the way of form, genre or structure, as she moved away from the academic Germanic style of her teachers and began to find and explore her strikingly original compositional voice. Her music bore traces of her international interests: *Der Wald* was indebted to the recent German popularity of *verismo* as well as to the Romantic and fairy-tale traditions, and *The Wreckers* adds a strong French element to this mix. But Smyth also began to draw increasingly on features which can only be described as English, such as folk materials and uniquely English subject matter and humour.

One could argue that Smyth's struggle to find and express her creative identity is embodied in the structures and style of her fourth opera *The Boatswain's Mate*. Composed just after she ended her two-year involvement in the battle for women's suffrage, it was premiered in wartime London on 28 January 1916. It can be seen as a pivotal work in her oeuvre, signalling the gradual realignment towards the English market that occurred in Smyth's life and career from the First World War on. The opera itself is stylistically fractured, and her struggle with the genre can be seen as representing Smyth's own divided allegiances to musical and theatrical traditions in Germany and England.

The Boatswain's Mate was the first large-scale musico-dramatic work Smyth embarked on after *The Wreckers* (composed 1903–4), and the first since Brewster's death. In the intervening years Smyth's involvement with the movement for women's suffrage had helped her find a new audience and new public identity. This built upon but also transcended her existing public persona. Smyth was known as an outspoken woman composer whose music appealed to traditional opera and high-art music audiences, which were based on aristocracy and high society. Through her interaction with women from different classes and educational backgrounds in the suffrage movement, Smyth discovered that her music could appeal to a broader audience, and these years of activism (1910–12) enabled her to move forward musically after Brewster's death.

The Boatswain's Mate shows Smyth looking both ahead and behind, struggling with convention on both the large and the small scale. Structured in one act, and two parts, Smyth called her new work a comic opera. Liz Wood delights in the parody and pastiche of the work, reading the score as "punctuated with operatic puns and parodic allusions that mock the musical rhetoric of High Art and masculine Genius".[13] Perhaps Smyth's involvement with the feminists of the suffrage movement liberated her to express a sense of play with the operatic tradition, while continuing her serious engagement with it.

Part 1 featured spoken dialogue and sung numbers, snappy comic material combined with moments of sentiment (whether this blend was considered seamless or arbitrary depended on the critic's point of view). Its style can be related to burlesque and ballad opera, as well as post-Romantic experiments with popular forms and contemporary settings. In terms of Smyth's own stylistic trajectory it points firmly forwards: toward her increasing focus on England, and the closer relationship she hoped to establish with the broader audience she had recently encountered.

Part 2, on the other hand, was through-composed, continuous, fully sung. Although aspects of its style, like the occasionally angular vocal writing and the big orchestral textures, connected it with contemporary operatic composers like Richard Strauss, it could be argued that this represented a backward glance to Smyth's Germanic training and the circles that had provided her first opportunities in opera.

Smyth composed the bulk of *The Boatswain's Mate* while on a working holiday in Egypt, where she wrestled first with being her own librettist, and then with composing music that was just right for her text. In letters to Mrs Emmeline Pankhurst, she spoke of the challenges of setting "contemporary life to music" for the first time,[14] but declared that "[p]ulling this opera together is huge fun".[15]

Smyth sometimes groaned at the difficulty of the compositional task,[16] but

[13] Elizabeth Wood, "Performing Rights: A Sonography of Women's Suffrage", in: *Musical Quarterly* 79 (Winter 1995), p. 629.
[14] Smyth, "A Final Burning of Boats", p. 201.
[15] Ethel Smyth, *Beecham and Pharaoh*, London 1935, p. 173.
[16] "This morning absolutely stuck in chorus. Felt whole opera ruined." Ethel Smyth, Letter to Emmeline Pankhurst, [March 1914?], quoted in: Louise Collis, *Impetu-*

also noted the way her perception of the work changed as she progressed through the scenes. She reflected that composing the second part would "be far harder and go more slowly, for everything is predestined by then – shape, colour, length, everything. But it will be awfully interesting, for as you travel through a first Act the perspective of Act II slightly changes."[17]

She consciously struggled with convention in composing the opera's closing scenes, telling Pankhurst that the "last scene before the final one" would be "the most difficult as she [Mrs Waters] does it all alone; quite a new idea for a finale".[18] Edward Dent may have dubbed *The Boatswain's Mate* Mozartian and a true ensemble opera,[19] but Smyth eschewed the ensemble finale, even deliberately avoiding the romantic cliché of closing with a love duet. She agonised over this scene in letters to Mrs Pankhurst, aware that she risked alienating audiences who looked for "a *great final duet* 'Love the Conqueror'; but that doesn't happen to be what I want."[20] Instead, she defied convention and left things up in the air between the potential couple, allowing Mrs Waters to reflect lyrically (but alone) on summer being the time for love, then dissipating any lingering sentimentality by closing the opera with the heroine scolding her gaping maidservant.

Smyth's struggle with her own past and future, represented by her competing allegiances to Germany and England respectively, can be read in the fractured body of *The Boatswain's Mate*, which was to become her most popular work. After the war she recognised that the world had changed, and that she could no longer rely on the high-status cosmopolitan audiences for whom her earlier operas had been composed and performed. So she re-arranged *The Boatswain's Mate* with flexible orchestration to make it more suitable for smaller touring companies, and it was performed in London and the provinces throughout the 1920s. Smyth's involvement with the women's movement and her constant drive for creative renewal helped her move beyond the elitism of her earlier career, and in her later life as a composer and a writer, she set her face squarely towards a broader audience.

---

ous Heart: the Story of Ethel Smyth, London 1984. p. 140. Collis gives no indication of date for many of the letters quoted in this chapter.

[17] Smyth, *Beecham and Pharaoh*, p. 118.
[18] Smyth, *Beecham and Pharaoh*, p. 153.
[19] Edward J. Dent, "A Commonsense Opera", in: *Nation and Athenaeum* 14 October 1922, p. 68.
[20] Smyth, *Beecham and Pharaoh*, p. 171.

Variation 3

And so we arrive at Variation 3 – the literary variation. Smyth had found her voice, but personal expression was not enough: she never relinquished her lifelong struggle to reach her audience. Despite setbacks and discouragement, she was always planning new ways to get her music played, heard, revived and broadcast.

The 1910s saw Smyth facing two new challenges that helped her forge a new direction. Just before the war, Smyth began to suffer from tinittus and distorted hearing, a condition that worsened into chronic deafness as her old age advanced. She grieved the loss of pleasure in listening to music, and it impaired her ability to take part in normal social intercourse. Settled in the countryside, outside the cultural hub that was London, Smyth encountered health problems in her last decades that further exacerbated what she perceived as her isolation from the musical world.

Smyth's published writings and her diaries betray that her battle for her music was a lonely one. In reference to the "jubilee" of performances held to honour her 70th birthday in 1928, she wrote:

> "The world thinks I have 'come into my own' but every detail was really inspired by me & but for my initiative not one of the events w[ould] have taken place! Now, when I am not trying for anything nothing will happen."[21]

But she did not give up.

When emerging financial problems forced her to find a new source of income, she discovered her "second string". Always a fluent correspondent, and having begun to write her memoirs while undertaking war-work as a radiographer in France, Smyth found that she could write professionally. This released a new aspect of her creative voice, and gave rise to a diverse range of writing from journalism to memoirs, musical anecdotes, cultural commentary, feminist polemic and travel writing.[22] Just as she had tackled the big forms in her music (Mass, operas, cantata etc), so too her writing ranged from letters and essays to full-length books and she is surely one of the most prolific and successful writers among composers. Writing for publication gave her a platform for independent expression – at last she was free of the systems of patronage which had dictated whether her music could gain a public hearing. Indeed journal editors sought her out and commissioned her to write for them.

---

[21] Ethel Smyth, Diary 3, 27 April 1928, p. 32 [ms., Special Collections, Harlan Hatcher Graduate Library, University of Michigan, Ann Arbor]
[22] See the contribution of Melanie Unseld in this volume.

In her volumes of autobiography, Smyth's stories of chasing performances trace her struggles with members of the musical establishment she described as the 'Machine', last-minute intervention by members of the social elite to rescue works from postponement to oblivion, and her constant frustration by theatre schedules that prevented her from getting a 'run', which would expose her work to audiences for long enough to find a permanent place in their affections.

Smyth created a narrative of struggle in her writings, performing her life through her memoirs. Like other famous performer / composers, such as Percy Grainger or Sergei Rachmaninov, she complained that the success of this performance (i.e. her writings) outshone the success of her music. Indeed, her books sold well, and brought her not only an attentive and supportive readership, but the broadest listening audience she ever reached. Reading Smyth's books drew people to her music, and her writing thus became an effective cross-promotional tool, enabling her to reclaim a space for her music in concert halls, theatres, and on the radio.

Smyth's main wish was that her music should reach an audience, and her conception of it changed as the English opera public became less socially homogeneous and she herself encountered a new public. Her books and articles provided her with direct access to her ideal audience, and Smyth became a modern composer, inasmuch as she used the modern media of mass dissemination – the radio and the press – to reach them. In her autobiographical writings and correspondence Smyth developed the idea that her music spoke to the 'common man', indicating her readiness to embrace the new post-war realities. She increasingly valued the idea that she could communicate directly and meaningfully with the people who wrote to her. In 1925, she expressed this in a letter to Edward Dent:

> "I remember a wise old man who used to be at Schotts saying to me 'You know how to talk to the *people* in music' (which is what Walter is forever saying – asking me if I realise how close to 'das Volk' I am in my grain – musically & otherwise) 'Stick to that! *You won't please the reviewers ... but that is where your strength lies.*'"[23]

Smyth had struggled to gain performance in theatres like Berlin's Hofoper and London's Covent Garden, battling prejudice against her sex and her nationality. She fought convention both in society and within her own creative process, never standing still in her own musical development. But she never lost faith

[23] Ethel Smyth, Letter to Edward Dent, 17 October 1925 [Edward Dent Collection, Rowe Music Library, Kings College, Cambridge, EJD/4/385], emphases in the original.

in her ability to engage with changing audiences, even in an age of such rapid transformation, and her gift to us – her contemporary audience – is her performance of struggle not just in her writing, but also in her music. In the words of her Hungarian doctor John Plesch, "Something of her great fighting spirit is in her music."[24] And Smyth herself knew that the integrity of her struggle, the creative possibilities it unleashed, was something she could communicate:

> "Well – I know now that this is true – that the *audiences* when I am allowed to get at them, understand what I am talking about. Catch the tone of my voice & feel 'that's true talk'[...]!"[25]

Abstract

Ethel Smyth kreieren. Variationen über das Thema des Kampfes
In ihren autobiographischen Schriften entwarf Ethel Smyth ihre Karriere als Komponistin rückblickend als eine Serie von Kämpfen. Der Feldzug, mit dem sie die Erlaubnis ihres Vaters für ihren Traum vom Studium in Leipzig erstritt, erwies sich dabei als Geplänkel im Vergleich zu den Schlachten, die noch folgen sollten. Obwohl es ihr gelang, all ihre Hauptwerke zu Gehör zu bringen, frustrierten sie die Bemühungen um weitere Aufführungen im Verlauf ihrer weiteren Karriere maßlos. Smyth kam zu dem Schluss, dass ihr schlimmster Feind die Presse sei, und zwar vor allem wegen der Vorurteile gegen komponierende Frauen. Die in den Memoiren anklingenden Kämpfe spielen sich vor dem Hintergrund dieser permanenten Kulisse der Geschlechterdiskriminierung ab, Szenerie und Details ändern sich jedoch: Vom Schauplatz der Familie wechselte Smyth auf die politisierten Bühnen der Theater und der Gesellschaft. Auch als sie ihre letzten Schlachten mit ihrer eigenen angeschlagenen Gesundheit und ihren Gehörproblemen ausfocht, hörte sie nie auf, die Anerkennung des Publikums zu suchen, und blieb zugleich standhaft gegenüber den Forderungen der Konvention. Dieser Aufsatz präsentiert drei Reflexionen über Smyths lebenslange Fortentwicklung ihrer kreativen Stimme sowie über das Nachleben ihres unbezähmbaren schöpferischen Geistes.

[24] John Plesch, *János, the story of a doctor*, transl. Edward Fitzgerald, London 1947, p. 443.
[25] The sentence ends: "as a quite simple man said to me the other day being the unmusical Dean of Worcester". Smyth, Letter to Edward Dent, 17 October 1925, emphasis in the original.

Melanie Unseld
Identität durch Schreiben. Ethel Smyth und ihre autobiographischen Texte

Als Komponist oder als Komponistin autobiographisch zu schreiben und zu publizieren, heißt, das eigene Metier, die Musik, zu verlassen und sich auf fremdes Terrain zu begeben, das der Schrift. Es heißt auch, sich selbst – primär die eigene Person, nicht das künstlerische Werk – ins öffentliche Licht zu rücken, mit der Darstellung des eigenen Lebens Aufmerksamkeit zu wecken, und zugleich ein Interpretationsfundament zu bieten, auf dem nicht zuletzt auch die Kompositionen betrachtet und gedeutet werden können. Und es heißt schließlich auch, ein Bild von sich selbst, der eigenen Künstleridentität zu inszenieren und der Öffentlichkeit zu präsentieren.[1]

Von diesen – zunächst recht allgemein formulierten – möglichen Funktionen einer Autobiographie haben zahlreiche Komponisten und einige wenige Komponistinnen Gebrauch gemacht:[2] von knappen Berufs- oder Gebrauchsauto-

[1] Zu Fragen von selbst- und/oder fremdinszenierten Musiker(innen)bildern vgl. u. a. Michael Heinemann, „Liszts Maskeraden", in: *Biographische Konstellation und künstlerisches Handeln*, hrsg. von Giselher Schubert (= Frankfurter Studien VI), Mainz 1997, S. 81–93; Marie-Agnes Dittrich, „Kein grollender Titan – Franz Schubert, der Österreicher", in: *Das Andere. Eine Spurensuche in der Musikgeschichte des 19. und 20. Jahrhunderts*, hrsg. von Annette Kreutziger-Herr (= Hamburger Jahrbuch für Musikwissenschaft 15), Frankfurt/M. 1998, S. 191–201; Beatrix Borchard, „Frau/Mutter/Künstlerin – Gedanken zum Thema Künstlerinnenbilder", in: *Bericht des Bruckner-Symposions Künstler-Bilder im Rahmen des Internationalen Brucknerfestes Linz 1998*, hrsg. von Uwe Harten u. a., Wien 2000, S. 103–116; Anselm Gerhard: „Verdi-Bilder", in: *Verdi-Handbuch*, hrsg. von dems. und Uwe Schweikert, Kassel/Stuttgart/Weimar 2001, S. 1–23; Melanie Unseld, „Lesarten einer Widmung. Gedanken zur autographischen Standortbestimmung der Komponistin Antonia Bembo", in: *Orte der Musik. Kulturelles Handeln von Frauen in der Stadt*, hrsg. von Susanne Rode-Breymann, Köln/Weimar/Wien 2007, S. 127–139; Janina Klassen: *Clara Wieck Schumann. Musik und Öffentlichkeit* (= Europäische Komponistinnen 3), Köln 2009.
[2] Vgl. dazu u. a. die Sammlung *Von Schütz bis Schönberg. Autobiographische Skizzen europäischer Musiker*, hrsg. von Reinhard Ermen, Kassel/Basel 1988 sowie Gabriele Busch-Salmen, „‚Dies ist mein Lebenslauf …' Musikerautobiographien: eine vernachlässigte literarische Gattung", in: *Österreichische Musikzeitschrift* 7 (2001), S. 8–22.

biographien³ bis hin zu dickleibigen Memoiren.⁴ Und gleich welchen Umfangs die Beschreibung des eigenen Künstlerlebens ist: Von Beginn an ist die Schaffung einer Künstleridentität und ihre Spiegelung in die Öffentlichkeit zentrales Anliegen. Hiervon legt Georg Philipp Telemann, der gleich mehrfach seine Autobiographie niederschrieb, ebenso beredtes Zeugnis ab⁵ wie die Memoiren von Hector Berlioz, Richard Wagner, Louis Spohr, Luise Adolpha Le Beau, Ernst Krenek u. v. a. Autobiographisches Schreiben dient – im Zusammenklang mit anderen Schriften und bildnerischen (Selbst)Inszenierungen – der öffentlichen Präsentation des Künstlers, die vor allem im Verlauf des 19. Jahrhunderts mit seiner Heroenhistoriographik, seinem bürgerlichen Öffentlichkeitsverständnis und seiner sich verändernden, ebenso kanonisierenden wie den Starkult pflegenden Musikkultur grundlegend an Bedeutung gewinnt.

Beginnt man die Lektüre von KomponistInnen-Autobiographien vor diesem Hintergrund, wird schnell deutlich, dass die Frage des Geschlechts eng mit jenen Faktoren zusammenhängt, die für das Künstlerselbstbild einerseits und seine Verortung innerhalb der bürgerlichen Musikkultur andererseits konstitutiv sind. Denn von der Geschlechterdichotomie, die das Bürgertum als gesellschaftsstabilisierende Kraft annahm und entsprechend zu fixieren trachtete,⁶ sind alle genannten Faktoren maßgeblich beeinflusst: die Heroengeschichtsschreibung im Sinne Heinrich von Treitschkes ebenso wie die Frage von Öffentlichkeit und Privatheit, Kanonisierungsprozesse, die Images der Virtuosinnen und Virtuosen und die Frage der unterschiedlichen Handlungsbereiche von Frauen und Männern in der Musikkultur. Nicht nur, da Autobiographien von Komponisten und Komponistinnen auf diese Bereiche *inhaltlich* zu sprechen kommen – von diesen Themen handelt ihr professionelles Leben –, sondern vor allem, da sie als Publikationen aktiv in diesen Dialog zwischen Künstler

---

3   Sammlungen von biographischen Artikeln, die weniger historisch intendiert waren, sondern vor allem dazu dienten, die (gegenwärtigen) Vertreter eines bestimmten Berufsstandes zu präsentieren.

4   Zur Unterscheidung von Autobiographie und Memoiren vgl. Michaela Holdenried, *Autobiographie*, Stuttgart 2000, S. 28–33. In diesem Sinne wäre im Fall der autobiographischen Schriften von Ethel Smyth treffenderweise von Memoiren zu sprechen, ein Begriff, den Smyth selbst häufig verwendet.

5   Vgl. dazu *Biographie und Kunst als historiographisches Problem. Bericht über die internationale Wissenschaftliche Konferenz anläßlich der 16. Magdeburger Telemann-Festtage Magdeburg, 13. bis 15. März 2002*, hrsg. von Joachim Kremer, Wolf Hobohm und Wolfgang Ruf, Hildesheim/Zürich/New York 2004.

6   Dazu noch immer grundlegend: Karin Hausen: „Die Polarisierung der ‚Geschlechtscharaktere'. Eine Spiegelung der Dissoziation von Erwerbs- und Familienleben", in: *Sozialgeschichte der Familie in der Neuzeit Europas*, hrsg. von Werner Conze, Stuttgart 1976, S. 363–393.

und Publikum, zwischen Selbst- und Fremdbild, zwischen Identität und Imagination eingreifen, ist eine gendersensible Lektüre dringend geboten.[7]

Gilt das bisher Gesagte für Autobiographien von Komponisten und Komponistinnen gleichermaßen, drängen sich in letzterem Fall manche dieser Fragestellungen in den Vordergrund, da hier mit erhöhter Brisanz (explizit oder implizit) über Fragen von Öffentlichkeit und Selbstdefinition als Komponistin verhandelt wird. Ein Beispiel: Hatten Komponisten im Vergleich zu anderen Kunstsparten zwar spät, aber immerhin im Verlauf des 18. Jahrhunderts den Status einer historiographiewürdigen Person erreicht, galt dies keinesfalls in gleichem Maße auch für Komponistinnen. Wenn Frauen überhaupt als öffentliche Personen der Musikkultur wahr- und in die Musikgeschichtsschreibung aufgenommen wurden, waren dies vor allem Interpretinnen.[8] Dezidiert als Komponistin autobiographisch in Erscheinung zu treten, wie dies Ethel Smyth ab 1919 mit einem umfangreichen Werk von 10 publizierten Bänden tat, verdeutlicht damit auch den Anspruch, Teil der Musikgeschichte zu sein und in den musikalischen Kanon aufgenommen zu werden. So selbstverständlich Komponisten diesen Anspruch mit der Publikation einer Autobiographie verbanden, für eine Komponistin war er Anlass für Rechtfertigungen. Und obwohl diese unterschiedlich ausfielen, lassen sich doch drei Rechtfertigungsstrategien in den Autobiographien von Komponistinnen des ausgehenden 19. und beginnenden 20. Jahrhunderts ausmachen: erstens

---

[7] Dies ist inzwischen zentraler Bestandteil der Autobiographie-Forschung. Einige der im Hinblick auf MusikerInnen-Autobiographien wichtigsten Titel seien an dieser Stelle genannt: Christa Bürger, *Leben Schreiben. Die Klassik, die Romantik und der Ort der Frauen*, Stuttgart 1990; *Geschriebenes Leben. Autobiographik von Frauen*, hrsg. von Michaela Holdenried, Berlin 1995; *Women, Autobiography, Theory. A Reader*, hrsg. von Sidonie Smith und Julia Watson, Madison/Wisconsin 1998; Michaela Holdenried, *Autobiographie,* Stuttgart 2000, S. 62–84; *LebensBilder. Leben und Subjektivität in neueren Ansätzen der Gender Studies*, hrsg. von Sabine Brombach und Bettina Wahrig, Bielefeld 2006; Martina Wagner-Egelhaaf, „Autobiografie und Geschlecht", in: *Erinnern und Geschlecht*, Bd. 1 (= Freiburger FrauenStudien. Zeitschrift für Interdisziplinäre Frauenforschung 19), Freiburg 2006, S. 49–64.

[8] Da die Bereiche musikkulturellen Handelns von Frauen sich oftmals nicht ausschließlich auf eine Tätigkeit fokussierten, bestand vor allem auch die Möglichkeit, komponierende Frauen primär als Interpretin darzustellen. Vgl. etwa La Mara [d. i. Marie Lipsius]: *Musikalische Studienköpfe*, 5. Bd.: *Die Frauen im Tonleben der Gegenwart*, Leipzig 1882. Vgl. dazu u. a. Melanie Unseld, „(Auto-)Biographie und musikwissenschaftliche Genderforschung", in: *Kompendium Musik und Gender*, hrsg. von Rebecca Grotjahn und Sabine Vogt (*Kompendien Musik*, Bd. 5), Laaber (Druck in Vorbereitung).

die offensive Thematisierung des Problems, als in die Öffentlichkeit tretende Komponistin Diskriminierungen ausgesetzt zu sein, zweitens die Strategie, den eigenen Lebenslauf nach dem (männlichen) Karriere-Modell auszurichten, um auf diese Weise die Frage des Geschlechts in den Hintergrund zu drängen,[9] und drittens – gewissermaßen als eine Strategie der Verweigerung – die explizite Ablehnung (auto)biographischer Darstellungen überhaupt.[10] Ethel Smyth verfolgte erstere Strategie, was ihre autobiographischen Schriften nicht nur zu wichtigen musikhistorischen, sondern auch zu überaus interessanten kultur- und geschlechtergeschichtlichen Quellen werden lässt.

Unter Fragestellungen einer gendersensiblen Autobiographik sollen im Folgenden einige Anknüpfungspunkte aus den autobiographischen Texten von Ethel Smyth herausdestilliert werden. Die Ausführungen verstehen sich als Ausgangspunkte, im Bewusstsein, dass die wissenschaftliche Aufarbeitung der Schriften Ethel Smyths – sowohl der autobiographischen als auch der musikkritischen und -historischen sowie der Briefe – weiterhin Forschungsdesiderat bleibt.

Übersicht: Publizierte autobiographische Schriften von Ethel Smyth
- *Impressions That Remained. Memoirs*, 2 Bde., London 1919
- *Streaks of Life*, New York 1922
- *A Three-Legged Tour in Greece [March 24– May 4, 1925]*, London 1927
- *A Final Burning of Boats etc.*, London 1928
- *Female Pipings in Eden*, Edinburgh 1933
- *Beecham and Pharaoh. Thomas Beecham (Fantasia in B# Major) Egypt Before England's Exodus (A Fragment of Autobiography)*, London 1935
- *Inordinate (?) Affection. A Story for Dog Lovers*, London [1936]
- *As Time Went On ...*, London/New York/Toronto 1936
- *What Happened Next*, London/New York/Toronto 1940

Überblickt man das autobiographische Werk von Ethel Smyth (vgl. Übersicht), fällt auf, dass sich die beiden ersten Bände (*Impressions That Remained*, 1919) deutlich von allen nachfolgenden unterscheiden: Nur in ihnen greift Smyth auf

---

[9] Diese Strategie ist bei Luise Adolpha Le Beau mit ihren *Lebenserinnerungen* zu bemerken, vgl. Luise Adolpha Le Beau, *Lebenserinnerungen einer Komponistin*, Reprint der 1. Aufl. von 1910, hrsg. von Ulrike B. Keil und Willi H. Bauer, Gaggenau 1999.

[10] Als Beispiele seien hier Lili Boulanger und ihre Schwester Nadia Boulanger genannt. Dazu: Melanie Unseld: „Biographical Research Versus Mystification: Interdependencies between Lili Boulanger's Life and Works", *Memorial-Day Lili and Nadia Boulanger 2003*, Royal Academy of Music London (unpublizierter Vortrag).

das charakteristisches Modell der Autobiographie im 19. Jahrhundert zurück: (weitgehend) chronologisch in der Darstellung – damit der Idee des Lebenslaufes folgend – und in enger Verwobenheit des schreibenden Ichs zu seiner Umwelt, oder, wie Wilhelm Dilthey formulierte, „ein Mensch [verhält sich] universalhistorisch zu seiner eigenen Existenz. [...] Er fühlt jede Gegenwart [...] als erfüllt und bestimmt von Vergangenem, als sich ausstreckend zur Gestaltung der Zukunft – das heißt aber als Entwicklung."[11]

Nach den beiden *Impressions*-Bänden wird keiner von Smyths autobiographischen Texten mehr diesem Modell folgen. Vielmehr greift Smyth schon in *Streaks of Life* auf, was sich in der autobiographischen Literatur der Jahrhundertwende immer deutlicher herausgebildet hatte: Sich der Vergeblichkeit von kohärenter Narration bewusst, greifen Autobiographinnen und Autobiographen immer häufiger zu darstellerischen Mitteln, die nicht auf die Vorstellung des eigenen Lebens als fortlaufendem Entwicklungsroman rekurrieren. Michaela Holdenried bemerkt – ihr Blick richtet sich dabei vorwiegend auf die deutsche Autobiographie, für England wäre gleichwohl Ähnliches zu konstatieren, etwa im Zusammenhang mit dem Bloomsbury Kreis – für das ausgehende 19. Jahrhundert Ansätze der Gattungserneuerung, die sich von kohärenten Erzählmodellen löst und, motiviert vor allem durch Irritationen in der Wahrnehmung von Individualität, nach neuen, adäquaten Ausdrucksformen sucht: Der Einbezug anderer literarischer Formen (Biographie, Essay) sowie eine kritische Auseinandersetzung mit autobiographischem Schreiben an sich führen, so Holdenried, zu einer „Öffnung der Form zu größerer Heterogenität. Die Literarisierung der Form umfasst nun auch Formen wie die Skizze, das Pasticcio, der Arabeske, die Humoreske, das Capriccio – Kleinformen, welche ebenso wie die Beschränkung auf bestimmte Lebensphasen [...] das Prinzip der Repräsentation in paradoxer Einschränkung retten"[12] und dabei nicht mehr das Lebensganze in den Blick nehmen, sondern gleichsam ‚Bausteine des Selbst' präsentieren. Dieses autobiographische Spiel mit neuen Formen wird durch die literarische Erfahrung, die sich unter dem Schlagwort ‚Krise des Romans' um 1900 fassen lässt, begünstigt, die wiederum als Widerspiegelung jener Tendenzen zu lesen ist, die sich um die Jahrhundertwende manifestieren, und denen ein grundlegender Zweifel an jeglichen rational begründeten Subjektivitätskonzepten eigen ist. Diese Grundirritation, der Verlust einer homogenen Identität und ihrer ebenso homogenen Darstellbarkeit, führte zu einer

---

[11] Wilhelm Dilthey: „Das Erleben und die Selbstbiographie", in: ders., *Der Aufbau der geschichtlichen Welt in den Geisteswissenschaften*, Frankfurt a. M. 1981, S. 235–251, hier S. 245.
[12] Holdenried, *Autobiographie*, S. 185f.

Vielfalt an unterschiedlichen, zum Teil erheblich dissoziierenden Erzählweisen: Zu dieser zählen u. a. polyphone oder polyperspektivische Darstellungstechniken und Techniken der Collage und/oder Montage sowie die Erzähltechnik des „stream of consciousness", die besonders die englischsprachige Romanliteratur der ersten Hälfte des 20. Jahrhunderts prägte und in loser, ungeordneter Folge Bewusstseinsinhalte einzelner oder mehrerer (Roman)figuren wiedergibt (James Joyce, *Ulysses*, 1922; *Finnegans Wake*, 1939; Virginia Woolf, *Mrs. Dalloway*, 1925; William Faulkner, *The Sound and the Fury*, 1929). Auch die Überschreitung von Gattungsgrenzen ist in diesem Zusammenhang zu nennen, etwa mit dem neuerlichen Hinweis auf Virginia Woolf und *Orlando* (1928), eine – wie es im Untertitel heißt – Biographie, die gleichwohl über alle Gattungsgrenzen hinweg vagabundiert, an Autobiographischem ebenso teilhat wie an Biographischem, an Historischem wie an Fiktionalem, und dabei auch über die Geschlechtergrenzen hinweggeht.

Der Hinweis auf Woolfs Identitäts-Camouflage im *Orlando* rückt einen wesentlichen Aspekt ins Zentrum, der vielfach als „eigene Geschichte"[13] der Autobiographik wahrgenommen wurde: die Autobiographik von Frauen. Denn in der Tat stehen die für die Jahrhundertwende virulenten schwankenden Identitätskonzepte für eine „Krise der Männlichkeit",[14] während zeitgleich die (gesellschafts)politischen Vorzeichen für Frauen durch die erste Frauenemanzipationsbewegung eher identitätsstärkende Impulse zeitigten, wobei von den schreibenden Frauen – anders als die männliche Autobiographik – ohnehin nicht auf ein kohärentes Identitätsmodell zurückgegriffen werden konnte.[15] Stattdessen, so Michaela Holdenried, rekurrierten Autobiographinnen und Schriftstellerinnen auf ein dekonstruktivistisches Verfahren – „weniger in einem radikal entsubjektivierten, als vielmehr in einem ästhetischen und ‚literaturpolitischen' Sinne", wenn etwa schreibende Frauen sich zwar „auf den männlichen Kanon bezogen, seine Strukturen übernommen, imitiert, sie aber auch subvertiert und ironisch de(kon)struiert"[16] haben. Bedeutsam in diesem Zusammenhang ist Gertrude Steins autobiographisches Schreiben, ihre *Autobiography of Alice B. Toklas* (1933) genauso wie *Everybody's Autobiography* (1937). Steins assozia-

---

[13] Vgl. die Kapitelüberschrift bei Michaela Holdenried: „Autobiographik von Frauen – eine eigene Geschichte?", in Holdenried, *Autobiographie*, S. 62.
[14] Vgl. dazu Jacques Le Rider, *Das Ende der Illusion. Die Wiener Moderne und die Krisen der Identität*, Wien 1990.
[15] Zur Frage des fehlenden kohärenten Identitätsmodells bei komponierenden Frauen vgl. Melanie Unseld: „Alma Mahler. Biographische Lösungen eines unlösbaren Falles?", in: *Leben als Kunstwerk: Künstlerbiographien im 20. Jahrhundert*, hrsg. von Christopher F. Laferl und Anja Tippner (Druck in Vorb.).
[16] Holdenried, *Autobiographie*, S. 83.

tionsreicher Parlandoton, versehen mit Ironie und Wahrnehmungsbrechungen, durchsetzt von narrativen, thematischen und chronologischen Sprüngen, unterläuft „die Fixierung auf die eigene Identität und den Gestus der Selbstsetzung"[17], zugleich unterläuft sie auch die Form der Autobiographie an sich, dabei sich „erheiternd und erhellend neue darstellerische Lösungen für knifflige identitäts- und subjekttheoretische Fragestellungen"[18] erschreibend.

Ethel Smyths autobiographisches Schreiben ist ohne diesen (knapp skizzierten) literarhistorischen Hintergrund nicht adäquat zu beschreiben. Wohlgemerkt geht es hier nicht darum, persönliche Zusammenhänge zu konstruieren, die (noch) nicht existierten – Smyth und Woolf lernten sich erst 1930 kennen[19] und von einer Bekanntschaft Smyths mit Stein ist (bislang) nichts bekannt. Es geht vielmehr um die Beobachtung, dass sich in den 1920er und 30er Jahren, jener Zeit, in der Smyth als Autorin an die Öffentlichkeit trat, der Gestus des weiblichen (autobiographischen) Schreibens in einer Weise veränderte, die auch in Smyths Schriften seit 1922 zu finden ist. Für eine solche Sichtweise spricht, dass sich Smyth mehrfach mit dem Thema des autobiographischen Schreibens in diesem Sinne auseinandergesetzt und dies zum Teil explizit formuliert hat. Hierzu einige Beispiele. Im Vorwort von *Streaks of Life* nimmt Smyth dezidiert zu Fragen moderner Autobiographik Stellung: "I call this collection of papers 'Streaks of Life' because although most of them are autobiographical there is no attempt at a connected story. Dealing with modern times, continuity is impossible unless you are prepared either to hurt feelings, or to dip your pen in purest solution of rose-coloured amiability."[20] In *Streaks of Life* gibt Smyth denn auch tatsächlich alle Kohärenz und den Anspruch auf Chronologie auf. Das Buch enthält eine Sammlung von Texten zu exponierten Ereignissen aus ihrem Leben sowie essayistische Texte, die man als ‚Reflexionen' bezeichnen könnte.

---

[17] Margot Brink, „Die Frage nach dem Subjekt – literaturwissenschaftliche Erkundungen", in: *Feministische Forschung – Nachhaltige Einsprüche*, hrsg. von Kathrin Zein und Barbara Thiessen (*Studien interdisziplinäre Geschlechterforschung* 3), Opladen 2003, S. 237–258, hier S. 253.

[18] Holdenried, *Autobiographie*, S. 83.

[19] Dass Woolf vor der persönlichen Begegnung mit Smyth deren *Impressions That Remained* offenbar kannte, weist Rebecca Grotjahn nach, vgl. ihren Beitrag in diesem Band. Ferner ist zu erwähnen, dass die Freundschaft der beiden Frauen dann maßgeblich auch das letzte veröffentliche autobiographische Buch von Smyth beeinflusste, wie der Widmungstext deutlich macht (vgl. Smyth, *As Time Went On ...*, Widmung [o. S.]).

[20] Smyth, *Streaks of Life*, S. 7.

Ein zweites Beispiel: *A Final Burning of Boats* erschien 1928, nachdem 1924 Smyths fast gleichlautender Artikel („A Burning of Boats") im *London Mercury* erschienen war. Diesen zitiert Smyth ausführlich im ersten Kapitel ihres Buches,[21] um ihn anschließend einer Überarbeitung zu unterziehen: „because a new situation demands a new analysis."[22] Nach der Re-Lektüre ihres eigenen Artikels beginnt somit eine aktualisierte Argumentation – wobei sie den Prozess der Re-Lektüre offenlegt. Eingebettet ist dies in das erste Kapitel, das mit „Autobiographical Sketch-Map with Key: 1889-1927" überschrieben ist und somit einen anderen zeitlichen Rahmen eröffnet, der zum Teil weit hinter die in *Streaks of Life* beschriebenen Episoden zurückreicht. Von einer auch nur im Ansatz vorhandenen Chronologie kann mithin keine Rede sein, vielmehr geht Smyth zeitlich sprunghaft, allein dem Gedankengang und der Argumentation ihrer Ausführungen folgend, vor, gemäß dem Motto „But life is a composite affaire"[23], das sie im Vorwort von *A Final Burning of Boats* formuliert – dabei spielerisch mit dem Wortspiel composite/composer arbeitend: Es sei ein großer Luxus, als Komponistin in der Autobiographie auch von nicht-musikalischen Belangen schreiben zu dürfen, das Leben also nicht als „composer" sondern als „composite affair" zu beschreiben.[24] Das eigene Leben als „composite affair" zu begreifen und es als solches zu schildern, ist auch in anderen Metaphern, die Smyth für das autobiographische Schreiben findet, zu greifen. So vergleicht sie diese Arbeit in *What Happened Next* (1940) mit dem Aufräumen alter, durcheinandergeratener Schulsachen: „Memoir-Writing is like tidying the schoolroom cupboard in the days of one's youth. [...] [Y]ou began to examine the objects piled higgledy-piggledy on the shelves, opening squashed cardboard boxes that contained you wondered what [...]."[25]

Hinter diesen Stand des autobiographischen Erzählens geht Smyth nach *Streaks of Life* (1922) nicht mehr zurück. Im Gegenteil sucht sie in jedem ihrer nun erscheinenden Bände neue formale und gestalterische Möglichkeiten, die jeweils aus dem Inhalt und dem Entstehungszusammenhang des Buches heraus entwickelt sind. Dabei ist das Material, das Smyth ausbreitet, heterogen. Es umfasst neben autobiographischem Material im engeren Sinne auch Memoiren-Anteile, allgemeine politische und kulturelle Betrachtungen, Reiseberichte, musikalische Reflexionen, biographische Porträts über andere Personen (darunter den Dirigenten Thomas Beecham, den Philosophen und

---

[21] Smyth, *A Final Burning of Boats*, S. 3–5.
[22] Ebd., S. 5.
[23] Smyth, *A Final Burning of Boats*, S. [1].
[24] Ebd., S. [1].
[25] Smyth, *What Happened Next*, Prologue, S. 1.

Dichter Henry Brewster und die Komponistin Augusta Holmès), Libretti und Originaldokumente wie Briefe sowie Abbildungen.

Im Zusammenhang mit der Selbstinszenierung der Komponistin Smyth in ihren autobiographischen Schriften ist es interessant, gerade auch die Abbildungen heranzuziehen, denn wie auch die Zusammenstellung unterschiedlicher Materialien, etwa die Integration von Briefen und Briefauszügen, einer überlegten Dramaturgie folgt, kann man auch bei der Analyse der abgedruckten Bilder von einer durchdachten „Komposition" sprechen. Auffällig ist dabei sowohl die relativ hohe Zahl an Bildern als auch ihre Auswahl: Bilder von Ethel Smyth selbst, vor allem aber Porträts ihr nahestehender Menschen, Landschafts- und Architekturaufnahmen (vor allem in *A Three-Legged Tour in Greece*) sowie auffallend viele Hundebilder. Es wird zu zeigen sein, dass die Bilder nicht nur rein illustrativen Charakter haben, sondern auch als Hinweis auf die Selbstkonzeption Ethel Smyths als einer in der Öffentlichkeit stehenden Künstlerin zu dechiffrieren sind. Auffällig ist zunächst vor allem, dass sich Ethel Smyth auf ihren insgesamt 14 abgedruckten Porträts (und diese sollen im Folgenden im Vordergrund stehen) nur in einem Fall dezidiert als Musikerin darstellt: am Flügel sitzend, zusammen mit Maurice Baring, in *What Happened Next*. Nicht weniger als 12 Bilder hingegen zeigen sie zusammen mit ihren Hunden (Abb. 1, S. 119). Doch was man als *spleen* einer Hundeliebhaberin, als die sie sich in *Inordinate (?) Affection* präsentiert, abtun könnte, ist möglicherweise doch auch Selbstinszenierungsstrategie einer ebenso resoluten wie emanzipierten modernen Künstlerin. Denn vergleicht man diese „Porträts mit Hund" mit anderen Fotografien aus den 1920er und 30er Jahren, auf denen sich Künstlerinnen wie Virginia Woolf, Gertrude Stein, Peggy Guggenheim, Annemarie Schwarzenbach, Tania Blixen, Gitta Alpár oder Victoria Sackville-West zusammen mit (zumeist großen) Hunden porträtieren ließen, wird deutlich, dass hier eine Ikonographie des modernen Künstlerinnentypus verhandelt wird.[26]

Eine zweite Auffälligkeit begegnet beim Betrachten der Illustrationen der autobiographischen Schriften von Smyth, eine Auffälligkeit, die besonders dann hervortritt, wenn man zeitgenössische Künstlerporträts oder auch solche aus dem späten 19. und frühen 20. Jahrhundert vergleichend hinzuzieht. Ihrem heraus-

---

[26] In der sich dem Vortrag anschließenden Diskussion wurde u. a. über diese Inszenierungsmuster gesprochen, vor allem auch über die Bedeutung des Hundes in diesem Zusammenhang: als Spiegelbild der sich mit dem Hund Porträtierenden oder als Metapher für Stärke, Bewegungsdrang, Wildheit und Kraft einerseits, für Treue und Freundschaft andererseits. Vgl. zu den Inszenierungen von Künstlerinnen der 1920er/30er Jahre mit Hunden auch die Anthologie von Britta Jürgs, *Schwarze Hunde – Bunte Hunde. Künstlerinnen & Schriftstellerinnen & ihre Hunde*, Berlin 2006.

gehobenen Status als Genie entsprechend wurden Komponisten in ernsthafter Pose porträtiert und selbst nachdem sich die Fotografie als (potentiell spontanes) Bildmedium verbreitet hatte, überwogen (selbstinszenatorisch lanciert) ernste Bilder. Umso erstaunlicher, dass als Frontispiz des zweiten Bandes von *Impressions That Remained* eine lachende Ethel Smyth begegnet (s. Abb. 2).

Abschließend, und das Terrain des Humors nicht verlassen, sei die Karikatur angesprochen, die Smyth im ersten Band der *Impressions* abdrucken ließ (s. Abb. 3). Sie stammt aus dem privaten Umfeld und ist damit nicht unter die üblichen Berufskarikaturen zu zählen, die über zahlreiche Komponisten wie Hector Berlioz, Richard Wagner, Johannes Brahms u. v. a. verbreitet wurden. Smyths Cousin zeichnete die Karikatur und zeigt sich dort selbst neben der jungen Ethel auf einem Eselskarren sitzend. Auf dem Rücksitz sieht man Ethel Smyths Schwester Mary. Das Mädchen Ethel lenkt den Wagen mit erhobener Peitsche, vom rasanten Tempo des Wagens und einem wilden Fahrstil zeugen der aufgewirbelte Staub, der geöffnete Mund der offenbar schreienden Wagenlenkerin, ihre wild fliegenden Haare und der sich ängstlich festhaltende Cousin. Von feiner Ironie ist auch die Bildunterschrift durchzogen: "Ethel (dolce) 'I guide him entirely by my voice! (fortissimo, con molto expressione) Gu-r-r- along yer-r- Br-rute!'" Diese Karikatur ließ Smyth nicht nur abdrucken, sondern kommentierte sie ausführlich auch im Text und gab ihr damit eine herausgehobene Bedeutung („one of my most cherished possessions"[27]), kulminierend in dem Satz "That picture has special mention in my Will."[28] Auf der Suche nach Gründen für die herausgehobene Bedeutung dieser Karikatur stößt man – neben dem Hinweis auf Smyths allenthalben deutlich hervortretenden Humor – auf zwei Aspekte, die wiederum den Kreis zu ihren Selbstinszenierungskonzepten als Komponistin schließen: Smyth nimmt die Karikatur zum Anlass, um ihren Charakter, vor allem ihre Unangepasstheit, zu dokumentieren und sie der Angepasstheit der Schwester gegenüberzustellen: "[the] sketch […] incidentally shows that strucutral differences in Mary's and my character […]. Calm and unmoved, neatly shod in the drab boots with shiny toes I remember so well, her [= Mary's] profile indicates the total detachment of a young lady out for an airing."[29] Die zweite Auffälligkeit der Karikatur liegt in den verwendeten musikalischen Attributen: Die junge Ethel schwingt eine sich in Violinschlüsselform windende Peitsche und ihre Sätze werden mit Quasi-Vortragsanweisungen notiert: zunächst ironischerweise mit „dolce", dann „fortissimo, con molto expressione". Ihr Cousin nimmt damit

---

[27] Smyth, *Impressions That Remained*, Bd. 1, S. 72.
[28] Ebd.
[29] Ebd.

auch Smyths früh deutlich gewordenes, in das ländliche Umfeld offenbar wenig passendes musikalisches Interesse aufs Korn, das – noch vollkommen „ungezügelt" – wichtiger Bestandteil des ausgeprägten Selbstbewusstseins des jungen Mädchens ist.[30] Diese Charakterisierung war Smyth offenbar wichtig. Sie legte damit nicht zuletzt auch eine Lesart ihrer Komponistinnenpersönlichkeit an, die sie als „Kämpferin" wahrnahm:[31] kraftvoll und eigenständig, willensstark und sich gegen Konventionen, vor allem gegen das weibliche Geschlechtermodell zur Wehr setzend, ein Bild, das durch Virginia Woolfs „Felsensprengerin"-Metapher weitergeführt wurde. Wichtig scheint mir festzuhalten, dass es aus dem Repertoire ihres Selbstkonzepts als Komponistin stammte, dass es von Beginn an als Gegensatz zu geltenden Vorstellungen von Weiblichkeit (Mary) wahrgenommen und so auch kommuniziert wurde und dass es eng mit der Fähigkeit zur Selbstironisierung verbunden war.

Ethel Smyth exponierte sich mit 10 Bänden autobiographischer Schriften. Der Umfang dieses literarischen Oeuvres ist für eine Komponistin ungewöhnlich, ebenso die Art des Schreibens, die deutlich auf Smyths aktive Auseinandersetzung mit aktuellen Fragen des autobiographischen Schreibens verweist: Smyth lag nicht nur daran, ihr Leben als Komponistin zu dokumentieren und sich damit in das kulturelle Gedächtnis, vor allem auch in die Musikgeschichte einzuschreiben. Sie hatte offenbar auch ein großes Interesse, am literarischen Diskurs ihrer Zeit teilzuhaben, sich damit als Autorin zu etablieren. Die Heterogenität ihrer Bücher spiegelt dabei einerseits die Schwierigkeiten autobiographischen Schreibens wider, die um 1900 – im Zusammenhang mit dem Zerfall der Ich-Identität – virulent wurden und in den 1920er und 30er Jahren zu einer Vielfalt alternativer Schreibformen führten. Andererseits konnte Smyth gerade aufgrund dieser Heterogenität ihr breites Interesse und ihr weitgefächertes literarisches Können zur Geltung bringen. Als Schreibende war Smyth mit den zeitgenössischen Strömungen in Literatur und Autobiographik offenbar eng vertraut. Mehr noch: Sie agierte souverän, positionierte sich mit großer Selbstsicherheit und zugleich – auch hier an zeitgenössische Diskurse anknüpfend – mit dem Bewusstsein, dass individuelle Kohärenz nicht darstellbar sei. Und sie ergriff die Möglichkeiten, durch autobiographisches Schreiben ihre Identität zu umreißen, formte daraus nicht zuletzt auch aktiv ihr Selbstbild als Komponistin: nicht monolithisch, als exponierte Komponistin, sondern diskontinuierlich und in einer polyperspektivischen Selbstkonzeption – gemäß ihrem Motto „life is a composite affaire".

[30] Zu Smyths späteren kompositorischen Auseinandersetzungen mit dem Thema Jagd/Reiten vgl. den Beitrag von Cornelia Bartsch in diesem Band.
[31] Vgl. hierzu auch den Beitrag von Elizabeth Kertesz im vorliegenden Band.

Identität durch Schreiben

Abb. 1 und 2: „Pan IV and E.S.", abgedruckt in *Inordinate (?) Affection. A Story for Dog Lovers (1936)*; Ethel Smyth, lachend. Frontispiz des zweiten Bandes der *Impressions That Remained (1919)*.

Abb. 3: Karikatur aus dem ersten Band der *Impressions That Remained (1919)*

Abstract

Creating Identity by Writing: The Autobiographical Oeuvre of Ethel Smyth
Ethel Smyth's autobiographical oeuvre is extensive and varied. The first two volumes, published by Smyth in 1919 (*Impressions that Remained. Memoirs*), were originally planned as a larger autobiographical series, a plan she never ultimately realised, however. Instead, Smyth published volumes consisting partly of autobiographical material but also, among many other items, of travelogues, letters from contemporaries, reflections and animal tales. A heterogeneous collection of texts developed, which despite (or possibly due to) its heterogeneity can be interpreted as constituting a work of artistic self-expression. However, such an understanding of this collection can only be founded upon a basis of methodological reflection on autobiographical writing. In this contribution, Smyth's autobiographical writings are first analysed with gender aspects in mind, before her artistic self-perception, as drawn from close examination of these considerations, is placed in a context embracing other artists also active around 1900.

Cornelia Bartsch
Schön Rohtraut und das Sattelpferd. Lyrisches und biographisches Ich in Ethel Smyths Liedkompositionen der 1870er Jahre

Für Franziska und für Julia

Der Begriff des „lyrischen Ichs" wurde von Carl Dahlhaus für die Musik eingefordert, und zwar im Zusammenhang mit Ludwig van Beethovens Sonate op. 81a, *Les Adieux*, dem musikalischen Lebewohl an den Erzherzog Rudolf.[1] Die Entlehnung aus der Literaturwissenschaft diente dabei gewissermaßen der Ehrenrettung eines Helden. Sie ermöglicht es, von einem in der Musik anwesenden „ästhetischen Subjekt" zu sprechen, das eine „Identifikation mit dem biographischen Subjekt nicht zulässt".[2] In Anpassung an das monumentale Beethovenbild einer auf der Idee des Heldischen beruhenden Musikgeschichtsschreibung wird so aus dem persönlichen Abschiedsgruß ein „Meisterwerk", dessen Wert sich gerade an der Entfernung von möglichen biographischen Implikationen bemisst, ein „Formprozess, der das programmatische Moment […] allmählich auslöscht"[3], wie Dahlhaus formuliert, und zugleich eine Rede an uns alle, an die Menschheit.

Nun steht eine solche Sicht mittlerweile längst auch im Rahmen verschiedener „Meisterdiskurse" in Frage. Die Auseinandersetzung mit semantisch aufgeladenen Chiffren etwa im Werk Johannes Brahms' oder Alban Bergs seit den 1980er Jahren ist hierfür paradigmatisch.[4] Dasselbe gilt auch bezogen auf Beethoven,[5] wie überhaupt Dahlhaus' Vorschlag als Reaktion auf das Paradox

---

[1] Vgl. Carl Dahlhaus, *Ludwig van Beethoven und seine Zeit*, Laaber 1987, S. 60ff.
[2] Ebd., S. 64.
[3] Ebd., S. 64f.
[4] Vgl. z.B. Douglas Jarman, „Alban Berg, Wilhelm Fliess und das geheime Programm des Violinkonzerts", in: ÖMZ 40 (1983), S. 12–21, Constantin Floros, *Alban Berg. Musik als Autobiographie*, Wiesbaden 1992, und *Johannes Brahms oder die Relativierung der „absoluten Musik"*, hrsg. von Hans-Werner Heister (= Zwischen/Töne Musik und andere Künste, Bd. 5), Hamburg 1997.
[5] Zu Beethovens musikalischer Kommunikation mit dem Erzherzog Rudolf vgl. insbesondere Birgit Lodes, „‚Von Herzen – möge es wieder – zu Herzen gehen!'. Zur Widmung von Beethovens ‚Missa solemnis'", in: *Altes im Neuen. Festschrift*

gelesen werden kann, dass ausgerechnet bei jenem Komponisten, der gewissermaßen zum „Monument der absoluten Musik" geworden ist, der Diskurs über die programmatischen Inhalte seiner Musik und deren Verbindung mit seiner umfang- und detailreich diskutierten Biographie von Anfang an mehr Regalmeter in den Bibliotheken eingenommen haben dürfte als „rein" analytische Arbeiten. Im Zusammenhang mit der Musik Ethel Smyths stellt sich die Frage nach dem biographischen und ästhetischen Subjekt jedoch sehr viel grundlegender, wie ich anhand von zwei Theoremen verdeutlichen möchte, um sie dann anhand einer Parallellektüre von Smyths frühen Liedern und ihren Memoirenbänden *Impressions that Remained* zu verfolgen.

Immer Ärger mit dem Subjekt

Das erste Theorem, das die Dimensionen der Frage nach ästhetischem und biographischem Subjekt in Bezug auf eine Komponistin am Ende des 19. Jahrhunderts ausleuchten soll, ist Theodor W. Adornos Begriff des musikalischen Materials – der Musikwissenschaft vertraut und von Ethel Smyths späten Kompositionen historisch nicht weit entfernt. Im Zusammenhang mit Arnold Schönberg führt Adorno bekanntlich aus, dass das Material der Musik nicht als „natürliches", geschichtsloses zu verstehen, sondern „selber sedimentierter Geist, ein gesellschaftliches, durchs Bewußtsein von Menschen hindurch Präformiertes" sei.[6] Wodurch es präformiert ist, erfahren wir in den folgenden Sätzen:

> „Als ihrer selbst vergessene, vormalige Subjektivität hat solcher objektive Geist des Materials seine eigenen Bewegungsgesetze. Desselben Ursprungs wie der gesellschaftliche Prozeß und stets wieder von dessen Spuren durchsetzt, verläuft, was bloße Selbstbewegung des Materials dünkt, im gleichen Sinne wie die reale Gesellschaft, noch wo beide nichts mehr voneinander wissen und sich gegenseitig befehden. Daher ist die Auseinandersetzung des Komponisten mit dem Material die mit der Gesellschaft, gerade soweit diese ins Werk eingewandert ist und nicht als bloß Äußerliches, Heteronomes, als Konsument oder Opponent der Produktion gegenübersteht."[7]

Theodor Göllner zum 65. Geburtstag, hrsg. von Bernd Edelmann und Manfred Hermann Schmid (= Münchner Veröffentlichungen zur Musikgeschichte, Bd. 51), Tutzing 1995, S. 295–305.

[6] Theodor W. Adorno, *Philosophie der Neuen Musik*, Frankfurt/Main ⁶1991 (¹1949), S. 39.

[7] Ebda, S. 39f.

Bezogen auf eine Komponistin, die dem historisch präformierten musikalischen Material gegen Ende des 19. Jahrhunderts als „Subjekt" gegenübertritt, verlieren diese Sätze ihre Vertrautheit und führen in ein Geisterhaus – oder vielmehr in ein „Spiegelkabinett", in dem das Ich und sein vielfach zurückgeworfenes Spiegelbild nicht mehr voneinander zu unterscheiden sind. Frauen waren nicht historische Subjekte des Prozesses, von dem Adorno spricht. Dennoch müssen sie Spuren in der Musik hinterlassen haben, denn sie waren Teil der Gesellschaft, deren Entwicklung in einem dialektischen Prozess auch zum Teil des musikalischen Materials geworden ist. Aber wer ist in diesem Fall „sie"? Ob wir versuchen, die geschlechterhistorischen Spuren im musikalischen Material mittels der Metaphorik der musiktheoretischen Terminologie von Adolph Bernhard Marx zu lesen oder ob wir sie subtiler in bestimmten kulturgeschichtlichen Entwicklungen suchen, wie beispielsweise in der Sehnsucht nach einem Ursprung, für den um 1800 „das Weibliche" bzw. die den Frauen zugeschriebene „Natürlichkeit" stand und der sich in der Musik unter anderem in Kompositionen niederschlug, in denen die Musik sich selbst neu zu erfinden scheint,[8] – oder ob uns dies zu spekulativ erscheint und wir uns lieber den Männlichkeits- und Weiblichkeitsbildern in der Oper oder im Lied zuwenden, für die freilich ein von Adorno nicht gemeinter erweiterter Materialbegriff vonnöten wäre: Wir werden mit dem Spuren dessen im Material konfrontiert, was als „weiblich" galt.[9] Dies trifft ungeachtet der Komponistinnen zu, von denen wir mittlerweile wissen, denn erstens ist die Rezeptionsgeschichte ihrer Musik bis ins 20. Jahrhundert hinein so brüchig, dass sie nicht Teil der Kompositionsgeschichte werden konnte, und zweitens schlossen die Merkmale „Frau" und „Komponist" vor dem Hintergrund der bürgerlichen Geschlechterordnung des 19. Jahrhunderts einander gewissermaßen aus.[10] Die misogynen Schriften, die um die Wende zum 20. Jahrhundert, zur Schaffenszeit Ethel Smyths also,

---

[8] Ein besonders eindrucksvolles Beispiel hierfür ist Mozarts „Dissonanzenquartett" KV 365. Zu der Thematik „Musik und Natur um 1800" – wenn auch nicht unter expliziter Berücksichtigung des Gender-Aspekts – vgl. Peter Schleuning, *Die Sprache der Natur. Natur in der Musik des 18. Jahrhunderts*, Stuttgart 1978, insbesondere Teil III „Aufbruch in eine andere Natur", S. 127ff.

[9] Dies trifft auch für das „Männliche" zu. Bei den Bildern des „Männlichen" handelt es sich jedoch um 1900 – jedenfalls wenn man die Bildproduktion als kollektiven Prozess einer Kultur betrachtet – um Selbstbilder und nicht um Fremdbilder.

[10] Dies spiegelt sich nicht nur in zeitgenössischen Rezensionen, die bei Musik von Frauen ohne den Hinweis aufs Geschlecht nicht auskommen, sondern auch in den Lebensgeschichten von Komponistinnen wie Emilie Mayer (1812–1883) oder Luise Adolpha Le Beau (1850–1927). Insbesondere in Deutschland ging kompositorische Professionalisierung fast zwangsläufig mit einer Entscheidung gegen Heirat und Familie einher.

gerade bei Intellektuellen Konjunktur hatten, verlegten den gesellschaftlichen Rollenkonflikt dann ins Innere und sprachen einer schöpferisch tätigen Frau die Weiblichkeit einfach per definitionem ab.[11]

Das zweite Theorem wird zumal in der deutschen Musikwissenschaft eher zögerlich rezipiert. Die Frage nach dem Subjekt des Schreibens, die für die Musik bei Adorno schon aufscheint, ist unter Einbeziehung poststrukturalistischer Theorien sowohl im Kontext der Gender-Studien als auch insbesondere in der angloamerikanischen Literaturwissenschaft zum zentralen Motor einer Theorie der Postmoderne geworden. Als weiterführend haben sich dabei jene Ansätze erwiesen, die nicht nach Kontinuitäten gefragt haben, also nicht nach vermeintlichen Ursprüngen der aus einem herrschenden kulturellen Diskurs Ausgeschlossenen gesucht, keine „Parallelgeschichten" konstruiert haben, sondern die Brüche in Augenschein genommen haben, welche unweigerlich entstehen, wenn eine Person in einen künstlerischen Diskurs eintritt, die vorher dessen Objekt war.[12] Der Literatur- und Kunsthistoriker Homi K. Bhaba, den diese Brüche vor allem bezogen auf Künstlerinnen und Künstler aus den ehemals kolonialisierten Ländern in der Migration interessieren, spricht im Rückgriff auf Jacques Lacan in diesem Zusammenhang von einem Akt der Verdopplung oder einer „Spaltung des Subjekts am historischen Ort seines Sprechens".[13] Dieser, so Bhaba, sei bei Schriftstellerinnen wie beispielsweise Toni Morrison „zu erkennen – am Spiel mit den metonymischen Figuren von ‚Vermißtsein' oder ‚Unsichtbarkeit', um die ihr Hinterfragen der Identität kreist."[14] „Im postkolonialen Text", so Bhaba, „kehrt die Frage der Identität wieder als anhaltendes Hinterfragen des Rahmens, des Repräsentationsraumes, in dem das Bild", oder wie er mit Bezug auf zwei zuvor zitierte Gedichte sagt, „der Vermißte, das unsichtbare Auge, das orientalische Stereotyp – mit seiner Differenz, seinem Anderen konfrontiert wird."[15]

[11] Otto Weininger zufolge gehörten schöpferisch tätige Frauen von Sappho über Clara Schumann bis George Sand nicht dem weiblichen Geschlecht, sondern „sexuellen Zwischenformen" an. Otto Weininger, *Geschlecht und Charakter. Eine prinzipielle Untersuchung*. München 1997 [Nachdruck der 1. Auflage Wien 1903], VI. Kapitel „Die emanzipierten Frauen", S. 79–93. Genialität galt für Weininger als „eine ideale, potenzierte Männlichkeit", ebd., S. 144. Vgl. hierzu den Beitrag von Rebecca Grotjahn in diesem Band.

[12] Vgl. die Einleitung von Elisabeth Bronfen und Benjamin Marius in: *Hybride Kulturen, Beiträge zur anglo-amerikanischen Multikulturalismusdebatte*, hrsg. von Elisabeth Bronfen, Benjamin Marius und Therese Steffen (=Stauffenberg Diskussion, Bd. 4), Tübingen 1997, S. 1–29, hier S. 7f.

[13] Homi K. Bhaba, „Die Frage der Identität", in: *Hybride Kulturen*, S. 97–122, Zitat S. 99, siehe auch S. 107ff.

[14] Ebd., S. 107.

[15] Ebd., S. 99.

Was hat dies mit Ethel Smyth zu tun, die vielleicht gerade deshalb zu ihren Lebzeiten so erfolgreich war, weil sie so erfrischend deutlich „Ich" sagen konnte, weil sie keine Scheu hatte, den Größen ihrer Zunft wie Gustav Mahler bzw. Bruno Walter ihre Opern vorzuführen und zumindest Letzteren für sich gewinnen konnte? Was – so ist diese Frage zu präzisieren – haben Theorien, die Schreibstrategien von Künstlerinnen und Künstlern in der Migration beschreiben, mit einer weißen höheren Tochter aus einem kolonialisierenden Land zu tun, noch dazu der Tochter eines Vaters, der als Offizier der Royal Army in Indien war?[16] Und last but not least: Was haben Theorien, die so stark um das Sehen kreisen, mit einer Kunst zu tun, in der es vornehmlich um das Hören geht?

„Something yet unvoiced"

Eine erste Brücke zur Beantwortung dieser Fragen kann ein Satz aus dem Essay *Female Pipings in Eden* bilden, mit dem Ethel Smyth offenbar auf Virginia Woolfs *A Room of One's Own* „antwortet".[17] Bezogen auf die Romane Woolfs schreibt Smyth dort:

> "a great woman writer of to-day has said of her books that they are all experiments. That is what I mean, only put in another form; I have always felt it must be, for women, a question of something yet unvoiced [...]."[18]

Als „something yet invoiced" – etwas noch Unausgesprochenes, etwas, das bislang keine Stimme hat, – definiert Ethel Smyth im letzten Abschnitt ihres Essays den Begriff der Originalität. Damit unterscheidet sie sich grundlegend von den zu ihrer Zeit herrschenden Vorstellungen, denen Originalität nicht bislang Unartikuliertes, sondern einen angemessenen Einschreibevorgang in einen jahrhundertealten künstlerischen Diskurs bedeutete. Die Kunst der Originalität bestand vielmehr darin, ohne epigonal zu sein an den vorangehenden Meister anzuknüpfen oder, um es mit Adorno zu sagen, als Subjekt in einen eigenständigen Dialog mit dem musikalischen Material zu treten, wie jener es hinterlassen hatte. Um zu beschreiben, wie eine „Komponistin an der Schwelle der Freiheit" – ein künstlerisches Subjekt also, das bislang keines sein durfte – in der Musik spricht, bedient sich Ethel Smyth interessanterweise des Be-

---

[16] Zu Smyths eigenem kolonialisierenden Blick vgl. den Beitrag von Pavel Jiracek in diesem Band.
[17] Zur Dialogizität der beiden Essays vgl. den Beitrag von Elicia Clements in diesem Band.
[18] Ethel Smyth, „Female Pipings in Eden", in: Dies., *Female Pipings in Eden*, Edinburgh 1933, S. 1–57, Zitat S. 55.

griffs „coarseness": Rauheit.[19] Mit diesem Attribut belegt sie sowohl den Weg einer Künstlerin, die ihre Stimme in einer männlich dominierten Welt finden will, als auch den Klang dieser Stimme selbst.[20] Denselben Begriff – Rauheit – verwendet Roland Barthes in seinem Essay *Le grain de la voix (Die Körnung/ Rauheit der Stimme)*, um eine musikalische Praxis jenseits der Repräsentation zu beschreiben.[21] Nun meint Barthes mit Rauheit die Anwesenheit des Körpers im Klang und ein unmittelbares Zusammenfallen von Klang und Sinn und damit, zeichentheoretisch gesprochen, ein Zusammenfallen von Signifikant und Signifikat. Ethel Smyth bezeichnet damit – um es in ihren eigenen Bildern weiterzuführen – Evas schräge Töne im Paradies, von denen ihre Produzentin, auch wenn Adam sich die Ohren zuhält, stolz sagen kann, dass es ihre eigenen seien.[22] Dennoch scheint es sich bei der gemeinsamen Begrifflichkeit um mehr als eine Koinzidenz zu handeln – und dies nicht nur, weil auch Barthes' Begriff der Rauheit auf etwas „Unartikuliertes" verweist. In der zeichentheoretischen Revision der Psychoanalyse durch Jacques Lacan, auf die Barthes sich bezieht, ist die symbolische Ordnung, für die die Sprache steht, vom Geschlechtsunterschied regiert. Als Netzwerk aus Differenzen und Voraussetzung für die Konstituierung des Subjekts repräsentiert sie das „Gesetz des Vaters". Allerdings zeigt schon Lacans Begriff vom Subjekt als „(der Sprache) Unterworfenes", dass es sich dabei keineswegs um eine stabile Position handelt. Vielmehr wird das Lacan'sche Subjekt permanent unterwandert. Durch das eigene Spiegelbild wird das Ich erst seiner selbst gewahr – und tritt damit von Anfang an als ein gespaltenes in Erscheinung, ein labiler Zustand, der sich in der Bedeutung des Anderen fortsetzt: Im Anderen sieht und begehrt das Ich das auf sich selbst gerichtete Begehren. Subjekt und Objekt verschieben sich so permanent, was sich für Lacan in der metonymischen oder metaphorischen Struktur der Sprache niederschlägt. Trotz dieser „Subversion des Subjekts" gibt es für Lacan kein Entkommen aus der Sprache. Anders gesagt: Das Vorsymbolische, das Lacan aufgrund seiner Bildhaftigkeit und „Spiegelbildlichkeit" das „Imaginäre"

[19] Ebd.
[20] Vgl. ebd., S. 53. Zur Illustration der Unterschiedlichkeit weiblicher und männlicher Erfahrung sowie der Schwierigkeiten der Frauen von ihrem eigenen – noch gar nicht bestimmbaren – Ort aus zu sprechen, entwirft sie zuvor das Bild von zwei auf entlegenen Inseln wohnenden Urvölkern.
[21] Roland Barthes, „Le grain de la voix", in: Ders., *L'obvie et l'obtus. Essais critiques III*, Edition du Seuil 1984, S. 236–245. Wörtlich übersetzt lautet der Titel „Die Körnung der Stimme". Diese wird im Text als Rauheit beschrieben, als Widerstand, die den Körper in der Stimme hörbar werden lässt.
[22] „Evas schräge Töne im Paradies" bilden die Rahmenerzählung des Essays, vgl. Smyth, *Female Pipings*, S. 3 und S. 56.

nennt, setzt zwar eine Dynamik von Sinnverschiebungen in Gang, die die symbolische Ordnung unterwandern, aber es spricht selber nicht – es sei denn in Zuständen von Psychose und Neurose. Julia Kristeva und Roland Barthes haben sich mit diesem Entwurf eines „Sprachgefängnisses" durch ihren Lehrer Jacques Lacan nicht abgefunden. In der Kunst, der poetischen Sprache und bei Barthes auch in einem Musizieren, das nichts sucht als die Lust an sich selbst – allesamt künstlerische Praxen, die in die Alltagswelt hineinragen – kommt das Vorsymbolische, in der Kristeva'schen Terminologie: „das Semiotische", zur Sprache.[23] Gerade bei Kristeva wird deutlich, dass dieses in Entgegensetzung zum „Gesetz des Vaters" auf den mit „dem Weiblichen" identifizierten, gleichermaßen beängstigenden wie beglückenden Zustand der Einheit mit der Mutter verweist, der der Subjektkonstituierung vorgängig ist.[24]

„Evas schräge Töne im Paradies" in Smyths Essay lassen sich auch vor diesem Hintergrund durchaus als „Klänge jenseits der Repräsentation" bezeichnen. Mit Bhaba gesprochen handelt es sich bei den „Rauheiten" ihrer Musik um jene Brüche, in denen Ethel Smyth den gegebenen Repräsentationsrahmen hinterfragt und durch die narrative Oberfläche hindurch sowohl Subjekt- als auch Sinnverschiebungen initiiert, mittels deren sie den objektivierenden Blick auf ihr Selbst mit seinem „Anderen" konfrontiert. Diese Brüche sind Indizien eines dem vormals verdinglichten Objekt des künstlerischen Diskurses angemessenen Einschreibevorgangs in die Geschichte des musikalischen Materials und folglich Qualitätsmerkmale ihrer Musik. Sogar im Sinne Adornos sorgen sie dafür, dass Smyths Musik „funktioniert".

---

[23] Julia, Kristeva, *Die Revolution der poetischen Sprache*, Frankfurt/Main 1978 (französische Erstausgabe Paris 1974).
[24] Kristeva nennt diesen Zustand in Anlehnung an Platons *Timaios* „chora"; diese strukturiere Triebfunktionen des Körpers im Verhältnis zur Mutter. Vgl. Kristeva, *Revolution*, S. 38. Judith Butler kritisiert jedoch die ontologische Bedeutung, die Kristeva dem Körper der Mutter zuschreibt, und zwar nicht zuletzt deshalb, weil diese an der binären Struktur einer „männlich" gedachten Kultur und eines vorkulturellen „Weiblichen" festhalte, vgl. Judith Butler, *Das Unbehagen der Geschlechter*, aus dem Amerikanischen von Katharina Menke, Frankfurt/Main [7]1991, S. 125. Damit geht Kristeva gewissermaßen hinter Lacan, der dem Vorkulturellen (Vorsymbolischen) eine genuine Ontologie abspricht, zurück. Um die durch das Geschlecht kodierten binären Strukturen der Sprache und hierauf basierend auch des Denkens besser zu verstehen, sind m. E. beide Theorien nach wie vor hilfreich.

Ich und Nicht-Ich

Nicht nur bezogen auf die oben gestellte Frage, inwiefern die stark vom Visuellen ausgehenden postkolonialen Theorien überhaupt auf Musik anwendbar seien, sondern darüber hinaus auch hinsichtlich der Frage nach dem Subjekt in Smyths Liedern, bieten Überlegungen Lawrence Kramers einige Anknüpfungspunkte. So beschreibt Kramer das romantische Lied des 19. Jahrhunderts als überraschend „kinematographische" Gattung, da es in seiner Verbindung von Gedicht und Musik kleine Szenen im Kopf der Zuhörenden erzeuge.[25] Diese wirken seiner Auffassung nach ähnlich wie im Film als Mittel zur Konstruktion von Subjektpositionen, die allerdings nicht zwingend die Identifikation mit einem fiktiven Charakter fordern oder auch zurückweisen, sondern eher Positionen innerhalb der Hierarchie von Wissen und Begehren darstellen, welche die Subjekte innerhalb der Erzählung miteinander verknüpfen. Als solche formen sie das Zusammenwachsen von individueller psychologischer und kultureller Identität: "Such positions model the coalescence of psychological and cultural identity, with particular emphasis on the interrelations of sexuality, gender differentiation, and discursive authority."[26] Besonders wirkungsmächtig seien diese Bilder, weil sie jenseits von Raum und Zeit angesiedelt zu sein scheinen. Diese „Ahistorizität" betrachtet er als immanenten Bestandteil der vom Lied ausgehenden Ideologieproduktion, welche die psychosexuellen „rites de passages" der bürgerlichen Gesellschaft als universell darstelle und ihnen dadurch Autorität verleihe.[27] Ausgehend von Rezeptionstheorien des Films ergeben sich für Kramer hieraus Fragen an das Lied, die mögliche Subjektpositionen sowohl der Rezipierenden als auch der Ausführenden oder des bzw. der Komponist/in in die Analyse einbeziehen und die aus diesem Grund für die Analyse der Lieder „einer Komponistin an der Schwelle der Freiheit" weiterführend erscheinen: Bin ich das im Lied angesprochene Subjekt und was, wenn ich es nicht bin? Inwiefern wird die Unterordnung meines eigenen Imaginären unter die narrative Hierarchie der szenischen Bilder verstärkt? Oder umgekehrt: Inwieweit gibt mir das mit Wünschen aufgeladene Imaginäre Lied die Möglichkeit, neue Subjektpositionen zu finden, die der symbolischen Ordnung der „Liederzählung" Widerstand entgegensetzen, ihr entkommen oder sie gar transformieren?[28]

---

[25] Lawrence Kramer, „The Lied as Cultural Practice", in: *Classical Music and Postmodern Knowledge*, Berkeley/Los Angeles/London 1995, S. 143–173, hier S. 145.
[26] Ebd., S. 146.
[27] Vgl. Kramer, „The Lied", S. 144.
[28] Ebd., S. 146.

Schon als Frau, die sich den „rites des passages" des 19. Jahrhunderts widersetzt, ist Smyth für das Lied gewissermaßen „unsichtbar", für die Komponistin als „erzählendes Subjekt" gilt dies doppelt. Wie gelingt es ihr – mit Bhaba gesprochen – ihr Unsichtbares mit seiner Differenz/seinem Anderen zu konfrontieren? Hierzu muss sie nicht nur die normativen „rites de passages" in ihren Liedern transformieren. Wie gelingt es ihr darüber hinaus, die narrativen Hierarchien der „symbolischen Ordnung des Liedes" aufzubrechen, um Raum für Wünsche jenseits der Norm und jenseits des gegebenen Repräsentationsrahmens entstehen zu lassen, in dem ihr „unsichtbares Auge" zugleich sieht und sichtbar wird?

Nimmt man im Hinblick auf diese Fragen zunächst die Auswahl der Texte in Augenschein, so fällt eine interessante Diskrepanz auf: Auf den ersten Blick scheint Smyth durchaus Gedichte gewählt zu haben, die gängige Themen der literarischen und musikalischen Romantik bedienen: verlorene Liebe, eine mit Sehnsucht besetzte Kindheit, Abschied und Vergänglichkeit. Fünf der zehn Lieder liegen Gedichte Joseph von Eichendorffs zugrunde, einem der am häufigsten vertonten Dichter der deutschen Romantik überhaupt.[29] Umso erstaunlicher ist der Befund, dass es sich mit einer Ausnahme bei allen Liedern um Erstvertonungen handelt. Bei zwei Liedern, Georg Büchners *Tanzlied* und dem ursprünglich plattdeutschen Gedicht *Nachtreiter* (*Nachtrüter*) von Klaus Groth, stellt sich sogar die Frage, wie Smyth auf die wenig bekannten Texte gestoßen ist.[30] Wenn man das Geschlecht des lyrischen Ichs entsprechend der

---

[29] Neben Eichendorff, sind mit Paul Heyse (*Nachtgedanken*) und Eduard Mörike (*Schön Rohtraut*) zwei weitere sehr häufig vertonte Dichter des 19. Jahrhunderts vertreten. Ernst von Wildenbruch (*Schlummerlied*) ist dagegen eine ungewöhnliche Wahl: Fünf der insgesamt nur neun nachgewiesenen Vertonungen seiner Gedichte stammen von der wenig bekannten Komponistin Ingeborg von Bronsart (1840–1913), die den bismarcktreuen Dichter möglicherweise über die preußische Offizierstradition ihres Mannes persönlich kannte.

[30] Für das Lied *Nachtreiter* gilt dies vor allem, wenn es schon in England entstanden sein sollte, ansonsten käme der mit Klaus Groth gut befreundete Brahms selbst als Überbringer des Textes in Betracht. Die plattdeutsche Erstfassung in Klaus Groths Gedichtband *Quickborn* erschien 1852: Klaus Groth, *Volksleben in plattdeutschen Gedichten dithmarscher Mundart; nebst Glossar mit einem Vor- und Fürwort von Pastor Dr. Harms*, Hamburg 1853, [1852]. Zwei Jahre später erschienen von Klaus Groth *Hundert Blätter. Paralipomena zu Quickborn*, Hamburg 1854, die neben weiteren Gedichten auch Übersetzungen ins Hochdeutsche enthalten. Die Quickborn-Gedichte nebst Übersetzungen fanden in Deutschland rasche Verbreitung, dürften aber aufgrund der Verankerung in der deutschen Volkskultur nicht ebenso schnell nach England gelangt sein. Möglicherweise lernte Smyth das Gedicht durch ihre deutsche Gouvernante kennen. Das Drama *Leonce und*

Geschlechterordnung der bürgerlichen Kleinfamilie „normativ" denkt, setzen zunächst nur zwei der ausgewählten Gedichte den typischen Geschlechterbildern des 19. Jahrhunderts deutlich Kontrapunkte entgegen: das schon erwähnte *Tanzlied* aus Georg Büchners Drama *Leonce und Lena*, in dem ein „normativ" weiblich zu denkendes lyrisches Ich sich der Erotisierung seines Körpers durch Todessehnsucht zu entziehen versucht, und Mörikes Ballade *Schön Rohtraut* über die Königstochter, deren erotische Anziehung auf den Knaben gerade darauf beruht, dass sie sich nicht „normativ weiblich" verhält und anstatt zu nähen und zu sticken lieber fischen und jagen geht – Letztere die erwähnte Ausnahme von der Regel der Erstvertonungen. Beide Lieder besetzen innerhalb ihrer Liedersammlung prominente Plätze: Das *Tanzlied* eröffnet die *Lieder* op. 4, *Schön Rohtraut* beschließt die *Lieder und Balladen* op. 3. *Schön Rohtraut* ist noch aus einem anderen Grund „prominent": Es ist das einzige Lied, das Smyth in ihren 1919 erschienenen Memoiren erwähnt, und zwar gleich mehrfach. Bei jeder dieser Erwähnungen spielt ihre Einführung in die Leipziger Musik liebenden Kreise eine Rolle, die für ihren Berufsweg als Komponistin entscheidend werden sollte. Dem entspricht auch die Widmung, die in anderer Hinsicht ein kleines Rätsel aufgibt: Die Lieder und Balladen op. 3 sind der Sängerin Livia Frege zugeeignet, die bis 1836 als Opernsängerin in Leipzig und Berlin aufgetreten war und nach ihrer Heirat von ihrer Sängerinnenkarriere Abschied nahm und zur zentralen Gestalt der musikalischen Geselligkeiten in Leipzigs privaten Bürgerhäusern wurde.[31] Die Lieder op. 4 hat Ethel Smyth ihrer Mutter gewidmet, die, wie sie in ihren Memoiren beschreibt, nicht nur hochmusikalisch war, sondern auch sang – und insgeheim die Pläne ihrer Tochter, in Leipzig Musik zu studieren gegen den Widerstand des Vaters unterstützte.[32] Das Rätsel betrifft die Reihenfolge: Eine dem Lebenslauf entsprechende Chronologie ließe erwarten, dass Smyth ihrer erste Liedersammlung der Mutter und erst die zweite einer professionellen Sängerin widmet. Ein Blick auf die Autographe führt diesbezüglich zu einem inter-

---

Lena, aus dem Büchners Tanzlied stammt, wurde zwar 1836 in einem Almanach gedruckt und erschien 1850 in Büchners nachgelassenen Schriften. Es wurde jedoch erst 1895 in München uraufgeführt und war auch in Deutschland wenig bekannt. Vgl. Georg Büchner, *Werke und Briefe*, nach der historisch-kritischen Ausgabe von Werner R. Lehmann. Kommentiert von Karl Pörnbacher, Gerhard Schaub, Hans-Joachim Simm und Edda Ziegler, 3. Auflage 1981, S. 369.

[31] Zu Livia Frege vgl. Karlheinz Merkel, „„... so innig harmonierten hier Seele und Hülle ...'. Livia Virginia Frege (13.6.1818–22.8.1891)", in: *Waldstaßenviertel*, Nr. 13, 1998, S. 40–44.

[32] Vgl. Ethel Smyth, *Impressions that Remained*, Bd. 1, London 1919, S. 110 und 124.

essanten Befund: Hier ist die Liedersammlung op. 3 tatsächlich der Mutter gewidmet und erst die zweite Sammlung op. 4 Livia Frege.[33] Offensichtlich hat Smyth die Widmungen für den Druck geändert. Ihr Beweggrund könnte ein inhaltlicher gewesen sein, denn die zweite Sammlung enthält gleich drei Vertonungen von Gedichten, die entweder Kindheitsbilder heraufbeschwören oder in denen die Mutter explizit genannt wird; im letzten Lied *Nachtgedanken* („Es rauben Gedanken den Schlaf mir, o Mutter") nach Paul Heyse wird die Mutter als Adressatin des lyrischen Ichs sogar immer wieder direkt angesprochen. Die inhaltlich plausiblen Widmungen der gedruckten Sammlungen stellen nun gewissermaßen deren Reihenfolge in Frage: Müssten nicht die Lieder op. 4 den Liedern und Balladen op. 3 vorangehen? In dem Fall würden die beiden Lieder, die die tradierten Geschlechterrollen offensichtlich in Frage stellen, den Rahmen aller zehn Lieder bilden, das *Tanzlied* würde den Anfang und *Schön Rohtraut* den Schluss bilden. Die hinter solchen Überlegungen stehende Hypothese, dass die zehn Lieder op. 3 und 4 einen zyklischen Zusammenhang bilden und dass ihre Folge eine biographisch motivierte Geschichte erzählt, ist einigermaßen gewagt, und dies nicht nur, weil die Entstehungskontexte der Lieder weitestgehend im Dunkeln bleiben. Sowohl im Blick auf die angebotenen Subjektpositionen und auf Rezeptionswege jenseits der erzählerischen Hierarchien als auch bezogen auf die Frage, ob und wie Smyth die „rites de passages" der bürgerlichen Gesellschaft des 19. Jahrhunderts durch die Gattung des romantischen Klavierlieds hindurch transformiert, erweist sich diese Hypothese jedoch als ausgesprochen interessante Versuchsanordnung. Dies gilt insbesondere, wenn man die Erwähungen der Ballade *Schön Rohtraut* in Smyths Memoirenbänden als Parallellektüre hinzuzieht.

Schön Rohtraut ...

Zumindest für die Ballade *Schön Rohtraut* liefern die beiden Bände von Smyths *Impressions That Remained* den Nachweis, dass sie lange vor dem Druck der Lieder 1886 und sogar noch vor den Leipziger Studienjahren in England entstanden ist. Ob und wieweit dies auch für die anderen Lieder gilt, ist nicht belegt. Es ist jedoch anzunehmen, dass Smyth nicht nur ein einziges Lied mit nach Leipzig brachte und dass weitere der Lieder bereits Jahre vor der Drucklegung komponiert waren. Allerdings soll es im Folgenden gar nicht darum gehen, konkrete biographische Kontexte der Entstehungs- oder Aufführungssituationen der Lieder zu finden. Abgesehen

---

[33] GB-Lb, Add 46861 Ethel Smyth, *Early Compositions and Sketches*, fols. 47r und 58r.

davon, dass auf Smyths Schriften in Datierungsfragen wenig Verlass ist,[34] sind Memoirenbände nicht als Dokumente „biographischer Wahrheit" sondern als Produkte von Identitätskonstruktionen zu lesen.[35] Gerade einer Lektüre, die dessen gewahr ist, erschließen sich jedoch interessante narrative Parallelen zu den Liedern und Balladen op. 3 und 4, die dann ebenfalls als Mittel einer spezifischen Ich-Konstruktion erscheinen. So wirken Smyths Erwähnungen der Ballade *Schön Rohtraut* nicht nur wie ein wiederkehrendes Motiv, das ihren „Weg nach Leipzig" gewissermaßen als „Travestie" eines normativen Übergangsritus kennzeichnet, sondern verbinden sich darüber hinaus mit weiteren Topoi, die auch in den Liedern und Balladen zentral sind.

Die erste Erwähnung von *Schön Rohtraut* befindet sich im letzten Kapitel des ersten Teils von *Impressions that Remained*, dessen Hauptthema Smyths endgültige Durchsetzung des Musikstudiums in Leipzig ist. Das Kapitel beginnt mit einem Rückbezug auf das vorhergehende, in dem Smyth ausführlich die Beschäftigungen einer „höheren Tochter" im heiratsfähigen Alter schildert: Besuche von befreundeten Familien und Bälle, deren eigentlicher Sinn weniger das Tanzvergnügen als der Heiratsmarkt ist. Darüber hinaus geht es um die Geschichte ihrer verunglückten Verlobung mit dem Bruder von Oscar Wilde, die für sich genommen schon wie die bewusste Travestie eines Übergangsritus wirkt.[36] „In spite of these social perturbations for I won't quite call them pleasures", so kommentiert Smyth diese Unternehmungen, "music ran her course more or less fitfully."[37] In der Passage, in die sie die Entstehung der Ballade *Schön Rohtraut* einflicht, greift sie die Motive „Tanz/Bälle", „Heirat" – bezogen auf die verheirateten Schwestern – auf und fügt diesen gewissermaßen als „Kontrapunkt" und als Zeichen für ihr unangepasstes Verhalten das des (wilden) Reitens bzw. Jagens hinzu.[38] Sie schließt mit einem Bekenntnis zu ihrem „Coming Out"[39] als professionelle Musikerin:

[34] Vgl. hierzu Barbara Eichner, „Love, Death and the Sea: Ethel Smyth's *Three Moods of the Sea* (1913) and Other Water Music", unveröffentlicher Vortrag beim Symposion *Ethel Smyth and her Generation* am 28. November 2008 in Oxford.
[35] Vgl. hierzu den Beitrag von Melanie Unseld in diesem Band.
[36] Die Verlobung fand während einer zufälligerweise gemeinsam unternommenen Eisenbahnfahrt statt. Willie Wilde brach dabei mit seinem provisorischen Sitzmöbel, einer Keksdose, auf der er seiner Auserwählten zu Füßen saß, zusammen. Obwohl Ethel Smyth, wie sie versichert, in ihn nicht verliebter gewesen sei als in den Eisenbahnmaschinisten, ging sie auf seinen Antrag ein, löste die Verlobung jedoch kurze Zeit später wieder auf. Vgl. Smyth, *Impressions*, Bd. 1, S. 115–117.
[37] Ebd., S. 121.
[38] Das Bild des wilden Reitens dient in Smyths Erinnerungen mehrfach der Illustration ihres unangepassten Verhaltens als Frau bzw. Mädchen. Vgl. hierzu auch den Beitrag von Melanie Unseld in diesem Band.
[39] Ethel Smyth verwendet den Begriff „Coming Out" im Zusammenhang mit den

„Of course too there were visits to the married sisters. While staying with Alice and Harry Davidson in Edinburgh I wrote the ballad 'Schön Rohtraut' with which I was soon to sing myself into musical circles at Leipzig – also went to balls, and was entranced by what I had never seen before, reels danced in costume and to perfection. On the way home I stayed with Mary and Charlie Hunter in Northumberland, going out hunting on the only animal that could be raised for me – a huge and heavy animal that drew old Mr. Hunter's coal cart, and was supposed never to have jumped a fence in its life. On that day it got over or through a good many – one could hardly call it jumping – and I enjoyed myself immensely. But all the time the conviction grew and grew that nothing was any good save one thing, and that go to Leipzig I must."[40]

Integriert in das Kapitel, in dem zusammen mit dem Besuch von Brahms in Leipzig erstmals Heinrich und Elisabeth von Herzogenberg genannt werden, befindet sich auch die zweite Erwähnung der Ballade an einer für Smyths Selbsterzählung ihres musikalischen Werdegangs gewichtigen Stelle. Wie schon die erste bezeichnet auch diese einen Übergang: Sie beschließt die Geschichte ihres Umzugs in ein möbliertes Zimmer, der der ungläubigen Familie in England klar machte, dass der Aufenthalt in Leipzig nicht nur eine Grille war. Dies geht erneut mit einer Bekräftigung sowohl ihres unangepassten und freiheitsliebenden Charakters als auch des gewählten Weges als Musikerin einher, wobei Smyth als Möglichkeit der Legitimierung nach außen – etwa durch ihre Mentorin und Nachbarin – auch ihre englische Nationalität ins Spiel bringt. Am Ende erhält sie ein Geschenk, das nicht nur ihre Person mit der Titelheldin ihrer Ballade identifiziert, sondern auch die Ballade selbst zum Bestandteil eines Initiationsrituals macht:

"It was of course quite unusual for girls of my class either to go to restaurants or walk about the streets alone at night, and at first friends used to implore me to let a servant see me home; but neither that nor any other

Lebensbeschreibungen ihrer Schwestern als Bezeichnung für den Eintritt ins gesellschaftliche Leben, vgl. z. B. Smyth, *Impressions*, Bd. 1, S. 78. In der Beschreibung ihres eigenen Lebenswegs lässt er sich auch auf das Offenlegen ihrer Leipziger Pläne beziehen: "Soon after this adventure [gemeint ist die Verlobung, C.B.] [...] I came out, but cannot remember what my then frame of mind was. I had never dreamed of putting through my musical plans till I should be really grown up – that would have been too unreasonable – nor, as I said, did there seem any need for special hurry. So I suppose I thought it well to take a look at the world of real balls and other festivities for which I was now qualified." Smyth, *Impressions*, Bd. 1, S. 117.

[40] Ebd., S. 122f.

curtailment of my liberty would I permit. [...] Reflecting on it all I am astonished to think how calmly, on the whole, my Mentor, now my neighbour [Fr. Prof. Brockhaus, CB], took my proceedings. [...] Moreover she was clever enough to see that though the 'nice people', by way of explaining their indulgence to her *protégée*, were for ever reminding each other feverishly that I was English [...], as a matter of fact I met with more than tolerance, and but for the circumstance that nothing really counted for me but my work, should have been in a fair way to become terribly spoiled. My little song 'Rohtraut', sung with a strong English accent, had a great success everywhere, and the Brockhaus boys presented me with a black velvet student's cap lined with red silk, round which was embroidered in gold and scarlet the music and words of the first line. I still have this treasure, which moths have respected, and of course adored the music-ridden German nation more than ever."[41]

Die folgenden beiden Erwähnungen befinden sich in Briefen an die Mutter im Appendix zum ersten Leipziger Winter bzw. zu den Jahren 1878–1881. Im Brief vom 12. August 1877 berichtet Smyth von Georg Henschels Lob ihrer Lieder und ihres kompositorischen Talents und anschließend vom Besuch eines musikalischen Nachmittags, bei dem sie aufgefordert wird, ihre Lieder vorzutragen. Auch hier wird die Ballade mit einem Initiationsritual verbunden:

"Of course Henschel was there and several other musicians, and I was asked to sing some things of mine. Mother! I wish you had been there. They were astonished, they all came round and said it was ‚merkwuerdig, wundervoll', and all the afternoon, when Henschel was strumming, as *he* only can strum, between the songs, he kept on coming back to the modulation at 'Schweig still, mein Herz' in 'Rohtraut', which pleased him hugely. Afterwards, when we still were all supping, our host proposed the health of the artists and coupled with the name 'of one who has but lately come among us and whom we hope to keep,' and once again I was fêted, and oh I wish you had been there! [...] The greatest musical genius I know has seen my work and so to speak has given his blessing, and it is well with me ...!"[42]

[41] Ebd., S. 182f.
[42] Ebd., S. 213. Der Diktion nach zu urteilen, dürfte Smyth mit dem Ausdruck „the greatest musica genius" auf Brahms anspielen. Ein eindeutiger Bezug ist in dem Brief jedoch nicht gegeben. Ihre erste Begegnung mit Brahms war durch Henschel vermittelt. Vgl. hierzu Smyth, *Impressions*, Bd. 1, S. 179f.

Diese Initiation stellt Smyth der eigentlich für eine Tochter aus gutem Hause vorgesehenen unmittelbar gegenüber. Denn in dem hierauf folgenden Brief erklärt sie ihrer Mutter, sie würde jeden Heiratsantrag – selbst den von Brahms – ausschlagen, um ihre musikalische Zukunft nicht zu gefährden.[43] Die vierte und letzte Erwähnung der Ballade schließlich steht im Kontext von Clara Schumanns Künstlerinnenjubiläum im Herbst 1878, das Ethel Smyth in Leipzig miterlebte. Sie imaginiert sich dabei in ihr eigenes Lied hinein, identifiziert sich jedoch nicht – wie es zuvor die Söhne ihrer Mentorin taten – mit ihrer Titelheldin, sondern mit dem Knaben. Ihr Gegenüber ist die berühmteste professionelle Musikerin, die sie persönlich kannte. Die Umdeutung der vorgesehenen „rites des passages" zur Initiation in die Berufswelt der Musikerin verbindet sich hier mit einer Travestie der Geschlechterrolle:

"At this minute up came Lisl [Elisabeth von Herzogenberg] and put her arm round me and said: 'Dieses ist mein Pflegekind!' Frau S[chumann] said, 'Wir waren Nachbarn im Concert aber da wollten Sie gar nichts von mir wissen.' Lisl said, 'sagen Sie dass [sic!] ja nicht! Ethel war viel zu bescheiden Sie *dort* anzusprechen.' Frau S[chumann] was so dear, said she hoped she would see me again, and I kissed her hand, feeling rather like the page-boy in Rohtraut – 'Ihr tausend Blaetter im Walde wisst ich habe schön Rohtraut's Mund gekuesst!' When Brahms comes in January I hope to see more of that grand women."[44]

... und das Sattelpferd

In insgesamt vier Liedern der beiden Sammlungen sind die Motive des Tanzes und des (wilden) Reitens bzw. des Jagens zentral, die in der ersten Erwähnung der Ballade alle eine Rolle spielen. Der umgekehrten Reihenfolge der beiden Sammlungen folgend sind dies das *Tanzlied*, *Nachtreiter*, *Der verirrte Jäger* und *Schön Rohtraut* selbst. Im Zusammenhang mit diesen vier Liedern möchte ich zunächst der Frage nachgehen, ob und wie Smyth mit den hiermit verbundenen musikalischen und auch literarischen Topoi spezifisch umgeht und ob dadurch Verbindungen zwischen den Liedern entstehen. Weiterhin möchte ich fragen, ob und wie Bedeutungsverschiebungen oder -überlagerungen sichtbar werden, die innerhalb der einzelnen Lieder, aber auch über diese hinausgehend für die Liedersammlungen Subjektpositionen jenseits normativer Geschlech-

---

[43] Ebd., S. 215. Der Brief ist zitiert im Beitrag von Amanda Harris in diesem Band.
[44] Smyth, *Impressions*, Bd. 2, London 1919, S. 36f.

terbilder anbieten und durch die narrativen Hierarchien hindurch Raum für nicht-normatives Begehren schaffen.

Das erste Lied, das *Tanzlied*, folgt, wie schon erwähnt, einem Gedicht, das vor dem Hintergrund der zu seiner Entstehungszeit geltenden Geschlechterbilder vor allem aufgrund der Einbeziehung körperpsychologischer Aspekte ausgesprochen „modern" wirkt. Es entstammt der dritten Szene des ersten Aktes aus Büchners *Leonce und Lena* und wird dort von Rosetta, der Geliebten des Prinzen Leonce und Gegenfigur zu Lena, gesungen, die sich an ihren durch den erotisierenden Blick von außen fragmentierten Körper wendet: an die Füße, die tanzen, die Wangen, die glühen und die Augen, die im Strahl der Kerzen blitzen sollen. Jede Strophe verweist auf den Tod als einzige Ausflucht aus dieser Lage. Entsprechend dieser Groteske eines Tanzes komponiert Smyth ein sehr „gebrochenes" Tanzlied. Am deutlichsten ist dies zunächst im Zusammenhang mit Rhythmus und Metrik: Bereits im Klaviervorspiel wird der in den 6/8-Takt integrierte Walzer-Rhythmus von Irregularitäten der Melodie begleitet. So bricht die weit ausholende und durchaus tänzerische erste Melodiephrase des Vorspiels in der Mitte des dritten Taktes unvermittelt ab, während der bloße Walzerrhythmus für eineinhalb Takte in die rechte Hand wandert. Mit dem zweiten Einsatz der Singstimme (T. 14) mutiert die Sechzehntelbewegung, die der Melodie zu Beginn gerade ihren schwungvollen Impuls gab, zu einem „Schluckaufsechzehntel", das den Melodiefluss unterbricht. In derselben oder leicht variierter Gestalt kehrt die Figur im Verlauf des Liedes wieder (T. 16–18, T. 24ff.) und initiiert eine ganze Reihe metrisch irregulärer Sechzehntel, die – wie bereits die umgekehrten Punktierungen der zweiten Melodiephrase des Klaviervorspiels (T. 7ff.) – die Melodie ins Stolpern bringen (vgl. hierzu und zum Folgenden Notenbeispiel 1).

Die metrischen Irregularitäten werden harmonisch unterstrichen. So beginnt das Lied quasi dominantisch über dem Grundton der Tonika. Diese wird im zweiten Takt zwar erreicht, von der Melodie aber zur Durchgangsstation auf dem Weg zur Doppeldominante erklärt. Der harmonisch gewissermaßen zu schwungvolle Anfang wird durch einen falschen Orgelpunkt gebremst: den Tonikagrundton, über dem der vorwärtsdrängende Dominantseptnonenakkord mit dem leeren Walzerrhythmus in der rechten Hand (T. 3 und 4) förmlich festzukleben scheint. Mit dem Einsatz der zweiten Melodiephrase in Takt 5 wird das *g* im Bass zwar endlich zum Grundton einer Dominante, zu einem richtigen Orgelpunkt also, dies jedoch nur, weil die „Tonika" als Dominantseptakkord erklingt und eine kurze Ausweichung zur Dur-Subdominante einleitet. Die wiederkehrenden Bordunbässe – wie schon eingangs der falsche Orgelpunkt – erzeugen zusammen mit den Vorschlägen in der linken Hand zu Beginn der ersten und dritten Liedstrophe einen szenisch anmutenden Effekt:

Schön Rohtraut und das Sattelpferd

Notenbeispiel 1: *Tanzlied*, T. 1–22

Sie erwecken den Eindruck, als spiele eine volkstümliche und nicht immer ganz sattelfeste Kapelle zum Tanz auf. Musikalische Zwistigkeiten wie zwischen dem Vorwärtsdrängen des verkürzten Dominantseptnonenakkord und der Stagnation auf dem Tonikagrundton in den Takten 3ff., verursachen dabei auch im weiteren Verlauf ein harmonisches Torkeln des Liedes: So wird die erste Liedstrophe zwar mit der ersten vollständigen Kadenz zur Tonika g-Moll eingeleitet, anschließend bleibt sie jedoch wie das Vorspiel zunächst zwischen Dominante und dem Tonikagrundton als Orgelpunkt hängen. Die Auflösung der Dominante erfolgt mit dem Einsatz der zweiten Melodiephrase nicht zur Tonika, sondern zur Tonikaparallele. Diese erklingt aber als Dominantseptakkord über einem nun korrekten Orgelpunkt, der am Phrasenende auch erwartungsgemäß mit einem Quintfall aufgelöst wird. Allerdings erklingt dazu die „falsche" Harmonie: nicht Es-Dur oder es-Moll, sondern c-Moll – mit einer zusätzlich irritierenden Sexte. Der Versuch einer Kadenz zur Tonikaparallele wird in der Überleitung zur letzten Melodiephrase wiederholt; er endet jedoch – passend zum Text, in dem hier das lyrische Ich erstmals die Todessehnsucht ausspricht – mit der Variante es-Moll. Der Beginn der zweiten Strophe ist anschließend nicht nur charakteristisch für die metrischen Irritationen, er ist auch dramaturgisch interessant. Gegenüber der ersten Strophe setzt die Singstimme hier um einen halben Takt verschoben, in der Taktmitte, ein.

Die ersten anderthalb Takte des Vorspiels erklingen zuvor leicht modifiziert als Zwischenspiel, so dass die Eingangsmelodie der rechten Hand, die im Vor-

Notenbeispiel 2: *Tanzlied*, T. 22–29

spiel in den leeren Walzerrhythmus mündete, nun den Anfangsimpuls für den Einsatz der Gesangsstimme gibt. Rückwirkend erweckt dies den Anschein, als hätte die Sängerin zu Beginn des Liedes ihren Einsatz verpasst bzw. – bezogen auf die folgende, den Liedbeginn wieder aufnehmende dritte Strophe – als verweigere sie diesen. Die Tänzerin, so scheint es, tanzt nur widerstrebend, sie lässt die Impulse der Tanzkapelle ins Leere laufen. Dieser Zwist zwischen Sängerin und Klavier – Tänzerin und Tanzkapelle – bestimmt auch den weiteren Verlauf der zweiten Strophe. So wirkt die Singstimme mit ihren Tonrepetitionen im Anschluss an die schwungvolle Melodie des Klaviers ausgesprochen müde, während umgekehrt die Sechzehntelsprünge auf dem jeweils zweiten Achtel des Walzerrhythmus zusammen mit den chromatischen Rückungen vorwärts drängen (vgl. Notenbeispiel 2).

Im Vergleich zum *Tanzlied* kommt das Lied *Nachtreiter,* das auch der musikalischen Illustration der in *Impressions that remained* beschriebenen wilden Reitvergnügen dienen könnte, leichtfüßig und fast tänzerisch daher. Dabei meint man einige Elemente aus dem *Tanzlied*, wie beispielsweise die nachschlagenden Sechzehntel, wiederzuerkennen, die hier im geraden Takt jedoch den gegenteiligen Effekt haben. Sie bringen das Lied nicht aus dem Fluss, sondern sorgen vielmehr für den vorwärtstreibenden Impuls, wie gerade am Ende des Vorspiels deutlich wird, wo sie sich in eine Sechzehntelkette auflösen und den Einsatz der Singstimme vorbereiten (vgl. Notenbeispiel 3).

Notenbeispiel 3: *Nachtreiter,* T. 1–7

Begleitung und Singstimme – Pferd und Reiter(in), wenn man eine Analogie zum *Tanzlied* herstellt – befinden sich im Einklang und auch der Topos des Reiterliedes wird, anders als der des Tanzliedes, erfüllt, wobei Smyth zwei verschiedenen Varianten des Reiterliedes miteinander verbindet: Die Rahmenstrophen haben in ihrer einfachen Rhythmik und Harmonik anfangs durchaus Kinderliedcharakter, während der Mittelteil zum Text der vierten Gedichtstrophe eher an musikalische Ritte erwachsener Reiter erinnert (vgl. Notenbeispiel 4).

Notenbeispiel 4: *Nachtreiter*, T. 16–20

Sollten Brahms' Lieder nach Texten von Klaus Groth Smyths Auswahl des zugrunde liegenden Gedichtes inspiriert haben, so fällt hinsichtlich des Motivs der Kindheit bzw. Jugend, das auch in Brahms Groth-Vertonungen bis 1877 zentral ist, ein Gegensatz auf: Während die Kindheit in Brahms' Vertonungen der Gedichte seines Freundes Klaus Groth dem romantischen Topos entsprechend als versunkenes Land der Sehnsucht erscheint, in das zurückzukehren unmöglich ist,[45] werden wir in Smyths Lied *Nachtreiter* ungestüm in den Bann der geschilderten Situation gezogen. Zwar handelt es sich hierbei gleichfalls um die Imagination eines Wunsches („Hätt ich ein Sattelpferd"), doch versetzt sich das lyrische Ich so lebhaft in diesen hinein, dass es im Mittelteil mit dem erdachten Ross wie mit den Zuhörenden durch Sturm und Wind reitet und zweifellos an seinem Ziel ankommt, beim „liebsten Kind". Melancholie oder Sehnsucht haben keinen Platz. Anders verhält es sich in Eichendorffs Ballade *Der verirrte Jäger*, in der annähernd dieselbe Szenerie unter umgekehrten Vorzeichen verhandelt wird. Der Jäger erreicht sein Ziel nie, das Hirschlein als Sinnbild der Geliebten erweist sich als Projektion der eigenen Wünsche und führt ihn in die Irre.[46] Wie im *Tanzlied* befinden sich Gesangsstimme und Klavier miteinander im Zwiespalt; während aber im *Tanzlied* das lyrische Ich der Gesangsstimme selbst deutlichen Impulsen des Klaviers nur widerwillig zu folgen scheint, ist dem „Ich" der Gesangsstimme im „verirrten Jäger" umgekehrt eine energische Aktivität eigen, die vom Klavier mit recht unverhohlener Ironie kommentiert wird. So verrät die Begleitung von Anfang an, wie es um den Jäger steht: Bereits das Klavierecho der Gesangsmelodie (T. 7, T. 10, T. 15) ist nicht nur ein naheliegende Gestaltungsmittel in einem Jagdlied, sondern weist auch darauf hin, dass der Jäger einem Trugbild folgt. Anstelle eines Gegenübers hört er nur seine eigene Stimme. Dies zeigt sich besonders eindrücklich der Mitte der ersten Strophe, wo das Klavier das Echo der Gesangsstimme mit harmonisch großer Geste fortspinnt und am Ende in den verfremdeten Hornruf des Jägers – als Tritonus integriert in einen Dominantseptnonenakkord

---

45 Bei den bis 1877 erschienenen Groth-Vertonungen von Johannes Brahms handelt es sich um das *Regenlied* („Walle Regen, walle nieder") und *Nachklang* („Regentropfen aus dem Bäumen"), op. 59, 3 und 4, sowie „Mein wundes Herz" und „Dein blaues Auge", op. 59, 7 und 8 (Erstausgabe Leipzig: Rieter 1873) und um die drei *Heimweh*-Lieder („Wie traulich war das Fleckchen", „O wüsst' ich doch den Weg zurück" und „Ich sah als Knabe Blumen blühn") op. 63, Nr. 7–9 (Erstausgabe Leipzig: Peters 1874). Weiter Groth-Vertonungen Brahms' erschienen zwischen 1886 und 1888 (Komme bald, op. 97,5 „Wie Melodien zieht es mir" op. 105, 1 und „Es hing der Reif im Lindenbaum" op. 106, 3).

46 In Eichendorffs Roman *Ahnung und Gegenwart*, in dem das Gedicht zuerst erschien, verweist der Protagonist Rudolf darauf, dass seine Geliebte ihn verlassen und das Lied vom „verirrten Jäger" gesungen habe. Das verfolgte Wild als Sinnbild der Geliebten ist schon im Volkslied verbreitet. Vgl. den Kommentar zu dem Gedicht in: Joseph von Eichendorff, *Sämtliche Werke*. Historisch-kritische Ausgabe, hrsg. von Hermann Kunisch und Helmuth Koopmann, Bd. 1, 2 *Gedichte* (Teilband: Kommentar), hrsg. von Harry Fröhlich, Berlin/Köln 1994, S. 669.

– überleitet (T. 9–11). Am Strophenende erweist sich dies als Vorwegnahme der letzten Gesangsphrase, in der der Jäger seinen Wunsch ausspricht („muss ewig nach ihm gehn"). Nicht zuletzt, weil diese Geste quasi im Kreis, nämlich zurück zur Anfangsphrase verläuft, verstärkt sich der Eindruck, das Klavier wisse schon hier, dass der Jäger in die Irre geht.

Notenbeispiel 5: *Der verirrte Jäger*, T. 1–14

Umso übertriebener erscheint dann die zweite Strophe, in der der Hornruf mit entsprechendem Text in die Gesangsstimme wandert, der Jäger sozusagen mit erhobener Stimme, in der Tonart der Dur-Subdominante, ins Horn bläst – und auch noch Verstärkung anfordert (vgl. Notenbeispiel 6).

Notenbeispiel 6: *Der verirrte Jäger*, T. 20–23 (Beginn der 2. Strophe)

Zu seiner musikalischen Charakterisierung trägt weiterhin auch die Überleitung zur folgenden dritten Strophe bei: In der abfallenden Triolenkette meint man ihn fröhlich trällernd in sein Verderben laufen zu sehen und auch hier ist das Klavier ihm wieder voraus: Die Figur nimmt die Überleitung zur zweiten Strophenhälfte und damit zugleich zur zweiten Liedhälfte vorweg, in der das Hirschlein die Führung übernimmt („Das Hirschlein führt den Jägersmann") und der Jäger endgültig seiner Schimäre aufsitzt. Trotz seines blinden Pathos und seiner Naivität wird der Jäger nicht der Lächerlichkeit preisgegeben. In der vierten Strophe, in der er sich in jeder Beziehung verirrt hat (in Cis-Dur hat er auch seine bislang für alle Strophen charakteristische Melodie verloren), erklingt im Anschluss an die unheimlichen Tremoli im Klavier ein letztes Mal sein Hornruf – dieses Mal jedoch so zaghaft, dass die sonst mit ihm demonstrierte übersteigerte Selbstsicherheit relativiert wird. Auch sein Wunsch selbst, für den gewissermaßen seine in dem Lied fast leitmotivisch wiederkehrende Eingangsmelodie steht, wirkt keineswegs lächerlich. In ihrer Mollfärbung und zugleich ihrem rüstigen – wo sie in Dur erklingt, sogar ausgesprochen munteren – Vorwärtsschreiten, das durch die Melismen dann wiederum gebrochen wird, wirkt die Melodie vielmehr auf kleinstem Raum sehr differenziert. Ironisiert wird jedoch das aufgesetzte Pathos, mit dem der Jäger seinem Trugbild folgt. Insbesondere wenn man das folgende und letzte Lied des „Viererzyklus" zum Vergleich heranzieht, erscheint dies als Dekonstruktion sowohl eines der Geschlechterordnung konformen literarischen und musikalischen Topos als auch eines übertrieben selbstbewussten männlichen Ichs. Denn die Ballade *Schön Rohtraut* verhandelt eine überraschend verwandte Szene: Auch hier finden die entscheidenden Ereignisse im Wald statt, es wird gejagt. Aber es hat eine wundersame Verwandlung stattgefunden: An die Stelle des Hirschleins, das als Sinnbild der Geliebten gejagt wird, tritt die Königstochter Schön Rohtraut, die lieber selbst auf die Jagd geht. Gejagt wird folglich gemeinsam. Statt der Echos, die die Stimme des Jägers zurückwarfen, wird nun miteinander gesprochen: *Schön Rohtraut* ist ein Dialoglied. Und anders als der erwachsene Jäger erreicht der Knabe sein Ziel: einen Kuss seiner Angebeteten. Er erreicht es gerade, weil er nicht seiner eigenen Projektion nachläuft, sondern Fremdes auszuhalten versteht und seine Angst überwindet. Gegen jedes musikalische Pathos spricht schon die schlichte äußere Gestalt der Ballade: Als einziges der vier Lieder handelt es sich um ein einfaches Strophenlied, während umgekehrt *Der verirrte Jäger* formal das komplexeste ist und im ersten Moment wie ein durchkomponiertes Lied erscheint. Dennoch scheint nicht nur die Szenerie des „verirrten Jägers", sondern auch dessen Leitmotiv in *Schön Rohtraut* verwandelt wiederzukehren. Zwar mag es noch der volksliedhaften Melodik der beiden Balladen geschuldet sein, dass beide Melodien mit einem Quartsprung zum Tonikagrundton beginnen und dann aufwärts fortschreiten, die auffallende Ähnlichkeit auch hinsichtlich des weiteren Melodieaufbaus lässt jedoch Zweifel daran aufkommen, dass es sich hierbei um puren Zufall handelt (siehe Notenbeispiel 7, T. 1–6).

Anknüpfungspunkt für *Schön Rohtraut* bildet offenbar gerade die zweite Strophe des „verirrten Jägers", in der die Melodie in der Tonart der Unterquinte in Dur erklingt und in das Hornmotiv übergeht. Nach Erreichen der Terz schreitet die Melodie in *Schön Rohtraut* im Verhältnis zu der des Jägers in Umkehrung weiter. Während die Jägermelodie über das Melisma zum Grundton zurückkehrt, springt die Melodie in *Schön Rohtraut* aufwärts zur Quinte, um anschließend ebenso wie jene in ein „Rufmotiv" überzugehen, das zentral aus einem Quartsprung zum Tonikagrundton gebildet ist. An die Stelle des Hornrufs, der in der ersten Strophe des „verirrten Jägers" in den Klavierechos als „innere Stimme" des lyrischen Ichs bereits vorweggenommen wurde, und also deutlich machte, dass der Jäger mit seiner Wunschprojektion alleine bleibt, tritt hier der Name des Gegenübers.

Auch Elemente aus den anderen beiden Liedern scheinen in der Ballade *Schön Rohtraut* wiederzukehren: So ist die Begleitfigur zu Beginn mit der des *Nachtreiters* verwandt. Wie im *Tanzlied* sind auch in *Schön Rohtraut* Orgelpunkte charakteristisch (T. 10–11 und T. 13–15); anders als dort dienen sie jedoch nicht dazu, den Zwiespalt zwischen Begleitung und Sängerin zu verstärken oder das Lied harmonisch „aus dem Takt" zu bringen, sondern sie unterstreichen eher den dramaturgischen Spannungsverlauf und enthalten – wie sich zeigt – dabei sogar einen musikalischen Kommentar zum Verhältnis der beiden Protagonisten. Sogar die „Stolperfigur" aus dem *Tanzlied* meint man wiederzuerkennen: als Jauchzer im Klavier in höchster Lage (T. 5 und 6, vgl. Notenbeispiel 7), während das „Gesangs-Ich" den Namen „Schön Rohtraut" ausspricht.

Notenbeispiel 7: *Schön Rohtraut*, 1. Strophe

Dieser Klavierjauchzer ist nur das erste Beispiel dafür, wie Smyth im Rahmen der äußerlichen Schlichtheit eines Strophenliedes eine erstaunlich differenzierte Charakterisierung der Personen gelingt: Das Lied beginnt schlicht im Wechsel von Tonika und Dominante, wobei in die ersten beiden Takte ein Hornquintenmotiv integriert ist, das als musikalisches Jagdmotiv eine ungleich gelassenere Entsprechung zum Hornruf des Jägers bildet. Der kleine Sprung, den die Melodie im zweiten Takt vollführt, entwickelt sich im fünften Takt der Klavierbegleitung zum nämlichen Jauchzer, der den ruhigen Fluss der Begleitung durcheinander bringt. Ähnlich wie in *Der verirrte Jäger* scheint das Klavier auch hier das „bewusste Ich" der Gesangsstimme zu kommentieren und sein Unbewusstes an die Oberfläche zu bringen: Während das Ich sich bezwingt, den Namen der Angebeteten ganz ruhig in tiefer Lage auszusprechen, lässt sich das Herz – in der Klavierstimme – ganz offensichtlich nicht kontrollieren und gerät aus dem Takt, und zwar in jeder Strophe aufs Neue, denn der Name „Schön Rohtraut" fungiert im Gedicht als Binnenrefrain. Bei der Frage nach dem unbotmäßigen Verhalten Rohtrauts („Was thut sie denn den ganzen Tag?") gerät auch das „bewusste Ich" der Gesangsstimme außer sich und erreicht binnen eines Taktes aus der tiefen Lage heraus in zwei Sprüngen den höchsten Ton der Melodie (T. 6/7). Harmonisch wird die Aufregung unterstrichen, denn während bislang fast ausschließlich Tonika und Dominante als einfache Dreiklänge sowie ein erster Dominantseptakkord beim Binnenrefrain zu hören waren, erklingt nun der Sekundakkord der Doppeldominante und anschließend die sehr spannungsreiche Version eines Dominantseptakkordes mit Nonenvorhalt. Während das Klavier zwischen dem zweiten und dritten Gedichtvers noch eine minimale Zäsur vorsieht, gehen Frage („was thut sie …?"), Erläuterung („da sie nicht spinnen und nähen mag") und Antwort („thut fischen und jagen!") in der Gesangsstimme fast überhastet ineinander über, wobei die harmonische Gestaltung wiederum bemerkenswert ist. Das Ende der zweiten Teilphrase, in der das nicht-normative Verhalten Rohtrauts beschrieben wird, schließt mit einer Kadenz zur Tonikaparallele, die aufgrund eines durchgehaltenen Orgelpunktes über ihrer Quinte erklingt (T. 10). Während man in dieser plötzlichen Wendung nach Moll Rohtrauts Unlust angesichts der ihr vermeintlich angemessenen Tätigkeiten hören mag, ist der folgende harmonisch unvermittelte verkürzte Dominantseptakkord über *a* wohl eher mit der Aufregung des Ichs der Gesangsstimme, des Knaben, in Verbindung zu bringen. Umso erstaunlicher ist dann das fast choralartig anmutende Ende der Passage. Mit einem über die Doppeldominante mit vollständiger authentischer Kadenz erreichten Halbschluss löst sich auch endlich der spannungsgeladene Orgelpunkt (T. 11). Rohtrauts unbotmäßiges Verhalten wird dadurch gleichsam von einer sakralen Aura umgeben. Zugleich steht der Halbschluss wie ein

Doppelpunkt vor dem folgenden Abschnitt, der textlich den geheimen Wünschen des lyrischen Ichs (in Strophe 1 und 2) sowie ihrer Erfüllung (in Strophe 3 und 4) gewidmet ist. Harmonisch bewegt sich das Lied weiter im Bereich von Dominante und Doppeldominante – letztere, klanglich der Ungeheuerlichkeit der ausgesprochenen Wünsche entsprechend, als verkürzter Dominantseptnonenakkord – und steht wie auch die vorausgehende Passage über einem Orgelpunkt, nun aber gewissermaßen dem „richtigen" – der Dominante. Die anschließende Rückkehr zur Tonika über den Refrain „Schweig still, mein Herz" knüpft an den „sakralen Ton" der Takte 11 und 12 an, mit dem Rohtrauts unkonforme Vorlieben gutgeheißen wurde, und enthält auch einen Anklang an die kurze Ausweichung nach Moll in Takt 10. Über die Molltonika wird in der Mitte des Refrains (T. 17/18) ein Trugschluss in Ces-Dur erreicht, aus dem der Septnonenakkord der Doppeldominante von Es-Dur, der zuvor für die innere Aufregung des Ichs der Gesangsstimme stand, auf wunderbar einfache Weise über eine vollständige authentische Kadenz zur Tonika – und dem entspannten Liedbeginn – zurückführt (vgl. Notenbeispiel 7).

„Es wandelt, was wir schauen"

Dreimal verwandelt sich dasselbe Bild: Aus dem imaginierten Ritt des jugendlichen Nachtreiters zum „liebsten Kind" wird der „wirkliche" Ritt des erwachsenen und geschlechtsrollenkonformen Jägers, der der Schimäre seiner Geliebten nachreitet, aus diesem wieder der gemeinsame Ritt des Knaben mit der ganz und gar nicht geschlechtsrollenkonformen „Schön Rohtraut". Das *Tanzlied* scheint hiermit nur durch den Gegensatz der Szenerie verbunden zu sein. Die Einbeziehung der übrigen Lieder stellt jedoch nicht nur eine Verbindung zwischen dem *Tanzlied* und dem *Nachtreiter* her, sondern macht auch für jede Sammlung ein übergreifendes Thema und weiterhin auch Symmetrien sichtbar, die die Idee eines beide Sammlungen umfassenden Zyklus stützen. Ähnlich wie bei den drei Szenerien des Reitens/Jagens werden dabei wiederkehrende Motive Verwandlungsprozessen unterworfen, die sowohl den Sinngehalt der Topoi und die Subjektpositionen der Lieder als auch die normativen Geschlechtsidentitäten verschieben. Bei umgekehrter Reihenfolge der beiden Sammlungen sind die vier Lieder, für die die Topoi des Tanzes bzw. des Reitens/Jagens zentral sind, ganz regelmäßig über die zehn Lieder verteilt; jeweils zwei der übrigen Lieder befinden sich zwischen den bisher besprochenen Liedern *Tanzlied*, *Nachtreiter*, *Der verirrte Jäger* und *Schön Rohtraut*. Innerhalb jeder Sammlung sind dabei jeweils eine Gruppe von zwei und eine Gruppe von drei Liedern dramaturgisch oder aufgrund der Übernahme literarischer Motive enger miteinander verbunden. Die Liedersammlung op. 4 beginnt mit einem Paar: Das *Schlummerlied* greift das Motiv des Schlafes aus der letzten Gedichtzeile des *Tanzliedes* auf, so dass der „ewige Schlaf" als Bild für den Wunsch zu Sterben, den das lyrische Ich dort in seiner Adressierung an die Augen ausspricht („Und schlieft im Dunkeln lieber aus von Euren Schmerzen"), sich in den behüteten Schlaf des Kindes im Arm der Mutter verwandelt: „O schlummre süß, o schlummre lind ..." lautet der erste Vers. Was in der Abfolge der beiden Lieder wie eine Umdeutung des Todeswunsches in einen regressiven Rückzugswunsch erscheint, beruht jedoch, wie sich im Verlauf des Liedes zeigt, auf der für die Liebeslyrik des 19. Jahrhunderts typischen Adressierung der Geliebten als „Kind". Obwohl der Geschlechterordnung dieser Zeit entsprechend das lyrische Ich folglich männlich, das Gegenüber weiblich zu denken ist, changiert die Geschlechtsidentität durch das Bild, mit dem das lyrische Ich sich in die Rolle der schützenden Mutter imaginiert. Wenn man hier erneut Smyths Memoirenbände und ihre Beschreibungen der Freundschaft zu Elisabeth von Herzogenberg als erotisierte Mutter-Kind-Beziehung hinzuzieht,[47] wird zugleich eine Verschiebung des heterosexualisierten Begehrens deutlich. Hierüber stellt sich eine Verbindung zum folgenden Lied her, denn die Ruhe im Arm der Mutter aus dem *Schlummerlied* verwandelt sich in dem Eichendorff-Lied *Mittagsruh* in einen Moment gleichermaßen beunruhigenden wie erkennenden Innehaltens, der auf dem Zenit eines geschäftigen Sommertages Unbewusstes an die Oberfläche treten lässt. *Mittagsruh* ist das erste einer Gruppe von drei Liedern, in denen es explizit um verborgene – im *Nachtreiter* auch offene – Wünsche oder Träume geht.[48] Der *Nachtreiter*, in dem der Wunsch durch die lebhafte Imagination des lyrischen Ichs quasi Realitätsgehalt bekommt, bildet dabei eine Achse, über die sich das mittägliche Gewahrwerden unbewusster Wünsche aus dem Eichendorff-Lied in der Heyse-Vertonung *Nachtgedanken* in einen nächtlichen Alptraum verwandelt. Über diese Gruppierung hinaus gibt es Motivverbindungen, die alle fünf Lieder wie ein Netzwerk miteinander verknüpfen und den Sinngehalt der literarischen Topoi verschieben. Im Lied *Mittagsruh* kehren im Zusammenhang mit den beunruhigenden Aspekten der unbewussten Wünsche erotisierte Bilder aus dem *Tanz-*

[47] Vgl. hierzu auch die oben zitierte Szene beim Jubiläumskonzert Clara Schumanns, in der Elisabeth von Herzogenberg Ethel Smyth als „ihr Pflegekind" vorstellt. Vgl. oben S. 13.
[48] In der Gegenüberstellung der beiden Lieder verschränkt Smyth zugleich die üblichen Zuschreibungen von Tag und Nacht und kehrt sie um: Üblicherweise steht die weiblich konnotierte Nacht für die unbewussten und verborgenen Wünsche, der Tag dagegen für Aktivität und Bewusstsein. Zu den Zuschreibungen und ihrer Geschichte vgl. Elisabeth Bronfen, *Tiefer als der Tag gedacht. Eine Kulturgeschichte der Nacht*, München 2008.

lied verwandelt wieder: So tritt an die Stelle des Kerzenscheins, in dem die Augen im *Tanzlied* blitzen müssen, hier das „schillernde Weben" und „Strahlen" „stiller Lust und tiefer Qualen". Aus der Hitze und „Schwüle", die vor allem die mittlere, die „heißen Wangen" ansprechende Strophe des *Tanzliedes* bestimmt, wird nun die „dunkelblaue Schwüle" des Mittags, in dem verborgene Lust und Qual „aus der unbewachten Brust" als „ewige Gefühle" verwandelt an die Oberfläche treten. Zu dem ausgesprochen kontemplativen Lied *Mittagsruh*, in dem das lyrische Ich explizit gar nicht genannt wird, bildet der *Nachtreiter* zwar einen Gegensatz, als Imagination eines Wunsches bleibt das Lied jedoch mit seinem Vorgänger verbunden: Aus der „stillen Lust" wird die wilde Lust des jugendlichen Reiters. Oder der Reiterin? Denn mit der Adressierung des geliebten Gegenübers als „Kind" knüpft der *Nachtreiter* an das *Schlummerlied* an, so dass die Geschlechterzuordnungen hier ebenfalls gegen die Norm changieren. Mit Traum, Schlaf, Lust und Qual sowie der Mutter, an die sich das lyrische Ich hier in jeder Strophe adressiert, kehren alle bedeutsamen Motive der vorangehenden Lieder im letzten Lied, *Nachtgedanken* wieder. Aus den „ewigen Gefühlen" und „unbewachten Wünschen" des Liedes *Mittagsruh*, die sich im *Nachtreiter* Raum schufen, sind nun nächtliche Schatten geworden, die das lyrische Ich in Alpträumen verfolgen. Die Ruhestätte im Arm der Mutter verwandelt sich in einen Kriegsschauplatz: „Es wird mein Bette dem Kampf zur Wiege/Dem Kriege, dem bösen Kriege zur friedlosen Stätte". Welcher Art das „Streben nach falschem Glücke" war, das das Gedicht als einzige Erklärung für den geschilderten Nachtmahr anbietet, bleibt offen. Dasselbe gilt für „die Geschichte" der Liedersammlung op. 4, als deren übergreifendes Thema auch über die letzten drei Lieder hinaus die Auseinandersetzung mit unbewussten Wünschen erscheint. Durch die Sinnverschiebungen der Topoi – wie etwa des Schlafes oder der Adressierung der Geliebten als Kind – wird dahinter auch ein Widerstreit (*Nachtgedanken*) zwischen dem nicht konformem Begehren des Imaginären – im Lied *Mittagsruh* sowie bei travestierten Geschlechterzuweisungen auch im *Schlummerlied* und im *Nachtreiter* – und den von Außen an das Ich herangetragenen Vorstellungen – im *Tanzlied* – erkennbar. Gegenüber dieser „modern" anmutenden Thematik erscheint die Liebe als Thema der Sammlung op. 3 für die Gattung des romantischen Klavierliedes ausgesprochen traditionell. Bei umgekehrter Reihenfolge der Sammlungen ergibt sich aus dem Zyklus aller zehn Lieder jedoch ein Hinweis auf das „falsche Glück", von dem im letzten Lied von op. 4 die Rede war – und sogar eine Korrektur. In den ersten drei Liedern von op. 3 geht es um die verlorene bzw. unerreichbare Liebe. Wie der *Nachtreiter* in op. 4 bildete hier *Der verirrte Jäger* die Mitte einer Dreiergruppe, über die die Szenerie des ersten Liedes sich verwandelt. Und ähnlich wie der Nachtreiter hebt sich auch *Der verirrte Jäger* von den umgebenden Liedern ab, anders als jener jedoch nicht durch die Suggestion eines höheren Realitätsgehaltes, sondern vielmehr durch seine Sinnbildlichkeit – während die anderen beiden Lieder das Thema unverklausuliert behandeln. Das dritte Lied *Bei einer Linde* kehrt dabei buchstäblich zur Szenerie des ersten Liedes zurück: Der „Baum dort vor dem Hause [...], wo wir gesessen haben", den das lyrische Ich im Eingangslied *Vom Berge* aus der Ferne betrachtet, rückt nun als gealterte Linde in den Mittelpunkt der Szene. Aus der gestorbenen Geliebten im ersten Lied wird im dritten Lied die verlorene Jugendliebe. Hierauf folgt das vierte Lied, *Es wandelt was wir schauen,* das in seinem kontemplativen Verhältnis zu den übrigen Liedern funktional dem Lied *Mittagsruh* aus op. 4 verwandt ist. Das lyrische Ich ist in einem die Zuhörenden ansprechenden „Wir" aufgehoben: „Wir müssen alle scheiden, von allem was uns lieb." Indem Ethel Smyth nur die ersten beiden Strophen des Gedichtes vertont und die eindeutig christlich konnotierten Strophen drei und vier weglässt,[49] wird es möglich, diese Aussage als Fazit zu den der vorausgegangenen Liedern zu verstehen. Im Verlauf der Sammlung op. 3 ist das vierte Lied seinem Titel gemäß jedoch selbst der Ort der Verwandlung – und verbindet sich auf diese Weise mit dem letzten Lied zu einer Zweiergruppe.[50] Denn aus der unerreichbaren wird in der Ballade *Schön Rohtraut* die gewonnene Liebe. Und wie die Parallellektüre der – fast 40 Jahre nach der Entstehung dieses Liedes erschienenen – Erinnerungen Ethel Smyths zeigt, travestiert der Kuss des Knaben nicht nur die normative Geschlechter-

[49] Das Gedicht entstammt dem Zyklus „Der Umkehrende" aus Eichendorffs *Geistlichen Liedern*. Zur vollständigen Textgestalt vgl. Eichendorff, *Sämtliche Werke*, hrsg. von Hermann Kunisch und Helmuth Koopmann, Bd. 1, Berlin/Köln 1994, S. 313f.

[50] Die Tonartenbeziehungen unterstützen die Dramaturgie, in der das vierte Lied aus op. 3 als Ort einer kontemplativen Besinnung die Verwandlung zum Ende herbeiführt: Das erste Lied *Vom Berge* steht in f-Moll und ist mit der folgenden Ballade *Der verirrte Jäger* (a-Moll) mediantisch verbunden, *Bei einer Linde* steht bezogen hierauf in der Tonart der Oberquinte und ist damit harmonisch – als Dominante des vorausgehenden Liedes – gewissermaßen „rückwärtsgewandt" – hin zur Gruppe der ersten drei Lieder. Der textlichen Zäsur zwischen dem dritten und dem vierten Lied entspricht auch ein Bruch in den Tonarten. Dabei verhält sich das c-Moll des betrachtenden Liedes *Es wandelt was wir schauen* zum vorausgehenden E-Dur harmonisch wie eine „Versunkenheitsepisode" – ein musikalischer Topos, der ebenfalls auf aus der Zeit herausgehobene metaphysische Betrachtung verweist (vgl. hierzu Bernhard S. Van der Linde, „Die Versunkenheitsepisode bei Beethoven", in: *Beethoven-Jahrbuch* 1973–77, hrsg. von Hans Schmidt und Martin Staehelin, Bonn: Beethovenhaus, S. 319–337). Die Ballade *Schön Rohtraut* verwandelt den Moll-Klang schließlich in seine Parallele Es-Dur.

ordnung. Es handelt sich zugleich um einen „travestierten Musenkuss": Hier küsst nicht die Muse den Künstler, sondern die angehende Künstlerin küsst ihre selbsterwählte Muse in Gestalt der berühmtesten Vertreterin ihrer Kunst.

Das Netzwerk aus musikalischen und textlichen Bezügen, die Bedeutungsverschiebungen literarischer Topoi wie musikalischer Motive initiieren – dies sei abschließend bemerkt – wird durch die vorgeschlagene „Versuchsanordnung" einer umgekehrten Reihenfolge der beiden Liedersammlungen nur deutlicher und fügt sich in eine Geschichte. Auch bei der gegebenen Reihenfolge bleibt es erhalten: dann mit dem „travestierten Musenkuss" im Zentrum.

Abstract

Schön Rohtraut und das Sattelpferd: the 'Lyrical and Biographical I' in Ethel Smyth's Early Lied Compositions

The term 'lyrical I' was introduced into musicological discourse by Carl Dahlhaus in the context of Beethoven reception. It served 'to save a hero's honour', since in defiance of the idea that discourse concerning musical masterpieces is to be free of the seamy sides of biography, programmatic and biographical traits were repeatedly being revealed in Beethoven's works. With reference to Ethel Smyth, however, the question of the 'lyrical and biographical I' has to be put much more fundamentally. How can a young Englishwoman, upon discovering around 1870 that her language was music, write herself as an artistic subject into a history for which a 'female I' does not exist, or at least does not *speak*? And how can she embark on this project in Germany, of all countries, where – at least since the establishment of the above-mentioned mode of Beethoven reception – musical genius was even more closely linked with the male sex than elsewhere? The question of the artistic self arises in a manner not unlike that posed today for artists from the formerly colonised countries. And – to express it through the title of a book by Salman Rushdie – Ethel Smyth's *imaginary homelands* seem to be rather complex ones.

Smyth's early songs and ballads, which – as far as can be proven from the scant evidence available on their genesis – were composed partially in England and partially in Germany, and which opened to her the doors of the Leipzig bourgeoisie with all its musical sociability, apparently pay tribute to German musical romanticism. But looking at (and listening to) them more closely reveals not only an unusual choice of texts but also some astonishing musical treatment of the well-known topoi and images of romantic poetry. A parallel reading of Smyth's memoirs *Impressions that Remained* and her early songs and ballads following the topoi of "dance" and of "riding and hunting" which emerge in both, leads to the thesis that the early songs and ballads are cyclical in design. As a cycle, they seem to reveal a narrative of Smyth's path to musical creativity, a self-narrative (self-construction) parallel to that found in her memoirs: using the given poetic and musical images and nonetheless in transformation of the gender-rules of her time, the composer tells her "own" story.

Pavel B. Jiracek
Empire zwischen den Zeilen. Eine postkoloniale Perspektive

> "Ideas, cultures, and histories can not seriously
> be understood or studied without their force,
> or more precisely their configurations of power, also being studied."[1]
> Edward Said

Das stolze Seereich Großbritannien, dessen einst weltumspannender Machtanspruch „Rule, Britannia! Britannia, rule the waves"[2] sich nicht nur militärisch niederschlug, sondern sich auch immer wieder bis in die Künste hinein seinen Weg ins soziokulturelle Geäst bahnte, war zu Lebzeiten Ethel Smyths noch immer auf einem Höhepunkt. Der britische Imperialismus mit seinem Kolonialismus und Orientalismus war eine treibende Kraft im alltäglichen Leben und mutet im Zusammenhang mit der Beschäftigung mit Werken und Taten derer, die innerhalb des Systems handelten, an wie der im Englischen sprichwörtliche Elefant im Zimmer, der zwar riesig groß ist und doch leicht übersehen wird.

Versucht man allerdings, sich aus einer westlichen Perspektive heraus insbesondere kolonialen Zusammenhängen zu nähern, läuft man leicht Gefahr, selbst zu einem sprichwörtlichen Elefanten zu werden – zu einem Elefanten im Porzellanladen, der auf vermintem Gebiet herumtrampelt, ohne dies zu beabsichtigen. Die Anmaßung, aus einer Position westlicher Hegemonie heraus über (oder für) Subalterne sprechen zu wollen – eine paternalistische Mission, deren „kolonialistisches Wohlwollen" das systematische Zum-Schweigen-Bringen der Subalternen verschleiert, das durch die Ordnung oder besser die Unordnung des eurozentrischen Diskurses entsteht[3] – birgt ähnlichen Zündstoff wie die Versuchung, unterschiedliche sozial-politische

---

[1] Edward Said, *Orientalism*, Harmondsworth 1978, S. 5.
[2] *Rule Britannia*, Gedicht von James Thomson (1700–1748), vertont durch Thomas Arne (1710–1778) für die Masque *Alfred* (1740)
[3] Gayatri Chakravorty Spivak, „Can the subaltern speak?", in: *Marxism and the Interpretation of Culture*, hrsg. von Cary Nelson und Lawrence Grossberg, Urbana 1988, S. 271–313.

und kulturelle Kontexte und verschiedene Orientalismen miteinander zu verknüpfen und damit oft undifferenziert zu betrachten – eine Praxis, die der Komplexität transkultureller Beziehungen und ihren jeweiligen spezifischen Umständen nicht gerecht wird, sondern stattdessen alt gediente Stereotype zu bekräftigen vermag.

Auch hat die Frage Stuart Halls nach dem zeitlichen Moment des Post-Kolonialen nach wie vor ihre Relevanz.[4] Es lässt sich kaum leugnen, dass das „Post" des Terminus Postkolonialismus nichts Vergangenes markiert, sondern einen quicklebendigen Prozess benennt, der wenig von seiner politischen Sprengkraft eingebüßt hat und dessen Mechanismen in unsere aktuelle Lebenswirklichkeit hineinreichen. So befinden wir uns 150 Jahre nach der Geburt Ethel Smyths im fünften Jahr einer militärischen Invasion im Irak, zu deren Rechtfertigung immer wieder das Stiften von Demokratie angeführt wurde und wird. War es denn nicht auch für den damaligen britischen Imperialismus die erklärte Absicht gewesen, bis in entlegene Winkel des Globus hinein Modernität zu stiften, Länder wirtschaftlich zu erschließen und den im Kant'schen Sinne „rohen Menschen" zu zivilisieren? War der Imperialismus denn nicht Großbritanniens „soziale Mission", die für die Repräsentation des Weltreichs nach außen sowie auch nach innen von größter Bedeutung war? Der erste Earl of Cromer, einst britischer Generalkonsul in Ägypten, bemerkte beispielsweise: „the special aptitude shown by Englishmen in the government of Oriental races pointed to England as the most effective and beneficent instrument for the gradual introduction of European civilisation into Egypt."[5]

Ägypten war ein Schauplatz, auf dem auch Ethel Smyth am Vorabend des Ersten Weltkrieges einige Monate ihres Lebens verbrachte. Ihre retrospektiv niedergeschriebene Darstellung dieser Zeit bietet für eine Suche nach Spuren des Empire zwischen den Zeilen einen – so scheint mir – geeigneten Ansatzpunkt und soll daher im Folgenden etwas näher betrachtet werden.

Zunächst sei jedoch die grundsätzliche Frage gestellt, in wieweit die Realität des britischen Empire tatsächlich Teil der Lebenswirklichkeit von Ethel Smyth war. Ihr Vater war Generalmajor in der britischen Armee gewesen, hatte lange Zeit in Indien gedient, und es war diese Tätigkeit im Dienste des Empire, die quasi die finanzielle Lebensgrundlage der Familie darstellte. Sie sorgte für eine privilegierte soziale Stellung der Smyths, die mit dazu beigetragen hat, dass

---

[4] Stuart Hall, „When was ,the Post-colonial'? Thinking at the Limit", in: *The Post-Colonial Question: Common Skies, Divided Horizons*, hrsg. von Iain Chambers und Lidia Curti, London u. a. 1996, S. 242–260.

[5] Evelyn Baring, 1st Earl of Cromer, *Modern Egypt*, 2 Vols., New York 1908, Vol. I. XVII–XVIII.

sich Ethel Smyth in jungen Jahren von ihren familiären und gesellschaftlichen Fesseln befreien und nach Deutschland gehen konnte und überhaupt in den Genuss der Erziehung durch eine Gouvernante kam, die in ihr den Wunsch zu wecken vermochte, das Komponieren zu erlernen.

Neben derartigen biographischen Fakten, die unmittelbar ins Auge fallen, ist vor allen Dingen das vorherrschende kulturelle Klima in Betracht zu ziehen, das zu Lebzeiten Smyths einen Nährboden schuf, auf dem beispielsweise Orientalismus gedeihen konnte – Orientalismus hier verstanden im Sinne Edward Saids „as a Western style for dominating, restructuring, and having authority over the Orient."[6] Über zahlreiche Aspekte dieses kulturellen Klimas und der westlichen Konsumierung des Orients im musikgeschichtlichen Zusammenhang ist bereits geschrieben worden.[7] Daher seien an dieser Stelle nur einige Schlagworte im Zusammenhang mit dem damals weit verbreiteten „Ägypten-Fieber" in Erinnerung gerufen.

Das populäre Interesse an Ägypten verdankte sich zu einem großen Teil der Archäologie, einem wichtigen Katalysator für Orientalismus. Ausgrabungsprojekte wie die des 1882 durch die Schriftstellerin und Ägyptologin Amelia Edwards gegründeten „Egypt Exploration Fund", der für eine Reihe wichtiger Expeditionen verantwortlich zeichnete und für den zu Beginn des 20. Jahrhunderts unter anderem der spätere Entdecker des Grabes Tutanchamuns, Howard Carter, tätig war, eröffneten mannigfaltige Projektionsflächen für Vorstellungen vom Orient. Nicht nur die durchschlagenden literarischen Erfolge der Zeit, etwa eines Henry Rider Haggards, zeugen von einem regen Interesse an Abenteuergeschichten in exotischer Kulisse – sondern auch das noch relativ junge Kino, das diverse Orientalismen transportierte und sich alleine zwischen den Jahren 1908 und 1918 fünf verschiedene Spielfilme über Kleopatra leistete, nebst einer Unmenge anderer im Orient verorteter Streifen wie biblische Filme, Fremdenlegionsfilme, arabische 1001-Nacht-Abenteuer und dergleichen.[8] Ethel Smyth selbst schreibt in ihren Erinnerungen über die ihrer Einschätzung nach vorhandene Fähigkeit des Kinos, über fremde Kulturen adäquat zu berichten.[9] Interessanterweise tut sie dies zu Beginn ihrer Aufzeichnungen über ihre Zeit in Ägypten, in Zusammenhang mit einer ihrer

---

[6] Said, *Orientalism*, S. 3.
[7] Z.B. Lawrence Kramer, „Consuming the Exotic: Ravel's ‚Daphnis and Chloe'", in: ders., *Classical Music and Post-Modern Knowledge*, Berkeley 1995, S. 201–25.
[8] *Visions of the East. Orientalism in Film*, hrsg. von Matthew Bernstein und Gaylyn Studlar, New Brunswick 1997.
[9] Ethel Smyth, „Egypt before England's Exodus", in: dies., *Beecham and Pharaoh*, London 1935, S. 88: „[...] film has brought home to sophisticated inhabitants of England what sort of life these islanders lead."

Orientexpedition vorangegangenen Reise nach Irland – ein Land, das sie als einen ähnlich exotischen Ort porträtiert wie später Ägypten.[10]

Zu Beginn ihrer Ägypten-Erinnerungen erwähnt Smyth auch ihren Besuch bei einer Vorstellung der „Ballets Russes" 1911 in London, die ebenso wie das Kino für die Visualisierung eines imaginierten Orients eine bedeutsame Rolle spielten, wie Gaylyn Studlar gezeigt hat.[11] Anlässlich dieses Vorstellungsbesuches lernt Smyth auch Ronald Storrs kennen, „at that time Lord Kitchener's Oriental Secretary at the British Agency at Cairo" und später ein wichtiger Kontakt für sie in Kairo.[12]

Die Exotik des Orients wird also in verschiedenen Bereichen der Künste und auch der Wissenschaften beschworen und sie wird dabei häufig mit Weiblichkeitsbildern und Sexualität in Verbindung gebracht – sei es in der Psychologie etwa bei Sigmund Freud, der die Frau als „dunklen Kontinent" bezeichnete, sei es in der Literatur, wo in Haggards „King Solomons Mines" die Geographie der fremden Umgebung mit der Physiognomie der Frau verglichen wird, oder sei es auf der Kinoleinwand, wo häufig zu erleben ist, dass Protagonistinnen in fremden Umgebungen gerne in gefährliche Situationen gebracht werden, die Raum bieten sowohl für Vergewaltigungs- als auch für Rettungsphantasien (wie beispielsweise in *King Kong*). Wie auch immer diese Weiblichkeitsbilder inszeniert werden, sei es subversiv oder gängigen Klischees von Weiblichkeit entsprechend: Der Orient ist fester Bestandteil europäischer Kultur und als das „Andere" für das eigene Selbstbild des Westens notwendig. Er ist sowohl ein Ort der Unterdrückungsphantasien des Westens als auch ein Ort der Sehnsucht nach Sinnlichkeit und Erotik.

Das kulturelle Klima der Zeit ist auch an Ethel Smyth nicht spurlos vorbeigegangen und so lassen sich in ihrem musikalischen Œuvre durchaus Anklänge an einen imaginierten Orient ausmachen, am deutlichsten vielleicht in dem Lied *La Danse* aus den *Four Songs* (1907). Anders als etwa im *Tanzlied* wird hier der Tanzfluss nicht gestört.[13] Anstelle des dort komponierten Stolperns steht der sinnlich verführerische Tanz im Mittelpunkt, dank „orientalisch" anmutender Instrumentierung mitsamt Flöte und Harfe.[14]

---

[10] Ebd.
[11] Gaylyn Studlar, „‚Out-Salomeing Salome': Dance, the New Woman, and Fan Magazine Orientalism", in: *Visions of the East. Orientalism in Film*, S. 99–129.
[12] Smyth, „Egypt before England's Exodus", S. 98f.
[13] Vgl. hierzu den Beitrag von Cornelia Bartsch in diesem Band.
[14] Die Harfe – eines der ältesten Musikinstrumente der Menschheit, mit Wurzeln in Ägypten – wird von Ethel Smyth an prominenter Stelle angeführt, um zu verdeutlichen, wie Frauen an die nicht-lukrativen Instrumente in einem Orchester verbannt werden – ein weiteres, trauriges Beispiel der systematischen, in diesem Falle öko-

Es ist jedoch vor allen Dingen Ethel Smyths literarisches Schaffen, durch das uns Einblicke in die Mechanismen des Imperialismus gewährt werden, insbesondere in dem bereits zitierten autobiographischen Fragment *Egypt before England's Exodus*. 1911 hatte Ethel Smyth sich der Suffragettenbewegung um Emmeline Pankhurst angeschlossen und während dieser Zeit ihre kompositorische Arbeit ruhen lassen. Zwei Jahre später „flieht" Smyth aus dem vertrauten Umfeld, um sich als Künstlerin wieder zu finden und der Versuchung zu widerstehen, ihrer Freundin Pankhurst im politischen Kampf bis zum Äußersten beizustehen und sich damit selbst in Gefahr zu bringen. Sie flüchtet in eine für sie exotische, weit entfernte Welt – den Orient.

Hier scheinen sich Kräfteverhältnisse, denen Smyth im eigenen Land unterworfen ist, zu verschieben. Es ist bemerkenswert, wie Ethel Smyth, auf der ein männlicher, „kolonialisierender" Blick lag, selbst zeitlebens vehement und mutig schaute, schrieb und kämpfte und ein eigenes Bild von sich zu konstruieren versuchte. Wie allerdings schaut, schreibt, kämpft die Kolonialisierte in einem Land, in dem sie selber als Teil der Kolonialmacht in Erscheinung tritt? Cornelia Bartsch hat gezeigt, dass die Schreibstrategien Smyths Ähnlichkeiten aufweisen mit den Strategien von Autorinnen und Autoren ehemals kolonialisierter Länder und hat dazu eingeladen, das Wirken Ethel Smyths unter dem Gesichtspunkt des Anknüpfens zu lesen, als ein dialogisierendes „Netzespannen", das es Smyth ermöglichte, sehr rasch an die unterschiedlichsten Gegebenheiten zu adaptieren – sei es in Form des Absorbierens eines Stils während ihres Studiums in Leipzig oder sei es die Mobilisierung aller möglichen Kräfte, um Aufführungen ihrer Werke zu erreichen.[15] Ich möchte dies unterstreichen, gleichzeitig aber auch behaupten, dass sich ihre Fähigkeit oder ihre Bereitschaft zum Dialog nur zu einem gewissen Grad auf diejenigen ausdehnte, die der Kolonialherrschaft Großbritanniens unterworfen waren und dass sich Smyths „Anknüpfen" im Orient um einiges komplexer darstellt, sowohl in künstlerischer als auch in sozialer Hinsicht.

Dies wird deutlich in Smyths Schilderungen ihrer Begegnungen mit „Einheimischen", insbesondere mit Frauen, über die sie sich abfällig äußert und

---

nomischen, Unterdrückung der Frau in einem patriarchalischen System (vgl. hierzu den Beitrag von Elicia Clements in diesem Band). Der Vergleich der Harfenistin mit der Regimentsziege, den Smyth heranzieht, um die Beziehung zwischen den männlichen Mitgliedern eines Orchesters und der Harfenistin zu charakterisieren, erscheint mir in seiner militärischen Dimension für eine postkoloniale Lesart als durchaus relevant und aufschlussreich, um sowohl die damaligen „imperialen" Machtverhältnisse im Orchester zu benennen als auch das nicht seltene Bemühen militärischer Metaphern der Majorstochter Smyth zu verdeutlichen.

15 Siehe hierzu den Beitrag von Cornelia Bartsch in diesem Band.

beispielsweise schreibt, dass "a very large proportion were simply animals, got up with fifteenth-rate European elegance, their hair dyed, their flesh purple-pink rolls of fat".[16] Smyth besinnt sich in solchen Momenten immer wieder auf die Suffragettenbewegung und ihre Freundin Emmeline Pankhurst, mit der sie während dieser Zeit in regem Briefkontakt steht. Den Kämpferinnen der Suffragettenbewegung stellt sie die ägyptischen Frauen gegenüber und schreibt: "I was very anxious about Mrs. Pankhurst, and could not help thinking with sombre rage of that huge pen full of female cattle, apparently content to be what they were ... and she's giving her life by inches for all women!"[17] Das Different-Machen nicht-westlicher Frauen hat dazu beigetragen, den britischen Kolonialismus als soziale Mission zu legitimieren. Smyth hat sich an diesem Different-Machen beteiligt – nicht nur in Hinblick auf ihre Beschreibungen der ägyptischen Frauen sondern auch der Männer. Am Tag ihrer Ankunft in Kairo etwa bekam Ethel Smyth Gelegenheit, eine jährlich zur Erinnerung an die Ermordung der Söhne des letzten Kalifen stattfindende rituelle Prozession mitzuerleben, und zwar anders als geplant nicht vom sicheren Balkon aus, sondern inmitten des Prozessionszuges. Verstört durch die Fremdheit des Rituals und die dazu gehörigen körperlichen Läuterungen der Teilnehmenden schreibt Smyth: "the narrow street was lined with raving maniacs, rolling their eyes, chanting, hacking each other with swords, and streaming with blood. A huge drop flew on to my cheek, and I never felt nearer going mad myself with horror and blood-exultation".[18]

Smyths negative Wahrnehmung und ihr scharfer Ton, der sich auch durch andere Passagen der Erinnerungen zieht, mag nicht grundsätzlich einer ablehnenden Haltung einer fremden Kultur gegenüber geschuldet, sondern durch eine Reihe von Faktoren begünstigt gewesen sein – wie beispielsweise durch die Tatsache, dass ihr das Klima und das fremde Essen zusetzten, was wiederum zu Schlafstörungen führte und ihre Stimmung trübte. Und doch lassen ihre Texte immer wieder eine eurozentrische Perspektive durchblicken, die von der Überlegenheit der „abendländischen" Kultur ausgeht:

> „Contemplating the Egyptian as he is today, involuntarily you account for nine hundred and ninety-nine thousandths of his artistic past. Geographically situated as the country is, Grecian airs were bound to blow across the water, and all the beauty you see in Egypt was borrowed, or directly imported from Greece. Otherwise this people seem to have gone on contentedly doing the same thing for one thousand five hundred years,

---

[16] Smyth, „Egypt before England's Exodus", S. 137.
[17] Ebd., S. 139.
[18] Ebd., S. 101.

apparently making no effort to get out of the rut. Dumped down as unprejudiced foreigner in their midst, and looking at them as they are today, your feeling is: ‚Of course! what else could one expect? As they are now so they were then.' This is the fact which that tiresome line of pyramids seems for ever proclaiming: and I suppose that is why everyone I have ever known loathes the Pyramids."[19]

Doch es sind nicht nur die baulichen Zeugen, die Smyth als Zeichen für den Stillstand und die Minderwertigkeit der ägyptischen Zivilisation zu interpretieren scheint und an die sie britisches Maß anlegt. So schreibt sie über die „fellaheen" (Arbeiter, Bauern): „these [...] have not a quarter the brains and character of either our schoolboys or our foxhounds"[20] und folgert daraus, dass Ägypten mit harter Hand regiert werden sollte:

"I remember when first I went to those parts wondering why all my countrymen, even conspicuously kind, gentle people [...] always seemed to be so angry with their underlings, giving their orders in such a very hard, stern voice. But I soon perceived that no other style penetrates those thick skulls, stirs those brutish wits [...]. I was assured – and I believe it – that, like dogs, natives prefer being spoken to sharply. [...]. Some day it may be the fellaheen's turn to bark at us, but at present it is our role to bark at them."[21]

Anstatt in einen „Dialog" mit der ägyptischen Bevölkerung zu treten, insbesondere mit den doppelt kolonialisierten ägyptischen Frauen, und anstatt auch musikalisch ihre Umwelt zu reflektieren, besinnt Ethel Smyth sich auf das Eigene. Sie genießt in vollen Zügen die Annehmlichkeiten des betont britischen Koloniallebens in Kairo, spielt Golf und Tennis, nimmt an Teestunden und Abendveranstaltungen teil und bekommt einmal wöchentlich das britische Magazin *The Suffragette* ins Haus gesandt, das sie über die neuesten Nachrichten der Bewegung daheim informiert. Während in den Jahren vor ihrer Reise in ihrer Musik durchaus orientalische Anklänge auszumachen sind (siehe *La Danse*), erscheint es bemerkenswert, dass eine Auseinandersetzung mit ihrer kulturellen orientalischen Umgebung in dem Werk, das sie während ihres Aufenthalts in Ägypten schreibt – *The Boatswain's Mate* – fehlt. In deutlicher Abgrenzung zur einheimischen Bevölkerung schärft Ethel Smyth ihr Bewusstsein für das Eigene und schreibt mit *The Boatswain's Mate* eine feministische

---

[19] Ebd., S. 161f.
[20] Ebd., S. 159.
[21] Ebd., S. 159f.

Oper. Als Ouvertüre verarbeitet sie hier ihren *March of the Women*, die Hymne der Suffragettenbewegung. Ein gewisses Unbehagen mag sich einstellen, hört man diese Oper vor dem Hintergrund ihrer ägyptischen Kulisse und in Anbetracht derer, die als Kolonialisierte vom *March of the Women* ausgeschlossen waren oder gar – im übertragenen Sinne – von ihm niedergewalzt wurden.

Abstract

Empire between the Lines: A Postcolonial Perspective

Like many British families at the threshold of the 20th century, the Smyth family profited from the existence of the British Empire. Its colonial territories provided arenas in which at least the male members of the family were able to make careers and money.

But traces of the Empire are not limited to Ethel Smyth's biography: the cultural and societal climate of the time provided a nurturing ground for orientalism – an orientalism that manifested itself musically, as well as thematically, in a number of works by Smyth. A point of departure for a postcolonial perspective of Smyth's oeuvre is provided by the recollections of her months spent living in Egypt, as depicted in the autobiographical fragment *Egypt before England's Exodus*. Encountering the alien North African culture, Smyth's view of the "self" is sharpened, while at the same time she is an equally sharp observer and critic of Egyptian society, which deems her uncivilised and brutish. On her search for "oriental charms", she sketches her impressions of Egyptian exoticisms. As she does so, she observes that power relations seem to be shifting: on the home front, British women are still fighting subjugation, whereas in Egypt they find themselves in a more powerful position, not only with regard to their individual freedom, but also in comparison to the female natives of the colonised countries.

Margaret R. Hunt
Same-sex Love before *Psychopathia Sexualis*: Or, What Young Ethel Knew

Ethel Smyth discovered her many callings – musician, writer, suffragist, lover, sportswoman, friend – in a world that was remarkably accepting of the love of women for other women. It was, however, a world in flux. For historians of sexuality one of the most important sign-posts of that change is the publication, in 1886, of Richard von Krafft-Ebing's *Psychopathia Sexualis: mit besonderer Berücksichtigung der conträren Sexualempfindung: eine klinisch-forensische Studie*. Krafft-Ebing's book was an exhaustive account of "abnormal" sexual practices that many argue helped "pathologize" women's same-sex love generally, and female homosexuality in particular. I want to devote this paper to love between women in the two centuries *before* 1886 – the world before Krafft-Ebing. Ethel Smyth turned twenty-eight in the year *Psychopathia Sexualis* appeared, so we may reasonably assume that that older world heavily influenced both her life and her loves.

The social terrain of women's same-sex love (1700–1886)

In the eighteenth and nineteenth centuries capitalist agriculture, proto-industry and, eventually, the factory system replaced subsistence and other small-scale economies across much of Europe. As a result, ever greater numbers of young Western European women – by some estimates up to half of them – began leaving home in their early teens or earlier to take up wage work in the cities or in rural industry. Some of these women seized the opportunity (or were forced by necessity) to set up house with other women. So for example, it was fairly common for French linen-drapers, seamstresses, and nurses to establish common households and remain permanently unmarried.[1] English and Dutch silkworkers and teachers did the same thing. And a rather surprising number of working-class women across Europe "passed" or sought to pass as men, some of them going so far as to marry other women. Maria van Antwerpen (1719–1781), going under the name of Machiel van Antwerpen, officially

---

[1] Clare Haru Crowston, *Fabricating Women: The Seamstresses of Old Regime France, 1675–1791*, Durham, NC 2001.

married Cornelia Swartsenberg in Zwolle in the Netherlands in 1762. At the time of the marriage Cornelia was pregnant, and she later became pregnant twice more, while Maria represented herself as the father.[2] In a 1793 case from Hungary, one "Ferenc" Horvath was arrested for having gotten a priest to officiate when she married her pregnant bride. "Ferenc" testified forthrightly: "I am a girl dressed up as a man and it has been three years since I married a gipsy girl. I have a man's and a woman's nature in me but I have never liked men, I have always loved women." Witnesses testified that they assumed she was a man because she served as a coachman and "she smoked and sang songs for dancing just as any man would."[3]

Women of the middle classes also saw their horizons change and expand over the course of the eighteenth and nineteenth centuries. Perhaps the most significant agent of change was the growth of women's education, and especially the proliferation of schools for middle-class and elite girls. Girls' schools were very rare in the latter part of the seventeenth century, especially in Protestant lands. But a century later there were hundreds of girls' schools, many of them proprietorial schools run by women. By 1872, the year Ethel Smyth went off to boarding school, there were tens of thousands of them across Europe. The rise of girls' schools is very significant for the history of same-sex love, because a large proportion of lovers of other women in the eighteenth and nineteenth centuries had their first romance with another girl or woman while in boarding school – this had already become a girls' school stereotype by the eighteenth century.[4] In addition, school-teaching became an important new job for middle-class women who wished to be self-supporting.[5] There were some other knock-on effects. Schools contributed to making middle-class female literacy virtually universal in Western Europe by the later eighteenth century and rising literacy led to an enormous amount of letter-writing by and between women. Middle-class literacy also helped create a mass market in women's literary genres, and novel-writing and journalism joined teaching as jobs for middle-class women. Both women writers and women school-teachers figured prominently as "lovers of other women" from the early eighteenth century on.[6]

[2] Rudolf Dekker and Lotte van de Pol, *The Tradition of Female Transvestism in Early Modern Europe,* New York 1989.
[3] István György Tóth, "Peasant Sexuality in Eighteenth-Century Hungary", in: *Continuity and Change* 6 (1991), pp. 43–59 at p. 55.
[4] Martha Vicinus, *Intimate Friends: Women Who Loved Women, 1778–1928,* Chicago 2004, pp. 206ff.
[5] Ibid., pp. 63–69.
[6] Susan S. Lanser, "Befriending the Body: Female Intimacies as Class Acts", in: *Eighteenth-century Studies* 32 (1998), pp. 179–198.

Women who loved women were also represented at the top of the social scale. Noble girls, especially the lesser nobility, also attended boarding schools in some numbers from the later seventeenth century on, and earlier in Catholic countries, so that we also see "girls' school" romances in this class. Noblewomen had a somewhat different relationship to heterosexual marriage than most of their social inferiors. Life-long celibacy was appreciably higher among the nobility, both male and female, than it was for other social groups in both Protestant and Catholic Europe in the eighteenth and into the nineteenth centuries, reaching twenty-five percent or more in some cohorts.[7] This, coupled with the prevalence of purely dynastic and loveless marriages, meant that noblewomen were often deeply committed to all- or largely-female political, religious, charitable or artistic coteries and clientage networks. In the eighteenth and nineteenth centuries noblewomen in many countries also enjoyed somewhat more sexual latitude – or at least greater freedom from punishment for sexual misdeeds – than other women. Perhaps for this reason some noblewomen were quite sexually adventurous, both in a hetero- and homosexual vein. An early eighteenth-century example was Henriette-Julie de Castelnau, Countess of Murat (1670–1716), who was constantly in trouble late in the reign of Louis XIV for writing (or cooperating in the writing) of a critical pamphlet about the court, as well as for her open affairs with other women ("a monstrous preference for people of her own sex") and for hosting dionysian parties. Like a number of obstreperous French aristocrats she was kept under police surveillance, and the spy reports on her (partly based on information supplied by an embittered ex-lover) contain several breathless dispatches devoted to chronicling the progress of the countess's love life and deploring her propensity to flaunt her erotic preferences in front of tradesmen and servants.[8]

After about 1700 people in the performing arts, especially actresses, singers and dancers, began to gain a much more prominent place in European society (this had, of course, begun earlier, particularly in Italy). These people were sufficiently hybrid as to their social origins, and, at least initially, sufficiently sexually unrespectable, to form what was, in effect, a distinct caste. This caste benefited immeasurably from the enormous increase, especially in the eighteenth century, in the number of theatres, resident theatre-companies,

---

[7] Llorenç Ferrer i Alòs, "Fratelli al celibato, sorelle al matrimonio. La parte dei cadetti nella riproduzione sociale dei gruppi agiati in Catalogna (Secoli XVIII–XIX)", in: *Quaderni Storici* 83 (1993), pp. 527–554.

[8] René d'Argenson, *Rapports inédits du lieutenant de police René d'Argenson (1697–1715)*, ed. Paul Cottin, Paris 1891, pp. 11–12, 89, 94.

purpose-built opera houses, and public and semi-public concert venues, and the seemingly insatiable demand for actresses, musicians and dancers to perform in them. The growing passion for and commercialization of culture soon bid up the price of labor. In the 1780s French actors and actresses at the *lowest* salary rung in provincial companies were making up to fifteen times the salary of a seamstress, and perhaps twenty-five times the salary of a female domestic servant. Of course the top actresses or opera singers from the Comédie-Française or the Paris Opéra were making much more than that, and acting was also one of the few fields where women – at least the stars – could fairly consistently command higher salaries than men.[9]

By the middle of the eighteenth century actresses had turned into public celebrities and some had grown enormously rich. Not surprisingly, legions of talented or pretty girls, mostly of working-class or lower middle-class origins, flocked into the performing arts in Italy, France, England, Spain, the Netherlands, the Austro-Hungarian Empire, Poland and many of the German states. It was an artistic variant of the great migration of young people to the city, and like its counterpart, characterized by a loosening of moral oversight. Women performers were notorious for their affairs with rich and, often, aristocratic men, men who, in return for these women's favors, paid for them to live in a style to which the performers – almost none of them born to wealth – were happy to become accustomed. Elite men also used their influence to press for better roles for their paramours, supplied some of the financial backing that permitted these women's own works to be performed, and generally became deeply involved in the politics of artistic production, especially in the larger, more expensive enterprises such as opera.[10] While the dominant pattern was for performers to take up with elite men there were also a number of examples of actresses and musicians who became involved with other women. To name just two examples among many, the most notorious French "sapphist" of the late eighteenth century was the wildly popular actress Mlle Raucourt (1756–1815) who lived for some time with the opera singer Sophie Arnould (1740–1802) whom she is supposed to have "married." Raucourt was also associated with a succession of other women, both noblewomen and other artists. In the nineteenth century the famed Shakespearian actress, Charlotte

[9] Lauren Clay, "Provincial Actors, the Comédie-Française, and the Business of Performing in Eighteenth-Century France", in: *Eighteenth-Century Studies* 38 (2005), pp. 651–679. On the pay disparities see especially pp. 656–657. I have supplemented Clay's figures with some of my own.
[10] See e.g., Jacqueline Letzter and Robert Adelson, *Women Writing Opera: Creativity and Controversy in the Age of the French Revolution*, Berkeley, California 2001.

Cushman (1816–1876) presided in Rome and London over a kaleidoscopic array of current and former women lovers, most of them actresses, musicians, artists or passionate fans.[11]

The character of same-sex love in the eighteenth and nineteenth centuries

There is no question that *some* lovers of other women engaged in full-bore lesbian sex of a kind perfectly recognizable to any modern person. They did not need late nineteenth-century sexologists to teach them how. How do we know this? Because some were quite explicit about it. Here is a not atypical entry from December of 1825 from the diary of the early nineteenth-century English gentry-woman Anne Lister (1791–1840). It involves a woman named Mrs. Barlow whom Anne Lister had recently succeeded in seducing. Lister has her own private language for talking about sex, and she usually uses the word "grubble" to mean manual stimulation of the genital area.

"Paris, January 3, 1825

> Mrs Barlow and I seemed left to ourselves. She had had a little pain in her back ... and had lain down but got up to tea, then had lain down again & I got into [bed with] her about ten & three-quarters [o-clock]. I soon took up her petticoats so as to feel her naked thighs next to mine. Then, after kissing [her] with my tongue in her mouth, got the middle finger of my right hand up her & grubbled her long & better than ever, she seeming rather more at ease than before & taking it with more emotion and apparent pleasure, which made me keep dawdling there a long time. She seemed more moist than before but really very nice. She hid her face on my shoulder & we lay a good while silent & as if half-dozing. At last said I, "have you not my affections & all my heart?"[12]

In spite of accounts like these historians have been understandably reluctant to assign the term "lesbian" across the board to love relationships between women in the era before Krafft-Ebing's *Psychopathia sexualis*. Despite what one reads in older histories of sexuality, this is not because the term "lesbian"

---

[11] For the association of actresses with sapphism see especially Emma Donoghue, *Passions between Women: British Lesbian Culture 1668–1801*, London 1995, pp. 143–147, 64–73.

[12] Anne Lister, *No Priest but Love: Excerpts from the Diaries of Anne Lister, 1824–1826*, ed. Helena Whitbread, Otley 1992, p. 68.

was unknown or meant something wholly different in earlier times. The word was in use at least by the late sixteenth century for women who had genital sex with other women, though variations on "sapphist", "tribade", or "fricatrice" – three other very old terms for essentially the same thing – were probably more common.[13] The real problems with terms like "lesbian", "tribade" etc. are more subtle. First, and most obviously, we often do not know whether a particular couple were really having "lesbian" sex even if the definition of that is fairly broad. (It is also fairly hard for historians to tell whether heterosexuals in the past were having sex either – unless the marriage or liaison produced children, and many marriages did not.) Second and more importantly, identifiers like "lesbian", whether they are being used today or in the sixteenth century, emphasize genitally-focused sex-acts to the virtual exclusion of other social, emotional, or erotic practices and arrangements that may well have been more important to women themselves. These terms, in short, narrow the analytic field in a way that makes historians – and indeed, anyone who appreciates erotic and emotional complexity – quite uneasy.

One might think that the problem of generalizing about women who loved women before Krafft-Ebing stemmed from a lack of evidence; in fact the opposite is true. This is thanks to the thousands upon thousands of poems, novels, diaries and letters – especially letters – written by eighteenth and nineteenth-century women to and about their loves, a phenomenon that, as we have seen, stems directly from the rise of middle class female literacy from the late seventeenth century on. If only *some* of the lovers of women pre-Krafft-Ebing engaged in lesbian sex – and there are many for whom we will never know one way or the other – we can be more confident about asserting that virtually all women who loved other women were expected to express that love using the passionate idioms and conventions of romantic friendship. Romantic friendship between women has received a lot of attention from women's historians, and there is not time to go in depth here into the various debates to which it has given rise.[14] Suffice it to say that part of its appeal was its enormous flexibility

---

[13] See Pierre Brantôme, *Lives of Fair and Gallant Ladies*, trans. A. R. Allinson, New York 1933, pp. 128–129. Brantôme was writing in the late sixteenth century. For the eighteenth century see Donoghue, *Passions between Women*, pp. 3–5.

[14] See e.g., Carroll Smith-Rosenberg, "The Female World of Love and Ritual: Relations between Women in Nineteenth-Century America", in: *Signs: Journal of Women in Culture and Society* 1 (1975), pp. 1–29; Lillian Faderman, *Surpassing the Love of Men: Romantic Friendship and Love between Women from the Renaissance to the Present*, London 1981; Vicinus, *Intimate Friends; Mit 1000 Küssen Deine Fillu. Briefe der Sängerin Marie Fillunger an Eugenie Schumann 1875–93*, ed. Eva Rieger in collaboration with Rosemary Hilmar, Köln 2002.

as a concept and an everyday practice. Romantic friendship was and is very difficult to pin down in physical, emotional and institutional terms. For one couple romantic friendship might mean tear-drenched partings; jealousy; writing to each other twice a day; wearing rings made from each others' hair; kissing; spending a lot of time wrapped around each other in bed; and a difficult break-up – but not involve genital, much less penetrative sex. Or it could involve living together, owning a home in common, calling one another "wife", sleeping together and being buried side-by-side, but keeping the relationship on a spiritual plane – by, say, organizing the relationship around a mutual devotion to Jesus Christ or by consciously sublimating physical passion – and physical sex – into the pursuit of "pure art."[15] Romantic friendship between women could also masquerade as platonic while being anything but – as was the case with Anne Lister. Lister took daily advantage of the fact that the people around her assumed that it was perfectly normal for two women to be deeply attached to one another, want to sleep and travel together, and even to move in together. And the impression one gets on reading her diary is *not* that it never crossed people's mind that these friendships had a strong erotic dimension – her close relatives and, obviously, her numerous ex-lovers, several of whom continued to be part of her social set, could have had little doubt about her erotic proclivities. Rather it was that most people were perfectly familiar with the outer trappings of romantic love between women and chose not to inquire too closely into the more intimate details of any one iteration of it, especially if the principals possessed both respectability and social position.

Many, indeed most women who loved other women were not in a position to set up house with them and some may not have wanted to. But as Anne Lister, Maria van Antwerpen, Ferenc Horvath, Charlotte Cushman and many others show, women across the social spectrum also practiced what was often, at the time, called "female marriage", relationships that closely mimicked heterosexual marriage in that the couple lived together, owned property in common, socialized as a couple, called each other "wife" (or, occasionally, "husband" and "wife" as did Lister and at least two of her lovers), had children together, made wills in each other's favor, passed through bitter "divorces" and asked to be buried side by side. Women's love for other women was certainly not new in the early modern period,[16] but its institutionalization and domestication

[15] Lia van Gemert, "Hiding Behind Words? Lesbianism in 17th-Century Dutch Poetry", in: *Thamyris* 2 (1995): pp. 11–44 is especially useful on this point.
[16] Valerie Traub, *The Renaissance of Lesbianism in Early Modern England* (Cambridge Studies in Renaissance Literature and Culture 42), Cambridge 2002; *Same Sex Love and Desire among Women in the Middle Ages,* ed. Francesca Canadé Sautman and Pamela Sheingorn, New York 2001.

into relations that look very like marriage almost certainly increased significantly from the eighteenth century on, largely due to the structural shifts in the nature and provenance of women's work discussed above, changes which made it far more feasible for respectable women to be independent and self-supporting.

The final characteristic that often played a part in the world of women who loved women was experimentation with cross-gender signifiers, especially clothes, and, to a lesser extent, other masculine markers like smoking or working with horses. Many of the actresses who participated in "female marriages" or who were known to have been great lovers of women – women like the eighteenth-century English actress, Charlotte Charke (1713–1760) – were also famous for playing travesty or breeches roles. In her case she also wore men's clothes offstage, passed for lengthy periods as a man, and lived with another woman under the pretense that they were man and wife. Anne Lister worked hard to make her clothes, accoutrements and gestures just masculine enough to attract women's attention, while still staying just inside the pale of upper-class female respectability. As she mused one day "… my manners are certainly peculiar, not all masculine but rather softly *gentleman*-like. I know how to please girls."[17] The Ladies of Llangollen, the most famous "romantic friends" of the late eighteenth and early nineteenth centuries affected a kind of hunting costume, complete with top hats. The association of lovers of women with riding costume, powerfully marked both as masculine and as upper-class (since it was largely rich people who owned horses), lasted well into the twentieth century. Perhaps the most iconic expression of this is the 1926 portrait of the Duchess de la Salle by the bisexual artist Tamara de Lempicka.

Public attitudes toward same-sex love before Krafft-Ebing

This essay began with the assertion that Ethel Smyth came of age in a world that was remarkably accepting of the love of women for other women. In some ways this is counterintuitive. European society in the eighteenth and nineteenth centuries was anything but gender egalitarian. Most women were pressured to marry and taught that they should subordinate their needs and desires to those of others. They also experienced constraints on their mobility, and were expected to obey men or higher-ranking women. When they failed to do so resort to violence, confinement and disgrace was often swift. The result was that women had far less freedom than men had about where

---

[17] Anne Lister, *I Know My Own Heart: The Diaries of Anne Lister*, ed. Helena Whitbread, New York 1992, p. 136.

they might place their affections. Yet even within this extremely inegalitarian world same-sex love between women was probably the least constrained kind of extra-familial female connection, and far from being viewed as a problem, it was often celebrated.

In a moment we will go into the logic of this, but before we do so it must be acknowledged that there are exceptions to the generalization that female same-sex love was broadly accepted. During the eighteenth and nineteenth century there were perhaps a half dozen to a dozen known cases where women who loved or married other women were arrested or punished for it, and one known case where a woman was actually executed. These cases were very unrepresentative, however. Most involved working-class women who came to the attention of the authorities because they committed some other quite serious crime (religious apostasy, murder, etc.). One Catharina Margaretha Linke was executed in Halberstadt in 1721 for religious apostasy and sodomy (i.e., using a dildo).[18] A trio of lesbians came to the attention of the Dutch authorities in the late eighteenth century because one of them murdered the rival for her lover's affections.[19] Almost all of the remaining cases were women who impersonated men and married other women (typically prosecuted as a crime of fraud). This was the case both for Maria van Antwerpen and, it seems, "Ferenc" Horvath, as well as for the British cross-dresser, Mary Hamilton, the subject of Henry Fielding's notorious pamphlet, *The Female Husband* of 1746.[20] And while it is undeniably true that women already deemed criminal who were also found – or believed – to have been practicing "indecency" with other women were punished more severely (as the case of Linke clearly shows), most women who sought to pass as men (and hundreds of women are known to have done so) were either ignored or simply admonished and sent home. Women who were caught trying to marry other women (or pretending already to be married to women) might be whipped or banished from their towns but few were executed, and some were simply ignored.[21] The overwhelming majority of women who loved other women in the eighteenth and nineteenth

---

[18] Brigitte Eriksson, "A Lesbian Execution in Germany, 1721: The Trial Records", in: *Journal of Homosexuality* 6, Special issue: Historical Perspectives on Homosexuality (1980/81), pp. 27–40.

[19] See e.g., Theo Van der Meer, "Tribades on Trial: Female Same-Sex Offenders in Late Eighteenth-Century Amsterdam", in: *Journal of the History of Sexuality* 1 (1991), pp. 424–445.

[20] Terry Castle, "Matters Not Fit to Be Mentioned: Fielding's *The Female Husband*", in: *ELH*, 49 (1982), pp. 602–622.

[21] On this issue see especially Dekker and van de Pol, *Tradition of Female Transvestism in Early Modern Europe*.

centuries, whether single, married to a man, or living with another woman, were neither punished for it, nor deemed to be especially out of the ordinary.

Actresses might seem to be the exception here. They played starring roles not just on the stage, but in the pornographic imagination of the day, and consequently there was much titillating talk by contemporary gossip writers about the stars or their female patrons' alleged sapphic proclivities. However even in these cases there is precious little evidence that the rumors ever harmed women's careers, and in some cases (as has been asserted with respect to Mlle Raucourt), it may have enhanced them.[22] In the final analysis most women who loved other women – especially middle and upper-class women – were more likely to encounter praise than blame or criticism. Victorian scholar Sharon Marcus has recently shown that passionate female friendship in the nineteenth century was most often seen as a *support* to normative heterosexual marriage rather than subversive of it. Writers of advice books for girls, far from being concerned about women's passionate friendships with other women, tended to think that they prepared them for marriage by teaching them patience, forbearance and selflessness, as it were, training their hearts to please others. Few people thought two women capable of anything that might actually be termed "sex."[23] Even "female marriages", the form of same-sex love that would seem to pose the most direct threat to marriage, seems to have been surprisingly readily assimilated. The passing woman Maria van Antwerpen's own brother stood god-father to the children she had with her "wife". When Ann Lister died in 1840 her obituary referred matter-of-factly and without other comment to her "friend and companion".[24] Some "female marriages" were actually celebrated as models for heterosexual marriage. The Ladies of Llangollen became icons of disinterested and chaste love, to such an extent that courting heterosexual couples came in huge numbers to pay homage to them and locals took to selling "Ladies of Llangollen" tourist trinkets. The Dutch novelists and devoted couple, Bettje Wolff (1738–1804) and Aagje Deken (1741–1804) attracted similar adulation on the continent.

The belief that women's passionate friendships could be a support to heterosexual marriage, and – it bears saying – were readily assimilated to female sub-

[22] See Pamela Cheek, *Sexual Antipodes: Enlightenment Globalization and the Placing of Sex*, Stanford, CA 2003, pp. 57, 60; and Karl Toepfer, "Orgy Salon: Aristocracy and Pornographic Theatre in Pre-Revolutionary Paris", in: *Performing Arts Journal* 12 (1990), pp.110–136.

[23] I owe this reminder to conversations with Birgit Kiupel, and her comments have also been most useful in guiding my revisions of this essay.

[24] Quoted in Sharon Marcus, *Between Women: Friendship, Desire, and Marriage in Victorian England*, Princeton 2007, p. 51.

ordination, also made it easier for some husbands not only to tolerate but to encourage their wives' relations with women. Much passionate correspondence between women was carried on perfectly openly, sometimes with correspondents' husbands attaching supportive little notes at the end. The notion that passionate female friendship between women could be fully consistent with, and indeed enhance heterosexuality, sheds considerable light on the apparently approving view Heinrich von Herzogenberg took toward the intense relationship between his wife, Lisl, and the young Ethel Smyth, as well as the openly supportive attitude of Ethel Smyth's friend and lover, Henry Brewster toward her passionate affairs with women. In later life Ethel Smyth's friend, Mary Benson, and her husband, Edward Benson Archbishop of Canterbury, actually brought Mary's woman lover, Lucy Tait to live with them – and, we are told, Mary and Lucy henceforth slept together in their own bed under Edward Benson's roof – for the next twenty-five years.[25] It is, of course, important to note, Smyth and her friends notwithstanding, that the ideal did not always match the practice. Some husbands undoubtedly tried to limit all their wives' connections, including their friendships with other women, in a bid to keep them under closer control – and both law and custom allowed a husband free rein to do so. Still, idealized or not, the assumption that female same-sex love was fully compatible with marriage and heterosexuality (though shorn of the association with female subordination) undoubtedly exerted a life-long influence on Smyth herself.

Same-sex love across the social divide

One of the most significant long-term changes affecting women's same-sex love in the two centuries or so before Krafft-Ebing was the gradual breaking down of social, affectional and erotic barriers between *some* women who might otherwise have remained apart due to class. There were a number of contributing factors at work. While women performers never entirely shed their bad reputation, this was increasingly trumped by their beauty, style and artistry – especially in the context of the more heterogeneous forms of sociability of the Enlightenment era. Disreputable associations diminished most rapidly with respect to women musicians, especially harsichordists, pianists and harpists – drawing room performers—and with respect to genres like lieder and chamber music. The continued suspicion of other kinds of women performers is well illustrated by the disapproval shown by Smyth's Leipzig patrons, the Herzogenbergs and their circle, for opera – even though,

[25] Marcus, *Between Women*, p. 95.

as we know, Ethel Smyth would end up embracing a broader compositional vision.

Another trend that helped break down social barriers was that, as artistic connoisseurship became a more central feature of aristocratic identity, aristocratic women began asserting their patronage power more. Partly due to the established link between artistic patronage and sex (see above), they also fell violently and often ostentatiously in love with actresses and other women of talent, and sometimes sought to become their "protectors" in much the same way that aristocratic men did. The Duchesse de Villeroy, arguably the most famous aristocratic lover of women of the later eighteenth century, may or may not have had a lesbian affair with Mlle Clairon, the most famous *tragédienne* of the eighteenth-century French stage, as the contemporary rumor mill claimed. But there is no question that she was in love with her. One of the great patronesses of both the theatre and music in the second half of the eighteenth century, de Villeroy had love affairs with both actresses and opera singers. She also held all-women dinners, to which she invited both noblewomen and actresses, and she is alleged to have staged "sapphic" entertainments afterwards.[26] Middle-class women writers, always more respectable than actresses, also began socializing with actresses. Rahel Varnhagen (1771–1833), the famous Berlin salonnière, had numerous actress friends and received them in her home, while the writer and arts patron Hester Thrale Piozzi (1741–1821) became close friends with the actress Sarah Siddons. Obviously it was only a matter of time before some middle-class as well as aristocratic women would start falling in love with actresses and woman musicians. Marie-Jeanne Riccoboni (1714–1792), the best-selling French woman novelist of the eighteenth century, who herself had a background in the theatre, took as her life partner an actress named Thérèse Biancolelli (1723–1795). The aristocratic sculptor Anne Seymour Damer (1749–1828) had a close relationship, rumored to be lesbian, with the most popular English comic singer-actress of the day, Elizabeth Ferren (1759?–1828).[27] And they were just a few among many.

As with other women's same-sex loves before the twentieth century, these relationships, in all their unpredictable diversity, were performed against the

---

[26] Toepfer, "Orgy Salon."
[27] Deborah Hertz, "Salonières and Literary Women in Late Eighteenth-Century Berlin", in: *New German Critique* 5 (1978), pp. 97–108. For Varnhagen and romantic friendship see Deborah Hertz "Inside Assimilation: Rebecca Friedländer's Rahel Varnhagen", in: *German Women in the Eighteenth and Nineteenth Centuries: A Social and Literary History*, ed. Ruth Ellen B. Joeres and Mary Jo Maynes, Bloomington, Indiana 1986, pp. 271–288; Donoghue, *Passions between Women*, pp. 145–148, 266–267; Lanser, "Befriending the Body."

backdrop of considerable public acceptance. And even when they were not – the association of women performers with sexual excess was, as we have seen, long-lived – the disapproval of people women artists felt increasingly empowered to call "philistines" seldom detracted greatly from these women's professional success. This is the world that Ethel Smyth was born into and that she made her own. In her case it translated into some very familiar patterns: boarding school loves; a passion for at least one opera star; endless letter-writing; a long-time love alliance with a man who seems to have been little threatened by her intense connections to women; numerous passionate female friendships some of which were clearly physical in the lesbian sense, and some of which, almost certainly, were not; mannish clothes; and a life-long attraction to noblewomen, women who themselves patronized, "protected", and formed passionate bonds with artists, writers, actresses and musicians, including Ethel herself.

Conclusion

During Ethel Smyth's lifetime the "lesbian" began to emerge as a modern category of psycho-sexual and political identity, helped along, for better or for worse, by Krafft-Ebing, as well as by people he influenced, most notably Magnus Hirschfeld and Sigmund Freud. It was characteristic of this new view that both celebrants and critics of love between women began to see it as centered on genital sexual gratification and incompatible with heterosexuality and marriage – both significant changes from earlier times, though the transition was not swift, nor, arguably, was it ever complete. In many ways Smyth bridges that era before *Psychopathia sexualis*, and the society it helped create. We have seen how comfortably she inhabited the older world, but she played a role in later developments too, through her involvement in the women's suffrage movement (which was already becoming associated with perverse sex) and in the public persona she created for herself through her music and her remarkable autobiographical writings. Interestingly, she was not involved in the efforts, which started first in Germany, to agitate for the right of "inverts", "uranians" and women and men of the "third sex" to love as they wished.[28] They were a different generation from Ethel Smyth, and one suspects their understanding of love and sexuality, so indebted to Krafft-Ebing, would not really have suited her more expansive and experimental vision. Ethel Smyth's intense desire to live her life in her own way still has much to tell us about women artists, their loves, and the women *and* men who loved them in return.

[28] *Lesbians in Germany: 1890's–1920's*, ed. Lillian Faderman and Brigitte Eriksson 2nd ed., Tallahassee, Florida 1990, pp. ix–xxi.

Abstract

Gleichgeschlechtliche Liebe vor Psychopathia Sexualis *oder Was die junge Ethel wusste*

Das lange Leben Ethel Smyths war eine Zeit großer Veränderungen der Geschlechterverhältnisse, in der sich insbesondere die Vorstellungen von Sexualität und sexuellen „Abweichungen" erheblich wandelten. Aber die Geschwindigkeit und Richtung der Veränderungen wichen nicht nur in den Ländern, in denen Ethel Smyth lebte, voneinander ab, sondern hatten auch auf Frauen und Männer sehr unterschiedliche Auswirkungen. In Deutschland entwickelte sich eine Sexualwissenschaft, und deutsche Forscher lieferten die frühesten „Ethnographien" gleichgeschlechtlicher Gemeinschaften, die – etwa bei Magnus Hirschfeld – Beobachtungen über die Liebe und Sexualität zwischen Frauen einschlossen. Im England des späten 19. Jahrhunderts war offene Homosexualität und das Eintreten für die Rechte Homosexueller eng mit dem utopischen Sozialismus und der Suffragetten-Bewegung verknüpft. Aber in Deutschland, England und Frankreich hatten sexuelle Non-Konformitäten (einschließlich „offener Ehen", Bisexualität und Homosexualität) eine wesentlich längere Geschichte, insbesondere am Schnittpunkt von Adel, Mäzenatentum und Kunst. Hierfür ist etwa Kreis um die Princesse de Polignac ein Beispiel, mit dem Smyth gelegentlich in Kontakt war. Der Aufsatz betrachtet diese Entwicklung in vergleichender historischer Perspektive. Dabei wird das Verhältnis zwischen den traditionellen Orten und Trägern einer sexuellen Non-Konformität (adliges Mäzenatentum, aber auch jahrhundertealte Praktiken erotisierter „romantischer Freundschaften" zwischen Frauen) und der „neuen", sozial heterogeneren Welt der Kämpferinnen für Frauenrechte und finanzielle Unabhängigkeit der Frau betrachtet und auch nach den Auswirkungen der Diskussion um sexologische „Identitäten" gefragt, von denen eine wachsende Anzahl selbsternannter „Liebender ihres eigenen Geschlechts" Anfang des 20. Jahrhunderts in ihrem Selbstverständnis geprägt wurde.

Kordula Knaus
Mere Mates or Mainly Monsters: Homoeroticism and Homosexuality in Operas Around 1900

On June 7, 2008 New York City Opera announced that it had commissioned composer Charles Wuorinen to create an opera based on the 1997 short story *Brokeback Mountain* by Annie Proulx.[1] The story about two cowboys falling in love with each other in the 1960s and struggling to live their passion in a society that would not let them do so had already served as the basis for the 2005 Academy Award-winning movie *Brokeback Mountain*, directed by Ang Lee. Though homosexual characters have occasionally – and during the last couple of years more frequently – appeared in opera[2], a same-sex love story being central to an opera plot seems quite extraordinary even in our day and is another sign (or even highlight) of the growing visibility of homosexuality in our culture. It is no coincidence that this opera has been announced at a time when same-sex marriage or equal substitutes for marriage are being legalized in a growing number of countries.[3]

Connections between the values of a society and what happened on an operatic stage have always been strong. However, down the centuries opera has always occupied a rather ambivalent position: It has reflected moral, religious, or political values, but it was also a place for upheaval, for the extraordinary, for a playful handling of borders, and for a sphere that had no place in real-life society.

My article aims to track down the connections between homosexuality or homoeroticism in operas[4] dating from around 1900 and a society that had

---

[1] Steven McElroy, *'Brokeback,' the Opera*, in: New York Times, June 9, 2008, URL: http://www.nytimes.com/2008/06/09/arts/music/09arts-BROKEBACKTHE_BRF.html; Date of access: November 12, 2008.
[2] For example, several characters in Hans-Jürgen von Bose's *63: Dream Palace* (1990), the protagonist and other characters in Stewart Wallace's *Harvey Milk* (2005), Kreon in Rolf Liebermann's *Freispruch für Medea* (2001), Louis Ironson, Prior Walter and other characters in Peter Eötvös's *Angels in America* (2003).
[3] See for example the ILGA-map on LGBTI-Rights. URL: http://www.ilga.org/map/LGBTI_rights.jpg; Date of access: November 12, 2008.
[4] Another repertoire worth investigating in relation to homoeroticism or homosexuality would be operetta around 1900. I can refer here only to first findings on this

embarked on an intense medical, psychological and legal discourse on homosexuality only a couple of years earlier. I do not want to provide a "gay or lesbian reading" of operatic characters – several publications have appeared in past decades on that topic[5] – but rather investigate how obvious cases of homoeroticism were constructed within operatic plots and received by the audience – an audience that was part of a society in which Ethel Smyth lived.

Operatic characters romantically and/or sexually involved with other characters of their own sex were extremely rare around 1900, if not to say nonexistent. The reasons are obvious: In a society where any practice of homosexual behaviour was seen as a sin by the church, as a crime by legal authority, and as an illness by the (newly established) science of psychology[6], homoerotic desire had no place in a representative art form like opera.

A striking example of the banning of homosexuality from the operatic stage was Richard Strauss's adaptation of Oscar Wilde's play *Salomé* (1893) for his opera of the same name, which was first performed in 1905. Both the play and the opera start with a conversation between a young Syrian (in the opera called Narraboth) and the Page of Herodias, the Syrian being obviously in love with Salome and the Page trying to prevent him from looking at her. To claim that the Page constantly warns the Syrian because he himself is in love with him is clearly only one way of reading this scene. But later on in Wilde's play the Page himself utters some details about his relationship to the young Syrian.

The first passage occurs immediately after the Syrian kills himself:

"The young Syrian has slain himself! The young captain has slain himself! He has slain himself who was my friend! I gave him a little box of perfumes and earrings wrought in silver, and now he has killed himself! Ah, did he not foretell that some misfortune would happen? I, too, foretold

---

topic in the collection of essays: *Glitter and be gay. Die authentische Operette und ihre schwulen Verehrer*, ed. Kevin Clarke, Hamburg 2007.

[5] See *Queering the Pitch. The New Gay and Lesbian Musicology*, ed. Philip Brett, Elizabeth Wood and Gary C. Thomas, New York/London 1994; *En Travesti. Women, Gender Subversion, Opera*, ed. Corinne E. Blackmer and Patricia J. Smith, New York 1995; *Queer Episodes in Music and Modern Identity*, ed. Sophie Fuller and Lloyd Whitesell, Urbana/Chicago 2002; Judith A. Peraino, *Listening to the Sirens. Musical Technologies of Queer Identity from Homer to "Hedwig"*, Berkeley 2006. On the contemporary view of female homosexuality see also the contribution by Margaret Hunt in this volume.

[6] See for example Wolfgang Till, "Über die Konstruktion männlicher Homosexualität zwischen Normalität und Pathologie, zwischen Männlichkeit und Weiblichkeit", in: *Körper – Geschlecht – Geschichte. Historische und aktuelle Debatten in der Medizin*, ed. Elisabeth Mixa et. al., Innsbruck/Vienna 1996, pp. 132–146.

it, and it has happened. Well, I knew that the moon was seeking a dead thing, but I knew not that it was he whom she sought. Ah! why did I not hide him from the moon? If I had hidden him in a cavern she would not have seen him."⁷

In the second passage, some lines below, he talks about the Syrian's importance to him:

"He was my brother, and nearer to me than a brother. I gave him a little box full of perfumes, and a ring of agate that he wore always on his hand. In the evening we used to walk by the river, among the almond trees, and he would tell me of the things of his country. He spoke ever very low. The sound of his voice was like the sound of the flute, of a flute player. Also he much loved to gaze at himself in the river. I used to reproach him for that."⁸

Even if one does not go as far as to interpret the flute as a phallic symbol and consequently the "flute player" as an allusion to the sexual practices of the Syrian and the Page, it is obvious that the Page was in love with the Syrian, felt closer to him than a brother, made him presents, listened to his stories, wanted to protect him, and was jealous of the Syrian's narcissistic attitude. In his adaptation for the operatic stage Richard Strauss cut all these passages and reduced the on-stage appearance of the Page to the first scene of the opera. As a result the Page does not react at all to the death of Narraboth, nor do we even know if he is still on stage, as Strauss provides no stage direction for his exit. After his last utterance, "O, was wird gescheh'n? Ich weiss, es wird Schreckliches geschehn" (occurring when Salome wants to persuade Narraboth to let her talk to the Prophet) he simply disappears from the operatic score. Thus, the Page's homoerotic desire for the Syrian that was obvious from his strong reaction to his death in the Wilde play is completely excluded from Strauss's libretto.

Following Katie Begley, in the 1896 premiere of Wilde's *Salomé* at the *Theatre de l'Oeuvre Paris* theatre director Aurélian Lugné-Poe chose an actress as the Page to "avoid the homosexual overtones of the Page's affection for the young Syrian, a choice imitated by several subsequent directors."⁹ The reason was clearly that Wilde himself had served a two-year prison sentence

7 Oscar Wilde, *Salomé. A tragedy in one act*, translated from the French by Lord Alfred Douglas, in: *Complete Works of Oscar Wilde*, Glasgow 1994, pp. 590–591.
8 Ibid., p. 591.
9 Katie Begley, *Salome. A tragedy in one act*, http://etext.virginia.edu/subjects/salome/prod.html, Date of access: November 12, 2008.

for a sexual offence. Strauss, too, composed the part of the Page for a woman singer, following a tradition of trouser role pageboys in operatic history. He thus created a relationship between Narraboth and the Page that could easily be interpreted as a heterosexual one, upon seeing a woman perform the Page and hearing a woman's voice as well.[10] However, the Page does not assume a prominent profile in the opera and is dramaturgically and musically reduced to foreseeing the terrible events to come, in particular because his warnings allude musically to Salome's demands for Jocchanaan's head.[11] Thus, not only his voice is a woman's voice but also the contour of his vocal line is associated with the female main protagonist in the piece.

If Narraboth and the Page could have been perceived as heterosexual because the Page was a trouser role, the apparent conclusion would have been that in consideration of the gender of the singer other trouser roles placed in a heterosexual setting within the play could have been perceived as homosexual. To stay with Strauss, the most obvious example is *Rosenkavalier*. Margaret Reynolds has recently shown how the piece could work as a means of identification and a vehicle for sexual desire for lesbians.[12] My interest here is to reveal early 20th century sources that make a homosexual reading a subject of public discussion.

In contrast to Strauss's *Salome* or *Elektra*, where discussions of the deviant plots played a prominent role in newspaper reviews, *Rosenkavalier* did not provoke much debate on that account. However, discussion did arise concerning the first scene, where the Marschallin (a married woman) and her young lover Octavian are seen in bed the morning after they have obviously been indulging in sexual activity (during the prelude is heard before the curtain rises). The fact that a woman was singing Octavian played an important role in the discussion of this immoral scene.

---

[10] Ulrich Linke (*Im Ton vergriffen? Homosexualität in der Oper*, p. 21–22, URL: http://www.schwur.net/ht2002/linke.pdf, Date of access: November 21, 2008) thus talks about aural heterosexuality, the pendant to the term "aural homosexuality" proposed by Dame Joke, "Unveiled Voices. Sexual Difference and the Castrato", in: *Queering the Pitch*, p. 147.

[11] See for example the Page's "Du siehst sie immer an" (p. 10, bar 4–5) and Salome's "Ich will den Kopf des Jochanaan" (p. 272, bar 7–8, p. 273, bar 1) or the Page's "Schreckliches kann geschehn" (p. 13, bar 1–3) and Salome's "Gib mir den Kopf des Jochanaan!" (p. 286, bar 9–10, p. 287, bar 1) in Richard Strauss, *Salome. Musikdrama in einem Aufzug*, Op. 54, Studienpartitur, Wien 1996.

[12] Margaret Reynolds, *Ruggiero's Deceptions, Cherubino's Distractions*, in: *En travesti*, pp. 132–151; on the question of lesbian narratives in operatic plots see also Marilyn R. Farwell, *Heterosexual Plots and Lesbian Narratives*, New York/London 1996, pp. 1–3.

In a fictitious dialogue with the Rosenkavalier a contributor to the *Straßburger Post* argued:

> „Also eine Hosenrolle! Ja, das ändert aber die Sache nicht unerheblich. Die erste Szene zum Beispiel beim Aufgehen des Vorhanges ist an sich doch ein bißchen bedenklich [...]. [Aber] die sonst höchst pikante erste Szene wird dadurch gemildert, daß Sie kein Mann sind. Unwillkürlich, so supponieren die Zuschauer unter Ihr schmuckes gräfliches Kavaliergewand zarte Mädchenglieder, und die Sache wird unanstößig."[13]

The writer's concern is clearly the indecency of this bed scene at the beginning of the piece – indecency that is fortunately reduced because Octavian is performed by a woman singer. In the eyes of the author, the absence of a male singer on stage means the absence of any sexual activity on stage. He does not concede the two women any sexual attraction to each other.[14]

For the *Badische Landeszeitung* Albert Geiger wrote an article voicing similarly deep concern with the beginning of the *Rosenkavalier*:

> „Ich bin nun schlechterdings kein Moralist. Sinnlichkeit und Leidenschaft sind für die Kunst so notwendig, wie für das Leben. Aber – diesen Anfang einer Oper finde ich ganz einfach unanständig. [...] Hofmannsthal und Strauß haben da freilich einen scheinbaren Ausweg gefunden, um das Widerliche und Perverse dieses Vorgangs abzuschwächen. Einen scheinbaren Ausweg. Dieser siebzehn- oder achtzehnjährige Bub ist ja gar kein Bub. Denn der ‚Rosenkavalier' ist ja eine ‚Hosenrolle'. Ich muß gestehen: diese Kombination macht mir die Sache noch widerwärtiger. Zumal dieses Weib in Männerkleidern doch für unsere Vorstellung äußerst männliche Dinge verrichten muß [...]."[15]

---

[13] Well, a trouser role! Yes, that changes things not inconsiderably. The first scene for example when the curtain opens is a little worrying [...]. [But] the otherwise highly risky first scene is softened because you are no man. Involuntarily, the audience assumes a female body under your decorated courtly Cavalier garment, and the matter gets decent. "Beim Rosenkavalier, ein Plausch", in: *Straßburger Post*, January 23, 1911. Anonymous article, collected by the Richard Strauss Institut, Garmisch-Partenkirchen, Zeitungsarchiv (Transl.: K. K.).

[14] One could probably also see the trouser role Jack in Ethel Smyth's *The Wreckers* in this context. The 15-year-old Jack, being in love with Avis, is only exploited and used by her. He is not established seriously as a lover.

[15] I am absolutely no moralist. Sensuality and passion are as important for art as they are for life. But – this beginning of an opera I simply find indecent. [...] Hofmannsthal and Strauss seemingly found a way to soften the disgusting and perverse in this occurrence. Seemingly a way out. This seventeen or eighteen year old

Geiger's conclusions are the opposite of those drawn by the writer in the Strassburger Post. For him, the fact that the scene is played by two women makes it even more disgusting. Interestingly, what disturbs him most is that a woman singer has to do "männliche Dinge" (masculine things) on stage. Geiger's rhetoric resembles the medical and psychological discourse about homosexuality and gender roles around 1900. Central to the discussion of female homosexuality that started in the 1860s with publications of Carl Friedrich Otto Westphal (arguing his famous case of Fräulein N. who had a "fury to love women"[16]) was a connection between homosexuality and the reversal of gender roles. In Richard von Krafft-Ebing's *Psychopathia sexualis* of 1886 and similar writings by other authors, homosexual women were said to take on male attitudes: they preferred boys' games, they rivaled men, they did not like needlework, cosmetics, perfume or sweets, and they loved to smoke, drink, do sports, wear men's clothes and engage in higher education.[17] As Sabine Mehlmann argues, Kraft-Ebbing set in motion a highly differentiated discourse on healthy sexual behaviour that was oriented around reproduction, and sexual deviations that were not.[18]

But these close connections between sexual preferences and gender roles were not only used by those who created a psychopathology of sexual deviations but also by those who fought for the acceptance of homosexuality. In 1904, Anna Rüling, one of the first prominent lesbian activists, held a speech on the topic "What is the interest of the women's movement in solving the homosexual problem?"[19] She argued that the homosexual woman has many characteristics, inclinations, and talents usually ascribed to men; she has a clear intellect, whereas for heterosexual women feelings are of greater importance. Consequently, Rüling's view is that homosexual women can play an

> boy is not a boy at all. Since the Rosenkavalier is a trouser role. I have to admit: this combination makes the thing even more disgusting. In particular because that woman in men's clothes for our understanding has to carry out explicitly masculine things. Albert Geiger, "Unpassende Worte", in: *Badische Landeszeitung* No. 160, 5 April, 1911. Article collected by the Richard Strauss Institut, Garmisch-Partenkirchen, Zeitungsarchiv (Transl.: K. K.).

[16] See Hanna Hacker, "'Patientin fühlt sich von jeher zu Weibern hingezogen'. Eine Einführung in die Beziehungsgeschichte von Medizin und Frauenliebe", in: *Körper – Geschlecht – Geschichte*, pp. 116–131.
[17] See Hacker, "Patientin fühlt sich von jeher zu Weibern hingezogen", p. 121.
[18] See Sabine Mehlmann, *Unzuverlässige Körper. Zur Diskursgeschichte des Konzepts geschlechtlicher Identität*, Königstein 2006, p. 180.
[19] Anna Rüling, "Welches Interesse hat die Frauenbewegung an der Lösung des homosexuellen Problems? Eine Rede", in: *Jahrbuch für sexuelle Zwischenstufen unter besonderer Berücksichtigung der Homosexualität* 7 (1905), pp. 131–151.

important role in the fight for women's rights. Though later in her speech Rüling clearly argues for more flexibility of gender roles and a participation of women in education, public and political life, she constructs the homosexual woman as a warrior for women's rights because she has masculine qualities.

So when Albert Geiger criticizes the fact that the woman singer of Octavian has to do 'masculine things' on stage, this clearly reflects the debates on gender roles and homosexuality of the time. Strangely enough, Krafft-Ebing himself relates homosexuality to operatic trouser roles in one passage of his book when he says: „Auch Schauspielerinnen und Operettensängerinnen sind nicht so selten Konträrsexuale, besonders solchen [sic], die in Hosenrollen brillieren, denn hier sind sie in ihrem Element und spielen ihren wahren, d. h. männlichen Charakter."[20]

The most prominent homosexual operatic character deeply embedded in these discourses is Gräfin Geschwitz in Alban Berg's unfinished *Lulu*. Berg started to compose *Lulu* in the late 1920s, but the first version of Frank Wedekind's play *Die Büchse der Pandora. Eine Monstretragödie* (*Pandora's Box. A Monster's Tragedy*) dating back as far as 1894. Because the editor Albert Langen did not want to publish the theatre play in this form, Wedekind made drastic changes to the play; the first part, *Erdgeist,* was published in 1895, and the second, *Die Büchse der Pandora,* in 1903. In 1913 Wedekind again made profound changes to the edition included in the first *Gesamtausgabe,* the source Berg referred to when adapting the work for his libretto. Thus, from Wedekind's unpublished manuscript in 1894 to Berg's libretto in the 1920s the character of Geschwitz changes profoundly. In the course of these twenty-five years Gräfin Geschwitz loses more and more of her sexual desire and drastic longing for Lulu and becomes a faithful and loving companion to her.[21] Without going into detail with this rather well known example I want to investigate another opera scarcely known today, in which similar patterns can

---

[20] Also actresses and operetta singers may quite often be sexually inverted, particularly those who prove to be brilliant in playing trouser roles, because here they are in their element and play their real, this is masculine, character. Richard von Krafft-Ebing, *Psychopathia sexualis. Mit besonderer Berücksichtigung der konträren Sexualempfindung,* 14th edition, ed. by Alfred Fuchs, Vienna 1912, p. 301. (Transl.: K.K).

[21] This is to be observed even in very small details, for example when with her first entrance Gräfin Geschwitz brings with her a bouquet of "Tuberosen" – a flower whose odour was said to seduce young girls. In later versions and also in Berg's libretto they are reduced to a white bouquet. See also Kordula Knaus, "Pathologischer Fall oder bedingungslos Liebende? Über den Umgang der Musikwissenschaft mit Gräfin Geschwitz in Alban Bergs Oper *Lulu*", in: *Musik mit Methode. Neue kulturwissenschaftliche Perspektiven,* ed. Corinna Herr and Monika Woitas, Köln etc. 2006, pp. 213–224.

be observed for a libretto adaptation.

In 1906, only one year after Richard Strauss's *Salome* appeared on stage, Camille Erlanger's *Aphrodite,* after a novel by Pierre Louÿs, received its premiere in Paris.[22] Erlanger's opera, with Mary Garden in the leading role, was a huge success at the Opéra-Comique and by 1926 it had played in Paris nearly 200 times.[23] To mention Erlanger's *Aphrodite* and Strauss's *Salome* in one and the same sentence makes sense from various perspectives. Not only are both their subjects placed in an antiquity steeped in decadence and brutality, but also the authors of the literary sources had close connections to each other, resulting for example in the dedication of Wilde's French *Salomé* publication to Pierre Louÿs.

Aphrodite tells the story of the painter Démétrios falling in love with the courtesan Chrysis. She demands three gifts from him: the silver mirror of the courtesan Bacchis, the ivory comb of the highpriest's wife and the necklace of pearls decorating the Aphrodite statue in the temple. Démétrios fulfils the wishes but feels guilty about his acts of robbery and the murder of the highpriest's wife. When Chrysis wants to fulfil a wish in return, he demands from her that she shows herself in public with the stolen goods. Chrysis is sentenced to death; Démétrios naturally grieves about her fate.

Obviously the main couple of the opera is heterosexual, and again homosexuality is found elsewhere in the plot, namely in the world of the courtesans who play a prominent role in the atmospheric background of the piece. The first act opens at the market place where the courtesans Myrto and Rhodis accompany the dance of Théano by singing and playing the flute. After Rhodis has collected money from the people for their performance, Théano leaves to perform for the rich Callidés. But Rhodis says to Myrto:[24] « Mais nous n'irons pas avec elle. » (But we will not go with her.) And Myrto answers: « Non, ma Rhodis, rentrons. Viens avec ton amie: Elle te bercera, dans ses bras endormie (*Elle la prend par la taille et l'emmène.*) » (No, my Rhodis, we go back. Come with your friend: She will rock you to sleep in her arms. [*She takes her by the waist and leads her away.*]) We can also find an allusion to the nature of their relationship in the third act when the courtesan Bacchis is giving a huge fes-

---

[22] I want to thank Ulrich Linke for bringing this opera to my attention.
[23] See Rainer Franke, Art. "Aphrodite", in: *Pipers Enzyklopädie des Musiktheaters. Oper – Operette – Musical – Ballett*, ed. Carl Dahlhaus, Vol. 2, München/Zürich 1987, pp. 155–156.
[24] Camille Erlanger, *Aphrodite. Drame Musical en 5 Actes et 7 Tableux, après le roman de Pierre Louÿs. Adaptation de Louis de Gramont*, Partition chant e piano, Paris 1905, p. 19. Thanks to Volker Klostius for reviewing my translations from the French.

tivity. Myrto says: « Verse-nous du vin de Lesbos: c'est le meilleur. » (Fill the glasses with the wine from Lesbos. It is the best.) Rhodis answers: « Celui qui fait le plus aimer! » (It is this which makes one love most!)[25]

Clearly, it is no coincidence that Myrto mentions the island Lesbos and Rhodis refers in her answer to love. Considering the fact that French dictionaries from the 19th century already use the term "sapphisme" for female homosexuality and the term "lesbienne" for the female homosexual, these references were clearly understood by audiences around 1900, in particular because Pierre Louÿs himself initiated the literary "lesbian" Sappho interpretation with his *Les Chansons de Bilitis* in 1895.[26]

It is worth making a short excursion into Jules Massenet's *Sapho* of 1897, which offers another example of homoerotic overtones being excluded in opera. In contrast to Gounod's or Pacini's *Sappho* operas, Massenet's *Sapho* is not about the poet Sapho. In Alphonse Daudet's novel *Sapho* dating from 1884, which was the literary source for Massenet's opera, we learn that the main character Fanny Legrand obtained her courtesan-nickname Sapho while being the lover of a woman. Moreover, this revelation is the dramatic climax of the scene where Jean Gaussin is reading the love letters of her former (male) lovers.[27] In Massenet's opera we simply do not discover why Fanny Legrand is called Sapho and the climax of the scene is the revelation that she has an illegitimate child from a man who is in prison. (In Daudet's book the mother of the child is not Sapho but an unknown woman, already dead.)

But back to Lesbos, Myrto and Rhodis in Erlanger's *Aphrodite*: Whereas one finds out about the intimate relationship between Myrto and Rhodis only from these four sentences in the whole opera, Pierre Louÿs dedicates a whole chapter to them in his novel.[28] We learn that they have known each other since childhood and have loved each other and shared a bed since they were 11 years old. They are no courtesans and the jealous Myrtokleia wants to protect the prettier of them, Rhodis, when she has to dance at social gatherings. We find out how difficult it is for them to protect their love in a world where girls are married at the age of 12. One passage even speaks of Myrtokleias's wish to marry Rhodis, as was customary in her country, Ephesos. Chrysis – with whom they have spent that night – tells them that one day

---

[25] Erlanger, *Aphrodite*, p. 133.
[26] See Harriette Andreadis, Art. "Sapphic Tradition", in: *Lesbian Histories and Cultures: An Encyclopedia*, ed. Bonnie Zimmerman, New York/London 2000, pp. 666–668.
[27] Alphonse Daudet, *Sapho. Moeurs parisiennes*, Paris [without date], p. 92.
[28] Chapter 6: "Les vierges" in Pierre Louÿs, *Aphrodite. Moeurs antiques*, Paris 1896, pp. 70–77.

they will change the law even in Alexandria. (Obviously the exclusiveness of their relationship only applies to men as they have a threesome with Chrysis).[29] In the opera Myrto and Rhodis assume a function similar to the Page's in Strauss's *Salome*. This is particularly evident in their duet at the beginning of the piece where they do not express their own feelings but sing a song for the crowd at the market place. The song is about the destroying (or in this case transforming) power of love.

> « Le chèvre pieds jusque au fleuve
> A chassé la Syrinx éperdue et farouche !
> Eros ! Eros ! le pâle Eros qui de larmes s'abreuvé,
> Au vol a baisé sa joue et sa bouche !
> Eros ! Puis, sur la tombe humide il a cueilli pour nous
> Les roseaux dont il fit la flûte, voix touchante
> D'une âme morte, O femmes, qui nous chante
> Le désir douloureux, le désir douloureux, douloureux et doux. »[30]

(The Satyr followed the desperate and shy Syrinx up to the river!
　Eros! Eros! the pale Eros, full of tears, who on the fly kissed her on cheeks and mouth !
　Eros! Then, from the moist tomb he picked for us old reed and built a flute, touching voice of a dead soul, oh women, who sings to us of painful desire, of painful desire, painful and sweet.)

The story about the nymph Syrinx, who on being chased by the God Pan asks the river nymphs for help, the latter transforming her into sea wood of which Pan builds his flute, introduces central topics of the later plot: the power of desire, seduction, and death. In this way, also Myrto and Rhodis "foresee" the events to come but do not express their own feelings, nor even their feelings for each other. The musical setting, with the ostinato in the orchestral accompaniment and the highly chromatic vocal lines, communicates both a distant exoticism and an unpleasant threat of future happenings:

---

[29] The meeting with Crysis occurs in Chapter 7: "La Chevelure de Chrysis" in Louÿs, *Aphrodite*, pp. 78–84.
[30] Erlanger, *Aphrodite*, pp. 10–12.

Ex. 1: Camille Erlanger, *Aphrodite*, p. 10 (extract)

As in the adaptations of *Salome* and *Lulu,* in *Aphrodite* homosexuality is considerably reduced in the libretto. However, in contrast to *Salome* it is not cut completely and, moreover, it is enriched by another complementary same-sex couple: the wealthy courtesan Bacchis and her slave Corinna. (Interestingly, this relationship was not obviously a same-sex relationship in Pierre Louÿs's book.) The release of Corinna is the reason for Bacchis's festivities in the third act. Again, diverse allusions inform us about the nature of their relationship, especially when the six sisters of Corinna complain about their lower status. In an ensemble they sing: « Toujours de tout travail elle fut dispensée! Oui, notre sœur fut toujour caressée! Pour elle les baisers, les cadeaux, les bijoux! Pour nous la besogne et les coups! » (All day she is free from work! Yes, our sister is caressed all day! For her, the kisses, the gifts and the jewelry! For us, the work and the blows!)

Corinna's position as the favourite and lover of Bacchis is shortlived. When Bacchis realizes someone has stolen her mirror, Corinna's jealous sisters claim that she and her secret (male) lover committed the crime. They want her to be crucified. Bacchis, believing herself to have been betrayed, actually orders her to be crucified and she herself even hammers the first nail into Corinna's hand. While all the courtesans simply go on with their drinking and partying, Corinna is dying on the cross, accompanied only by Timon, who pities her.

Erlanger's opera offers very different types of same-sex couples. Myrto and Rhodis are the only couple in the whole piece whose relationship is not dominated by materialistic demands and hierarchies, whereas the liaison between Bacchis and Corinna ends with the one slaughtering the other in the most brutal way.

So how can we interpret these two couples against the backdrop of early 20th century culture? First of all, both couples are placed within a demimonde of courtesans where conventional morals obviously had no relevance. Bacchis can easily be seen as another monstrous woman (as were Lulu, Salome, Judith and others) who murders her – in this case female – lover. This couple represents only another facet of the orgiastic and deviant society depicted in the third act of the piece.

With Myrto and Rhodis the case is a little different because their relationship is positive and harmonious. So why were they not shown as pathological or obsessive characters as was the case with other lesbian characters appearing on stage at that time? Several arguments seem to deliver the answer to this question.

On the one hand, we find in fin-de-siécle France an increasing tradition for the leading male part being (again[31]) taken by woman singers. Jules Massenet, for example, composed the Prince in *Cendrillon,* Jean in *Le Jongleur de Notre Dame* and Cherubin in *Cherubin* for woman singers. This affinity for trouser role lovers could serve principally to demonstrate the perspective that the turn-of-the-century audience perceived two women performing on stage as a pair of lovers as being nothing out of the ordinary.

On the other hand, the non-existence of an autonomous female sexuality guarantees the decency of the lesbian couple. As we have already seen in the *Rosenkavalier* review, the contributor to the *Straßburger Post* did not perceive two women on stage as being possibly sexually involved with each other. He interpreted the scene as harmless and innocent. Of course, he was not alone in holding this opinion. In general, the medical and psychological discourse at that time claimed that women sensed no sexual desire at all – or very little, when compared to men – and if they demonstrated too much, they were said to be pathological. For Krafft-Ebing one of the reasons for the invisibility of female homosexuality in society is "weil das Weib an und für sich und jedenfalls auch das konträrsexuale nicht so sinnlich und aggressiv in der Erreichung

---

[31] Earlier traditions include Italian opera at the beginning of the 19th century (for example Tancredi in Rossini's *Tancredi* or Romeo in Bellini's *I Capuleti e i Montecchi*) or operetta between 1860 and 1880 (for example Fantasio in Jacques Offenbach's *Fantasio* or Wladimir Samoiloff in Franz von Suppe's *Fatinitza*).

des Geschlechtsbedürfnisses ist, wie der Mann, so dass der konträr-sexuale Verkehr unter Weibern nicht so auffällig ist und vom Laien als blosse Freundschaft gedeutet wird."[32]

Myrto and Rhodis with their rather tender than sexual scenes could easily be seen as a "mere friendship" that did not threaten the common ground of compulsory heterosexuality. Precisely this web of arguments provides the answer to the question of why not a single male gay character appeared on the operatic stage around 1900. It provides the answer to the question as to why, when compared with their literary sources in all operas I have mentioned, homosexual desire or passion is reduced to an account that is hardly noticeable. And it provides the answer to the question of why Ethel Smyth avoided placing any direct homosexual allusions or overtones in her operatic plots.[33] Neither mere friends in the manner of Myrto and Rhodis nor pathological cases such as Geschwitz or Bacchis would have served her as a means for identification.

Abstract

Harmlose Freundschaft oder pathologische Monstrosität. Homoerotik und Homosexualität in Opern um 1900

Opercharaktere die als homosexuell definiert werden können, oder Operninhalte, die homoerotisches Begehren offen zeigen, sind um 1900 zwar rar, aber in diesem Zeitraum treten die ersten prominenten Beispiele auf. Der Beitrag befasst sich mit der Darstellung dieser Charaktere und ihrer Rezeption durch das Publikum. Zu den Beispiele zahlen Richard Strauss' *Salome* (1905), wo homoerotisches Begehren zwischen dem Pagen und Narraboth bewusst ausgespart wird, außerdem zwei lesbische Paare in Camille Erlangers Oper *Aphrodite* von 1906 sowie die Gräfin Geschwitz in Alban Bergs unvollendeter *Lulu*. ein weiteres Augenmerk liegt auf der Frage, ob und wie die Hosenrolle

---

[32] [...] because woman (whether sexually inverted or not) is by nature not as sensual and certainly not as aggressive in the pursuit of sexual needs as man, for which reason inverted intercourse among women is less noticeable, and by outsiders is considered mere friendship. Krafft-Ebing, *Psychopathia sexualis*, p. 297. Translation cited from Krafft-Ebing, *Psychopathia sexualis*, New York 1906, p. 395.

[33] Elizabeth Wood showed in several articles how Smyth "masked" herself in male operatic characters or created "strong" women's characters as figures for identification, see Elizabeth Wood, "The Lesbian in the Opera: Desire Unmasked in Smyth's Fantasio and Fete Galante", in: *En Travesti*, pp. 285–305; Elisabeth Wood, "Performing Rights: A Sonography of Women's Suffrage", in: *The Musical Quarterly* 79 (1995), pp. 606–643.

vom Publikum des frühen 20. Jahrhunderts als eine Zurschaustellung homoerotischen Begehrens interpretiert wurde. Die fast vollständige Abwesenheit männlicher Homosexueller auf der Opernbühne und die Darstellung weiblicher Homosexueller als entweder harmlose Freundinnen oder pathologische Monster werden im Licht des medizinischen, psychologischen und rechtlichen Diskurses über Homosexualität interpretiert, der im Umfeld der Entstehung dieser Opern mit besonderer Intensität gepflegt wurde.

Christa Brüstle
Hell, dunkel, männlich, weiblich: „So shall I at last be whole". Musik und Homosexualität bei Michael Tippett

In seiner 1991 erschienenen Autobiographie, in der Michael Tippett relativ offen über Homosexualität spricht und seine homosexuellen Beziehungen schildert, gibt es einen kurzen Abschnitt, in dem er über die Wirkung seiner ersten großen Liebe zu dem Maler und Bildhauer Wilfred Franks berichtet. Das tiefe Gefühl und die überwältigende Erfahrung dieses Ereignisses (ab 1932) habe unter anderem auch die Basis für die „Entdeckung" seiner eigenen musikalischen „Sprache" gebildet, ohne dass er dies allerdings kompositionstechnisch in Worte fassen könne. Das starke emotionale Erlebnis habe sich im langsamen Satz seines ersten Streichquartetts niedergeschlagen: "all that love flowed out in the slow movement of my First String Quartet, an unbroken span of lyrical music in which all four instruments sing ardently from start to finish."[1]

Das erste Streichquartett ist datiert am 23. September 1935 und wurde 1943 überarbeitet: Aus dem ursprünglich viersätzigen Werk mit einem langsamen Kopfsatz quasi als Einleitung wurde ein dreisätziges Stück, bei dem die langsame Einleitung weggelassen wurde. Diese hatte ohnehin Aspekte des Mittelsatzes vorweggenommen, so dass der von Tippett genannte langsame Satz, umgeben von zwei schnellen Rahmensätzen, nun tatsächlich als Kontrast hervortreten konnte. Auch in der Tippett-Literatur, so etwa in der ersten großen Monographie von Ian Kemp, wird das erste Streichquartett Tippetts als Zäsur herausgestellt, hier noch beinahe literarisch umschrieben, es stelle eine fast unerklärliche Metamorphose von einer Raupe zum Schmetterling dar („a metamorphosis as remarkable as that between a caterpillar and a butterfly").[2] Auf die besondere Rolle des langsamen Satzes kommt Kemp ebenfalls zu sprechen und erklärt, dass Tippett über seine bisherige Themenbildung hinausgegangen sei, insbesondere bei der Gestaltung der „unendlichen" melodischen Linien: "their shaping is wholly individual and symptomatic of his willingness

---

[1] Michael Tippett, *Those Twentieth Century Blues. An Autobiography*, London 1991, S. 58.
[2] Ian Kemp, *Tippett. The Composer and His Music*, London 1984, S. 85.

to take the 'volutionary jump', to go beyond the forbidden corner and find himself in some unexpected paradise."³

Charakteristisch für den langsamen Satz des ersten Streichquartetts (*Lento cantabile*) sind nun nicht nur die individuell rhythmisch gestalteten und selbständig „ausgesungenen" Stimmen, die miteinander kombiniert werden, sondern vor allem die harmonischen Resultate und Wirkungen dieser Kombinationen. Innerhalb eines „tonalen" Rahmens (Des-Dur), der jedoch erst am Ende mit einer klaren Kadenz hervorgehoben wird, ergeben sich – vor allem durch Vorhaltsbildungen und Synkopen – Sekund- bzw. Septimreibungen, die kaum aufgelöst, sondern zumeist weitergetrieben werden. Binnenabschnitte sind überwiegend nicht durch Kadenzen markiert, sondern durch den melodischen und dynamischen, expressiven Verlauf, so dass die Abschnitte auch mit unaufgelösten Dissonanzen enden können. Gerade diesen Momenten, aber auch besonderen Spannungssteigerungen, folgen dann – jeweils mit „aufhellender" Wirkung – Fortführungen oder neue Ansätze in relativ entfernten Dur-Bereichen (so etwa nach dem Steigerungszug Takt 4 D-Dur oder nach dem Abschnittsende Takt 10 G-Dur, im zweiten Teil nach dem melodischen Aufschwung aus b-Moll Takt 20 E-Dur, später eine Bestätigung von G-Dur Takt 27; im dritten Teil wird in Ges-Dur zwei Mal Es-Dur als markante Zäsur gesetzt, bis die ausdrucksvolle Kadenz von As nach Des *molto lento* den Gesang abschließt). Ian Kemp wies zu Recht darauf hin, dass Tippett damit einen eigenen, individuellen Gebrauch von „Tonalität" als „expressive Farbgebung" entwickelt habe („Tippett's idiosyncratic use of tonality as expressive colour"), den er von hier aus systematisch weiterverfolgt habe.⁴ Kemp erklärte ferner, dass die verschiedenen Tonartenbereiche nicht funktional zu verstehen seien, sondern: "These tonalities are heard instead as sonorities, evoking associations from an inherited language of feeling" (Kemp spricht dort auch von „neo-romanticism of the adagio").⁵

Im vorliegenden Rahmen kann nicht näher darauf eingegangen werden, welche weiteren kompositorischen Aspekte Tippett damals auf einem neuen Niveau behandelte. Es ging vorrangig, wie bereits angedeutet, um die rhythmische und melodische Ausprägung, motivische Entwicklung und Individualisierung der Stimmen sowie um die Verstärkung der Arbeit mit rhythmischem und „dissonantem" Kontrapunkt (unter Einfluss zuerst von Paul Hindemith, dann von Béla Bartók).⁶

---

3   Ebd., S. 122.
4   Ebd., S. 123.
5   Ebd., S. 124.
6   Vgl. bei Kemp auch S. 76–78 zu den vorangegangenen kompositorischen Versuchen von Streichquartetten („a struggle to reproduce Beethovenian gestures", S. 78) sowie zu Tippetts harmonischen Neuerungen S. 95.

Notenbeispiel: Michael Tippet, String Quartet No.1, Satz II, *Lento cantabile*

Musikalisch hatte sich Tippett damit von der Jahrhundertwende schon relativ weit entfernt, aber gerade für seine Kompositionen ab den 1930er Jahren stellt sich zunehmend die Frage nach der Bedeutung von Reminiszenzen und Allusionen, die auf die musikalische Sprache des 19. Jahrhunderts zurückgehen beziehungsweise, die in einer modernen, rhythmisch motorisch getriebenen und/oder dissonant geprägten Umgebung als romantische Topoi wie Inseln aus einer fernen, „paradiesischen Welt" erscheinen. Es zeigt sich ein musikalischer „Dualismus", eine Polarisierung von Modernität und Romantik (um es sehr plakativ in Worte zu fassen), die sich für Tippett zu einem lebens langen Arbeitsfeld entwickelt hat. Dieses Arbeitsfeld bestand nicht zuletzt darin, in der Musik Vermittlungen zwischen diesen Polen zu finden. Dabei ging es zunächst in den Streichquartetten und Orchesterwerken um eine Polarisierung/Kontrastierung von Tonarten und Rhythmen sowie Konsonanz/Diatonik und Dissonanz/Chromatik. Seit den 1960er Jahren änderten sich die Mittel der Polarisierungen und Kontrastierungen, indem Tippett den Orchestersatz radikal fast nur auf Bläser und Schlagzeug reduzierte, neue Klangfarben wie beispielsweise E-Gitarre heranzog und somit die klangfarblichen Differenzen sowie „musikalische Gesten", also markante Themen und Motive zum Teil aus verschiedenen Musikrichtungen (Jazz, Pop, Blues), als charakteristische Definitionen von Gegensatzpolen benutzte. Tippett begann außerdem, mit Überlagerungen von verschiedenen Ausdrucksdimensionen und einer Mosaiktechnik sowie Kombinationen aus den unterschiedlichen strukturellen Modellen zu arbeiten, die sich vor allem in den Orchesterwerken zunehmend zu musikalischen „Landschaften" entwickelten.[7]

Doch ist die Vermittlung zwischen gegensätzlichen Dimensionen bei Tippett nicht nur ein kompositionstechnischer Aspekt, sondern sie lässt sich auch mit Lebensanschauungen verknüpfen, wie zum Beispiel aus einem frühen Radiovortrag vom Mai 1945 hervorgeht, in dem Tippett nicht das Kriegsende thematisiert, sondern – vielleicht gerade absichtlich – seinen Standpunkt als Komponist verdeutlicht.[8] Man vertrete als Komponist die Welt der Kunst, der Phantasie, der Natur, des Unbewussten, der Träume, der Hoffnung, der Wahrheit und der Schönheit. Diese stehe, so Tippett, der modernen Welt der Technik, der Entdeckungen und Erfindungen, der Alltags- und Arbeitswelt am Fließband, also der neuzeitlichen, industriell geprägten „zivilisierten" westli-

---

[7] Vgl. dazu David Clarke, *Language, Form, and Structure in the Music of Michael Tippett*, 2 Bände, New York/London 1989.

[8] Siehe Michael Tippett, „A Composer's Point of View", in: ders., *Moving Into Aquarius*, London 1959, S. 7–12. Vgl. dazu David Clarke, *The Music and Thought of Michael Tippett. Modern Times and Metaphysics*, Cambridge 2001.

chen Welt gegenüber, die den Menschen seiner Gefühle, seiner Imagination und seiner Seele entfremdet habe. Die Musik sei als Medium der Regeneration beziehungsweise der Möglichkeiten zu verstehen, sich diese „innere Welt" zu bewahren oder sie wieder zurückzugewinnen. Einige Jahre später nahm er dazu erneut Stellung und beendete seinen Text über die „gesellschaftliche Stellung der Musik" mit folgendem Statement: „Wir sind moralisch und emotional geschwächt, wenn wir unser Leben ohne künstlerische Nahrung verbringen; ja, unser Gespür für das Leben läßt nach. In der Musik spüren wir am unmittelbarsten jenen inneren Fluß, der unserer Psyche beziehungsweise der Seele Kraft gibt."[9] Auf Grund solcher Äußerungen, die ganz „unzeitgemäß" das Bild des romantischen Genies ebenso wie (seit der Antike bekannte) ethische und therapeutische Vorstellungen über die Wirkung von Musik ansprechen, ist Tippett in den vergangenen Jahrzehnten sowohl Eskapismus als auch Popularismus vorgeworfen worden. Dessen war er sich durchaus bewusst. Seine Homosexualität allerdings wurde in der Öffentlichkeit mit dieser sehr idealistischen Haltung, die bei Tippett Pazifismus und zeitweise Kommunismus/Sozialismus einschloss, nicht in Verbindung gebracht. Und auch Tippett selbst verknüpfte sie nicht explizit damit, obwohl er dieses Thema, wie eingangs angedeutet, in seiner Autobiographie recht freizügig behandelt hatte.[10] Dass sich Tippetts Plädoyer für die Wertschätzung von „inneren Werten", von Harmonie, Phantasie, Wahrheit und Schönheit allerdings gleichermaßen auf ein Plädoyer für die Liebe, und in seinem Fall für die gleichgeschlechtliche Liebe bezieht, dürfte außer Zweifel stehen. So sahen sich seit Mitte des 19. Jahrhunderts in vielen homosexuellen Zirkeln der gehobenen sozialen Schichten vor allem Intellektuelle und Künstler mit dem Hinweis auf einen besonderen Bezug zur Kunst, zu Schönheit, vorzugsweise zur Musik und zu einer „ästhetischen Lebensausrichtung" in einer Sonderstellung, die ihnen selbst ihre Gegner zugestanden. In dem lesenswerten Band *A Gay History of Britain*[11] werden die Anfänge einer „modern gay movement" mit folgenden, sich überlappenden Tendenzen beschrieben: Es habe sich um eine „artistic movement" seit den 1880er Jahren gehandelt, die unter dem Begriff „aestheticism" bekannt wurde. Obwohl

---

[9] Michael Tippett, „Zur gesellschaftlichen Stellung der Musik" (1961), in: ders., *Essays zur Musik*, hrsg. von Meirion Bowen, übersetzt von Meinhard Saremba, Mainz 1998, S. 32f.

[10] Vgl. Clarke, *The Music and Thought of Michael Tippett*, S. 229–231; vgl. dazu etwa Edward Venn, „Idealism and Ideology in Tippett's Writings", in: *Michael Tippett. Music and Literature*, hrsg. von Suzanne Robinson, Aldershot 2002, S. 35–59.

[11] *A Gay History of Britain. Love and Sex Between Men Since the Middle Ages*, hrsg. von Matt Cook, Oxford/Westport Connecticut 2007.

damit kein offenes Bekenntnis zu Homosexualität verbunden gewesen sei, wurden unter dieser Bewegung vor allem die viktorianischen Moralvorstellungen angegriffen. "Instead aestheticism replaced the notion that art should perform some moral function with a love of art for art's sake, a passion for intense feeling and an embrace of classical Greece, including its subtly homoerotic ideals of beauty."[12] Zu dieser idealistischen Aufwertung der Kunst, auch im Sinne der Steigerung und Anerkennung „anderer" sinnlicher Erfahrungen (in Deutschland etwa vergleichbar mit dem Kreis um Stefan George), kam hinzu, dass zeitgleich in der Naturwissenschaft Studien entstanden, die belegen sollten, dass Homosexualität eine „natürliche Variante" der menschlichen Sexualität darstelle, die sich vor allem auf das soziale Verhältnis unter Männern günstig auswirke (im Sinne einer Idealisierung von Männernetzwerken und Kameradschaft, die um die Jahrhundertwende vor allem im Kontext von Wirtschaft und Krieg hervorgehoben wurde).[13]

In den 1920er und 1930er Jahren verband sich die „Sonderstellung" einer „ästhetischen Lebensausrichtung", zu der auch teilweise – um diesen wichtigen Punkt nicht zu vergessen – eine Betonung „weiblicher Ideale" (Schönheit, Emotionalität etc.) gehörte, mit einem gewissen „upper-class"-Bohemien-Bewusstsein. War man(n) als Künstler Außenseiter der Gesellschaft, doch zunehmend toleriert als Teil der kulturellen Unterhaltung, so ließen sich darunter unausgesprochen auch die verschiedensten Lebensführungen subsumieren, solange der Staat nicht Gründe suchte oder an die Hand bekam, gesetzlich einzugreifen.[14]

Nachdem noch zu Anfang des 19. Jahrhunderts Männer auf Grund ihrer Homosexualität in England hingerichtet werden konnten – die letzte Hinrichtung von zwei Männern fand 1835 statt – und nachdem zwischenzeitlich unzählige Menschen auf Grund dieses „unnennbaren Vergehens" zu Gefängnisstrafen oder Zwangsarbeit verurteilt worden waren (darunter 1895 Oscar Wilde), wurde privat praktizierte Homosexualität unter Erwachsenen in weiten Teilen Großbritanniens erst seit 1967 (*Sexual Offences Act*, erweitert 1980/82) legalisiert.[15] In seiner Autobiographie, die trotz der sich in den späten

---

[12] H.G. Cocks, „Secrets, Crimes and Diseases, 1800–1914", in: *A Gay History of Britain. Love and Sex Between Men Since the Middle Ages*, hrsg. von Matt Cook, Oxford/Westport Connecticut 2007, S. 108.

[13] Vgl. dazu ebd., S. 108f.

[14] Vgl. Matt Houlbrook, *Queer London. Perils and Pleasures in the Sexual Metropolis, 1918 – 1957*, Chicago/London 2005.

[15] Siehe Matt Cook, „Queer Conflicts. Love, Sex and War, 1914–1967", in: *A Gay History of Britain. Love and Sex Between Men Since the Middle Ages*, S. 145–177, insb. S. 176.

1980er Jahren durch das Aufkommen von AIDS drastisch veränderten Atmosphäre insgesamt als Symbol für die befreienden Veränderungen gelesen werden kann, fand Michael Tippett vielleicht gerade für diese Situation ein Sinnbild. Er schildert dort am Ende den Traum von einem Haus, das ihm Meirion „Bill" Bowen, sein Lebensgefährte von 1974 bis zu seinem Tod 1998, gebaut hatte. Es war ein Haus mit vielen Zimmern, in denen genau das zu finden war, was augenblicklich gebraucht wurde. Es war belebt von glücklichen, jungen Menschen, die sich frei darin bewegten, „a house that is free and open".[16]

Bleibt also in Tippetts Musikessays, die 1959 und 1974 (*Moving into Aquarius*), 1980 (*Music of the Angels*) und 1995 (*Tippett on music*) gesammelt veröffentlicht wurden, die Verbindung von kulturidealistischen und zivilisationskritischen Ideen mit privaten Erlebnissen nur in indirekter Form herauslesbar, so können wir nun weiterhin fragen, inwiefern sich nach dem langsamen Satz im ersten Streichquartett Tippetts Homosexualität über den vagen Ausdruck der ersten Liebe hinaus in seinen Werken manifestiert hat, und in welcher Form und in welchen Zusammenhängen. Zur Beantwortung dieser Fragestellung ist es naheliegend, konkrete Inhalte aus der Vokalmusik und hauptsächlich den Opern heranzuziehen, auf die darum im Folgenden etwas näher eingegangen wird. Tippett komponierte fünf Opern, *The Midsummer Marriage* (1947–52, uraufgeführt 1955 in London), *King Priam* (1958–61, uraufgeführt 1962 in Coventry), *The Knot Garden* (1966–70, uraufgeführt in London 1970), *The Ice Break* (1973–76, uraufgeführt in London 1977) und *New Year* (1985–88, uraufgeführt in Houston 1989). In jeder der Opern geht es, kurz zusammengefasst, um das Bestehen von Konflikten zwischen Menschen – zwischen Generationen, zwischen Mann und Frau, zwischen Menschen aus unterschiedlichen gesellschaftlichen Schichten – und um die Lösung oder Auflösung der Konflikte. In *Midsummer Marriage* beispielsweise, für die nicht nur, aber zum bedeutendsten Teil Mozarts *Zauberflöte* als Vorbild diente, ist es das Paar Jennifer und Mark, das sich quasi selbst auf die Probe stellt. Jennifer begreift sich als reine, unschuldige „Lichtgestalt", die Mark als leidenschaftliche, „dionysische" Figur der Erde zurückweist. Doch beide werden dazu gebracht, sich in die Regionen des jeweils anderen hineinzuversetzen, so dass sie am Ende nicht ihre Gegensätzlichkeit vertiefen, sondern ihre Ähnlichkeit erkennen und das Begehren des Anderen als Verlangen nach einem erfüllten Leben oder Ausleben aller Dimensionen ihres eigenen Selbst aufzufassen in der Lage sind.[17]

---

[16] Tippett, *Those Twentieth Century Blues. An Autobiography*, S. 278.
[17] Zu den Opern vgl. Eric Walter White, *Tippett and His Operas*, London 1979, Angelika Fisher, *Die Bühnenwerke Michael Tippetts* (= Europäische Hochschul-

Um eine ähnliche Anerkennung der unterschiedlichen Facetten einer Persönlichkeit geht es in Tippetts zweiter Oper *King Priam*, in der Homers *Ilias* die Basis der Erzählung darstellt. König Priamus verliert seinen Heldensohn Hector im Kampf gegen Achilles, so dass die Rache Paris zufällt, dem ungeliebten Sohn, der in den Augen des Vaters ein Schwächling und Feigling ist. Der Vater muss jedoch erkennen, dass beide Söhne Persönlichkeitsstrukturen verkörpern, die von ihm selbst ausgehen. Als Nebenschauplatz deutet Tippett in *King Priam* im zweiten Akt (Anfang 2. Szene) eine Beziehung zwischen Achilles und Patroclus an. Patroclus wurde von Hector umgebracht, daher stellt sich Achilles dem Kampf mit Hector, dem Mörder seines Freundes. Diese Episode bleibt allerdings, wie erwähnt, eine Nebenhandlung, obwohl sie musikalisch in und mit einem Duett zwischen Achilles und Patroclus ausformuliert ist und in Inszenierungen entsprechend betont werden kann. Die Szene, die von Kriegslärm umgeben ist, bildet eine Insel des Privaten. Sie beginnt zunächst mit einem einfachen, durch Gitarre begleiteten Lied von Achilles, der die Kriegssituation und die Abwesenheit von der Heimat betrauert, zeigt also die „schwache Seite" des Kämpfers. (Die „starke Seite" des Helden wird erst durch den Tod seines Freundes wieder entfesselt.)

In der dritten Oper *The Knot Garden*, in der Tippett Figuren und Szenen aus Shakespeares *Sturm* mit dem Plot einer Familientherapie verbindet, spielen sich labyrinthische Verwicklungen zwischen einem Ehepaar, einem homosexuellen Paar sowie zwei weiteren Frauen und dem Familientherapeuten Mangus ab, letzterer fungiert quasi als Spielleiter (vergleichbar mit Prospero).[18] In dieser Oper über den „Irrgarten" und das „Labyrinth" hat Tippett der Figur des Musikers Dov autobiographische Züge verliehen. So scheitert (im 1. Akt in der 10. und 11. Szene) die Beziehung zwischen dem schwarzen Dichter Mel und dem weißen Musiker Dov auf Grund der Hinwendung Mels zu einer Frau, ähnlich dem Ende der Partnerschaft Tippetts mit Wilfried Franks 1938. Auch der Musiker Dov bleibt danach einsam zurück, findet dadurch allerdings zur eigenen musikalische Sprache (vgl. 2. Akt, 5. und 6. Szene; 3. Akt, 9. Szene). Die Musik und die Erfahrung von Musik wird hier übrigens mit den Liebeserfahrungen sowie mit den schmerzhaften Erfahrungen der Trennung unmittelbar verbunden, wenn nicht sogar gleichgesetzt.

schriften: Reihe 36, Musikwissenschaft; Bd. 100), Frankfurt a.M. 1993, sowie Richard Elfyn Jones, *The Early Operas of Michael Tippett. A Study of the* Midsummer Marriage, King Priam *and the* Knot Garden, Lewiston 1996.

[18] Vgl. Fisher, *Die Bühnenwerke Michael Tippetts*, S. 111–121.

The Knot Garden, 2. Akt, 5. Szene (Ausschnitt):

FABER
Heartbreak: good grief?
And dare I guess
The cause, the agent;
That man of honey:
Mel?

DOV
Not honey: bitter.
Or bitter-sweet;
Like music.

Tippett hat in einem Text über seine Opern zur Deutung der Figur des Musikers festgehalten, Dov sei eine Figur in *Knot Garden*, die schließlich den anderen fern bleibe, sogar letzten Endes isoliert sei und bloß von dem impotenten Mangus bedauert werde. „Für mich", so schreibt Tippett, „schien eine Identifikation mit Dov, dem Sänger und Musiker, der großem Leid Ausdruck verleiht, immer naheliegend". Seine Schlüsselszene findet sich im 2. Akt, als er von Mel dazu gezwungen wird, den Bruch ihrer Beziehung zu akzeptieren; ja, gezwungen, all seine Kräfte als Musiker aufzubieten. Mel sagt zu ihm: "Stop howling now. / Become yourself. / Go turn your howls to music" (Ende der 6. Szene im 2. Akt). „Auf diese Weise", so Tippett, „wird Dov mit seinen zukünftigen Aufgaben als Sänger und Komponist konfrontiert."[19] In dieser Figur des Dov spiegeln sich also einerseits sicherlich einige wesentliche Aspekte der privaten und professionellen Situation und Entwicklung von Tippett selbst, doch andererseits verglich sich Tippett, gerade im Blick auf diese Oper, auch mit der Figur des Mangus, der alle Handlungsfäden bestimmt, verstrickt und letztlich löst, der insofern eine Außenperspektive einnimmt, die ihn erhaben über die Geschicke der Figuren walten lässt.[20]

In der vierten Oper *The Ice Break* werden Konflikte zwischen Generationen, zwischen Einwanderern und Einheimischen, zwischen Schwarz und Weiß ausgetragen, und auch hier scheinen die Konflikte in einer Figur gebündelt zu werden: in dem jungen Mann Yuri (Sohn des Einwanderers), der am Ende seine

---

[19] Siehe Michael Tippett, „Träume der Macht, Träume der Liebe", in: *Essays zur Musik*, hrsg. von Meirion Bowen, übersetzt von Meinhard Saremba, Mainz 1998, S. 280.
[20] Vgl. ebd., S. 275.

Identitätskrise überwindet und damit eine Wiedergeburt erleben kann. In der letzten Oper *New Year* schließlich geht es ebenfalls um eine Wiedergeburt, hier allerdings wird sie durch den Kontakt mit Außerirdischen beziehungsweise Besuchern aus der Zukunft ermöglicht, die dem Waisenkind Jo Ann Wasser aus dem „See des Erinnerns" verabreichen, so dass die junge Frau selbstbewusst ihr Leben zu meistern beginnt, während die Besucher in die Zukunft zurückkehren.

Fasst man die Inhalte der Opern zusammen, so wird deutlich, dass es auch in diesem Kontext um Polarisierungen geht, die letztlich als Teile eines Ganzen begriffen werden sollen. Es ist im vorliegenden Rahmen nicht möglich, auf die Verankerungen dieser Gedanken in den tiefenpsychologischen Schriften C. G. Jungs einzugehen, die Tippett (gerade nach seinem Bruch mit Franks 1938) sehr intensiv studierte.[21] Bereits in seinem Oratorium *A Child of Our Time*, das 1944 uraufgeführt wurde und Tippetts internationalen Ruf begründete, erhielten sie große Bedeutung, in dem der Komponist das Schicksal des verzweifelten jüdischen Flüchtlings Herschel Grynspan zu einer psychologischen Deutung positiver und negativer Beweggründe menschlichen Tuns wandelte. Das Finale kulminiert in einem Plädoyer für die Akzeptanz gegensätzlichster Erfahrungen: "I would know my shadow and my light, so shall I at last be whole." Gemäß der erwähnten Arbeit mit unterschiedlichen Regionen von Tonarten, die verschiedene expressive Dimensionen definieren und symbolisieren, gestaltete Tippett in diesem Finale des frühen Oratoriums – in einer Variation des Einleitungschorsatzes (gewendet an das Kollektiv der Zuhörer) – eine tonartliche „Aufhellung", die von h-Moll ausgeht und über F-Dur in ein strahlendes A-Dur mündet (erst solistisch, dann in Wiederholung mit dem Chor). Dass in solchen Anordnungen die „Bewegung" im Quintenzirkel eine große Rolle spielt, gerade in den Werken bis in die 1940er und 1950er Jahre (unter Rückgriff auf die Theorien von Vincent d'Indy), kann hier ebenfalls nur am Rande erwähnt werden.[22] Jedenfalls verband Tippett im Finale des Oratoriums – wie in den späteren Bühnenwerken – mit dem Plädoyer für die selbst-

---

[21] Vgl. dazu Clarke, *The Music and Thought of Michael Tippett*, S. 13–35.

[22] „The principal lesson learnt from d'Indy [*Cours de Composition Musicale*, 1897–1900] however concerned the control of modulation, or the structural use of tonality. This is seen in relation to an ascending or a descending cycle of fifths, the former creating a ‚clarté', the latter ‚obscurité'", Kemp, *Tippett. The Composer and His Music*, S. 89f. Vgl. dazu auch Kenneth Gloag, *Tippett. A Child of Our Time*, Cambridge 1999; sowie Verf., „Michael Tippett (1905–1998): A Child of Our Time", in: *Geschichte der Musik im 20. Jahrhundert: 1925–1945* (= Handbuch der Musik im 20. Jahrhundert, Bd. 2), hrsg. von Albrecht Riethmüller, Laaber 2006, S. 271–277.

bewusste Akzeptanz der eigenen Licht- und Schattenseiten eine Hoffnung auf Erneuerung, Veränderung zum Guten, die auch musikalisch zum Ausdruck kommen soll –, ein Impuls, den der Komponist nicht aus den Augen verloren zu haben scheint.

Zum Abschluss sei festgehalten, dass die Frage nach der Relevanz der Homosexualität Tippetts für seine Musik nicht eindeutig beantwortet werden kann. Es scheint überwiegend eine indirekte, abstrakte Thematisierung oder Auseinandersetzung mit Homosexualität zu geben, mit Ausnahme der erwähnten Episoden in der Oper *The Knot Garden*, wobei hier allerdings die Ergebnisse des Geschehens im Vordergrund stehen. Tippett setzte sich persönlich sehr mit seiner Homosexualität auseinander, wie seine Autobiographie nahe legt. Daraus scheint er das allgemeine und für seine Werke in vieler Hinsicht bestimmende Resümee gezogen zu haben, dass schonungslose Selbstanalyse und Selbsterkenntnis sowie kompromisslose Anerkennung der sich daraus ergebenden Resultate ethisch-moralisch, ganzheitlich dazu verhelfen könnten, die Lebenssituation des „modernen Menschen" auszugleichen.

Thesen aus der „Gay and Lesbian Musicology", so etwa von Philip Brett oder Suzanne Cusick, legten in den letzten Jahren nahe, dass zu überlegen ist, ob und wie sich die Identität als Musiker und Komponist nicht doch viel enger als angenommen mit der sexuellen Identität verbinde. Dabei stünde zum Beispiel die Musik für „das Weibliche" oder „Andere" und für die Intensität von „anderen" sexuellen Erfahrungen.[23] Es erscheint mir schwierig, diesen Aspekt für oder bei Tippett zu entscheiden, doch klar ist, dass Tippetts Sicht auf die Bedeutung von Musik in der Gesellschaft und für die Gesellschaft (auch wenn sie abstrakt umgesetzt ist) nicht von seinen eigenen Erfahrungen als Teil der (britischen) Gesellschaft und auch als Teil der „homosexual community" zu trennen ist.

Abstract

Light, Dark, Male, Female: "So shall I at last be whole" – Music and Homosexuality in the Works of Michael Tippett
Looking at the oeuvre of Michael Tippett (1905–1998), and considering thereby not only his vocal music and his operas but also his instrumental works, one detects that his compositions were led by a principle which doubtless also belonged to the principles by which he lived: he created polarity in order to

---

[23] Vgl. dazu die Beiträge in *Queering the Pitch. The New Gay and Lesbian Musicology*, hrsg. von Philip Brett, Elizabeth Wood, Gary C. Thomas, New York/London (2. Auflage) 2006.

show that opposites are part of a whole and not mutually exclusive. Already in his oratorio *A Child of Our Time*, which was premiered in 1944 and established Tippett's international reputation, the composer transformed the fate of the despairing young Jewish fugitive Herschel Grynspan into a psychological analysis of positive and negative motives for human action. The finale ends with a plea for the acceptance of opposing experiences: "I would know my shadow and my light, so shall I at last be whole." Among the opposites which, from Tippett's point of view, have to be reconciled are not only the light and dark sides of life, but also the polarity of "male" and "female". *The Midsummer Marriage* (premiered in 1955) was the first of a series of operas in which he dealt with this aspect. Tippett tended to allow his male characters, in particular, to incorporate "femininity" as well, or presented male characters who discover their "femininity" (their "other side") and accept it for themselves, for example in *King Priam* (premiere 1962). It seems clear that this is to a great extent influenced by the biography of Tippett himself, who analysed his own homosexuality with the help of C. G. Jung's studies. The question arises, however – and this applies not only to Tippett but to many other male and female composers as well – to what degree a composer's life and oeuvre can be seamlessly linked. What hints may be found in the instrumental pieces, for example, taking Tippett's *Concerto for Double String Orchestra* (1938/39) and his four symphonies (1944/45, 1956/58, 1970–72, 1976/77) as a basis? Can the principle of polarity and the search for synthesis in the instrumental pieces be similarly attributed to Tippett's biography, and what evidence is there to support such attribution?

Erik Dremel
„All there was in my heart". Ethel Smyth, ihre *Mass in D* und ihre Freundschaft zu Pauline Trevelyan

Die *Mass in D* ist eines der bekanntesten Werke Ethel Smyths. Um die Bedeutung der Komponistin herauszustellen, wird stets auf die Messe verwiesen, denn diese gehört neben den Opern zu jenen Werken, die man im Englischen „large-scale" nennt, die also einen großen Aufführungsapparat erfordern und zugleich einen hohen ästhetischen Anspruch erheben. Es scheint eine gewisse Emphase hörbar zu werden, wenn es heißt, Smyth habe eine Messe für Soli, Chor und Orchester komponiert oder wenn sie selbst schreibt: "I was composing a Mass."[1] Das Werk wurde am 18. Januar 1893 in der Londoner Royal Albert Hall durch die Royal Choral Society und das Albert Hall Orchestra unter der Leitung von Sir Joseph Barnby uraufgeführt. Die Widmung der *Mass*, "Written for Pauline Trevelyan", scheint auf den inneren Anlass für die Komposition zu verweisen. Oft wurde vermutet, dass die Messe durch die Freundschaft mit Pauline motiviert wurde, was auf den ersten Blick einleuchtet, da Pauline Trevelyan römisch-katholisch war.[2] Im Folgenden soll dieser Spur nachgegangen und das Verhältnis von Trevelyan zu Smyths *Mass* und natürlich auch zu Ethel Smyth als Person und Künstlerin befragt werden. Zugleich wird der Versuch unternommen, die Geschichte der Entstehung der Messe mit Hilfe der autobiographischen Schriften von Ethel Smyth zu rekonstruieren. Dass es sich bei diesen Texten Smyths um ein Unternehmen der Selbstkonstruktion – mehr als dreißig Jahre nach den Ereignissen – handelt, ist evident.[3]

---

[1] Ethel Smyth, *Impressions that Remained*, Memoirs Vol. II "In the Desert", London 1919, S. 238.
[2] Vgl. z.B. Meinhard Saremba, *Elgar, Britten & Co. Eine Geschichte der Britischen Musik in zwölf Porträts*, Zürich, St. Gallen 1994, S. 130f; vgl. CD-Booklet *Ethel Smyth: Mass in D*, Audite Mus B0000268B4, S. 4; vgl. *Komponistinnen des 19. und 20. Jahrhunderts. Eine Dokumentation,* hrsg. von der Hochschule für Musik und Theater Hannover, Frauenbüro (Birgit Fritzen). Konzeption und Redaktion: Susanne Rode-Breymann und Katharina Hottmann, Hannover 1999, S. 68.
[3] Vgl. dazu den Beitrag von Melanie Unseld im vorliegenden Band.

Gleichwohl werden sie hier zum Zweck der Annäherung an das komplexe Phänomen als ernstzunehmende und authentische Quellen behandelt. Nur so ist – jenseits der vermeintlich „historisch-realen" Geschehnisse – eine Annäherung an die mentale Wirklichkeit Smyths möglich.

Die Messe: Fragen an eine Gattung

Bei der Beschäftigung mit anglikanischer Kirchenmusik in den Dekaden vor 1900 fällt auf, dass es für einen britischen Komponisten oder eine Komponistin um 1890 recht ungewöhnlich war, eine Orchestermesse zu komponieren. Kaum andere Werke dieser Gattung sind bekannt, was auch für Länder außerhalb Großbritanniens gilt, also in typischerweise „katholischen" Kernlanden. Dies dürfte mit dem Cäcilianismus nach 1860 zu tun haben, der – so bedeutend er für die katholische Kirchenmusik war – Orchestermessen gerade nicht motivierte. Ähnliches lässt sich über die anglikanische Kirchenmusik des 19. und frühen 20. Jahrhunderts sagen, denn was in dieser Zeit reichlich entsteht, sind zwar Vertonungen des englischen Messtextes, allerdings in deutlich kleineren Besetzungen (Orgel mit 4stimmigem Chor) und in Komposition und Aufführung wenig aufwendig. In der Intention solcher Messen liegt es, gerade den Gemeinden und Chören kleinerer und mittlerer Kirchen der Vorstädte und Dörfer Stücke zur Verfügung zu stellen, die mit geringen Mitteln, also mit dem eigenen Gemeindechor (gleichgültig ob gemischt oder als Knabenchor) und mit dem Organisten realisiert werden können. Eine Orchestermesse, die mit großer Besetzung und hohem technischen Anspruch den Anforderungen für die gottesdienstliche Praxis anglikanischer Vorstadtgemeinden keinesfalls gerecht wird, lässt sich daher nicht in diese kirchenmusikalischen Bestrebungen englischer Komponisten einpassen. Für die Praxis anglikanischer Gemeinden also ist die *Mass* gewiss nicht konzipiert und auch nicht für die römisch-katholische Gottesdienstpraxis, sondern eindeutig für den Konzertsaal. Damit stellt sie sich erkennbar in die Tradition von Beethovens *Missa solemnis* (1823), die ebenfalls in D(-Dur) steht.[4]

Wie außerordentlich Ethel Smyths Unternehmen war, lässt sich auch an einer anderen Tatsache erkennen. Im selben Jahr, in dem Smyths *Mass in D* in London unter großer Beachtung der Presse und der musikalischen Öffentlichkeit uraufgeführt wurde, begann der aktivste englische Komponist dieser Zeit, der als Komponist, Dirigent, Professor und Musikfunktionär das britische Musikleben maßgeblich bestimmte, Charles Villiers Stanford, ebenfalls

---

[4] Die Beziehung der beiden Werke zueinander wäre in der Forschung noch zu klären.

eine Orchestermesse zu schreiben.⁵ Dass Stanford sich in seinem Unternehmen von Smyths *Mass* inspirieren ließ, kann vermutet werden.

Zu klären ist noch der Begriff des „Katholischen". Pauline Trevelyan entstammte einer römisch-katholischen Familie und lebte diese Konfession fromm und leidenschaftlich. Damit gehörte sie und ihre Familie einer Minderheit in Großbritannien an, denn zwar gab es auch nach der Trennung der Church of England von Rom im 16. Jahrhundert zahlreiche römische Katholiken, deren gesellschaftliche Stellung jedoch als problematisch angesehen werden muss. So durften sie lange Zeit keine politischen Ämter übernehmen und keinen (Land-)Besitz haben bzw. vererben und waren durch die Bindung des Wahlrechts an Grundbesitz von den Wahlen wie auch vom Militärdienst ausgeschlossen. Erst eine ab 1778 sukzessiv veränderte Gesetzeslage beendete letztlich 1829 diese Situation (*Catholic Relief Act*). Eine intensive theologische Auseinandersetzung zwischen dem römischen Katholizismus und der Church of England gab es in den 1830er Jahren und im ganzen 19. Jahrhundert. Nach der Jahrhundertmitte bildete die „Oxford Movement", eine hochkirchlichen Erneuerungsbewegung innerhalb der Church of England, eine starke und gesellschaftlich extrem einflussreiche Strömung in Großbritannien. Diese auch als „High-Church-Movement" bezeichnete Richtung betonte das Katholische – im Sinne des Allumfassenden, Allgemeingültigen und die abendländische Kirche kultisch Zusammenhaltenden. So wie die Church of England sich schon im 16. und 17. Jahrhundert in „High Church" und „Low Church" einteilen ließ und sich erstere schon in dieser postreformatorischen Epoche selbst gelegentlich als „katholischer" als die Römische Kirche bezeichnete, gab es Mitte des 19. Jahrhunderts eine innerkirchliche Bewegung, die dieses „katholische" Element besonders betonte und in ihren Gottesdiensten auch demonstrativ zeigte. Man spricht in England diesbezüglich von „Anglo-Catholic". Diese Bewegung, durch das „Oxford Movement" ausgelöst, hatte eine weite Verbreitung und starke gesellschaftlich-kulturelle Prägekraft. In den anglo-katholischen Gottesdiensten wurde teilweise die lateinische Sprache für die Liturgie verwendet, was allerdings nicht erklärt, warum Smyth in der *Mass* (mit diesem englischen Titel) den lateinischen Messtext vertonte. Das Lateinische der *Mass in D* stellt eine Relation zur Römischen Kirche her, aber eine, die durch die Oxford-Bewegung und die liturgischen Bestrebungen der Anglo-Catholics ohnehin schon bestand.

Dass sich Smyth eventuell auf diese Form des Katholischen bezog, ist an der Stellung des Satzes „Gloria in excelsis Deo" zu erkennen, der gemäß der

---

5   Vgl. Stephen Banfield, *The Early Renaissance – Mackenzie, Stanford and Smyth*, in: British Opera in Retrospect, hrsg. von der British Music Society, London 1986, S. 63–68.

Liturgie des *Book of Common Prayer* nicht an zweiter, sondern an fünfter Stelle steht. Diese liturgische Reihenfolge, die das *Book of Common Prayer* im Zuge der Loslösung von Rom propagierte, bezieht sich auf die theologische Legitimation dessen, was im oben ausgeführten Sinne als katholischer als die römische Kirche bezeichnet wurde. Vermeintlich nach mittelalterlichen englischen Formularen rekonstruiert, sollte diese Stellung des *Gloria* eine Distanz zur römischen Liturgie demonstrieren, die durch die historische Legitimation „älter als die römische" artikuliert wurde. Daraus folgt, dass die gelegentlich geäußerte Deutung, Smyth habe ein musikalisch wirkungsvolles „Finale" gewollt und darum aus musikdramaturgischen Gründen eine Umstellung der Sätze vorgenommen,[6] nicht ganz triftig ist: Für in der Church of England sozialisierte Engländer im 19. Jahrhundert war die von Smyth geforderte Reihenfolge nichts Ungewöhnliches. Festzuhalten ist aber auch, dass es ihr an keiner Stelle um einen echten liturgischen Bezug geht: Weder in einem römisch-katholischen noch in einem anglo-katholischen Gottesdienst sollte das Werk je erklingen oder formalen Strukturen der Liturgie „dienen".[7] Vielmehr geht es in der Messe um eine innere Religiosität, die Smyth selbst formuliert: "Into that work I tried to put all there was in my heart."[8]

Smyth und das Religiöse

Mehrfach finden sich in den autobiographischen Veröffentlichungen Smyths Aussagen zur Religion, naturgemäß vor allem zum Christentum.[9] Sie schreibt, dass sie als junge Frau vom „Oxford Movement" fasziniert, ja geradezu gefesselt gewesen sei: "I had been very High Church".[10] In den Memoiren ist deutlich erkennbar, dass diese Begeisterung für das „very High Church" – wenn sie auch schon zuvor begonnen hatte –, insbesondere für die Zeit in München, also die Zeit der Begegnung mit Pauline Trevelyan, von großer Bedeutung war.

---

[6] Vgl. CD-Booklet Smyth: *Mass in D*, S. 5; vgl. *Komponistinnen des 19. und 20. Jahrhunderts*, S. 72.
[7] Christopher St. John, *Ethel Smyth. A Biography*, London 1959, S. 187.
[8] Smyth, *In the Desert*, S. 238.
[9] Auf Bemerkungen zu anderen Religionen kann hier nicht weiter eingegangen werden. Es ist indes anzumerken, dass die Frage der Religion und des Religiösen am Ende des 19. Jahrhunderts und um 1900 in England wie in ganz Europa eine entscheidend große kulturelle Rolle spielte. In Hinsicht auf die sog. „Weltreligionen" – im Übrigen eine englische koloniale Konstruktion des 18. Jahrhunderts – ist festzustellen, dass europäische Konzepte gegenüber den fremden Religionen eine hohe Attraktivität besaßen.
[10] Smyth, *In the Desert*, S. 233.

Smyth nennt diese Zeit in ihren autobiographischen Schriften gerne „Munich mood". Diese „München-Stimmung" ist dabei stets religiös konnotiert in einer engen Personalbeziehung zu „Christus" und bezieht sich im autobiographischen Rückblick zugleich auf die Nähe zu Pauline Trevelyan. Wie es biographisch zu dieser Verknüpfung kommt, wird noch zu erörtern sein.

Immer wenn Smyth auf Religiosität zu sprechen kommt, betont sie ihre Begeisterung für das „very High Church". Sie erkennt selbst, dass es sich dabei um eine religiöse Euphorie handelt (die in religionspsychologischen Stufenschemata der frühadoleszenten Entwicklungsphase zugeordnet wird[11]) und schreibt auch, dass diese religiöse Euphorie später verblasste. Allerdings hält sie fest, dass der hochkirchliche Aspekt des Anglikanismus auch weiterhin für sie seine Anziehungskraft behielt und einen bemerkenswerten Zugriff auf ihre Imagination hatte und dass alle Anschauungen der „Low church" ihr immer mehr zuwider wurden.

Grundsätzlich spricht die Smyth-Biographik mit Blick auf die mittleren und späten 1880er Jahre von einer langandauernden Krise, die durch die Trennung von der Familie Herzogenberg – vor allem von Elisabeth von Herzogenberg –, durch fehlende berufliche Erfolge und durch Enttäuschungen und Orientierungslosigkeit ausgelöst war.[12] In der Folge wuchs in Smyth ein Gefühl von Heimatlosigkeit. Rastlose Reisen zwischen England und Deutschland waren die Folge und trugen ihrerseits zu diesem Gefühl der Entwurzelung bei. Smyth erkennt selbst zwar ihre enge Bezogenheit auf England und ihre Familie, zugleich wird ihr jedoch klar, dass sowohl das Familienleben als auch das englische Musikleben zu eng und für ihr Fortkommen nicht förderlich sind. Daher rührt ihr ständiges Bedürfnis, England und ihre Familie stets schnell wieder zu verlassen.

Im Herbst 1889 reist sie wieder nach Deutschland, diesmal nach München. Hier ist sie im Hinblick auf die Religion besonders fasziniert von den „last found traces of religion on a German scene"[13]. Selbst in München, besonders aber in den ländlichen Gebieten Bayerns finde sich noch „a certain fantastic element",

---

[11] Vgl. James W. Fowler, *Stages of Faith. The Psychology of Human Development*, New York 1981; *Christian Perspectives on Faith Development*, hrsg. von Jeff Astley, Grand Rapids 1992; Heinz Streib, *Hermeneutics of Metaphor, Symbol and Narrative in Faith Development Theory*, Frankfurt am Main 1991.

[12] Vgl. Saremba, *Elgar, Britten & Co.*, S. 129, ebenso in Louise Collis, *Impetuous Heart. The Story of Ethel Smyth*, London 1984; vgl. auch Erik Dremel, „,Always Germany, the obsessive comparison'. Englische Musiker an deutschen Konservatorien im 19. Jahrhundert", in: *England & Deutschland. Beiträge zur Musikforschung, Jahrbuch der Bachwochen Dill*, München und Salzburg 2002, S. 21–37.

[13] Smyth, *In the Desert*, S. 205.

das der römische Katholizismus mit sich bringe und das sie aus dem eher strengen und nüchtern lutheranischen Leipzig nicht kannte.[14] In München gäbe es sogar noch eine Hexe in der Stadt, mit einer enormen Anzahl von Kunden. Dieses „fantastic element" des Religiösen hatte es ihr angetan, der Aspekt des Irrationalen, Rätselhaften, dem sich zu nähern eher mit Methoden von Mystik und Mysterium gelingt als mit der Ratio. Hier ist dasselbe Motiv erkennbar, das bei Engländern eine Begeisterung für das Archaisch-Kultische des Anglo-Catholic evozierte.[15] Dass sich die Faszination bei Smyth wenige Jahre später vom Mystischen weg und zum Poetischen hin entwickelt, ist nicht verwunderlich.

„Munich mood"

Mit dieser Gesamtdisposition persönlicher Religiosität, die offenkundig reflektiert war und mit Freunden und Familie diskutiert wurde,[16] hängt die genannte „Munich mood" zusammen. Hier scheint sich die religiöse Phase von Smyth räumlich und zeitlich begrenzbar zuzuspitzen. Smyth schreibt in Bezug auf die „Munich mood" später von „a new religious conviction"[17], die zwar in einem bereits vorher existierenden Kanal floss, aber eben doch neu war. Diese „new conviction" wird nicht explizit erläutert, gleichwohl ist klar, dass sie auch mit der römischen Katholizität der Trevelyans zusammenhängt – und mit einem Buch, das Pauline Trevelyan vergessen hatte, worauf später noch einzugehen sein wird.

Dass sie in München aufgrund ihrer religiösen Gesamtdisposition zwar vom Römisch-Katholischen fasziniert war, das Anglikanische aber nicht vollständig verdrängt oder überlagert wurde, lässt sich aus zwei Stellen der Memoiren schließen. Erstens zitiert Smyth die befreundete Mrs. Benson (die Gattin des Erzbischofs von Canterbury), die in Bezug auf Pauline gesagt habe: "If *she* hasn't made a Roman of you you must indeed be a good Anglican."[18] Zweitens gibt es in *Streaks of Life* eine Episode, in der Smyth beschreibt, wie sie Queen Victoria Teile aus der Messe vorspielt. Nachdem Smyth den Raum verlassen hat, spricht die Königin die ebenfalls anwesende Empress Eugénie an: "'I hear

[14] Ebd., S. 205.
[15] Vgl. Nigel Yates, *Anglican Ritualism in Victorian Britain*, Oxford 1999; vgl. John S. Reed, *Glorious Battle. The Cultural Politics of Victorian Anglo-Catholicism*, London 1996; vgl. Martin Wellings, *Evangelicals Embattled. Responses of Evangelicals in the Church of England to Ritualism, Darwinism and Theological Liberalism (1890–1930)*, Carlisle 2003.
[16] Vgl. ebd., S. 244.
[17] Smyth, *In the Desert*, S. 233.
[18] Ebd., S. 236; vgl. die Parallelstelle in Ethel Smyth, *As Time Went on*, London 1936, S. 60.

she is going to turn Roman Catholic,' to which she [the Empress] had replied: 'I dont't think that is at all likely.' Here I broke in, being at that time much preoccupied with religious questions, and exclaimed that she might surely have added: 'On the contrary, she is an enthusiastic Anglican.'"[19] Es geht also im Zusammenhang mit der *Mass* nicht einfach um einen römisch-katholischen Bezug, der durch Pauline Trevelyans römischen Katholizismus ausgelöst oder motiviert worden wäre, sondern um eine wesentlich komplexere Beziehung von individueller Religiosität und Katholizismus. Die kleine Wendung „being at that time much preoccupied with religious questions" ist aufschlussreich und verweist auf das, was Smyth immer wieder als „Munich mood" beschreibt.

Zu dieser „Münchner Stimmung" gehören nicht zuletzt Fragen des Komponierens und Musizierens. In München arbeitet Smyth mit dem Dirigenten Hermann Levi zusammen, der sie unterstützte und förderte. Im gemeinsamen Studium ihrer eigenen wie auch anderer Partituren, namentlich der *Serenade* und der Ouvertüre *Antony and Cleopatra*, erkennt sie selbst noch Schwächen, die sie bearbeiten will. Ein konkreter Anlass für ein intensives Arbeiten in München bestand unter anderem darin, dass August Mann, Direktor der berühmten Londoner „Crystal Palace Concerts", ihr aufgrund ihres Streichquartetts zugesagt hatte, im Frühjahr 1890 ein Orchesterwerk von ihr aufzuführen, wenn er bis zum 1. Januar 1890 eine Partitur vorliegen hätte. Zugleich nimmt Smyth als Zuhörerin am Münchner Musikleben teil, besuchte die Oper und hörte Konzerte. Das ist das äußere Setting im November 1889.

Die Trevelyans

Bei einer Aufführung von Richard Wagners *Lohengrin* im November 1889 in München entdeckt Smyth im Publikum einige Mitglieder der englischen Familie Trevelyan – Freunde ihrer Schwester Mary Hunter, die sie im Sommer desselben Jahres kennengelernt hatte.[20] Die Trevelyans sind ein altes englisches Adelsgeschlecht mit Stammsitz in Cornwall, ihm entstammen mehrere Wissenschaftler und Politiker, die im 19. und frühen 20. Jahrhundert wichtige Positionen (z.B. als Minister, Gouverneure in Übersee usw.) innehatten. Lady Trevelyan gehörte einer der ältesten irischen Adelsfamilien an, deren Abstammung aus der mythologischen Genealogie der Milesier hergeleitet wird. Die Familie Trevelyan war römisch-katholisch, Smyth beschreibt sie als „devout Catholics", also fromme, praktizierende Katholiken, „but of the Old English type".[21]

---

[19] Ethel Smyth, *Streaks of Life*, London 1921, S. 101.
[20] Vgl. Smyth, *In the Desert*, S. 209ff.
[21] Smyth, *In the Desert*, S. 210; damit meint sie eine den Auffassungen des Galli-

In ihren Memoiren schildert Smyth diese Familie als „one of the most original and delightful of personalities".[22] Alle Mitglieder seien äußerst musikalisch, und ihre Ansichten über Kunst stimmten mit ihren eigenen so vollkommen überein,[23] dass es eine große Freude sei, mit ihnen zu diskutieren. Zudem besäßen sie ein untrügliches Gefühl für Musik, wüssten viel und urteilten gründlich.[24] Die drei Töchter hätten Musik studiert, wohl auch in Deutschland, worauf Smyth allerdings nicht weiter eingeht. Die irische Abstammung der Mutter spräche für ihre Musikalität und ihren Kunstsinn,[25] und Sir Alfred Trevelyan – zwar Engländer, aber wie die ganze Familie „unlike the ordinary Englishman in his views and tastes" – sei „one of the most original and delightful of personalities".[26] Pauline, die älteste der drei Töchter, war nach Smyths Urteil „probably the most musical of the party, anyhow the chief executant".[27] An anderer Stelle schreibt Smyth über sie: „Servant of two Passions, religion and music",[28] und: Pauline Trevelyan lebe in „twin realities, religion and music".[29] Die ganze Familie schere sich nicht um Gesellschaft oder Konvention, sondern „they thought for themselves and belonged to no set in particular, which is perhaps the only receipt for keeping a really fresh mind."[30] Smyth fügt sogar noch hinzu, sie seien „real artists at heart".[31]

Bei der ersten Begegnung waren Sir Alfred und Pauline noch nicht dabei, sie kamen erst zu einer Aufführung von Wagners *Ring des Nibelungen* hinzu, was für Smyth eine beachtliche Veränderung mit sich brachte. Die Anwesenheit der nun fünfköpfigen Familie „made all the difference for the time being, and we revelled in music together".[32] Besonders eine Aufführung von Beethovens *Missa Solemnis*, immer noch im November 1889, war ein Schlüsselereignis: Smyth beschreibt ihre emotionale Involviertheit und erhöhte Sensibilität. Auf-

---

kanismus zuneigenden Katholizität, die das Königtum als natürliche Leitung der Kirche versteht. Diese ist zugleich eine ältere Katholizität als jene, die durch die zahlreichen Konversionen des 19. Jahrhunderts quasi neu entstanden ist.

[22] Smyth, *In the Desert*, S. 209.
[23] Vgl. ebd.
[24] Vgl. ebd.
[25] Irland war um 1900 für englische Künstler/innen aller Disziplinen ein idealisiertes und verzaubertes Traumland. Man bedenke, wieviele englische Komponisten sich mit irischen Sujets in ihren Werken beschäftigten.
[26] Ebd., S. 209.
[27] Ebd., S. 210.
[28] Smyth, *As Time*, S. 60.
[29] Smyth, *In the Desert*, S. 217.
[30] Ebd., S. 210.
[31] Ebd., S. 222.
[32] Ebd., S. 210.

grund ihres damaligen „state of mind" habe sie das Gefühl gehabt, „it seemed to me I had never heard it [*Missa Solemnis*] before".[33] Diese erhöhte Aufmerksamkeit wird verstärkt durch ein Treffen mit Hermann Levi am Morgen nach der Aufführung, der mit ihr das Werk (oder zumindest Passagen daraus) am Klavier analysiert und bespricht.

Was ist dieser „state of mind"? Er bezieht sich wahrscheinlich zunächst auf die Verliebtheit in Pauline Trevelyan; zugleich aber scheint eine religiöse Orientierungssuche im Spiel zu sein, die durch die persönlichen Krisen und Lichtblicke ausgelöst oder verstärkt wurde. Wie bedeutend Pauline Trevelyan für diese Stimmungen ist, wird immer wieder angedeutet: "During these weeks began what [...] was destined to be an eventful relation, my friendship with Pauline."[34] In den Monaten zuvor war Ethel Smyth in depressive Zustände verfallen, nachdem sich ihre Beziehung zu Elisabeth von Herzogenberg getrübt hatte. Welche Rolle Pauline Trevelyan für Smyths Gefühlsleben spielte, wird aus einem Satz ihrer Memoiren deutlich: "But little did I dream that when all else had failed, when, with the cheapening of what had been my great treasure[35] life seemed almost worthless, a miracle would be wrought by what one calls change … and that the agent, humanly speaking, was to be Pauline."[36]

Pauline

In Smyths Schriften finden sich verschiedene Beschreibungen Pauline Trevelyans, die offenbar mehr über Smyths Blick auf die Freundin aussagen als über letztere selbst. Smyth beschreibt die Ruhe ihres Wesens: "I often noticed how, quite unconsciously, she imposed her ways on all around her – merely by the penetrative strength of *'a gentle noble temper, a soul as even as calm'*."[37] Diese Ruhe, die sich gelegentlich auch als Schweigsamkeit äußert, löst in Smyth das Gefühl aus, angenommen zu sein und verstanden zu werden, was ihr in ihrer Krisensituation gut getan haben dürfte:

> "The quality of her spirit sometimes put her beyond one's reach; I did not always understand her, but was invariably and perfectly understood. There seemed to be no limit to her instinctive grasp of life and its intricacies; essential rays that got broken and dispersed on the rough surface of

---

[33] Ebd., S. 210.
[34] Ebd., S. 216.
[35] Damit ist die Trübung der Beziehung zu Elisabeth von Herzogenberg gemeint.
[36] Ebd., S. 210.
[37] Smyth, *In the Desert*, S. 217.

> other minds passed easily and unbroken into hers. You could have been silent with her all your days and yet know you have become part of her mind. Assurances were neither given nor needed … her quiet reticence bred a faith that nothing could trouble."[38]

„Faith" meint den religiösen Glauben, erschöpft sich aber nicht darin, sondern bezieht sich im Sinne von Vertrauen auch auf die zwischenmenschlichen Bereiche. Schon diese Beschreibung ist eine Liebeserklärung an Pauline Trevelyan; darüber hinaus überträgt Smyth ihre Zuneigung auch auf deren Mutter, die ihre Tochter selbst anbetete („worshipped") und ihr so ähnlich war („resembled Pauline").[39]

Wie so oft in ihren autobiographischen Schriften verpackt Smyth ihre Vorstellungen gelegentlich in die Berichte und Beschreibungen Dritter (die womöglich auch so stattgefunden haben können, es ist aber auffällig, dass dies eine durchgängige Technik der Reminiszenz ist). So gibt sie wieder, wie Lady Trevelyan ihre Tochter mit einer Art Traumsequenz charakterisiert: "If I were to go into Pauline's room, [...] and find she had suddenly vanished, melted into air leaving no trace, it would hardly suprise me."[40] Smyth kommentiert diesen Satz:

> "There was neither sentiment nor apprehension in her manner, it was merely a characterization that conveys what for lack of a better word one might call the *unearthly element* about Pauline. Her extreme gentleness and delicate beauty had something to do with it, but these were only the garments of her soul. Full of enjoyment of life, a grand laugher – and this I think stands high on the list of merits – there was yet the abiding suggestion of a visitant from another planet lent to this world for the time being … and as it turned out not lent for long."[41]

Das erwähnte „unearthy element" ist ein Indiz für eine sublimierende religiöse Überhöhung der Person Pauline Trevelyans. Die Verklärung geht noch weiter: "It was strange to realize that this most serene and contented of beings had been acquainted with physical pain from youth upwards, indeed was seldom free from it; here then was one key to her *saintliness*."[42] Auch Pauline Trevelyans erotische Anziehungskraft wird beschrieben: "But

---

[38] Ebd., S. 217f.
[39] Ebd., S. 218.
[40] Vgl. ebd., S. 216.
[41] Smyth, *In the Desert*, S. 216, Hervorhebung ED.
[42] Ebd., Hervorhebung ED.

on another point enlightenment of a less distressed kind awaited me; it appeared that every man she met fell in love with her – generally two men at a time – and the lives of her mother and sisters, so they said, were sometimes made a burden to them by Pauline's disconsolates."[43] Nie habe sie jedoch aus dieser Anziehungskraft einen Vorteil gezogen oder Freude an der Macht über andere Menschen gehabt. Auch diese Zuschreibung deutet auf eine Stilisierung als eine Art Heilige hin.

All diese Beschreibungen und Charakterzeichnungen lassen gewiss nicht mehr als nur vorsichtige Vermutungen über das Verhältnis zwischen Pauline Trevelyan und Ethel Smyth zu. Viele Formulierungen mögen klischeehaft erscheinen, klingen jedoch so liebevoll und offenherzig, dass man von ihnen angerührt wird. Und sie alle geben Aufschluss über den „Munich mood". Da die Trevelyans bereits am 29. November 1889 gemeinsam mit Smyth aus München in Richtung Wörishofen abreisten,[44] hielt dieser Zustand lediglich etwa vier Wochen an. Wie diese Zeit gestaltet war, wie oft Begegnungen stattfanden und was gemeinsam unternommen wurde, lässt sich ebenfalls nur bruchstückhaft rekonstruieren. In den Memoiren ist von regelmäßigen Konzert- und Opern-, aber auch Gottesdienstbesuchen die Rede, daneben gab es Treffen, Gespräche und dergleichen. Mitte Dezember reiste die Familie weiter nach Cannes.[45] Zurück blieb eine verwirrte und tieftraurige Ethel Smyth, die zu genau dieser Zeit aus ihrer Wohnung ausziehen muss, weil der Hauswirt – sie verwendet das schöne Wort „Hausherr" in deutscher Sprache – nicht an alleinstehende Damen vermietet. Sie zieht noch vor Weihnachten zweimal um, wird krank und immer deprimierter. An die Freundin Nelly Benson schreibt sie am 21. Dezember 1889:

> "Yes, you are right, I am ill; [...] Seeing what the Trevelyans' relation to God and the world is, loving Pauline at once almost as I did (I swear to you chiefly because of that[46] but also because of herself), feeling the brokenhearted when they went away, finding my vaunted strength and calm gone, coming back to this miserable lodging ... all this brought about a crisis."[47]

---

[43] Ebd., S. 216.
[44] Ebd., S. 211.
[45] Ebd., S. 219.
[46] Damit ist die Trennung von Elisabeth von Herzogenberg gemeint, auch der Halbsatz vor der Klammer dürfte ein Vergleich mit der Beziehung zu der einstigen Freundin sein.
[47] Smyth, *In the Desert*, S. 221.

Mystik

Bei all dem ist der religiöse Aspekt nicht zu vernachlässigen, der in den ja deutlich später festgehaltenen Aufzeichnungen eine große Rolle spielt. Eine kleine, aber wichtige Episode macht die Verquickung von Verliebtheit und religiöser Suche und Verwirrtheit deutlich. Pauline Trevelyan hatte bei der Abreise aus dem Hotel ein Büchlein vergessen und bittet Smyth, es dort abzuholen, um es für sie aufzubewahren.[48] Das Buch stellt damit quasi ein Pfand für das Wiedersehen dar, aber auch – so deutet es Smyth – einen Anstoß, das römisch-katholische Andachtsbuch selbst zu lesen. Ethel Smyth aber verliert das Büchlein auf dem Heimweg auf der Straße und ist verzweifelter als zuvor. Auf ein Suchinserat hin erhält sie das Buch zurück, wie sie Nelly Benson berichtet: "last night it came back, almost like a message from him whom the book is about."[49] Sie fährt fort: "Then this book came back and I feel as if I had been purposely driven into my last entrenchments. I give in and am ready and longing to try and learn there is another refuge and strength than human love and my own powers. I know it will take long but I believe it won't be denied in the end."[50]

Offensichtlich spielte dieses Buch in den religiösen „convictions" Smyths eine entscheidende Rolle. Es handelt es sich um *Imitation of Christ*[51] von Thomas von Kempen (Thomas à Kempis) aus dem frühen 15. Jahrhundert, einem der am meisten rezipierten mystischen Bücher überhaupt. Das Buch zählt zur deutsch-niederländischen mystischen Schule des 14. und 15. Jahrhunderts und war unter Katholiken ebenso wie später unter Protestanten verbreitet. Es gehört zum Kanon der Exerzitien des Jesuitenordens und auch John Wesley, der Begründer des englischen Methodismus, berief sich auf *De Imitatione Christi* als Motiv für seine Bekehrung. Das Werk ist eine Kompilation von Gedanken, die als suggestive Setzungen stehen bleiben und nicht argumentativ schlüssig ein- oder weitergeführt werden. Inhaltlich geht es um Demut und Leidensbereitschaft. Tragender Gedanke aller Reflexionen ist der Rat und die Anleitung zur Selbstaufgabe. Dieses Buch liest Smyth in den Tagen kurz

---

[48] Vgl. ebd., S. 221.
[49] Ebd.
[50] Ebd., S. 222.
[51] Das Werk, im Original *De Imitatione Christi* (Die Nachfolge Christi), in gereimten Versen verfasst, ist vermutlich eines der am weitesten verbreiteten Bücher des Christentums. Ein englischer Druck wurde erstmals 1502 publiziert, es folgten zahllose Auflagen. Thomas a Kempis (um 1380–1471) war Augustiner-Mönch und ein Mystiker des 15. Jahrhunderts, auch Dichtungen und Kompositionen werden ihm zugeschrieben.

vor Weihnachten, dessen Nahen sie ein wenig fürchtet, da sie das Fest gänzlich allein in einer fremden Stadt, ohne Familie und ohne Pauline Trevelyan, wird verbringen müssen.[52] Die Lektüre dürfte die eigentliche „Crisis", den Gipfel- und Wendepunkt der psychischen Situation, mit ausgelöst haben. Bei einem Gottesdienstbesuch am Weihnachtstag bricht sie emotional zusammen: "I stayed there in a dark corner, weeping, weeping... stayed on while others were communicating."[53] In den Memoiren beschreibt sie, was ihr im Moment des psychischen Zusammenbruchs klar wurde, und dies steht offenkundig im Zusammenhang mit der Botschaft von *De Imitatione Christi*, dem Prinzip der „Selbstaufgabe" als Inbegriff erfüllten Lebens:

> "Now all was clear to me; I had always thought of myself, and of nothing else... [...] always myself. No wonder I had failed; no wonder all I had touched [...] had turned into dust and ashes; no wonder that even Lisl was lost to me and that I had gone into the desert in vain. Now my path was clear... music must be thrown overboard too, there was only one road to happiness, renunciation."[54]

Nachdem sie in der englischen Kirche noch zur Messe gegangen ist, ohne zu kommunizieren ("I did not communicate myself, but went home full of a great peace"[55]), verlässt Ethel Smyth am zweiten Weihnachtstag krank und unter schwierigen äußeren Umständen München in Richtung England – eine Reise, die sie später „that nightmare return to England" nennt.[56]

Im Anschluss an die Beschreibung der Münchner Ereignisse und ihrer Rückkehr folgen in Smyths Memoiren mehrere Seiten, in denen sie die Zeit ihrer Rekonvaleszenz und ihre familiäre Situation schildert, insbesondere die Hochzeiten ihrer fünf Schwestern und die damit verbundenen Wohnortswechsel. Auch von künstlerischem Erfolg ist die Rede: August Mann löste sein gegebenes Versprechen mit der Aufführung der *Serenade* im April 1890 ein. Auf diese Episode folgt ein bezeichnender Satz: "And through it all Pauline burned like a steady light beside me, warm and quiet, helpful and practical."[57] Die Autorin schildert dann die Umstände der Aufführung und die folgenden neuen Projekte, für die sie nun die notwendige Kraft aufbringt. Und dann kommt wieder ein einzelner Satz, der – ohne dass Pauline erwähnt würde – doch als eine Aufrechterhaltung der inneren Verbindung zu ihr interpretiert werden

---

[52] Vgl. Smyth, *In the Desert*, S. 224.
[53] Ebd., S. 225.
[54] Ebd.
[55] Ebd.
[56] Ebd., S. 254.
[57] Ebd., S. 227.

kann: "For one thing at last I was at peace; the Munich mood was no passing one, and for the next eighteen months, in spite of arduous work, at the bottom of my soul was one thought only – Christ."[58]

The Mass

In den folgenden 18 Monaten arbeitet Smyth an ihrer Messe. Sie muss sich wohl zumindest gelegentlich mit Pauline Trevelyan getroffen und die Familie im Herbst 1890 in deren Haus in Nettlecombe besucht haben, obwohl sie davon kaum Konkretes berichtet.[59] Solche Begegnungen lassen sich aber aus einer Bemerkung schließen, die sie viel später – nach der Hochzeit Pauline Trevelyans im Jahr 1891 – macht: "Pauline and I did not meet as often as formerly."[60] Über diese Treffen und ihre Häufigkeit gibt sie bezeichnenderweise keine Auskünfte, aber allzu viele kann es nicht gegeben haben, da Smyth im Sommer 1891 mehrere Monate in Cap Martin an der französischen Riviera nahe Monaco bei Empress Eugénie verbringt,[61] was der Grund dafür gewesen sein mag, warum sich Eugénie später aktiv für die Aufführung der Messe einsetzte. Durch ihre Vermittlung kam es dazu, dass Smyth – wie erwähnt – das Werk Queen Victoria singend und klavierspielend vorstellen durfte, was wiederum von entscheidender Bedeutung für die Möglichkeit einer Aufführung der *Mass* war. Denn nach dem Vorspiel wurde der Königin durch die Frau des Privatsekretärs der Königin, Sir Henry Ponsonby, deutlich gemacht, dass der Leiter der Royal Choral Society, Joseph Barnby, die Messe zwar grundsätzlich zur Aufführung angenommen hatte, allerdings kein konkretes Datum oder Anlass ins Auge gefasst worden war, wodurch die Vorbereitung der Aufführung stockte. Es war Smyth durchaus klar, dass eine Messe sich kaum in Konzertprogramme des Londoner Musiklebens einpassen ließ. In *Streaks of Life* bemerkt sie, dass ein alttestamentlicher Stoff (wie er für englische Oratorien beliebt war) leichter den Weg in ein Programm einer der zahlreichen Chorvereine oder der diversen Choralfestivals gefunden hätte. Dem hält sie aber als Argument die „everlasting beauty" des Messtextes entgegen, der ihr soviel bedeute. Daraus lässt sich zugleich schließen, dass sie neben religiösen Konnotationen den Text auch als poetischen Text versteht.[62] Dennoch ist deutlich, dass die Komposition der *Mass* aufs Engste mit der „Munich mood" zusam-

---

[58] Smyth, *In the Desert*, S. 228.
[59] Vgl. ebd., S. 244.
[60] Ebd., S. 256.
[61] Vgl. Ethel Smyth, *As Time*, S. 37.
[62] Smyth, *Streaks of Life*, S. 110.

menhängt und insofern teils religiös, teils zwischenmenschlich, wenn nicht erotisch konnotiert ist. In *In the Desert* heißt es:

> "In order to round off the story of this phase of intense belief [...] I ought to say that during this [1890] and the ensuing year [1891] I was composing a Mass, which was eventually produced in London in 1893. Into that work I tried to put all there was in my heart, but no sooner was it finished than, strange to say, orthodox belief fell away from me, never to return."[63]

Versuch einer Deutung und ein Modell homosexueller Konstruktion

„All there was in my heart", so ist zusammenfassend festzuhalten, meint offenbar eine sich gegenseitig beeinflussende Kombination religiöser und zwischenmenschlicher Gefühle. Für den beschriebenen Verlust des „orthodox belief" führt Smyth Gründe an, die wiederum etwas von den Spannungen ihrer Gefühle erahnen lassen: „and ridiculous as it seems, the fact that Thomas à Kempis would have condemned Shakespeare's sonnets had a great deal to do with it."[64] Hier stehen die Shakespeare'schen Sonette wohl als Symbole für Kunsthaftigkeit, Sinnlichkeit, Liebe und Ästhetik. Die Gedanken der *Imitatione* lassen sich, so Smyth, nicht mit dem Leben einer Künstlerin vereinbaren und auch nicht mit den vielen Seelenbewegungen, die eben nicht nur in die eine Richtung gehen, in die Kempis sie kanalisieren wollte. Schließlich aber heißt es doch: "Only this will I say, that at no period of my life have I had the feeling of being saner, wiser nearer truth. Never has this phase [...] seemed overwrought, unnatural, or hysterical; it was simply a religious experience that in my case could not be an abiding one."[65] An anderer Stelle schreibt sie über die Zeit der Komposition der *Mass*: „I was absolutely in love with God and the Church".[66]

In *In the Desert* bemerkt Smyth über die „Munich mood", Pauline Trevelyan sei dazu bestimmt gewesen, „to walk with me through a stretch of life in which we did not see eye to eye".[67] Könnte das nicht ein Hinweis darauf sein, dass die Bedeutung Pauline Trevelyans für Ethel Smyth auch in Smyths Selbstkonstruktion ihres Lebens zu suchen ist? Das Denken an und Träumen von Pauline mag eine Wirklichkeit generiert haben, die vielleicht wirklicher

63 Smyth, *In the Desert*, S. 238. Zu der im Zitat erwähnten Aufführung vgl. Smyth, *As Time*, S. 43 und S. 60.
64 Ebd., S. 238f; vgl. S. 229.
65 Ebd., S. 239.
66 Smyth, *As Time*, S. 40f.
67 Smyth, *In the Desert*, S. 219.

war als die unwirtliche „Realität". Zusammenfassend lässt sich über die interpretierten Zitate aus den autobiographischen Schriften sagen: Das Motiv, der innere Anlass für die Komposition der *Mass* ist nicht allein in der Verliebtheit zur Widmungsträgerin zu suchen. Wirksam war vielmehr ein religiöses Gefühl, das sich auch in der Zuneigung und Liebe zu einem Menschen kristallisiert. Zugleich erweisen sich alle diese Äußerungen als Aussagen und Fragen einer Frau, die sich weder auf ein bestimmtes Motiv des Christlichen oder Religiösen reduzieren lassen will noch auf eine explizite Erotik in Hinsicht auf einen anderen Menschen. Hier zeigt sich eine Persona, die mit einer heftigen Sehnsucht auf der Suche nach etwas ist, das mehr ist – höher ist – als die als eng und eindimensional erlebte Welt einer limitierenden Gesellschaft. Dass die Liebesbeziehung zu Pauline Trevelyan in mancher Hinsicht wohl unerfüllt geblieben sein wird, spricht nicht gegen die Wirklichkeit dieser Liebe für Ethel Smyth. Dass homoerotische Sexualität im Kopf stattfand und sich homosexuelle Sehnsucht einerseits in mystischer Religiösität und andererseits in künstlerischen Werken äußerte, kann als ein Modell unerfüllter Homosexualität in England um 1900 angesehen werden.

Dies zeigt auch der Parallelfall des fast gleichaltrigen Dichters Alfred E. Housman (1859–1936) beispielhaft.[68] Housmans lebenslange unerwiderte Liebe zu einem Oxforder Mitstudenten kanalisierte sich in einem poetischen Œuvre, das Landschaften benennt, in denen der Dichter nachweislich nie gewesen ist, und Lebensformen besingt, die er nie erfahren hat. Hier werden innerliche Landschaften an- und ausgesprochen, die bei Housman zu einem gelebten, in eine Realität umgesetzten Selbstentwurf führen, die den emotional gebrochenen Mann vor einer Ent-Täuschung seiner Lebenskonstruktion bewahrten. Die Wirklichkeit der innerlichen Traumlandschaften zeigt sich an der Beobachtung, dass Housman in ihnen sogar täglich spazieren ging und dabei reale Personen seines Alltagslebens ignorierte. Bei Smyth sind es schriftlich festgehaltene autobiographische Konstruktionen einer die Realität überragenden Liebe unter anderem zu Pauline Trevelyan, die parallel zu religiösen Gefühlen als metaphysisch „höher" als das real Geschehene gedeutet werden. Dass Erotik im Kopf stattfindet und die mentale Konstruktion von Liebes- und Sexualbeziehungen zur Identitätsgenese moderner bzw. postmoderner Personae gehört, ist nicht nur als Modell homosexueller Erotik evident. Versus den oft gebrauchten Begriff der Selbstinszenierung – der suggeriert, dass Personae in der Realität eigentlich ganz anders sind als in ihrer eigenen Inszenierung – könnte treffender von Selbstkonstruktion gesprochen werden,

---

[68] Vgl. Erik Dremel, *Pastorale Träume*, Köln/Weimar 2005, Kap. 7.3 „Männer", S. 236–250.

weil dann deutlich wird, dass der Inhalt der Konstruktion echte und wirksame Auswirkungen auf die Wirklichkeit des Lebens eines Menschen hat – und „das Leben", im Sinne einer Lebensgeschichte, niemals etwas anderes ist als eine erzählte Konstruktion.

Ende des Jahres 1891 heiratet Pauline Trevelyan den entfernten Cousin Gilbert Heathcote, einen Offizier des elitären Infanterieregiments „Cameronians". Smyth schreibt dazu lapidar, sie hätten sich nun nicht mehr so oft wie zuvor gesehen, weil das frischvermählte Paar im Rahmen der militärischen Einsätze Heathcotes zunächst im Ausland lebte und Smyths Leben ebenfalls sehr anstrengend war. Pauline Heathcotes stirbt 1897 aufgrund eines ärztlichen Fehlers. Ethel Smyth hat sie kurz zuvor noch ein letztes Mal besucht.

Abstract

"All there was in my heart": Ethel Smyth, her Mass in D, *and her Friendship with Pauline Trevelyan*

The *Mass in D* (1891) is one of Ethel Smyth's more famous and more widely disseminated compositions, one that played a remarkable role in the reception and appreciation of her work and persona. This Englishwoman, who trained in Germany, studied the Catholic Mass outside the liturgical practice of her time and the area in which she lived. This raises questions which can be discussed from many different biographical perspectives and perspectives of cultural history. Combined in what Smyth named a 'Munich mood', the dedication of the work to her Roman Catholic friend Pauline Trevelyan and the strong influence Catholicism and spiritualism exerted on the composer seem to explain the motivation and intent behind the work. Hence the Mass has to be discussed in relation to questions of Smyth's religiosity, not only in relation to the High Church movement in particular, but also with regard to the individual situation of Ethel Smyth in Munich and her relationship to Pauline Trevelyan.

Aidan J. Thomson
Decadence in the Forest: Smyth's *Der Wald* in its Critical Context

Ethel Smyth's second opera, the one-act *Der Wald*, received its premiere on 21 April 1902 at the Berlin Königliches Opernhaus. This was a most appropriate venue for a work replete with *topoi* of German Romanticism, as an examination of the plot will make clear.[1] Set in a forest, the opera opens with Waldgeister, freed from earthly temporality, "engaged in ritual observances round an altar in the wood", singing of "their own eternity and the brevity of things human".[2] As they fade away, the story proper begins. A peasant girl, Röschen, the daughter of the woodman ("Waldbauer") Peter, is engaged to be married the next day to a woodcutter, Heinrich; she receives flowers from her friends, a pedlar sells his goods, and the scene concludes with a dance. At this point the party hears the horn of Iolanthe, the mistress of the local Count Rudolf, a "woman of cruel instincts and unbridled passions, supposed to be a witch and dreaded with superstitious fear". The peasants flee, and Röschen and Heinrich "invoke the protection of the forest" in a lengthy love duet. As Röschen leaves for the village, Iolanthe arrives, and on seeing the handsome Heinrich attempts to persuade him to leave Röschen and "enter into her service at the Castle". Count Rudolf, who has followed Iolanthe, is unhappy with this idea; so, too, is Heinrich; but Iolanthe is determined, and she is given a further chance to get her man. Earlier in the story Heinrich had killed a deer, the property of the Count, and had hidden it in a well. Rudolf's huntsmen discover the beast and accuse the pedlar of having committed the crime; the ped-

---

[1] Elizabeth Wood has aptly observed that *Der Wald* is "a romantic-magic work that belongs to the timeless spirit and folk world of Weber's *Silvana* (1812) or E. T. A. Hoffmann's *Undine* (1815), where the rites and spirits of the natural world dominate a simpler human one; in which the forest itself is the 'mother' [...] that nurtures, protects, and regenerates yet which has spawned evil from nature's womb." See Elizabeth Wood, "Gender and Genre in Ethel Smyth's Operas", in: *The Musical Woman: An International Perspective*, vol. 2 (1984–85), New York 1987, pp. 493–507, at p. 495.
[2] This synopsis paraphrases H[enry] B[rewster], "Argument", in E. M. Smyth, *Der Wald*, London: Schott, 1902, iii. All the quotations in this paragraph prior to footnote 3 are taken from Brewster's synopsis.

lar, under pressure from the huntsmen, reveals that it was Heinrich who was guilty. Iolanthe therefore gives Heinrich a choice: he must renounce Röschen to work for her, or else be killed for slaying the deer. Heinrich chooses love and death rather than a loveless life, and is stabbed to death by the huntsmen; Röschen, who has returned, falls lifeless on his body. The stage darkens, and the Waldgeister of the prologue return to continue their earlier ritual, "where it was interrupted by the incursion of things transient". The idea of the opera, Smyth explained, was that

> "the short, poignant tragedy which for a moment interrupts the tranquil rites of the Spirits of the Forest is but an episode, the real story being the eternal march of Nature – Nature that enwraps human destiny and recks nothing of mortal joys and sorrows."[3]

The plot and meaning of *Der Wald* was Smyth's own creation, although the genesis of the work owed much to her collaborator and lover, Henry Brewster, as the title-page dedication – "To Henry Brewster, the onlie begetter, I dedicate my part in this work" – makes clear: "the spirit of [*Der Wald*]", Smyth explained, "was a result of continual association with a mind like his".[4] The libretto was also Smyth's own work, although she tells nothing in her published memoirs of how she wrote it,[5] or why it was in German (although Louise Collis offers a plausible explanation for the latter, namely that Smyth's "most useful musical connections were continental"; thus a German libretto would increase the chances of the opera receiving a performance in Germany).[6] Of the composition of its music she reveals only that in February 1900 she was "absolutely intoxicated with work" on it.[7] The story of how *Der Wald* eventually made it to the stage, however, is related by Smyth at considerable length, and with characteristic élan, in *Streaks of Life*. In a chapter entitled "A Winter of Storm", she tells how the opera was initially accepted and then rejected at Dresden; how it was then accepted in Berlin by Georg Pierson, the director of the Königliches Opernhaus; how Pierson's death in February 1902 led to the date of the premiere being postponed; how a lack of cooperation from the principal singers and poor man-management by the theatre Intendant, Count Hochberg, nearly stymied the later rehearsals; and how anti-British feeling in

[3] *The Memoirs of Ethel Smyth*, abridged and introduced by Ronald Crichton, Harmondsworth 1987, p. 237.
[4] Ibid., p. 255.
[5] Her letters to Henry Brewster, which may well contain references to the process, are held in private possession.
[6] Louise Collis, *Impetuous Heart: the Story of Ethel Smyth*, London 1984, p. 75.
[7] Ibid., p. 230.

Germany over the Boer War contributed to the opera's negative reception at the first performance.[8] *Der Wald* nevertheless received four performances in Berlin that spring; at the last of these, according to Smyth, the audience "undisguisedly showed its approval", a marked improvement on the booing and hissing that had greeted the work at its premiere.[9] These performances attracted enough interest in Britain for *Der Wald* to be added belatedly to the 1902 Covent Garden season, and it received its first London airing on 18 July, as part of a double bill that also featured the second performance of *La Princesse Osra*, a recently premiered opera by another British composer, Herbert Bunning.[10] Critical reaction to Smyth's opera in Britain was mixed, but certainly sometimes positive; indeed, the critic of *The Times* expressed his hope that

> "this beautiful and poetic drama may pass into the regular repertoire of Covent Garden […] So many operas already exist which of themselves are too short for an entire evening's entertainment, that there is every practical reason why Der Wald should be preserved, while the fact that its intrinsic value as a work of art is very much greater than that of any of the shorter operas of recent years should be an extra inducement to the authorities to retain it on their list."[11]

But these hopes came almost to nothing: *Der Wald* received two more performances in England in 1902 and 1903, three in the United States in 1903 (two in New York and one in Boston), one at the Stadttheater Straßburg in 1904,[12] and thereafter dropped out of the repertory altogether.[13]

Why this neglect? The most obvious answer would seem to be that *Der Wald* was quickly superseded by works that were dramatically more convincing and musically much more advanced. *Pelléas et Mélisande* received its

---

[8] "A Winter of Storm", in Ethel Smyth, *Streaks of Life*, London 1921, pp. 139–205.
[9] Ibid., p. 203.
[10] (George) Herbert Bunning (1863–1937) was music director of the Lyric Theatre, Hammersmith, from 1892, and of the Prince of Wales Theatre from 1895. *La Princesse Osra* is a setting of a French libretto by Maurice Bérenger, based on part of Anthony Hope's novel, *The Heart of Princess Osra*; musically, it is reminiscent of Massenet. See "Obituaries: Mr. Herbert Bunning", in: *The Times*, 29 November 1937, p. 16; "The Royal Opera: Mr. Herbert Bunning's 'La Princesse Osra'", in: *Musical Times* 43/714 (1 August 1902), p. 539.
[11] "Reviews", in: *The Times*, 21 July 1902, p. 8.
[12] See Meinhard Saremba, *Elgar, Britten & Co.*, Zürich 1994, p. 135. See also the contribution of Rebecca Grotjahn in this volume, footnote 1.
[13] Smyth wrote that her opera "was as out of place in America as one of the Muses at a football match" (quoted in Collis, *Impetuous Heart*, p. 83).

world premiere just nine days after *Der Wald*, and the decade that followed saw the first performances of, inter alia, *Jenůfa*, *Madama Butterfly*, *Salome* and *Elektra*. Alongside these psychologically raw and tonally adventurous works the conservatism of *Der Wald* would have seemed relatively bland. But that alone does not explain the almost immediate neglect into which *Der Wald* fell. Operas like Stanford's *Shamus O'Brien* (1896), for instance, were no more advanced, musically, than Smyth's piece, yet achieved popularity and critical acclaim almost at once; indeed one commentator of the period considered that its premiere marked an important new chapter in the history of British music.[14] *Shamus*, however, had three advantages over *Der Wald*: it was a comic opera that mixed individual musical numbers with passages of spoken dialogue, a genre that had a long and rich tradition in Britain, exemplified most recently by the Savoy Operas of Gilbert and Sullivan; its libretto was in English; and its plot concerned an event in British (or, more accurately, Irish) history that had resonances with contemporary British society, namely the question of Irish home rule.[15] *Der Wald*, by contrast, was a serious, all-sung, through-composed work, an idiom in which British opera was conspicuous only by its absence; moreover, it had a German libretto and scenario that owed little, if anything, to British culture. Thus the fate of *Der Wald* depended not only on its musical and dramatic merits but also on how it engaged with the cultural politics of early-twentieth-century British opera, something that may be inferred from the reviews of the work by British music critics. This engagement was problematic for three reasons, as we shall now see: Smyth's status as a female composer, and the extent to which this cast doubt on her originality; the absence of public institutional support for composers of British opera; and the fact that *Der Wald* was perceived as Wagnerian, a word that implied as much about the work's ideological and moral position as about its musical style.

[14] "Had I to place the date of the *renaissance* I should mention the year of the production of 'Shamus O'Brien.' From thenceforth English music became less and less German and more English" (Common Time, "Musical Gossip of the Month", in: *Musical Opinion* (hereafter "MO") 25/295 (1 Apr 1902), pp. 509–510, at p. 510).

[15] *Shamus O'Brien* is set shortly after the unsuccessful Irish rebellion of 1798; the eponymous hero of the opera is a rebel in hiding from British soldiers. *Shamus* was sufficiently popular among nationalist Irish audiences that, from around 1912 until his death, Stanford, who was an Anglo-Irish Protestant Unionist, imposed a ban on the work "as it has sometimes led to a political misunderstanding" (Herbert Antcliffe, "Sir Charles Stanford", in: *Musical Student* 9 (1916–17), pp. 211–215, quoted in Paul Rodmell, *Charles Villiers Stanford*, Aldershot 2002, pp. 388–389).

Critical reaction and gender

That Smyth's gender coloured the critical reception of her work is indisputable; as Elizabeth Kertesz has noted, music criticism in the nineteenth century presupposed "a belief in women's lesser creative strength" and was often couched in the "all too familiar language of sexual discrimination".[16] A good example of this occurs in an article that appeared in *The Musical Standard* less than two months before Smyth's opera received its premiere. Entitled "Women and Originality," the article argued that women were essentially "copyists rather than creators" as a result of their education, which neglected the qualities of "pertinacity, endurance, and industry" that were necessary to master music at the highest level: "They have accepted form in music as they have found it, [and] have written after a pattern not invented by themselves, which probably explains their comparative failure."[17] This spurious relationship between gender and musical creativity thus placed a female composer in a vicious circle: if her work was poor, this could be explained on grounds of gender; if her work was good, it must somehow be unoriginal or else dismissed with a patronizing aside.

Such discourse features in early British reviews of *Der Wald*, even favourable ones. For example, the pseudonymous "Beckmesser" in *Monthly Musical Record* seemingly circumvents questions of gender in observing that *Der Wald* was "an opera which, for strength of workmanship and solidity of texture, is by far the most important contribution to operatic art which has come from British pens, either of men or of women". But then comes the backhanded compliment: the theme of the opera – that is, the contrast between the calmness and permanence of nature and the transience of the human tragedy that takes place within it – "called for big treatment. Here one might have thought that a woman composer would fail, but it is precisely here that Miss Smyth has succeeded".[18] Among unfavourable reviews, the issue of gender is raised more prominently. Writing in *Musical News*, Walter Willson Cobbett, whose series of chamber music competitions in the first decade of the twentieth century ironically would attract many entries from female composers, claimed that the

---

[16] Elizabeth Kertesz, "Gender and Beyond: Talking About the Critical Reception of Ethel Smyth", in: *Gender Studies and Music*, ed. Stefan Fragner, Jan Hemming and Beate Kutschke, Regensburg 1998, pp. 65–74 at p. 66.

[17] "Women and Originality", in: *The Musical Standard* (hereafter "MSt") 62/1963 (15 March 1902), p. 171. For more on the relationship between gender and creative genius, see Christine Battersby, *Gender and Genius: Towards a Feminine Aesthetics,* London 1989.

[18] Beckmesser, "The Opera", in: *Monthly Musical Record* (hereafter "MMR") 32/8 (Aug 1902), pp. 154–55 at p. 155.

declamatory vocal style that constituted the majority of the work was "unsuited to a woman" (Smyth's earlier vocal music, by contrast, was "admirable, and besides a certain dignity it has something of the femininity which we have a right to look for in a woman's compositions").[19] Perhaps the most excoriating critique came from Charles Maclean in the *Zeitschrift der internationalen Musikgesellschaft*. Maclean stated that Smyth was "head and shoulders above"other female composers "for accomplished musicianship", but it soon becomes clear that this is damnation with faint praise. Maclean was impressed by Smyth's orchestration and chorus writing, but "to pass beyond this to questions of general style or creativeness is to condemn the work, for in these in fact it is entirely (if cleverly) hollow." Hollow and, in his view, unoriginal. The opening, Maclean observed, was reminiscent of Brahms's *Schicksalslied*; the fête music that follows had overtones of Weber and Marschner; and the rest of the work was "one of the dreariest specimens of pseudo-Wagner ever presented to an audience on a first-class occasion." Warming to his theme, Maclean perorates with a damning broadside, only just stopping short of attributing Smyth's alleged lack of creativity to Eve's being created out of Adam's rib:

> "There is a toy by which one enters a dark dome, and on the table passes in shadow but in active motion the whole of the real outside surrounding world. The image on the table is this opera, painted to the life, but by reflection only. Mimeticism will never call down the moon from its sphere, nor cause the cold-blooded snake to burst in the field."[20]

It should be noted, however, that other critics, whilst acknowledging the same influences as those identified by Maclean, did not necessarily share his views. "Common Time", a columnist for *Musical Opinion*, and E. A. Baughan, the

[19] W[alter] W[illson] C[obbett], "Der Wald", in: *Musical News* (hereafter '*MN*') 23/595 (26 July 1902), p. 72. Under the auspices of the Worshipful Company of Musicians, Cobbett ran a series of competitions in 1906, 1907 and 1909 in which competitors submitted a single-movement 'phantasy' of twelve minutes or less for particular designated instruments (a string quartet in 1906, a piano trio in 1907, and a violin and piano duet in 1909); the first competition was won by William Hurlstone, the second by Frank Bridge, and the third by John Ireland. Charles Maclean noted that two women were shortlisted for prizes in these competitions (Alice Verne Bredt, who came fourth in 1907, and Mrs Henry Gibson, who came fifth in 1907 and fourth in 1909), and that many of the 134 manuscripts submitted in the 1909 competition were written by women. See Charles Maclean, "A New Form in English Music", *Zeitschrift der internationalen Musikgesellschaft* (hereafter "*ZIMG*") 12/6 (March 1911), pp. 149–153, at p. 151f.

[20] Charles Maclean, "'La Princesse Osra' and 'Der Wald'", in: *ZIMG* 3/12 (Sept 1902), pp. 482–488, at p. 486f.

editor of *The Musical Standard*, detected the influence of Brahms, Weber and Wagner – and, in the case of Baughan, Humperdinck as well – but heard in Smyth's music an original synthesis, not pale imitations of her predecessors: "The styles of Brahms and Wagner have been amalgamated [...] It represents an individual outlook: Miss Smyth has brought the reflective spirit of absolute music into music-drama; and the result is a work which is dramatic in the extreme and yet is saved from mere theatricality".[21]

Why, then, was Maclean's response to *Der Wald* so vitriolic? One reason was a personal dislike for its composer, for his comments about Smyth are often downright catty; for instance, his perception that she "has always had, and made use of, aristocratic influence" whilst neglecting to mention her musical education in Leipzig, paints a false picture of Smyth as a society dilettante.[22] But there is more to his scepticism than simply personal animosity, and to explain this we have to consider his position within British musical society. Firstly, Maclean moved within the circles of the "renaissance" group of composers and critics associated with the Royal College of Music, and broadly shared its pro-Brahmsian and anti-Wagnerian bias. This group included composers such as Stanford and Parry, whose art, Maclean claimed, "[stood] above that of his fellows, as the Drachenfels above the Rhine", and critics such as J. A. Fuller-Maitland, the editor of the second edition of Grove's *Dictionary of Music and Musicians*; it did not, however, include the overtly Wagnerphile Elgar, to whom Maclean was frequently hostile.[23] Consequently, it is reasonable to assume that Maclean's views about Smyth may well have reflected those of others within this highly influential circle: a circle that, through its scholarship and criticism as much as through its music, attempted to fashion the nation's musical taste in its own image. Secondly, as British group editor of the monthly *Zeitschrift der internationalen Musikgesellschaft* (and a frequent columnist within it), Maclean played an important role as a spokesman for British music to the journal's readership: the members of the Internationale

---

[21] E. A. B[aughan], "The Opera", "Miss Smyth's 'Der Wald'", *MSt* 62/1982 (26 July 1902), pp. 53–54, at p. 53. See also Common Time, "Musical Gossip of the Month", *MO* 25/299 (August 1902), pp. 817–819, at p. 818.

[22] Ibid., p. 486. A decade later, Maclean would add the political to the personal, when he "deplored" Smyth for being employed in the "truly nefarious cause" of the suffragette movement (Charles Maclean, "London Notes", in: *ZIMG* 14/12 (September 1913), p. 370–371), although it should be noted that in 1902 Smyth had not yet taken up that cause.

[23] Charles Maclean, "Hubert Parry's Latest Work", in: *ZIMG* 4/12 (September 1903), pp. 676–680, at p. 676. Elgar, in Maclean's opinion, trusted "little if at all to intellect" and "rushe[d] wholly on impulse" (ibid., p. 679).

Musikgesellschaft, a recently formed (1899) organization one of whose original aims was the promotion of the best music of each nation or region within an increasingly diverse international musical world.[24] A particular concern for him was promoting a nationally coherent English school to a readership that was predominantly German, and which, for the most part, would have considered England to be "Das Land ohne Musik"[25]. It is striking that his article on *Der Wald* begins with a Herderian credo of musical nationalism that merits quotation in full:

> "One principle is the natural fact, which will become plainer as the world grows older, that music seemingly of human composition only is in fact attached to localities, and dependent on soil and climate; nor is this less so, because that which makes the distinctions between music indigenous here and there is found on analysis to be nothing but what is technically called harmony. Another principle is that the human agent through which such products find expression, is able to issue them either by force of race and heredity, or through scarcely sensible contact with perceptional surroundings, or again through mere mimeticism; and here all the work finally adjudged best comes from the first impulse, while what the world infallibly in the long run pronounces weakest comes from the third impulse."[26]

By labelling Smyth's work as mimetic, Maclean thus not only assigns *Der Wald* to the weakest category of artworks, but also implicitly denationalizes it: the opera had "nothing whatever to do with our native art". "For our own native operatic development", Maclean concludes, in some frustration, "we are waiting".[27]

---

[24] According to its founder, the German musicologist Oskar Fleischer, the Internationale Musikgesellschaft aimed to be "a federation of the musicians and musical connoisseurs of all countries, for purposes of mutual information on matters of research or on more current matters" (Charles Maclean, "International Musical Society", in Eric Blom (ed.), *Grove's Dictionary of Music and Musicians*, 5th edition (1954–61), vol. 4, 518). See also Aidan J. Thomson, "Elgar's Critical Critics", in: *Edward Elgar and His World*, ed. Byron Adams, Princeton 2007, pp. 193–222, at p. 198.

[25] See, for instance, the title of the following book: Oscar A. H. Schmidt, *Das Land ohne Musik: Englische Gesellschaftsprobleme*, München 1914. (Its popularity is demonstrated by the fact that it was published in its 8th edition in 1929.)

[26] Maclean, "'La Princesse Osra' and 'Der Wald'", pp. 482f.

[27] Ibid., p. 488. The same complaint was made by Maclean of Bunning's *La Princesse Osra*, a work that was if anything even more dependent on Massenet than Smyth on any of her models, and which was hampered by a weak libretto and lacked dramatic punch, but which Maclean inexplicably preferred to *Der Wald*.

All this vindicates Elizabeth Kertesz's persuasive thesis that when discriminatory language occurs in writing on Smyth's music it is "combined in the minds of [her] critics" with other factors (she names style, nationalism and Smyth's persona as three examples of this tendency).[28] As I shall now show, Maclean's views on two such factors – the institutional context of national opera in Britain, and the influence of Wagner and Wagnerism – may be used to explain both his reaction to *Der Wald*, and, by implication, those of other negative critics of the opera.

The institutional context

Like many other early-twentieth-century British music critics, Maclean was acutely conscious of the absence of an English tradition in grand (as opposed to comic) opera. This concern was a long-running sore in British musical circles, and was attributed by many to the absence of a permanent national opera house artistically committed to the promotion of grand opera, by British composers, and in English. Several unsuccessful attempts had been made at creating such an institution during the nineteenth century, the most recent being Richard D'Oyly Carte's Royal English Opera House at Cambridge Circus, which opened in 1891 with the premiere of Sullivan's *Ivanhoe*, but which failed to make the necessary impact and by 1892 had been sold and reopened as a variety theatre.[29] Partly because of this failure, and partly because the syndicate that ran the Royal Opera House had no vested interest in promoting British composers at Covent Garden, the need for a national opera remained an important issue. Certain logistical issues were regularly debated within the musical press: whether there should be a purpose-built theatre to be used only for opera, and, if so, where; and whether this building and the company's subsequent running costs should be funded privately by a syndicate, like Covent Garden, or through public funds (either national or municipal). Early in 1902, two proposals for a new opera house were outlined: Lord Dysart advocated the building of a new purpose-built, privately run opera house costing £500,000 (towards which he would contribute £10,000); and around the same time a Conservative MP, William Johnson Galloway, published a pamphlet entitled *The Operatic Problem* that called for a somewhat cheaper national opera house that would promote English composers, and which would receive a public subvention from both parliament and London County Council.[30] Re-

[28] Kertesz, "Gender and beyond", p. 74.
[29] Eric Walter White, *A History of English Opera* (London: Faber, 1983), pp. 323–25.
[30] See Common Time, "Musical Gossip of the Month", in: *MO* 25/293 (Feb 1902),

action to their proposals varied: some commentators argued that England was an essentially non-operatic country and that both schemes were destined to fail; others, including the editor of *The Musical Standard*, E.A. Baughan, favoured a new opera house, but opposed public subsidies, which, he felt, "essentially belong to absolute monarchies"; others again, notably Stanford and Mackenzie, argued that a subsidized opera house would give British works a hearing, thereby educating the public, whose eagerness to re-hear these works would ensure the theatre paid for itself after a few years.[31]

Maclean belonged in the final category, frequently using his *Zeitschrift* column to keep the issue in the international musical eye long after both plans had been abandoned. "'National Opera' means an organization, where superior governmental or quasi-governmental authority makes subsidy to a theatrical enterprise", he claimed. "No country except America which lacks an indigenous opera to protect, and England which is so infatuated with the haphazard of individualism, thinks of entrusting so delicate a product as indigenous opera to the risks of uncontrolled private commercial enterprise".[32] His motives might not have been entirely disinterested: in 1895, his son, Alick, won the first competition organized by the Moody-Manners opera company with a verismo-influenced work, *Petruccio*, which was performed at Covent Garden, but failed to remain in the repertory thereafter. Nevertheless, his concern for the future of English opera appears genuine, although he was less vocal than some about the need for opera to be sung in English (possibly because of his despair at the quality of many English librettos). But in aspiring to create a national grand opera tradition almost *ex nihilo*, neither he nor anyone else seemed able to define what the essential artistic characteristics of English opera were. As Cecil Forsyth would note in 1911, since the eighteenth century English opera had been divided between pale imitations of all-sung

pp. 350–51; "Comments and Opinions", in: *MSt* 62/1954 (11 Jan 1902), pp. 19–21; "Musicians on the Opera Scheme", in: *MSt* 62/1955 (18 Jan 1902), pp. 41–42; "Comments and Opinions", in: *MSt* 62/1957 (1 Feb 1902), pp. 67–69; W. Johnson Galloway, *The Operatic Problem*, London 1902.

[31] The arch-pessimists included one "Bombardo", who argued not only that "the Anglo-Saxon race is constitutionally indifferent to opera", but that "the art of opera itself is an anachronism" (see Bombardo, "Rambling Reflections. On Opera", in: *MSt* 62/1957 (1 Feb 1902), p. 71). See also "Musicians on the Opera Scheme", p. 41.

[32] Charles Maclean, "Mackenzie's Colomba", in: *ZIMG* 11/5 (February 1910), pp. 142–45, at p. 145. Maclean supported Charles Manners' proposals for an English opera company in 1908, but disagreed with Manners's belief that the scheme could be made to work through solely private means; see Charles Maclean, "Moody-Manners English Opera Company", in: *ZIMG* 10/3 (December 1908), p. 83.

Italian (or, latterly, French) opera, and part-sung/part-spoken English ballad opera: in other words, between opera that was grand but not stylistically English and opera that was stylistically English but not grand.[33] Maclean's conception of what English opera should be exemplifies this paradox. His main desideratum for English opera was that the musical weight should be carried by lyrical vocal melodies, reflecting the indigenous tradition of ballad opera, rather than declamatory recitative.[34] But beyond an English libretto, and possibly an English scenario there was seemingly little to distinguish such works from those by contemporary French and Italian composers; and even English scenarios were more a feature of comic opera than serious works, which were more likely to be drawn from historical novels by European authors or, in some cases, from Celtic mythology.[35] Perhaps tellingly, Maclean's exemplar for national opera, Mackenzie's *Colomba*, is essentially a French grand opera, complete with ballet, based on a tale by Mérimée, but with English words; his advocacy of it was based on its music evoking the most universal and least national of all sentiments, "human nature".[36]

[33] See Cecil Forsyth, *Music and Nationalism: a study of English opera*, London 1911, especially chapter 4 ("The Eighteenth Century and After"), pp. 91–123. Forsyth adds that neither type of opera had produced a sufficient number of works remaining in the repertory by 1900 to be considered a 'school', the most notable exceptions being Balfe's *The Bohemian Girl* (1843) and Wallace's *Maritana* (1845).

[34] "[England has] never taken kindly to recitative in English, for phonetical reasons" whereas "all the successes of our composers have been of a lyrical cast" (see Charles Maclean, "London", "Mitteilungen der Internationalen Musikgesellschaft: Ortsgruppe", *ZIMG* 15/7 (April 1914), 197).

[35] Eric Walter White lists 55 operas by British composers that were first performed between 1875 (the year of the premiere of *Trial By Jury*, the first of the Savoy operas) and 1900; of these, 27 were comic works and 28 were serious. Around two thirds of the comic works were set in England, the remainder being set either elsewhere in Europe (including, in the case of Stanford's *Shamus O'Brien*, Ireland) or, in three cases, Asia. But of the serious operas, only six took place in historical (and none in contemporary) British settings – and three of those were based on plots by the long since internationalized Sir Walter Scott. The remainder included four that were based on Celtic (or at least pre-Anglo Saxon) mythology (Joseph Parry's *Blodwen* (1878) and *Sylvia* (1895), Granville Bantock's *Caedmar* (1892) and Hamish MacCunn's *Diarmid* (1897)), six that are set in France, nine in other parts of Europe, two in Asia, and one in Mexico. See Eric Walter White, *The Rise of English Opera*, London 1951, pp. 255–261.

[36] Its music was "neither comedy nor tragedy" but "simply human nature; and that is exactly what is wanted as the goal of English opera, unless the symptoms of our national life and progress are pointing all awry" (Charles Maclean, "Mackenzie's *Colomba*", in: *ZIMG* 11/5 (February 1910), p. 145.

Given Maclean's views on British opera – the need for lyricism, and the need for a publicly subsidized opera company devoted to works that were English in both origin and spirit – one can perhaps understand his frustration on listening to *Der Wald*: a work by an English composer whose German text and setting, and predominantly declamatory style, did not sound 'English' to his ears at all. Admittedly, Smyth could hardly be blamed for writing a German libretto, given that the work had been written for performance in Germany. But that fact illustrated perfectly that there wasn't a market in Britain for native opera composers: a most inconvenient truth for those pushing for a publicly-subsidized national opera house. Ironically, Smyth would reveal almost twenty years later, during which time the reality of a publicly-funded national opera had barely advanced, that she herself strongly favoured such a subsidy; in her view, "a grant would place [opera] beyond the reach of those two greatest enemies to art – the un-Heavenly Twins, Commercialism and Snobbery".[37] Whether she had always held this view or had come round to it as a result of the difficulties she had encountered in getting her operas performed in the intervening years is a moot point; she certainly remained unapologetic about the fact that she had made Germany her first port of call, and encouraged young composers to aim for the foreign rather than the domestic market (as she herself had done for her first three operas, all of which were premiered in Germany). England, she wrote, was "operatically speaking, non-existent"; native works which did receive performances were chronically under-rehearsed and/or poorly balanced, and singers were reluctant to learn parts that they knew they would probably only ever sing once.[38] But it is unlikely that, if she was of this opinion in 1902, Maclean knew that these were her views; all he would have seen was a seemingly *déraciné* lady making use of her considerable connections to get her opera added to the Covent Garden schedule after the opera season had begun.[39]

In short, Maclean was looking for an English *Freischütz*: a work whose musical and dramatic power and recognizably national qualities would simultaneously revitalize national opera artistically and make the case for a publicly subsidized national opera house unanswerable. He had, he thought, identified such a work the previous year, namely Stanford's *Much Ado About Nothing*, which he had reviewed enthusiastically in the *Zeitschrift*, even to the extent of

---

[37] Ethel Smyth, "The Opera Fiasco" (written July 1920), in: *Streaks of Life*, pp. 206–230, at p. 230.
[38] Ibid., pp. 215–21, quotation at p. 206.
[39] As late as 26 April, *The Musical Standard* stated that *La Princesse Osra* was the only new work in the Covent Garden schedule.

drawing direct parallels with Weber's opera; but *Much Ado* was withdrawn after only two performances at Covent Garden, and thus the search for a trailblazing English opera continued.[40] Unfortunately for Smyth, *Der Wald*, in Maclean's view, was not that opera.

Smyth as Wagnerist (1): ideology

This, however, does not wholly explain the vehemence of Maclean's criticism, for which one must instead consider the implications of his claim that *Der Wald* was "one of the dreariest specimens of pseudo-Wagner ever presented to an audience on a first-class occasion." The most obvious interpretation of this statement is that Smyth was influenced by Wagner stylistically, and the extent to which this was the case is something to which I shall return later. But for Maclean and other early-twentieth-century British critics, 'Wagner' connoted not just the Bayreuth master's compositional idiom but the ideology that he and his followers espoused. As Byron Adams, Emma Sutton and others have noted, *fin-de-siècle* Wagnerism in Britain was associated specifically with the 'decadent' movement in art and literature, a movement that occupied a prominent place in British aesthetics until the conviction of Oscar Wilde in 1895, after which (and largely as a result of which) it fell into disrepute. Adams has drawn attention to how in the years immediately following 1895, "the 'aestheticism' of both the heterosexual Pre-Raphaelites and the homosexual Wilde was now banished, and a new, more self-consciously "masculine" aesthetic took its place".[41] For many composers, that meant retreating from Wagner, both stylistically and ideologically; those who did not ran the risk of being

---

[40] Charles Maclean, "Stanford's New Opera", in: *ZIMG* 2/10 (July 1901), pp. 338–341. "Without presumption, there are points of parallel between 18th June, 1821, Berlin Opera-house, and 30th May, 1901, Covent Garden. At the former date an almost wholly French-Italian stage [was] invaded by a native German-libretto work; at the latter a French-Italian-German stage [was] invaded by a native English-libretto work. In each case the composer [had been] waiting some years for a spring, and in each case a national interest [was] at stake" (p. 339). *Much Ado* was performed only twice at Covent Garden before being withdrawn (Rodmell, *Charles Villiers Stanford*, p. 207).

[41] Byron Adams, "'No Armpits, Please, We're British': Whitman and English Music, 1884–1936", in: *Walt Whitman and Modern Music: War, Desire and the Trials of Nationhood*, ed. Lawrence Kramer, New York: 2000, pp. 25–42, at p. 31; see also Byron Adams, "Elgar's Later Oratorios: Roman Catholicism, Decadence and the Wagnerian Dialectic of Shame and Grace", in: *The Cambridge Companion to Elgar* eds. Daniel Grimley and Julian Rushton, Cambridge 2004, pp. 81–105; and Emma Sutton, *Aubrey Beardsley and British Wagnerism in the 1890s*, Oxford 2002.

tarred with a Wagnerian brush by critics like Maclean, who, although an admirer of Wagner's music, was appalled by the composer's politics, personal immorality and, in the case of *Parsifal*, blasphemy. "Once [one] is out of the wholesome or harmless circle of *Die Feen, Rienzi, Fliegende Holländer, Tannhäuser, Lohengrin*, and *Meistersinger*, he finds the baffling, moidering word 'redemption' at every turn flung in his face to push him off the stool", Maclean grumbled. "In one respect the word seems just synonymous with getting one's own way".[42]

It was such lack of wholesomeness that Maclean detected in *Der Wald*, whose 'natural' order and value-system are diametrically opposed to his socially conservative one. Smyth, Maclean humourlessly observes, "appears to see no harm" in Heinrich's shooting dead a deer that did not belong to him, while in commenting that "it is doubtful whether any healthy young peasant-woman of the latter part of the middle ages would be able to quit life so easily", he implicitly aligns Röschen's death with the 'unhealthy' values associated with late-nineteenth-century British Wagnerism. He makes no comment on Iolanthe, but since Iolanthe transgresses the most 'natural' convention of nineteenth-century opera – she lives, Heinrich dies, and her actions are, as Elizabeth Wood has noted, 'vindicated' by her return into the forest at the end of the work – it is reasonable to assume that Maclean would have been similarly unimpressed.[43] What made this subversive imagery worse for Maclean was the composer's decidedly un-British philosophical posturing. Smyth, he noted, had claimed that "there has been no tragedy, the feverish importance that human joys and sorrows assume is an illusion".[44] Maclean, in response, noted:

> "Now it is needless to say that Europe still holds to Christian practicality and has by no means given itself up to Pantheistic abstraction-processes, whether of Schopenhauer or Buddha; and that it does not regard the doctrine of ῥεῖ τὰ πάντα as any guide whatever for human action. The philosophy of the play therefore is incongruous; or, if taken seriously, offensive."[45]

---

[42] C[harles] M[aclean], Review of Ernest Newman, *Wagner* (London: Wellby, 1904), "Kritische Bücherschau", in: *ZIMG* 6/10 (July 1905), pp. 443–444, at p. 444; see also Charles Maclean, "Music and Morals", in: *ZIMG* 8/12 (September 1907), pp. 461–464.
[43] Elizabeth Wood, "Sapphonics", in: *Queering the Pitch*, eds. Philip Brett, Elizabeth Wood and Gary C. Thomas, London 1994, pp. 27–66, at p. 50.
[44] Quoted after Beckmesser, "The Opera", p. 155.
[45] Maclean, "'La Princesse Osra' and 'Der Wald'", p. 487. Maclean alludes to Heraclitus's theory of ῥεῖ τὰ πάντα' ("everything is in flux").

All this is a long way from "human nature" (for which read "Christian practicality", for which, in turn, read 'English common sense'). Admittedly Smyth's philosophizing actually impressed other critics: "Beckmesser" claimed that the message of the work was "in a sense, [...] the teaching of Wagner's 'Ring', only Miss Smyth takes a simple and less transcendental stand" whilst "Common Time" claimed that "the philosophic undercurrent actually conditions the music; so that the opera as a whole is a kind of symphonic poem on nature and mankind. It was in this spirit that Wagner wrote his music dramas".[46] But such references to Wagner were a decidedly double-edged sword in a society that was drawing back from Wagnerism and the cocktail of metaphysical speculation, political subversion and moral laxity for which it supposedly stood.

Maclean's comments would therefore seem to be an over-reaction to a plot whose "real story", according to Smyth above, was that well-established trope of Romanticism, the "eternal march of nature".[47] But one could be forgiven for thinking that, in making that claim, Smyth was being somewhat disingenuous (as was "Common Time" in describing the work as a "symphonic poem on nature and mankind"); for, with the exception of the Prologue, the Epilogue, and a brief section at the end of scene 4 when Heinrich and Röschen invoke the protection of the forest – the scenes that feature the chorus of Waldgeister – the opera focuses entirely on the human tragedy of the doomed lovers and the duplicity of Iolanthe in bringing this about (something that the Waldgeister, unconcerned as they are with the day-to-day concerns of humanity, would appear to condone). So does Maclean's charge of "offensive" Wagnerism have some substance to it? To answer this question requires an examination of the score: firstly, to ascertain whether the work is as Wagnerian stylistically as Maclean and the other critics appear to believe; and secondly, to investigate how the music can shed light on the relationship between nature and humanity in the opera.

Smyth as Wagnerist (2): structure and key symbolism in *Der Wald*

Maclean's description of *Der Wald* as "pseudo-Wagner" does not necessarily mean that Smyth employed a systematic use of leitmotifs or a particular combination of structure and chromatic harmony; as W. F. Apthorp, a contemporary of Maclean, observed, Wagner's influence on contemporary composers was less technical than generic: the development of lyric drama characterized

---

[46] Beckmesser, "The Opera", p. 155; Common Time, "Musical Gossip of the Month", p. 818.
[47] See full quotation on p. 219 above, footnote 3.

by the "recognition of text and action as the sole musical form-determining principles".[48] It was therefore possible for early-twentieth-century critics to designate a through-composed opera "Wagnerian" even if it contained sections that were obviously based on traditional operatic numbers (arias, ensembles, choruses, even ballets), as long as these numbers could be justified dramatically. Such a work was stylistically less likely to resemble *Tristan* or the *Ring* cycle than *Tannhäuser* or *Lohengrin*, which were performed far more often in early-twentieth-century Britain than any of the mature music dramas.[49] *Der Wald* is this type of work: although Smyth designated it a 'Musik-Drama', it is more a hybrid of music drama and German Romantic opera.

Smyth's opera is broadly symmetrical in terms of structure: the Prologue and Epilogue frame two large-scale tuttis that feature several soloists plus a chorus; and these in turn frame two lengthy duets. For the purposes of analysis, I have divided *Der Wald* into four sections which reflect this symmetry, conjoining the Prologue and Epilogue with the sections that they precede and succeed respectively; thus Section I comprises the Prologue and opening tutti (scenes 1 to 3), Section II the duet between Heinrich and Röschen in scene 4, Section III the duet between Heinrich and Iolanthe in scene 5, and Section IV the closing tutti (scenes 6 to 9) and Epilogue. These sections differ from each other not only in terms of which and how many characters appear on stage, but also musically, both in terms of form and musical style and, as we shall see, tonality.

Smyth's approach to the question of form, and specifically whether to write self-contained 'numbers' or free declamatory lyric drama, varies from section to section. In Section I, the Romantic opera 'number' element is most transparent. After the Brahmsian chorus of Waldgeister disappear at the end of the Prologue, general pauses and brief passages of recitative separate a succession of choruses, one solo song from a minor character (the pedlar), and a set piece dance (see figure 1, p. 247-8, column a); the folk-like character of the pre-nuptial celebrations suggests as an antecedent not Wagner but *Der Freischütz*. The appearance of Iolanthe's horn call and the chromatic

---

[48] W. F. Apthorp, *The Opera Past and Present: an Historical Sketch*, London 1901, pp. 194-195.

[49] In the opening number of the *Zeitschrift der internationalen Musikgesellschaft*, Maclean lists the operas in the permanent repertory of Covent Garden; among Wagner's works are *Der fliegende Holländer*, *Tannhäuser*, *Lohengrin*, *Die Meistersinger*, *Siegfried* and *Die Walküre*, but not *Das Rheingold*, *Götterdämmerung* or, perhaps surprisingly, *Tristan*. The 1899-1900 Covent Garden season included six performances of *Lohengrin*, five of *Tannhäuser*, four of *Tristan*, three of *Walküre* and two of *Meistersinger*. See Charles Maclean, "Music in England", in: *ZIMG* 1/1 (1899), pp. 9-25, at p. 10f.

Ex. 1. Smyth, *Der Wald*, scene 2, 10 bars before rehearsal figure 23: Iolanthe's horn call.

Ex. 2. Smyth, *Der Wald*, scene 2, 5 bars after rehearsal figure 24 (Peter and chorus omitted): Iolanthe's danger motif.

Ex. 3. Smyth, *Der Wald*, scene 5, rehearsal figure 49 (Iolanthe omitted): Iolanthe's seduction motif.

'danger' motif at the end of scene 2 and scene 3 (ex. 1 and ex. 2) respectively) coincides with a change of style to freer recitative, but for the most part the melodic interest occurs in the vocal parts; the orchestra does not introduce leitmotifs. In Section II (figure 1b), the divisions between musical numbers are slightly more blurred. Heinrich sings a lied in which he boasts of his killing the deer, but Röschen's response is more arioso than aria; here the orchestra plays a more active role than previously, depicting Röschen's fears by recalling Iolanthe's horn call. The closing duet, in which Heinrich and Röschen make their farewell to each other, concluding with their apostrophe to the forest, "O heilger [sic] Wald", is contrapuntally the densest music in the opera so far, with orchestral motifs often competing for attention with the vocal lines; but even here the main melodic interest lies with the singers. In Section III (figure 1c), however, the duet between Heinrich and Iolanthe consists largely of declamatory recitative with little or no motivic development (or even any recollection of earlier motifs) in the orchestral accompaniment. The main exception to this is the motif that first appears when Iolanthe hands Heinrich her drinking horn, and which thereafter is associated with her attempts to seduce him. This motif (ex. 3), which recalls both the Valhalla theme from *Das Rheingold* melodically and the 'magic fire' music from *Die Walküre* in its accompaniment, appears three times; on the first and third occasions Iolanthe sings lyrical passages that, like Röschen's solo in the previous scene, are best described as arioso. In Section IV (figure 1d), Smyth alternates passages of declamatory recitative with passages of arioso for Rudolf, a fugal chorus for the huntsmen that again hints at *Der Freischütz*, and, in the final scene, two duets – one between Röschen and Iolanthe and one between Röschen and Heinrich – that are lyrical in the vocal parts and largely motif-free in the accompaniment. A passage of recitative portrays the deaths of the peasant lovers, before the Waldgeister return in the Epilogue.

Thus *Der Wald* is perhaps less 'Wagnerian' in a strictly musical sense than might appear to be the case at first: although the vocal writing is predominantly declamatory, the orchestra generally reflects the stage action, with the aid of reminiscence motifs, rather than providing an independent musico-dramatic narrative. On the other hand, Smyth was undoubtedly influenced by Wagner in her approach to tonal planning. Scholars such as Robert Bailey, Patrick McCreless and Warren Darcy have shown how the voice-leading principles of Schenkerian theory can be applied to music drama just as effectively as to instrumental or small-scale vocal music, and how Wagner could use tonality, as well as leitmotifs, as a semantic tool (so-called 'associative tonality').[50] As a through-com-

[50] See Robert Bailey, "The Structure of the *Ring* and its Evolution", in: *19th-Century Music* 1 (1977), pp. 48–61; Patrick McCreless, *Wagner's* Siegfried: *Its Drama, History, and Music*, Ann Arbor 1982; Warren Darcy, *Wagner's* Das Rheingold, Oxford 1993. These sources, and others, are listed in J. P. E. Harper-Scott, *Edward*

posed work whose key centres are fixed from the outset, *Der Wald* lends itself to this sort of analysis. This does not mean, *pace* "Common Time", that we should conceive of this opera as a texted symphonic poem (an analytical approach that Carolyn Abbate and others have rejected);[51] but equally, it would be remiss to ignore the tonal coherence found within each of the four sections of the opera, for which reason I have included the tonics of each musical number or musical-dramatic period of the opera in the right-hand column of figure 1. The results of this analysis are sometimes musically and dramatically revealing.[52]

The Prologue establishes E major both as the tonic of the opera, and, because of its association with the Waldgeister, as the 'key of nature': a sylvan counterpart to the E♭ major that opens *Das Rheingold*.[53] But there the similarities to *Das Rheingold* end, for within the prologue Smyth hints at some of the tonal conflict to come. A case in point is the quick (if brief) progression to the flattened supertonic, F major, in bar 8 (ex. 4), which, as we shall see, becomes an important secondary tonic in Section II. For the moment, however, its presence is merely a surface detail within a section that, as a whole, may be heard as an extended progression in E major. The Prologue concludes in that key; the two scenes that follow it proceed via the cycle of fifths through A major, D minor (the song of the pedlar) and D major to G major (the presentation of the peasants' gifts to Röschen). From here the music returns, via A major, to E major for the peasants' dance and chorus: a positive affirmation of the 'natural' social order of the forest, and of vitality in a setting that does not yet know danger.

At the end of the dance Iolanthe's horn call is heard for the first time. Initially, the music remains in keys that are close to E (A minor and, by the start of scene 3, F sharp minor). But with the pedlar's ironic "ich fürcht mich nicht vor Frau Iolanthe!" in the middle of that scene (ex. 5) the music suddenly switches into a very foreign key: C minor, the hexatonal polar opposite of E major, and a key

Elgar, Modernist, Cambridge 2006, p. 6, n. 9. In this monograph, Harper-Scott makes successful use of both Schenkerian and associative tonal approaches in an illuminating analysis of Elgar's *Falstaff*.

[51] Carolyn Abbate, "Opera as Symphony, a Wagnerian Myth", in: *Analyzing Opera: Verdi and Wagner*, eds. Carolyn Abbate and Roger Parker, Berkeley and Los Angeles 1989, pp. 92–124.

[52] Sections predominantly in the minor mode but occasionally shifting into the major mode, especially at the end of a section, are denoted thus: d/D (or similar). Passages of modulation are denoted by an arrow, while significant secondary tonics within a number appear in brackets.

[53] An alternative, and perhaps better, *Ring* association is the E major that ends Act II of *Siegfried*, and also provides the tonic for *Siegfried Idyll*.

Ex. 4. Smyth, *Der Wald*. Prologue: opening motif.

with funereal associations in both Wagner's *Ring* and Beethoven's 'Eroica'.[54] This switch anticipates the tonal territory in which the musical and dramatic events of Section II are played out; for, with the arrival of Heinrich in scene 4, the music moves decisively flatwards. The scene begins with a passage of recitative for the two lovers that opens in D minor, moves to F minor, and ends with the dominant chord of A♭ major, the key of Heinrich's lied, which follows immediately afterwards. Röschen's response is to recall her fear on hearing Iolanthe's horn; here the harmony shifts from the dominant of A♭ to that of F minor, and eventually resolves into the tonic chord of the latter at the start of her

[54] For more on hexatonal tonal space, see Richard Cohn, "Maximally Smooth Cycles, Hexatonic Systems, and the Analysis of Late-Romantic Triadic Progressions", in: *Music Analysis* 15 (1996), pp. 9–40.

Ex. 5. Smyth, *Der Wald*, scene 3, 5 bars before rehearsal figure 26 (Peter's words from the upbeat to the final bar are omitted).

arioso, "O glaub mir, nie fühlt' ich solch Noth und Sorg'". This arioso confirms F as the tonal centre of the scene; although there are forays into D♭, B♭ and G in the section that follows it, in which Heinrich attempts to allay Röschen's fears (and introduces the 'O heilger Wald' motif in the process), these prove to be transitory destinations, and the passage ends on a V7 chord of F major. This chord forms the foundation for an increasingly ecstatic love duet between Heinrich and Röschen, which eventually, thirty-nine bars later, at "O heilger Wald", cadences in the tonic F major: the same F major that was anticipated in bar 8 of the Prologue, only this time with a greater sense of permanence (ex. 6).

This, however, is misleading. Röschen's departure at the end of the duet signals the start of scene 5. Here Smyth adopts another Wagnerian musico-dramatic technique, namely a sudden tonal shift at the start of a new scene, rather than a gradual transition; for, with the arrival of Iolanthe, the music soon returns to 'sharp' keys.[55] The scene is structured as four sections of dialogues between Iolanthe and Heinrich that are separated by the three appearances of the Valhalla-like seduction theme mentioned above. The first section begins in D minor (the relative of F major), but quickly shifts, via G major and E minor, to E major, though at no point is there a perfect cadence in the tonic (like Wagner, Smyth prefers to imply her tonic through a judicious use of dominant pedals). The conversation ends with Iolanthe giving Heinrich her drinking horn, at which point the Valhalla-like seduction theme sounds for the first time. The passage is trance-like, seldom straying far from C# major harmony that is underpinned by tonic and dominant pedals, and which is capable only of repeating itself over and over again: a musical depiction of the bewitching effect Iolanthe is beginning to have on Heinrich that is reminiscent of the tonal stasis of "O sink hernieder" in Act II of *Tristan*. Besides this intoxicating dramatic effect, however, the passage also functions tonally as a prolonged interrupted cadence (C# is VI of E major), which is resolved only when the second section of dialogue quickly returns to E, and thence to B (the dominant of E). This section also concludes with a brief statement of the seduction theme, this time in C major (VI of E minor, thus another prolonged interrupted cadence), as Iolanthe asks Heinrich "willst du meinem Dienste dich weih'n?" Heinrich's faltering reply is in A minor; Iolanthe, in turn, responds in D major, concluding with the longest and most tonally adventurous statement of the seduction theme.

[55] For more on this particular Wagnerian technique, see Barbara Eichner, "In träumerischer Entrückung auf pfadlosen Wegen: Verwandlungsmusiken in *Der Ring des Nibelungen* und *Parsifal*", in: *Verwandlungsmusik: Über komponierte Transfigurationen*, ed. Andreas Dorschel (= Studien zur Wertungsforschung, vol. 48, Vienna 2007, pp. 273–307, as cited by J.P.E. Harper-Scott, "Medieval Romance in the Ring", in: *19th-Century Music* 32/3 (2009), pp. 211–234, at p. 228.

Decadence in the Forest

Ex. 6. Smyth, *Der Wald*, scene 4, figure 42 (Röschen's and Heinrich's words at the beginning of that bar are omitted).

Beginning with two bars in B major, and initially coloured by chromaticism, the theme eventually confirms D major as the local tonic at the pause after rehearsal figure 56, and climaxes triumphantly with Iolanthe's appeals to the Wood God ("Heil dir Wald Gott!") and to Heinrich ("Heinrich, o Heinrich komm'!"; see ex. 7). The role of D major here is different from the previous appearances of the seduction theme: it functions not as a submediant but rather as the subdominant of the subdominant of E. And it is to E (minor) that the music returns, via D and A minor, by the end of the scene, by which time Heinrich has rejected Iolanthe's advances.

Von dem Zauber der Iolanthe berauscht ist Heinrich ihr immer näher und näher getreten. Er ist drauf und dran ihr zu verfallen, als er plötzlich, das Häuschen erblickend, sich fasst, und von ihr mit Entsetzen und Verwirrung zurück weicht.

Ex. 7. Smyth, *Der Wald*, scene 5, 7 bars after rehearsal figure 56 (Heinrich's word at the end of the last bar of the excerpt is omitted).

The primacy of keys closely related to E, rather than to F, is confirmed in the final section of the opera. This begins in scene 6: Rudolf's dialogue with Iolanthe, and his self-reproachful arioso ("Was blickst du so kalt mich an"), where the tonic is E minor. At the end of the scene this shifts to D for the *Freischütz*-like hunters' chorus in scene 7, from where the music shifts first to F (for the interrogation of the pedlar by Rudolf and his huntsmen, during which the pedlar reveals that Heinrich killed the deer), and then to C minor in scene 8, when Rudolf passes sentence on Heinrich. But scene 9 returns to E and keys that are close to it: Iolanthe's and Röschen's duet is in E minor; Heinrich's and Röschen's final duet is in the subdominant, A (both minor and major); and then, following a brief shift to C minor for Iolanthe's final appeal to Heinrich to leave Röschen, the music returns to E minor for the death of the lovers. As the forest becomes shrouded in darkness again, E minor gives way to E major for the Epilogue, and the opera ends in that key, just as it began.

Many meanings may be inferred from Smyth's use of tonality, but two perhaps are particularly significant. The first is that F major is the key associated with humanity and human love in *Der Wald*: as the tonic of Section II it underpins a positive, life-affirming love duet. Heinrich, like Siegfried, is a fearless alpha male, who boasts of his hunting exploits; Röschen is a nervous young woman, anxious for male protection, who articulates her fears; Heinrich comforts her, and they sing "O Macht der Liebe" confident that with the protection of the forest they can overcome the obstacles before them. But unfortunately for the lovers, they have invoked the forest in the wrong key. As with Strauss's *Also Sprach Zarathustra* – a work composed only a few years earlier, which Smyth would surely have known – humanity and nature in *Der Wald* exist an irreconcilable semitone apart from each other. The forest is truly at peace with itself only in E major, the key of nature in which the opera begins and ends, not in F major; and this fact is underlined by the Waldgeister singing "Vergänglich ist der Sterblichen Lust" in F major as the lovers embrace each other before parting. Significantly, this is the only point in the opera outside the Prologue and Epilogue at which the spirits appear; as voices of eternal wisdom and (one presumes) truth, they give the lie to the happy future for Heinrich and Röschen that the prolonged perfect cadence in F major seemed to proclaim. (Moreover, the only time later in the opera when F major is the tonic is also connected with the lovers' fate: the pedlar's revelation of Heinrich's guilt.) Thus at the very moment that the opera seems to celebrate the triumph and transcendent power of human love, the imminent fate of Heinrich and Röschen is laid bare before us.

The second meaning concerns the character of Iolanthe, a figure who, as Elizabeth Wood rightly observes, "embodies both [human and natural] worlds: witch and whore, possessing demoniac and supernatural powers and the bold, seductive, carnal adventurousness of the woman – once betrayed – who must destroy": in short, a Kundry figure.[56] Appropriately, the tonalities associated with Iolanthe reflect the ambiguity of a character who embodies both humanity and nature: the first mention of her name in the opera precipitates the shift away from the E major of the first three scenes to the F major of scene 4, whilst her physical arrival at the start of scene 5 signals the return to E. But this return is by no means absolute; for in the first two statements of the 'seduction' figure Iolanthe alludes to the tonal territory that Heinrich has just vacated: the statement in C# major recalls the D♭ major in which the "O heilger Wald" figure is first introduced, and the C major statement hints strongly at the F major in which scene 4 finished. By doing this, Iolanthe aims to confuse Heinrich: her voice is (almost) that of Röschen – the ascending fourths in the vocal counterpoint to the first statement of the 'seduction' theme recall similar patterns in 'O glaub mir' – but her words and her body manifestly are not. By the third statement of the seduction theme, Iolanthe is singing in a key, D major, that has no prior connection with Heinrich, but by this point it makes no difference: Heinrich is sufficiently confused (or beguiled) that he almost succumbs to her spell. Iolanthe is thus in control of the events of this scene, both dramatically and tonally, in a way that the passive Röschen was not in scene 4. And because Iolanthe's 'natural' key for most of the scene is E major, we may infer that her values, carnal and opportunistic though they might be, are supported by the forest spirits in a way that Heinrich's and Röschen's apparently more noble human values are not.

In short, the idea of nature as it is portrayed in the Prologue and Epilogue pervades the opera unseen because of the frequent recurrences of the key with which it is associated, E major. Initially, the connotations of this are positive (the peasant dance in scene 2 is in E major, for instance), but they become considerably less so in Sections III and IV, when the association of E with Iolanthe demonstrates that nature is 'beyond good and evil': it cannot (or will not) make a moral choice in favour of one party or another, but by its inaction vindicate those with the power to exploit others. For a Victorian Christian moralist like Maclean, this Nietzschean conclusion would have been downright unpalatable. By contrast, the key of humanity, F major, is consistently subservient to nature: from its inability to establish itself as an alternative key centre at the beginning of the Prologue to the haste with which it is dispatched at the end of scene 4. As with Strauss's *Zarathustra*, it is nature that gets the last word – and for the Macleans of this world, it is a subversive, even decadent one.

[56] Elizabeth Wood, "Gender and Genre in Ethel Smyth's Operas", p. 495.

Conclusion

To return to the original question: why did *Der Wald* fail? Undoubtedly the conservatism of Smyth's musical style was a contributory factor: there is little in the score that could not have been written fifty years earlier; and, as 'Beckmesser' observed when the work was revived in 1903, "Miss Smyth's debt to Brahms and Wagner seems heavier than one had at first imagined, and the opera seems less original and spontaneous".[57] But to attribute the work's failure solely to this would be an oversimplification. As I have shown above, other issues, both textual and contextual, also need be taken into account. Gender is one such issue; Smyth certainly suffered at the hands of critics who called her originality into question because she was a woman. But a bigger issue may have been Smyth's alleged Wagnerism which, whilst surface deep in terms of musical style, is more pervasive with regard to associated tonality; and, as I suggest above, the message that may be inferred from Smyth's key symbolism is perhaps far more modernist than the Romantic clothing of *Der Wald* might initially suggest. It would certainly have been too subversive for critics searching for a national opera style that they could not define but felt sure they would recognize when it arrived, given that that elusive national style depended as much on the projection of particular essentialized national characteristics and values as it did on a coherent, unique musical idiom.

And this, in many ways, is the heart of the problem. Because 'British opera' in this period is itself a contested term, and because there was no continuous performing tradition of grand opera in English (or because this was perceived to be the case), there was no clear consensus on what British opera should sound like: it existed more as an idea than as practice. In the absence of any publicly funded institutions where the *raison d'être* was the promotion of national opera, the future direction that the genre might take depended in part on how effectively critics were capable of imposing their ideas – in other words, their wills – in British and international musicological discourse (that the 'practical Christian' Maclean should so often be a practitioner of this most Nietzschean of concepts is particularly ironic). Any work that did not fit the model of a 'British *Freischütz*' – an elusive national style that critics could not define but would recognize when they heard it – was likely to be swiftly

---

[57] Beckmesser, "The Opera Season", in: *MMR* 33/8 (Aug 1903), p. 155. "Beckmesser" added: "But it is a good example of what good taste, skilled workmanship, and real poetic insight can achieve, even when marked originality and individuality are absent."

rejected; as a work that came into this category, *Der Wald* perhaps suffered simply from having been written at the wrong time.

As Smyth's bitter remarks in "An Opera Fiasco" testify, institutional reform in British opera would remain a contentious issue long after *Der Wald* had been forgotten; ultimately, it was only after World War Two, with the creation of the Arts Council and its public funding of Sadler's Wells Opera, that a viable solution was implemented. But for Smyth, who died in 1944, it was a necessary reform that took place just a little too late.

(A) Section I			
Scene	Characters	Number/Period	Key
Prologue	Waldgeister	Chorus	E
Verwandlung Scene 1	Peasants, later joined by Röschen	Orchestral transition Chorus	→ a/A
Scene 2	Pedlar	Recitative Song (AA‹B)	→ d (D during 'B' section)
	Youth Youth and Peasants, later joined by Röschen	Recitative Chorus	→ G
	Peter and Röschen, later joined by peasants Peasants	Recitative Dance and chorus (ABA')	G→D → E (first dance) A (second dance) E (first dance reprise, sung)
	Pedlar, Peter, Röschen + chorus	Recitative (Iolanthe's horn) (Iolanthe's danger theme) Recitative	e→ a →
Scene 3	Peter, Pedlar, Röschen		f# → c
	(exit Peter) Röschen	Hymn (Sancta Maria)	Eb d

(B) Section II			
Scene	Characters	Number/period	Key
Scene 4	Röschen, Heinrich Heinrich	Recitative Song (loosely ABA‹)	d →F/f→ Ab
	Röschen, Heinrich Röschen	Recitative Arioso	Ab→f f
	Röschen, Heinrich Röschen, Heinrich	Recitative Duet ('O heilger Wald')	Db(→G→Bb)→V7/F F

(C) Section III			
Scene	Characters	Number/Period	Key
Scene 5	Iolanthe, Heinrich Iolanthe	Recitative Recitative (Iolanthe's seduction theme)	(d →D→G→e)→E C#
	Iolanthe, Heinrich Iolanthe	Recitative Arioso (ends with Iolanthe's seduction theme)	c#→E→ B (C)
	Iolanthe, Heinrich Iolanthe	Recitative Arioso (Iolanthe's seduction theme)	a→d/D→ (B→)D
	Iolanthe, Heinrich	Recitative	d →D (→V/e)

(A) Section IV			
Scene	Characters	Number/Period	Key
Scene 6	Rudolf, Iolanthe Rudolf Rudolf, Iolanthe later joined by Pedlar and Huntsmen	Recitative Arioso Recitative	e e e→a e →
Scene 7	Pedlar, Huntsmen Huntsmen	Chorus Chorus	D F
Scene 8	Rudolf, Pedlar Rudolf	Recitative Arioso	F→V/c c
Scene 9	Iolanthe, Röschen Iolanthe Röschen, Heinrich	Recitative/duet Recitative Duet	e e a(→C#→a/A)
Epilogue	Iolanthe, Röschen Heinrich Iolanthe, Röschen Waldgeister	Recitative Recitative Recitative Chorus	c e (→c#→)e E

Figure 1. Musical-dramatic structure of *Der Wald*: (A) Section I (Prologue, Scenes 1-3); (B) Section II (Scene 4); (C) Section III (Scene 5); (D) Section IV (Scenes 6-9, Epilogue).

Abstract

Dekadenz im Wald. Smyths Der Wald im Kontext der Kritik

Ethel Smyths Oper *Der Wald* aus dem Jahre 1902 stieß nach ihrer Premiere in Berlin auf gemischte Reaktionen. Viele Faktoren spielten hierbei eine Rolle, nicht zuletzt die von Smyth selbst beobachtete antibritische Stimmung in

Deutschland aufgrund des zweiten Burenkrieges. So hätte man erwarten können, dass die Oper bei ihrer britischen Erstaufführung am 18. Juli im Londoner Covent Garden wohlwollender angenommen würde. Doch auch hier gingen die Meinungen der Kritiker auseinander. Während selbst positive Rezensionen nicht frei von geschlechtsbedingter Diskriminierung waren, verurteilten andere Kritiken die Oper als zu wenig originell, als zu „deutsch" und vor allem zu „wagnerianisch". Aber was genau ist mit „wagnerianisch" gemeint und was lässt sich aus dieser Einschätzung folgern? Der Beitrag beantwortet diese Frage in drei Schritten. Erstens geht er dem Begriff „wagnerianisch" nach, der im öffentlichen Gebrauch – zumindest in England Anfang des 20. Jahrhunderts – nicht die Verwendung von Leitmotiven oder die durchkomponierte Struktur im Gegensatz zur ‚Nummernoper' meint, sondern einfach ein lyrisches Drama, das in seiner Struktur Text und Handlung folgte. Dabei bezog das britische Publikum seine Wagner-Kenntnisse nicht etwa aus den späten Musikdramen, sondern vor allem aus *Tannhäuser* und *Lohengrin*. Vor diesem Hintergrund wird zweitens die Musiksprache in *Der Wald* analysiert, insbesondere die Tonartenstruktur. Das zentrale Liebesduett zwischen Heinrich und Röschen steht in F-Dur und damit in größtmöglichstem Abstand zur Grundtonart E-Dur der Oper, die den Wald und damit die Natur im Allgemeinen charakterisiert. Die folgende Szene – die versuchte Verführung Heinrichs durch Iolanthe – leitet jedoch die Rückkehr zur Grundtonart ein. Entscheidend ist dabei die Einführung der Figur Iolanthe, deren Kundry-artige Persönlichkeit die eher konventionellen Machtverhältnisse der vorangegangenen Szene umkehrt. In einem dritten Schritt werden die hermeneutischen Konsequenzen dieser Umkehrung ‚natürlicher' Werte verfolgt, indem die Oper in den Kontext der so genannten dekadenten Bewegung gestellt wird, mit der der Wagnerianismus im Großbritannien des *fin de siècle* in Verbindung gebracht wurde. Diese Bewegung kam nicht zuletzt durch das Gerichtsverfahren gegen Oscar Wilde 1895 in Verruf. Ein Werk wie *Der Wald*, das eindeutig in der Tradition Wagners stand, geriet somit schon aufgrund dieser Verbindung in die Gefahr, in ‚Sippenhaft' genommen zu werden: Der Stil (und, in großen Teilen, auch der Inhalt) erinnerte an eine Ästhetik, die in Misskredit geraten war.

Jürgen Schaarwächter
A British Choral Symphony? Ethel Smyth's *The Prison* in Context

On Thursday, 19 February 1931 Ethel Smyth conducted the first performance of *The Prison* at a Reid Orchestral Concert given at the Usher Hall, Edinburgh, a performance painstakingly prepared and rehearsed by Donald Francis Tovey.[1] The work had already been published in January[2] and lengthy articles written prior to the first performance, by W. R. Anderson for the *Musical Times* and Robert Hoare Hull for the *Monthly Musical Record*.[3] *The Prison* was to be performed occasionally in Britain in the years to follow, under Adrian Boult at the Queen's Hall, London with the Bach Choir on 24 February 1931 and under Sir Thomas Beecham in Manchester on 29 November 1934, amongst others;[4] it was also Beecham who conducted the performance on the occasion of Smyth's 73rd birthday on 23 April 1931. Smyth had already become fairly hard of hearing, so it was only natural that she now increasingly stepped back from conducting, choosing to leave this to colleagues.

The literary source Ethel Smyth drew upon in 1929–30 was *The Prison*, "a dialogue between a group of friends who are discussing a manuscript supposed to have been left behind by some unknown prisoner",[5] originally published in 1891.

[1] The soloists were Elsie Suddaby (soprano) and Stuart Robertson (baritone), the chorus is unnamed in the first performance programme. Programme, Edinburgh, 19 February 1931 (Reid Music Library, University of Edinburgh)
[2] The vocal score was on sale from J. Curwen & Son Ltd. – the full score and parts remained unprinted and on loan only (nowadays from ChesterNovello).
[3] W. R. Anderson, "Dame Ethel Smyth's *The Prison*", in: *The Musical Times* LXXII (1931), p. 37f.; Robin Hull, "Ethel Smyth's *The Prison*", in: *The Monthly Musical Review* LXI/722 (1931), p. 41f.
[4] I am very grateful to Rebecca Grotjahn for supplying the programme notes of Ethel Smyth to the performance mentioned, which differs only in minor respects from the premiere performance programme notes. *The Hallé Concerts Society. Seventy-Seventh Season. 1934–1935. Guest Conductor: Sir Thomas Beecham. Seventh Concert. November 29th, 1934. Programme With Historical and Analytical Notes*, [Manchester] 1934. (Ethel Smyth Archiv, Musikwissenschaftliches Seminar Detmold/Paderborn, without shelfmark.)
[5] Programme Edinburgh 1931 (see footnote 1).

University of Edinburgh.

THE SIXTY-EIGHTH SESSION OF
REID ORCHESTRAL CONCERTS
INSTITUTED IN 1841

REID SYMPHONY ORCHESTRA

FIFTEENTH SEASON

SIXTH CONCERT

USHER HALL, THURSDAY, 19TH FEBRUARY 1931
at 8 p.m.

Conductors

PROFESSOR DONALD FRANCIS TOVEY
DAME ETHEL SMYTH

Leader of Orchestra—Mr WATT JUPP

Concert under the direction of
PATERSON, SONS & CO. LTD., 27 George Street, Edinburgh

Prospectus for Series and all information from
Messrs PATERSON, SONS & CO. LTD., 27 George Street
METHVEN, SIMPSON LTD., 83 Princes Street
R. W. PENTLAND, 28 Frederick Street
TOWNSEND & THOMSON, 79 George Street

Fig.: Programme note, Edinburgh, 19 February 1931 (Reid Music Library, University of Edinburgh)

The text had been written by Henry B. Brewster (1850–1908), known as Harry, husband of the sister-in-law of Smyth's former teacher Heinrich von Herzogenberg. Harry Brewster had fallen in love with Ethel in 1882, and eventually this was reciprocated. After his death from liver cancer, it comes as no surprise that he was to retain his central position of significance in her life for many years to come, and she wrote about him at length in her memoirs. When Smyth tried to get Brewster's text republished to coincide with the first performance of her composition,[6] Leonard Woolf, Virginia Woolf's husband, strongly opposed the idea since he considered it "utter rubbish".[7] He was not alone in holding this opinion; the *Musical Times* critic, Frank Howes, was to describe it after the Bach Choir performance in February 1931 as "the kind of thing which gives philosophy a bad name – vague speculation which is neither metaphysics nor poetry."[8] And although both Smyth and her supporters regularly stressed that the text bore no relation whatsoever to Cardinal John Henry Newman's (1801–1890) poem *The Dream of Gerontius* (1865), set to music by Elgar in 1899–1900, the similarity – not only of topic – is striking. Of course, Ethel Smyth knew Elgar's Catholic oratorio, and although her composition is rather a-religious (or pantheist),[9] the general layout and construction of both "libretti" are similar. In a prefatory note to the score, also reprinted in the concert programme, the composer wrote: "The book records the struggle of one called 'The Prisoner' to escape from his bonds, and the motto printed on the title page of the vocal score and quoted by Andrew Lang as the last words of Plotinus, exactly sums up its essence: 'I am striving to release that which is divine within us, and to merge it in the universally divine.'"[10] The extracts set to music by Smyth are taken from the Prisoner's last utterances. As Elizabeth Wood has shown, *The Prison* deals, like several of her last compositions, with death, and with past sounds and traditions, as a kind of "musical recollection" similar to her literary memoirs, and I think it will be essential to bear this concept in mind when trying to understand *The Prison* as a composition in its own right and in context.[11]

---

[6] Henry Brewster, *The Prison. A Dialogue. With a Memoir of the Author by Ethel Smyth,* London [1930].
[7] Cf. Louise Collis, *Impetuous Heart. The Story of Ethel Smyth*, London 1984, p. 183 (without reference).
[8] Frank Howes, "The Bach Choir", in: *The Musical Times* LXXII (1931), p. 361.
[9] The research of "pantheist" music aesthetics in Britain would require a publication of its own.
[10] Programme Edinburgh 1931 (see footnote 1)
[11] See Elizabeth Wood, "On Deafness and Musical Creativity: The Case of Ethel Smyth", in: *The Musical Quarterly* 92 (2009), p. 33–69. (An abridged version of this article was read at the Ethel Smyth conference in Detmold 2009.)

The Prison consists of two parts approximately equal in length: *Close on Freedom* and *The Deliverance*. The course of the narrative has been summarized by Robert Hoare Hull as follows:

> "Part I: (a) The Prisoner communes with his Soul; (b) Voices sing of immortality; (c) The Prisoner asks the secret of emancipation; (d) His Soul (echoed by Voices) replies; (e) He asks in what shape emancipation will come; (f) The Voices reply; (g) Orchestral Interlude: The first glimmer of dawn; (h) The Prisoner understands his own immortality: he sleeps.
>
> Part II: (a) Organ music sounds from the Chapel. The Prisoner awakes; (b) His Soul tells him that the end of the struggle is at hand; (c) He hears his guests (the elements of his personality) moving to depart; (d) Pastoral-sunset calm; (e) He disbands his ego; (f) Voices sing the indestructibility of human passions; (g) Death calls him; glorying, he obeys the summons; (h) his farewell; his triumph; his peace."[12]

Why did Ethel Smyth call the work a symphony? She is quite explicit about this from early on in her performance notes: "In Greek and Roman times the word Symphony merely meant a 'concord of sweet sounds.' Even to-day some composers still think this a desirable end, so perhaps one may be pardoned for using the word in its original sense – if only as indicating an aspiration."[13] It is interesting to see that Donald Francis Tovey's entry on the Symphony in the *Encyclopaedia Britannica* begins with a broadly similar sentence, unfolding in the subsequent paragraphs the entire tradition of the term "symphony" from Schütz to Mozart.[14] But how is this essentially non-nineteenth-century use of the term to be understood?

W. R. Anderson wrote: "Dame Ethel Smyth's *The Prison* is entitled a 'symphony,' but I cannot see how it conforms to symphonic shape."[15] Neither several-movement nor one-movement compositional designs are in evidence, and while the succession of individual scenes might evoke individual movements of a symphony, these could just as well be movements of a suite or oratorio (thus it is not surprising that Louise Collis, like many others, calls the work just this[16] – and indeed Collis was not alone in doing so; the composer herself

[12] Hull, "Ethel Smyth's *The Prison*", p. 41
[13] Programme Edinburgh 1931 (see footnote 1).
[14] Donald Francis Tovey, "Symphony", in: Donald Francis Tovey, *The Forms of Music. Musical Articles from the* Encyclopaedia Britannica, 1943, New York 1956, pp. 238–239.
[15] Anderson, "Dame Ethel Smyth's *The Prison*", p. 37.
[16] Louise Collis, *Impetuous Heart*, p. 177.

called *The Prison* a "large choral work"[17]). Still, the tradition of the late-nineteenth-century "Sinfonia sacra" of Parry (*The Soul's Ransom, The Love that Casteth out Fear*, etc.), in consequence to the Schütz tradition, may indeed be an important case in point. Hubert Parry (1848–1918) had come to know twenty-three-year-old Ethel Smyth at a lawn tennis party and thought highly of her, although he described her as "the most extreme Wagnerite I had ever met. She knows a wonderful lot about music, is intimate in the highest musical circles, has most remarkable gifts, and is open and unsophisticated".[18] Parry is in fact one of the first composers whose "choral symphonies" survived nineteenth-century Britain. His "Sinfonie sacre" of the early 20th century were actually moral cantatas (or even spiritual cantatas in light of their text) with a relatively independent orchestral component. In formal terms, however, they are clearly derived from a concept of "symphony" similar to that of Schütz, Hammerschmidt, or Gabrieli's Symphoniae sacrae, and, as such, relate to a period well before other symphonies were being composed, namely to the end of the sixteenth and the beginning of the seventeenth century. So Parry was not in fact trying to produce a symphony in the more contemporary sense of the term, and it is very probable that Smyth was well aware of Parry's works.

Just as Parry's works have been reproached for not being successful in their formal construction, it has been doubted whether Smyth was able to fill such a form consistently. W. R. Anderson writes: "Her work suffers from its mixture of styles. No composition of hers that I know is anything like consistent."[19] And Frank Howes had the suspicion that the composer "had not digged [sic] much below the surface of the text, but had rather been prompted to illustrate it with more or less felicitous word-painting."[20] Powerfully orchestrated ariosi or recitatives adjoin orchestral imitations of birds (in the first orchestral interlude "The Glimmer of Dawn"); an organ chorale prelude is juxtaposed by carefully set choral counterpoint; and Greek melodies, in addition to the best sections of score, stand alongside the finali of both parts. Some listeners may find allusions to Mahler, early Schönberg and English symphonism in the work, while others

---

[17] Ethel Smyth, postcard to Emil Hertzka (Universal Edition), 1 January 1931: „Ich dirigiere + führe zum 1 Mal auf mein neues [insertion: grosses] Chorwerk 'The Prison' am 19 Febr – & am 24 Feb ist die Londoner Aufführung unter Boult" (Universal Edition Archive, Smyth Letters, No. 722). This postcard was exhibited at the Exhibition "Ethel Smyth – Impressions and Correspondence" at the Lippische Landesbibliothek Detmold from 6 November to 09 January 2009.

[18] Quoted in Hubert Foss, *Two Women Composers*, in: *Music Magazine*, ed. Anna Instone/Julian Herbage, London 1953, p. 73.

[19] Anderson, "Dame Ethel Smyth's *The Prison*", p. 37.

[20] Howes, "The Bach Choir", p. 361.

may stress the strong prominence of Smyth's very own voice. It may well be that also in this respect, as Elizabeth Wood has suggested, Smyth consciously (or unconsciously) incorporated such "musical recollections" at a time when, due to her deafness, she was almost entirely cut off from the contemporaneous British music scene as exemplified by Walton, Bliss, or Constant Lambert.[21]

Anderson's view is more than harsh (taking the vocal score as the basis for his judgment):

> "In simple illustration of words, or suggestion of mood, she is almost always happy, if restless; but I cannot feel that her music is really inseeing, or that it suggests more than the poem does: and if it fails to suggest more, why set the poem? Music can only serve words by raising them to higher power, not in patches, but consistently; and it is that weakness in working up a big-scale, consistent piece of unified architecture, that shows up in all this composer's work that I know. Her energy pushes too hard; her lovable eagerness, which, in her writings on unruled paper, braces and delights us, does not quite know, in music, how and when to thrust and when to be quiet. Her grasp of what her implements can do is always firm: she does not fumble, and for that we should be grateful. The trouble is, that after it is over, we ask of her work, 'Was it quite worth doing?' – and I, for one, am rarely convinced that it was."[22]

Hull's view is much more favourable:

> "'The Prison' is a greatly ambitious treatment of a formidably difficult theme. The reader of the score is struck by an excess of recitative, awkward verbal writing, and occasional breaks in continuity – due mostly to the problems set by the libretto – and the inventive power fluctuates. But the composer has poured her heart and soul into the work, and it is her triumph to have given to what might have been mere cold abstractions a sense of ardent reality."[23]

The "dramatic" style, which is so characteristic of *The Prison*, refers strongly to its origin in the Handelian oratorio, and philosophical topics receive treatment there as well (*L'Allegro, il Penseroso ed il Moderato*). Equally, it may well be that Smyth had been inspired to some extent by oratorios and cantatas she came to know when studying in Germany. Thus, unlike a "real" symphony, the work defies formal analysis, but can instead be gauged by the conciseness

---

[21] See Wood, "On deafness".
[22] Anderson, "Dame Ethel Smyth's *The Prison*", p. 38.
[23] Hull, "Ethel Smyth's *The Prison*", p. 42.

of the content-related concept, which is based on the notion, formerly widespread, of "per aspera ad astra".

Especially with respect to her (at least reported) egocentrism, it is not easy to say with any certainty which of her contemporaries' compositions Smyth actually knew; in her recollections she mentions very few, if any. It might be deemed probable that she knew the choral (and possibly also some of the orchestral) symphonies of Parry; she may also have known more of what was going on within the British music scene. Since Parry quite considerable developments had taken place in the field of the British choral symphony, and I would like to look at this tradition, in which *The Prison* must be seen to take its place, in somewhat greater detail. A far more remote connection than to Parry's *The Love that Casteth out Fear* and *The Soul's Ransom* (of 1904 and 1906 respectively) is to be found in respect to more genuinely symphonic choral symphonies such as Henry Walford Davies' Sacred Symphony *Lift up your Hearts* op. 20 of 1906, Edgar Leslie Bainton's *Before Sunrise* of 1907, or Granville Bantock's monumental Festival Symphony *Christus* of 1897–1907. But I am mentioning the works nevertheless, since Smyth may have been acquainted with these works – which had been published and were regularly performed by choral societies and at choir festivals. The form of the Bantock work underwent change over time and was later performed in separate sections, others now being lost, while *Lift up your Hearts* was soon forgotten. The influence of Bainton's *Before Sunrise* (on a text by Algernon Swinburne and dedicated to Charles Villiers Stanford) might have been stronger, although more in spirit rather than in its detailed conception; it is a kind of atheist discourse with complex content. It has rarely been performed since the First World War, although its compositional qualities are obvious. And whereas Vaughan Williams's *Sea Symphony* (1909), on texts by Walt Whitman, tries to reconcile Parry-esque choral part-writing with symphonic thinking, Smyth pursues an altogether different path.

Another work for orchestra and chorus composed as a kind of philosophical discourse is Josef Holbrooke's *Apollo and the Seaman* op. 51 of 1907, on a text by Herbert Trench, but Holbrooke, much more so than is the case with Smyth, transferred the literary content into the orchestral writing with the intention of strengthening the work's consistency. Sadly, Holbrooke and his son later prevented performances of the music so that most of Holbrooke's output is now forgotten.

Likewise, Granville Bantock's all-choral (i.e. a cappella) symphonies *Atalanta in Calydon* (1911) and *Vanity of Vanities* (1913) remained entirely without influence on Smyth's compositional approach. Three most important British choral symphonies are most unlikely to have been familiar to Smyth, though she might possibly have had access to the scores inspite of their not (yet) being in print in 1930: Bernard van Dieren's *Choral Symphony* op. 6 (1914, premiered only in 1935), Kaikhosru Shapurji Sorabji's First *Choral Symphony* (1921–22, unpublished and unperformed) and Havergal Brian's *Gothic Symphony* (1919–27, unpublished until 1932 and premiered only in 1961).

There was, however, at least one British choral symphony that might have had model character for Smyth, had she been in a position to take an interest in it[24] – Gustav Holst's First Choral Symphony op. 41 of 1923–24. It is a work known nowadays to have been a mile-stone in British choral-orchestral word-setting. After Bernard van Dieren had already explored the more profound possibilities of word-setting, overcoming external effect, Holst followed him down this path to an increasing extent in the 20th century, much to the regret of his own daughter. It is perplexing to note the degree to which Imogen Holst disliked the Choral Symphony, even though it bears a kind of linkage to Benjamin Britten's *Spring Symphony* op. 44 of several decades later, and hence to a composer Imogen Holst greatly admired. It is, however, rather improbable that Ethel Smyth consulted the score or was ever able to attend a performance.

It is still more confusing to see how close Smyth is in spirit to another British choral symphony of 1930, Arthur Bliss's *Morning Heroes*.

The 1933 *Radio Times* printed the following remarks by Ethel Smyth:

> "The present writer is old-fashioned enough not to shrink from drawing a moral. In closest connection with the subject of this article is a point in which, were it feasible to do so all the steam power, all the electric power, available on this planet should be brought to bear, for it is impossible to drive it in too deeply – namely, the childish folly, the mad, grown-up criminality of war. [...] The Aidin Inscription,

[24] We learn more with respect to Smyth's growing hearing problems from Elizabeth Wood; whether or not she might still have been able to read new scores without being able to hear them physically would require additional research. See Wood, "On deafness".

with other priceless remnants of the culture of Ancient Greece, was housed in the Museum at Smyrna. Well for civilisation that casts of this unique stone had been taken! – for in 1922, when the withdrawal of France and England's promises of help caused the Greeks to be driven out of Asia Minor Smyrna was burned to the ground by the Turks and the Museum and all its contents perished in the flames! [...] If my use of this exquisite melody should indirectly contribute to bring home to the world-crowd of indifferents the hideous, stupid waste of war, if it should put one spark more life into their vague, half-hearted will for peace, then, whether the musical *Prison* finds favour today, tomorrow, or never, it will not have been written in vain."[25]

Where Smyth uses an inscription, Arthur Bliss goes a step further by utilising – in his anti-war choral symphony *Morning Heroes* composed simultaneously to *The Prison* – poetry ranging from Li Tai-Po and the *Iliad* to Walt Whitman, Wilfred Owen and Robert Nichols. The mixture of poems was intended to express several aspects of war in all its devastating force, thus supplying a more immediate treatment of an aspect also evident in *The Prison*. It is probably as ambitious as *The Prison*, but Bliss structures his composition more in line with recent concepts of symphonism – using, unexpectedly, an orator instead of singing soloists, thus avoiding recitative and arioso in favour of melodrama. So this is a composition not far removed from Smyth's, yet it is probable that both composers knew about each others' compositional efforts only after the first performances (whether Smyth ever eventually got to know *Morning Heroes* remains a matter of doubt).

Norman Demuth, a well-known contemporary English composer, described Ethel Smyth's "beautiful choral and orchestral 'symphony', *The Prison*" as "one of her last works and one of her best".[26] And it well may be that it is indeed, as Robin Hull put it, "Ethel Smyth's highest achievement".[27] Still, with regard to contemporaneous British symphonism, it takes a step back, following a path trodden some twenty-five years previously, at least. Smyth ignores the achievements of Vaughan Williams, Bainton or Holst, to name but a few, and there were to be no successors to her approach. It was not destined to have a lasting effect on British music – but in this *The Prison*, like many other British choral symphonies and even large-scale choral compositions of the period, does not stand alone.

[25] "Notable music of the week. The Prison of self", in: *The Radio Times*, London, 29 December 1933, p. 938.
[26] Norman Demuth, *Musical Trends in the 20th Century*, London 1952, p. 113.
[27] Hull, "Ethel Smyth's *The Prison*", p. 42.

Abstract

Eine britische Chorsinfonie? Ethel Smyths The Prison *im Kontext*

Norman Demuth, ein bekannter zeitgenössischer englischer Komponist, bezeichnete Ethel Smyths „wunderbare ‚Sinfonie' für Chor und Orchester" *The Prison* (1930) als „eine ihrer letzten und besten Kompositionen". Eine ihrer umfangreichsten nichtbühnengebundenen Kompositionen, erlebte *The Prison* seine Uraufführung 1931 in Edinburgh unter Smyths Leitung nach Einstudierung durch Donald Francis Tovey. Der Textvorwurf stammte von Heinrich von Herzogenbergs Schwippschwager Henry B. Brewster (1850-1908), mit dem Smyth Ende des 19. Jahrhunderts eine intensive Beziehung pflegte. Formal durchaus eigenständig, hat das Werk gleichzeitig seinen Platz in der Tradition britischer Chorsinfonik zwischen Hubert Parry und Arthur Bliss. Angesichts der dramatischen Hörprobleme gegen Ende ihres Lebens ist es aber unwahrscheinlich, dass Smyth die ungefähr zeitgleich mit *The Prison* entstandenen Chorsinfonien etwa von Havergal Brian oder Gustav Holst kannte.

Die Autorinnen und Autoren

CORNELIA BARTSCH, Wissenschaftliche Mitarbeiterin am Musikwissenschaftlichen Seminar Detmold/Paderborn. Sie studierte Schulmusik, Germanistik und Politologie in Osnabrück und Berlin und promovierte 2006 mit *Fanny Hensel geb. Mendelssohn Bartholdy. Musik als Korrespondenz* (Kassel 2007). Derzeit Arbeit an einem Habilitationsprojekt über *Musik Erinnerung Gender in Ost- und Mitteleuropa*. Weitere Forschungsschwerpunkte u. a.: Männlichkeitskonstruktionen in der Beethovenrezeption, Felix Mendelssohn Bartholdy, Ethel Smyth, Sofia Gubaidulina, Musik im jüdischen Akkulturationsprozess, Musik und Medialität, Musik und Migration im 20. Jahrhundert.

CHRISTA BRÜSTLE, Wissenschaftliche Mitarbeiterin im Sonderforschungsbereich „Kulturen des Performativen" an der Freien Universität Berlin. Sie studierte Musikwissenschaft, Germanistik und Linguistik in Freiburg i. Br. und Frankfurt a. M. und promovierte 1996 über die Rezeptionsgeschichte Anton Bruckners an der Freien Universität Berlin. 2007 Habilitation mit *Konzert-Szenen: Bewegung – Performance – Medien. Musik zwischen performativer Expansion und medialer Integration 1950 – 2000* ebendort. Weitere Forschungsschwerpunkte u. a.: Musik in England im 20. Jahrhundert, Geschichte der Musikphilologie, Musik in der NS-Zeit, Musik nach 1945, Gender studies.

GUNILLA BUDDE, Professorin für deutsche und europäische Geschichte im 19. und 20. Jahrhundert an der Carl von Ossietzky Universität Oldenburg. Sie promovierte 1993 am Friedrich-Meinecke-Institut der Freien Universität Berlin mit *Auf dem Weg ins Bürgerleben. Kindheit und Erziehung in deutschen und englischen Bürgerfamilien, 1840–1914* (Göttingen 1994). Habilitation 2003 (*Frauen der Intelligenz. Akademikerinnen in der DDR, 1945 bis 1975*, Göttingen 2003) ebendort. Forschungsschwerpunkte: Geschichte des europäischen Bürgertums, Gender history, Geschichte der DDR, Konsumgeschichte, Politik und Musik in der Geschichte.

ELICIA CLEMENTS ist Assistant Professor für englische Literatur- und Kulturwissenschaften an der York University Toronto (Kanada). Ihre wichtigsten Forschungsschwerpunkte sind die Werke Virginia Woolfs sowie Beziehungen zwischen Literatur und Musik. Sie schrieb eine Monographie über die Behandlung von Sprache, Musik und Klang in Woolfs Novellen (Druck i. V.), außerdem befasste sie sich mit dem Einfluss Ethel Smyths auf Woolf, mit musikalischen Strukturen in *The Waves,* mit der Oper *The Mother of Us All* von Gertrude Stein und Virgil Thomson sowie mit dem viktorianischen Essayisten Walter Pater.

Erik Dremel, Universitätsdozent für Geschichte der Kirchenmusik, Hymnologie und Liturgik an der Martin-Luther-Universität Halle-Wittenberg sowie an der Hochschule für Kirchenmusik Halle. Er studierte Musikwissenschaft, Theologie, Philosophie und Literaturwissenschaft in Hamburg und Birmingham und promovierte 2004 mit einer Studie über die englische Musik des frühen 20. Jahrhunderts. Weitere Forschungsschwerpunkte: lutherische und anglikanische Kirchenmusik des 17.-19. Jahrhunderts, Liturgiegeschichte, Kirchenmusikalische Erneuerungsbewegung im 20. Jahrhundert, Theorie der Kirchenmusik, Ästhetik der Instrumentalmusik um 1800.

Rebecca Grotjahn, Professorin für Musikwissenschaft am Musikwissenschaftlichen Seminar Detmold/Paderborn. Sie studierte Schulmusik, Musikwissenschaft, Gesang und Deutsch und promovierte 1997 an der Musikhochschule Hannover mit *Die Sinfonie im deutschen Kulturgebiet zwischen 1850 und 1875* (Sinzig 1998). Habilitation 2004 an der Universität Oldenburg. Forschungsschwerpunkte u. a.: Geschichte des Singens, Musikstars, musikalische Sozial-, Alltags- und Institutionengeschichte des 19. und 20. Jahrhundert, Musik in der NS-Zeit, Robert Schumann. Sie ist Sprecherin der Fachgruppe Frauen- und Genderstudien in der Gesellschaft für Musikforschung.

Amanda Harris lehrt an der University of New South Wales, Sydney, und der University of Western Sydney. Nach ihrem Musikwissenschaftsstudium promovierte sie 2009 an der University of New South Wales mit *Composing Women and Feminism at the Turn of the Twentieth Century in England, France and Germany*. Ihre Forschungsinteressen liegen in der Schnittmenge von Musik, Kultur, Gesellschaft und Politik. Sie befasste sich mit den Themen Nationalismus und Rassismus in der Musik und im Musikleben und speziell mit Musik der Zeit um 1900, insbesondere Ethel Smyth, Lili Boulanger und Louisa Adolpha Le Beau, sowie mit australischer Musik.

Margaret Hunt, Professorin für Geschichte und Frauen- und Geschlechterstudien am Amherst College in Massachusetts. BA in Musik an der Harvard University, Promotion in Europäischer Geschichte an der New York University. Sie schrieb *The Middling Sort, Commerce, Gender and the Family in England, 1680-1780* (1996) und *Women in Eighteenth-Century Europe* (2009). Weitere Forschungsschwerpunkte: vergleichende Gesetzesgeschichte (mit Fokus auf Frauen und islamische Gesetzgebung); Militärgeschichte und Geschlechtergeschichte, besonders Homosexualität. Sie ist Präsidentin der Berkshire Conference of Women Historians.

PAVEL B. JIRACEK studierte Musikwissenschaft in Oxford und Hannover sowie Arts Administration an der Universität Zürich. Regiehospitanzen und -assistenzen, u. a. bei Peter Konwitschnys Inszenierung von Luigi Nonos *Al gran sole carico d'amore* (2004, Hannover). 2005/06 Dramaturgieassistent an der Staatsoper Hannover und Produktionsleiter der Reihe *zeitoper*. Stipendiat der *Akademie Musiktheater Heute* (2004–06), der *Richard Wagner Stipendienstiftung* (2006) und der *Byrd Hoffman Watermill Foundation* von Robert Wilson (2008). Derzeit arbeitet er an einem Promotionsprojekt zu Ethel Smyth an der Hochschule für Musik Köln.

ELIZABETH KERTESZ lehrt und forscht als Gastdozentin an der Fakultät des *Victorian College of the Arts (VCA) and Music* der University of Melbourne. Sie promovierte im Jahr 2001 an der University of Melbourne (Australien) mit *Issues in the Critical Reception of Ethel Smyth's Mass and Early Operas in England and Germany*. Ihr gegenwärtiges Forschungsinteresse gilt der spanischen Unterhaltungskunst (Tanz und Musik) im späten 19. und frühen 20. Jahrhundert. Ihr gemeinsam mit Michael Christoforidis verfasstes Buch *Carmen: Cultural Authenticity and the Shaping of a Global Icon* erscheint in Kürze im Verlag *Oxford University Press*.

KORDULA KNAUS, Wissenschaftliche Mitarbeiterin am Institut für Musikwissenschaft der Universität Graz. Sie studierte Gitarre (Konzertfach) an der Kunstuniversität Graz und Musikwissenschaft an der Karl-Franzens-Universität Graz und promovierte 2003 mit *Gezähmte Lulu. Alban Bergs Wedekind-Vertonung im Spannungsfeld von literarischer Ambition, Opernkonvention und „absoluter Musik"* (Freiburg 2004). Derzeit Arbeit an einem Habilitationsprojekt über gegengeschlechtliche Besetzungspraxis in der Oper des 17. und 18. Jahrhunderts. Weitere Forschungsschwerpunkte: Wagner, Strauss, Operette, Opernregie, Theorie der Musikanalyse, Gender studies.

JÜRGEN SCHAARWÄCHTER ist Wissenschaftlicher Mitarbeiter des Max-Reger-Instituts Karlsruhe. Er promovierte mit *Die britische Sinfonie 1914–1945* (Köln 1995), die mit dem Preis der Offermann-Hergarten-Stiftung ausgezeichnet wurde. Er ist sowie Vorstandsvorsitzender der Robert Simpson Society und Redakteur des *Journals der Robert Simpson Society Tonic* sowie der *Mitteilungen der Internationalen Max-Reger-Gesellschaft e. V.*, außerdem deutscher Repräsentant der British Music Society und kontinentaleuropäischer Kontakt der Havergal Brian Society. Zahlreiche Publikationen von Purcell und Bach bis Britten, daneben Rezensenten- und Übersetzertätigkeit.

AIDAN THOMSON ist Lecturer an der School of Music and Sonic Arts der Queen's University in Belfast. Nach seinem Studium am Magdalen College in Oxford und am King's College in London sowie seiner Promotion über die Rezeption Edward Elgars in England und Deutschland (2002) lehrte er an den Universitäten Oxford und Leeds. Er veröffentlichte u. a. Beiträge in *19th-Century Music*, *Edward Elgar and His World* (2007) and *Elgar Studies* (2007) und ist Mitherausgeber von *The Cambridge Companion to Vaughan Williams*, außerdem gewähltes Vorstandsmitglied der Royal Musical Association und der North American British Music Studies Association.

MELANIE UNSELD ist seit 2008 Professorin für Kulturgeschichte der Musik an der Carl von Ossietzky Universität Oldenburg. Sie studierte Musikwissenschaft, Literaturwissenschaft, Philosophie und Angewandte Kulturwissenschaft, Promotion 1999 an der Universität Hamburg („*Man töte dieses Weib!" Weiblichkeit und Tod in der Musik der Jahrhundertwende*, Stuttgart/Weimar 2001). Stipendiatin des Lise Meitner-Hochschulsonderprogramms, 2005–2008 Wissenschaftliche Mitarbeiterin an der Hochschule für Musik und Theater Hannover. Sie ist Mitherausgeberin der Reihe *Europäische Komponistinnen* (Böhlau Verlag Köln).

SUSAN WOLLENBERG ist Reader an der Fakultät für Musik der Universität Oxford, (an der sie den Themenbereich „Komponistinnen" ins Curriculum einführte,) Fellow und Tutor von Lady Margaret Hall und Dozentin im Fach Musik im Brasenose College. Sie veröffentlichte u. a. *Music at Oxford in the Eighteenth and Nineteenth Centuries* (Oxford 2001); *Concert Life in Eighteenth-Century Britain* (Ashgate 2004, als Mitherausgeberin) und *The Piano in Nineteenth-Century British Culture* (Ashgate 2007, mit Therese Ellsworth). Sie organisierte eine Tagung zu Fanny Hensels 200. Geburtstag, deren Beiträge sie in *Nineteenth-Century Music Review* 4/2 (2007) herausgab.